POPULATION CHANGE
IN CANADA

POPULATION CHANGE IN CANADA

The Challenges of Policy Adaptation

Roderic Beaujot

Foreword by Monica Boyd

M&S

Canadian Cataloguing in Publication Data
Beaujot, Roderic P., 1946–
Population change in Canada

Includes bibliographical references and index.
ISBN 0-7710-1158-X

1. Canada – Population.   2. Political planning – Canada.   I. Title.

HB3529.B42 1991   304.6'0971   C91-093728-1

McClelland & Stewart Inc.
The Canadian Publishers
481 University Avenue
Toronto, Ontario
M5G 2E9

Printed and bound in Canada

CONTENTS

To my parents, Leon and Dorothy Beaujot,
in Kipling, Saskatchewan.

FOREWORD

Population processes have a long association with policy concerns. Historically, the collection of population data owes much to the desire of governments to tax and to conscript. Colonization not only represented the social and economic aspirations of migrants but also the potential realization of economic and political agendas held by ruling elites. Long linked to perceptions of military strength and the creation of wealth, migration, death, marriage, and births were – and remain – of great importance to many governments.

The association of population issues with policy development is not merely an historical one. In the 1930s, North American demographers wrote extensively on the economic implications of slow population growth and the concept of optimum population. The resurgence of interest in population and ecology in the 1960s and early 1970s reflected the decolonization of the areas outside of North America and Europe and growing awareness of the social, economic, and political implications of the population explosion at a global level. During the 1970s and 1980s, industrial democracies experienced precipitous declines in fertility levels, rising percentages of elderly in their populations, and increasing movements of people within and across their borders. These changes in fertility, mortality, population age structure, and population movements occurred alongside growing government involvement in the provision of education and social services, health care and income security.

The growth of the welfare state has strengthened the importance of basic population processes for policy-making for two reasons. First, population processes underlie the age, sex, ethnic, and racial composition of a society and together these provide the bases for problem definition. In turn, problem definition is an essential first step in developing public policy. For example, a society with a high fertility rate and low mortality rate is also a country with a high percentage of children in its population. This demographic context may generate concerns over educating youth and how the educational system will meet the needs of this new generation. By encouraging the derivation of educational objectives, the demographic context of high youth dependency may ultimately influence the development of a public policy regarding education. In addition to its impact on social policy, the demographic context also may underlie the development of a demographic policy. For example, if high (or low) fertility levels are seen as problematic, this may stimulate the development of policies to reduce (or raise) fertility levels.

The second reason for the link between population issues and public policy is that the direction of influence also can be reversed. Public policies may be defined generally as a set of objectives and courses of action designed by government, or the state more broadly defined, to address pre-defined problems. Such policies can have direct demographic objectives, such as reducing high fertility, controlling immigration, or otherwise altering the processes and composition of the population in question. However, public policies with non-demographic objectives also can have indirect impacts on population processes. For example, a policy designed to increase the educational levels in a country may well contribute to declines in fertility indirectly through its impact on values and its influence on social and economic roles.

The links between population and public policy are of great interest to Canadian demographers and policy analysts. They are also much discussed at the public level in Quebec as a part of the more general discourse on nationalism and sovereignty. Throughout Canada, considerable media attention has promoted a general awareness of immigration, immigration policies, and multiculturalism issues. However, the relations between other aspects of population and public policy implications are less well understood by the public. Part of the reason lies in the large scope of such an exercise. The study of population alone can fill several hundred pages of text. But part of the reason also arises because of a relative neglect of the association between population and policy. Excluding those experts in immigration, in family planning, and/or in Quebec demography, many Canadian demographers paid little attention to policy implications of their research until recently. Most non-academic policy analysts displayed an equally restricted focus, concentrating on specific policies and their evaluation.

This separation of the two worlds of population and public policy has blurred during the past decade. The Review of Demography was an especially important catalyst in increasing awareness of linkages between the two areas. On April 20, 1986, the federal government approved the creation of the Review of Demography and Its Implications for Economic and Social Policy. Run by a small secretariat within Health and Welfare Canada, the review commissioned a number of studies on changes in the size, structure, and composition of the Canadian population, on their impacts on social and economic conditions, and on the policy and program responses of other countries.

The report was published in December, 1989. Titled *Charting Canada's Future*, it consisted of seventy-four pages, including seventeen pages of references and forty pages primarily of charts, as well as a list of 167 commissioned studies. The graphic visuals enhanced its accessibility to non-experts, and the report overall increased demographic awareness among non-demographers. So did the actual undertaking of the review, since extensive consultations occurred with government departments, academics, and other groups. However, the brevity and style of the report precluded extensive reporting of the commissioned studies and in-depth analyses of Canadian demographic trends and their implications for public policy.

In *Population Change in Canada: The Challenges of Policy Adaptation*, Roderic Beaujot fills the void. Through an exhaustive review of commissioned studies, scholarly works, and policy papers, Professor Beaujot has brought together population and policy issues in a comprehensive summary. In presenting material on Canadian demography, he not only informs the reader about population issues but also indicates where demographic trends and processes are problematic. Problem definition and problem specification are essential first steps in any policy discussion, and they are among the major contributions of this book. However, Professor Beaujot goes further. Arguing that two types of responses exist with respect to Canadian population issues, he explores how demographic processes can be altered through policies and, alternatively, how population change and composition provide the contexts and rationales for social policy responses.

These themes of problem definition and policy implications are applied to virtually every substantive field of Canadian demography: mortality and health; international migration; population distribution and internal migration; population growth; population aging; families and households; social, economic, and cultural composition. In each area, Professor Beaujot reviews demographic themes and places them in the Canadian context. Depending on the history of policy development in each field, Professor Beaujot then discusses policy issues, implications, options, and/or responses associated with the specific demographic topic. The breadth of coverage is enormous. As the first Canadian book of its kind, *Population Change in Canada* represents an invaluable sourcebook for students and policy-makers who want to examine further the relationships among population events, processes, and policy issues.

Monica Boyd
Social Science Chair in Public Policy
University of Western Ontario

PREFACE

This book attempts to cover the full range of areas relevant to the study of population, from mortality, fertility, and migration to size, distribution, and composition. Beginning with the basic historical and contemporary trends, each chapter then suggests interpretations by way of putting these in a broader context. After proposing a framework for analysing policy, the discussion then proceeds to raise policy issues associated with each demographic component.

By trying to keep in mind both the whole population and its various components, one starts to appreciate the complexity of policy questions and the associated tradeoffs. Former Minister of Health and Welfare Monique Bégin has noted that among the principal groups vying for social policy attention, the elderly have been most successful, women have had intermediate success, and children have been least successful. There is a series of other competing interests: living longer or improving health, fertility vs. immigration, charter groups and visible minorities, families and individuals, economic growth and regional development. It is one thing to pick a specific interest and to follow it through to policy suggestions, but another to try to balance off the interests of one sector against others. The focus on the whole population and its components forces one at least to try to do justice to the rival interests. I am sure that no one will agree with all the positions I have taken, but my purpose will have been served if the discussions can be advanced with maximum recognition of the entire demographic context.

I owe debts of gratitude to many people. First to Betty Macleod, who invited me to make a presentation on "population policy development and Canadian demography" on the occasion of the tenth anniversary of the Canadian Population Society. This 1984 assignment spurred my interest in the interplay of population and policy. Second to Leroy Stone, who developed a course at the University of Western Ontario on "Canadian Population and Social Policy," then after a few years left it for me to teach. In effect, my greatest gratitude is to the students of Soc. 150, who over the years have contributed much to the discussions presented in this book.

In terms of the materials used here, the main vote of thanks goes to the Review of Demography and Its Implications for Economic and Social Policy. This small secretariat, based in Health and Welfare Canada and consisting of Mike Murphy, Gordon Smith, Louis Rouillard, and Krystyna Rudko, has done much to sponsor research and thinking on the ramifications of demographic questions. They have been particularly open to sponsoring various kinds of research that has enhanced our information and understanding. More broadly, I am indebted to all the researchers whose work I have used. At the same time, I am sure that I have not always done justice to the work of others, and the responsibility is mine for any incorrect interpretations or conclusions.

Thanks to Employment and Immigration and to Health and Welfare for sponsoring some of my own research that has found its way into this book. I have much benefited from the dedication of Suzanne Shiel and Lorraine Schoel at Western's Population Studies Centre. My appreciation also goes out for the support received from the editors at McClelland & Stewart, especially Michael Harrison and Richard Tallman. Particular thanks to Monica Boyd, Tom Wonnacott, and to two anonymous reviewers for their helpful comments on earlier versions. Finally, thanks to the taxpayers, who make it possible for professors to spend sabbaticals quietly musing over manuscripts, and to Elisabeth, Ariel, Natalie, and Damien, who have been very accommodating.

LIST OF TABLES

LIST OF FIGURES

INTRODUCTION

The demographic events of birth, death, and geographic movement mark a person's life course. As such they are events experienced by individuals. However, aggregated together these phenomena also demarcate the life courses of societies over history. Because of this social side, human groups take interest in the evolution of demographic events, especially over the long term.

At the group level, fertility and immigration are the basic mechanisms through which populations, countries, societies, or communities are regenerated. These regeneration processes not only add numbers to the population, ensuring demographic continuity in the face of departures through death and emigration, they also change the character of the population and thus of the society. The character of the population is changed in terms of age and sex structures, socio-economic composition, cultural make-up, and regional distribution.

Given the fundamental nature of these demographic processes to societies and their regeneration, the society has a vested interest to ensuring that the processes operate to produce an overall net benefit (see Demeny, 1988a). All societies or human groups will attempt to shape the decision-making framework of individuals in order to promote this common benefit. On fertility, certain types of behaviour will be promoted while others are constrained. On mortality, behaviour that will prolong a person's presence in the society will be encouraged, and often the society will take some responsibility for the health and safety of its citizens. On immigration, the society as a whole will typically establish structures, policies, and rules through which entry and sometimes exit are controlled, encouraged, and/or constrained to produce a social benefit.

One issue is how many new members are to be added to the society and by what means. Another question is how the benefits and costs of new admissions are distributed among existing members. How do given societies distribute the costs and benefits of children between the families of procreation and the larger extended family, community, and society? Similarly, how are the costs and benefits of immigration to be distributed between the immigrants themselves and their sponsoring families, on the one hand, and, on the other, the receiving country, province, city, or community? For mortality the question becomes the extent to which health and safety are the responsibility of the individual or the surrounding society. These are among the political questions all societies must address.

In Canada, as in many other countries, recent and anticipated demographic changes encourage a new look at some of these fundamental questions. Let us briefly enumerate these elements of change. In so doing, we will identify the major questions underlying this book

Much of the change takes its point of reference in families. The title of a book published in 1989 captures the idea well: *The Family in Crisis: A Population Crisis?* (Légaré *et al.*, 1989). Family trends have changed rather extensively in the past twenty years: lower marriage rates, more common-law unions, older ages at first marriage, higher divorce rates, lower remarriage rates, and lower levels of childbearing. At the level of the structure of households and families, more people are living alone and there are more single-parent families. Among two-parent families there is a strong increase in the two-earner category. Since both adults and children are less likely to be living in husband-wife families, there is a push for the society to take further responsibility for child welfare, especially in cases where the family security net is inadequate. The growth of both the single-parent family and the double-income family (often with no children) means it is difficult to have programs and services that treat all families equally, since some are much more self-sufficient than others.

These changes in our families are interrelated and, from the point of view of the regeneration of society, they imply lower levels of fertility. Fewer marriages, older ages at marriage, more cohabitation, more divorce all imply fewer births. As marriage provides a less secure environment, people are prone to have fewer or no children. Having to depend on their own resources, men and women especially are prone to ensure that career questions are secure before children become part of the picture.

Lower fertility has brought us to what some have called a "demographic turning point" involving lower population growth and significant population aging. This has implications for the labour force as it grows less rapidly and gets older, making it difficult to maintain flexibility and dynamism. Just as the labour force growth slows down, the growing proportion of older people means an increasing dependence on those in the labour force. Stated differently, the momentum to increase transfer payments to pay for health and pension programs means more taxes for the working population. At the same time, the society can hardly afford to ignore the needs of families with children. Transfers that benefit the aged are transfers away from workers, who are the ones who would normally have children.

Given lower birth rates, there is a tendency for immigration to take a larger role in "demographic recruitment." This is partly an accounting question: even at constant immigration, fewer births will mean that population growth will become more a function of immigration. There is also a tendency to think of immigration as a "solution" to lower births. This solution is not without its problems, however, or at least it requires adaptation on the part of the receiving society. The process of socialization into the receiving society is more complete when the new arrivals are infants. In addition, because immigrants have been previously socialized in another society or community, immigration introduces a greater element of newness or difference, it brings the "outside in," and it also promotes a link to the sending country, community, and family. Stated simply, immigration has a tendency to increase the diversity in Canada and to heighten the links with the world beyond.

Lower levels of births are also related to higher labour force participation on the part of women. In fact, with fewer young people entering the labour force and with more demands to have those in the labour force support a larger number of elderly, there is pressure for greater participation on the part of women. As the society tries to accommodate to the presence of both women and men in the labour force, policy issues are raised in various domains, including equity and child care.

Other demographic changes require us to take a new look at the evolving society. Migration within the country tends to favour Ontario in the East and British Columbia and Alberta in the West. This brings strains on interprovincial arrangements, especially as some provinces become so much smaller than others and yet need to somehow count equally within the Canadian federation. At another level, internal movement now favours the fringes (sometimes rural fringes) of large metropolitan areas. This prompts considerations both of renewing inner cities and of rapid transportation from the outer reaches.

In terms of cultural composition, there is not only the diversity brought by immigration but the tendency for the English language to increase at the expense of French. Regionally, there is a decline in both the English minority in Quebec and the French minority outside of Quebec, reducing the extent to which minority groups can help hold a bilingual country together.

Demographic change typically has both positive and negative aspects. For instance, in some regards lower fertility is very liberating: there are less unwanted births and the energies of adults (especially women) can be used for other pursuits. One might argue that lower population growth and an aging population are to be interpreted positively because they result from increases in real standards of living, growing social security, and more individual choice. However, we must also note that "good" things can sometimes have negative consequences. For instance, a higher use of energy has increased our standard of living. Nonetheless, it can also have negative impacts on our environment, especially if it causes a climatic change that would reduce the potential for human habitation on this planet. Similarly, the consequences of slower growth and aging may have both positive and negative aspects, and these may be different in the short term and long term.

As another example, we can speak of both the benefits and the problems of numbers. In one sense, larger numbers mean more competition for scarce resources. If there are more people, will there be enough jobs? If there are more old people, will there be enough services for them? Higher numbers mean "crowding" in various ways. People who are in a crowded situation can suffer a relative disadvantage in the competition for resources, whatever these may be. In another sense, larger numbers mean more strength, more people to deal with the problems. For instance, more scientists could discern better and more efficient approaches that would more than compensate for scarcities in natural resources. Crowding can intensify positive aspects: larger cities present more amenities of various kinds. The "grey power" groups certainly realize that numbers mean strength to change the social arrangements to their benefit. Especially in a democracy, larger numbers can have more weight. Quebec, for example, may be concerned that its relative share of the Canadian population has been declining, reducing its relative weight in national decision-making.

If I were alone in this world, in a sense I would be very rich because I would have everything. In another sense, I would have to do everything for myself and life would hardly be worth living, if I could live at all. Typically, the optimum lies somewhere in between small and large numbers. However, defining such an optimum, let alone the means of getting there, is very difficult. Regardless of the difficulty of the problem, societies need to face the question of numbers as they think of their future.

Facing the question of numbers, or demographic questions more broadly, can take two forms. Governments can try to influence the demographic developments or they can adapt the society to the changing demographics. If low fertility is judged to be problematic, the government can try to raise births or to increase immigration. Alternatively, institutional structures must be changed to accommodate an aging population, for instance by lowering the retirement benefits or by increasing taxes from workers. Each of these has its benefits and drawbacks, to the point that a government might want to work at all fronts. In effect, this book will look at both policies that might influence demographic trends (especially Chapters 2 to 5) and policies that might adapt to changing trends (especially Chapters 7 to 10).

CANADIAN POPULATION GROWTH IN THE WORLD CONTEXT

We can describe the world population growth of the last two and a half centuries as involving two major expansions, first the expansion of the regions now considered to be more developed, over the period 1750-1950, and later the expansion of the populations of the Third World (Merrick, 1986). In 1750, the world population was about 0.8 billion, of which 25 per cent was located on the continents of Europe (including all of the U.S.S.R) and North America, plus Oceania and Japan. By 1950 the latter had increased to 33 per cent of the world total of 2.5 billion. It was mostly after 1950 that the populations of Asia, Latin America, and Africa began to grow more rapidly. By 1990 the populations of Europe, North America, Oceania, and Japan were back to 23 per cent of the total world population of 5.3 billion (United Nations, 1989a and 1989b).

Broadly speaking, Canada has followed the pattern of the more developed regions. From the end of New France (1760) to Confederation (1867) the non-native population of Canada increased at an average rate of 3.68 per cent per year, from 70,000 to 3,341,000 (Beaujot and McQuillan, 1982: 111; Statistics Canada, 1990b: 28; Charbonneau, 1984: 45). By 1950 the population had increased to 13,712,000, for an average growth of 1.67 per cent per year. Such rates are amazingly high in historical context. Before the Second World War, an annual growth rate of even 1 per cent might have been considered high. In the period since 1950, growth in Canada has been more rapid than the average for Europe, North America, and Oceania, bringing the total to 26,525,000 in 1990, for an average growth over 1950-90 of 1.66 per cent per year.

According to the medium variant population projections from the United Nations (1989b), the world population would grow from 5.3 billion in 1990 to 8.5 billion in 2025. In this period, Europe, North America, Oceania, and Japan would increase by an average of 0.33 per cent per year, while Asia, Latin America, and Africa would increase by 1.60 per cent per year. By 2025, the populations of Europe, North America, Oceania, and Japan would comprise 16 per cent of the world total. Once again, the Canadian growth would be larger than the average for Europe, North America, and Oceania. The average Canadian growth over 1990-2025 would be 0.54 per cent per year according to these projections.

Taking the whole period since Confederation, Figure 1 compares growth in Canada with that in the United States, the United Kingdom, France, and the world. While the world population has multiplied by 3.8 over these 123 years, that of Canada has multiplied 7.7 times. At 3.5

million, the population of Canada was relatively small in 1867. Roughly speaking, it was about one-tenth the size of each of the United States, France, and the United Kingdom. While Canada retains this relationship to the United States, it is now closer to half the size of France and the United Kingdom. One could argue that this rapid population growth has helped to increase the relative status of Canada in the world. According to the United Nations projections, by 2025 Canada's population would be 11 per cent of that of the United States, 56 per cent of that of the United Kingdom, and 53 per cent of France (see also Keyfitz, 1987).

The population dimension gives Canada a certain uniqueness in the world community. Only 2.3 per cent of the world population lives in countries with higher life expectancy than Canada's, and only 7.5 per cent in countries with lower fertility (Population Reference Bureau, 1990). In addition, the relatively high and diversified immigration promotes a "cultural mosaic" in Canada. In other ways, Canada shares in the slower population growth and the consequent population aging that characterizes the more developed countries. Canada is on one side of an important demographic divide that distinguishes the developed countries from the rapidly growing and relatively young populations of the Third World. By receiving some two-thirds of its immigrants from Asia, Latin America, and Africa, this may help to retain a common sense of destiny with the other three-quarters of humanity.

HISTORY OF CONCERN ABOUT POPULATION SIZE IN CANADA

Summarizing population policy over the past 150 years in Canada, Marr (1987) concludes that until recently this policy had been quite simple: "Canada had a small population relative to her needs and so that population should be enlarged." The policy orientation to enlarge the population was especially visible in the 1820s, for the whole period of 1860 to 1930, and in the 1950s and early 1960s (Marr and Peterson, 1980). Especially before the turn of the century, emigration to the United States frustrated the attempt to promote population growth (Lavoie, 1972). The last clear policy statement favouring population growth is the 1966 White Paper on immigration (Manpower and Immigration, 1966: 7):

Immigration has made a major contribution to the national objectives of maintaining a high rate of population and economic growth. . . . Without a substantial continuing flow of immigrants, it is doubtful that we could sustain the high rate of economic growth and the associated

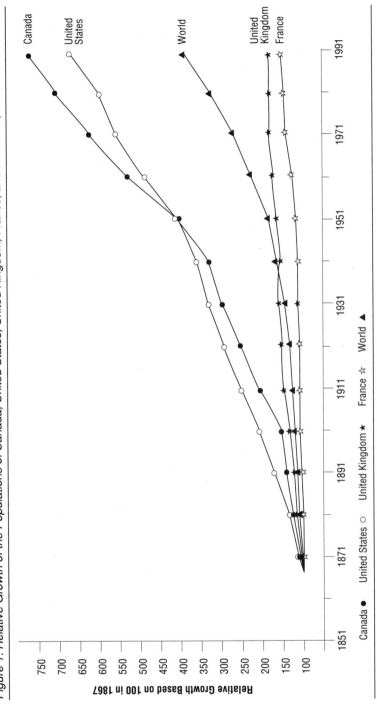

Figure 1: Relative Growth of the Populations of Canada, United States, United Kingdom, France, and the World, 1867-1990

Canada ●   United States ○   United Kingdom ★   France ☆   World ▲

SOURCES: Beaujot and McQuillan, 1982: 114; United Nations, 1989b.

cultural development which are essential to the maintenance and development of our national identity beside the economic and cultural pulls of our neighbour to the South.

It becomes harder to read the policy in the decades of the 1970s and 1980s. Certainly some sources argued for slower growth. A publication by the Conservation Council of Ontario and the Family Planning Federation of Canada (1973: 54) came out in favour of reducing growth: "Canada is already over-populated"; there is an "urgent need to ... reduce ... the absolute size of the human population of this country"; "even today, Canada has more people than it can support comfortably on a sustainable basis." With the benefit of hindsight, one can suggest that the concern was based on questionable assumptions. For instance, they observe that the "planet's supply of recoverable fossil fuels is unlikely to last much beyond 2000 A.D." In a recent review of such questions, Demeny (1988b) calculates that fossil fuel reserves will last another 280 years. The potential for population growth also seems to have been exaggerated by the Conservation Council of Ontario. It was suggested that migration could increase the total population by some 25 million by the year 2000. Such a scenario would have required some one million net immigrants per year, which should have hardly seemed probable.

Other voices expressed similar concerns. Barrett and Taylor (1977: 39) reviewed the different viewpoints regarding population and tended to favour an environmentalist approach that would work toward a "levelling off of further growth." In a report on "Population, Technology and Resources," the Science Council of Canada (1976) argued for reducing growth to maintain a long-term stable population size. Marsden (1972: 142) argued that there was a need for a comprehensive policy: "a policy concerning numbers, distribution and what we intend to do about them is essential." Her orientation was clearly in favour of slower growth: "We have not shown that continued growth is economically, politically, ecologically or socially desirable or necessary for the continued harmonious development of Canada" (p. 133).

At the level of the federal government, the 1974 Green Paper on immigration provides the clearest statement in favour of slower growth (Manpower and Immigration, 1974: 6): "it would probably be a not unfair assessment of our understanding of the economic consequences of higher against lower population growth rates ... to conclude that the evidence in favour of higher rates is uncertain." Stone and Marceau (1977: 60) cite this Green Paper to suggest that the "federal government favours, at least in the short term, a slowdown of growth." These authors also cite the Green Paper in noting the difficulties in setting definite targets and the uncertainties in implementing policies: "there are few firm handholds for policy in the field of demographic planning" (p. 67).

After the recession of the early 1980s, some government voices have implied that population growth should be sustained. This is especially the case in Quebec where concern about low births has clearly entered the political agenda and some policies have been introduced to encourage births. At the federal level, the clearest indication comes from the annual *Report to Parliament on Immigration Levels*, which over the period 1985-90 has argued for "moderate controlled growth" in immigration levels. These levels have in fact increased year by year from 84,000 in 1985 to 212,000 in 1990 (Howith, 1988; Dumas, 1990b: 37). There has been considerable support for this orientation on the part of the opposition parties; in effect, the discussions they introduce tend to say "why not more?"

RESEARCH ON POPULATION AND POLICY

It can be argued that until recently not much Canadian demographic research had been aimed at policy concerns (Beaujot, 1985). The Macdonald Royal Commission on the Economic Union and Development Prospects for Canada (1985, II: 668) found that population represented an area of Canadian policy that was "little debated, under-researched, and extremely important."

There has since appeared a considerably larger volume of literature. A special issue of *Cahiers Québécois de Démographie* was devoted to population and policy. For instance, Latouche (1988) observed that we have policies in various areas, but not in demography, yet the problems are serious and require attention. A special issue of *Population Research and Policy Review* was devoted to "Population Issues in Canadian Public Policy." In his "Editorial Introduction," Eric Moore (1989) noted a number of changing demographic phenomena that have consequences for public policy: declining growth, aging, family structures, urbanization.

In a publication by the Institute for Research on Public Policy, one of three major sections pays attention to "the nature of policy responses to demographic change" (Seward, 1987c). Consideration is given to the demands placed on programs by demographic change like population aging, declining fertility, changing family structures, and increased participation of women in the labour force. Iacobacci (1987: 24) observes that there is an "inability of the political system to recognize and respond to the complex requirements engendered by demographic change." The article in this collection by Bégin (1987) on "Demographic change and social policy" focuses on the competition for spending priority between three main client groups: the elderly, who have been most successful; women, who have had intermediate success; and children, who have been the least successful. She also presents an overview of issues relating to immigration, native peoples, and health care, as seen from the point of view of a former minister of Health and Welfare.

Internationally, the volume of literature has also increased. Without doing a full survey, one can note the special issue of the *European Journal of Population* (1987) on "Demographic change in Europe and its socio-economic consequences." Three other major publications that should be cited are: *The Fear of Population Decline* (Teitelbaum and Winter, 1985), "Below-Replacement Fertility in Industrial Societies: Causes, Consequences, Policies" (Davis *et al.*, 1986), and "Population and Resources in Western Intellectual Traditions" (Teitelbaum and Winter, 1988).

A number of countries have instituted public commissions or inquiries on the impact of demographic change. Focusing on twenty-eight countries that have total fertility rates of 2.3 births per woman or lower, Destin (1988) finds sixty-nine such inquiries since 1960 in twenty-four of the countries. This overview concludes that: (1) developed countries take an interest in their demographic change and its consequences and frequently have committees, commissions, work groups, or conferences to help make informed decisions, and (2) they do not always reach the same conclusions, for instance, low fertility and aging are sometimes seen as a danger, sometimes as a concern, sometimes as not a problem, sometimes as a good thing. However, "the most frequent conclusion nonetheless is that sustained below replacement fertility has more disadvantages than advantages in the long term . . . and that it would be desirable to have fertility go back to replacement levels."

Canada has had one major inquiry into demographic questions. Instituted by the federal government in 1986, the Review of Demography and Its Implications for Economic and Social Policy released its major report, *Charting Canada's Future*, in 1989. At the time of this release, the Review had sponsored some 167 reports by 160 demographers, economists, and other social scientists (Kettle, 1990). In effect, it is one purpose of the present book to provide a summary of this and other literature, which has become considerably more voluminous.

CONFLICTING QUESTIONS:
TO CHANGE OR TO ADAPT

In his book on *Population Change and Social Policy*, Keyfitz (1982) begins by noting that the issues are very complex: "whether we should be concerned about the low birth rate, about immigration, about age distribution in relation to social security, each involves a host of conflicting questions." While discussions of policy questions are needed, we must also realize, as Ryder (1985) has put it, that governments are by and large minor actors in the onrush of social change. Also, some of the adjustment can occur automatically. However, if there is concern about population dynamics, a key question is to know whether to try to influence these dynamics or to adapt to the changing population.

Hohn (1987) has observed that there is the potential for considerable conflict between the aims of various policies. While she favours policies that have explicit demographic aims, she points out that these can often be in conflict with other policies. She provides an argument in support of both immigration and pro-natalist policies. Pro-natalist approaches are those that would encourage more births. However, she also notes that both immigration and pro-natalist strategies tend to conflict with the goals of other important and powerful social and economic policies. For instance, many of the factors reducing fertility are rooted in the very emergence and expansion of the welfare state: the expansion of education has reduced the extent to which parents can profit from the labour of young children; social security for health and old age has reduced the dependence of elderly on their own children; and the emancipation of women has given them opportunities outside of family and child-care roles. More broadly, low fertility and long life expectancy reflect an enhanced quality of life. These blessings of the welfare state can be enjoyed even without children, from the individual point of view. But taken at the level of the society as a whole, children are of course needed (Hohn, 1987). Consequently, part of the conflict is between the goal of maximizing individual welfare in the short term and maximizing social welfare in the long term. Children are in many respects present pain for future gain. While social security allows the individual to avoid this dilemma, it cannot be avoided at the level of the society.

Chesnais (1987) speaks of the conflict as one between production and reproduction. Production and wealth are maximized, both at the individual and collective level, by maximizing the time spent in the labour force. But reproduction also takes time. Therefore there needs to be an adjustment between production and reproduction, and that adjustment has increasingly been to the detriment of the latter. In effect, it is mostly women who have made the adjustment and this has enhanced their status. Chesnais observes that the improvement of women's status has involved three stages: it began with access to education, as secondary and higher education became more democratically available; the second stage involved a quest for financial independence as women entered the labour market; the third stage involves a search for equal opportunities to men in daily life. There is room for considerably more change, because the second stage is not yet finished and the third is just beginning. These changes are also part of the modernization of society. However, the social cost of this democratization process is a growing scarcity of children. This poses problems at the level of the society, in particular with regard to the organization of gender roles to allow for both emancipation and reproduction.

In reviewing these trends, Lesthaeghe (1987) concludes that the new demographic regime will produce major strains on various social structures and ultimately on individual welfare. Chesnais (1987) is even more forceful, noting that the present situation is "unprecedented in peacetime." Nonetheless, as Lesthaeghe further observes, there is "room to manoeuvre." That manoeuvring, as Teitelbaum and Winter (1985) have well defined, includes possibilities of trying to influence fertility and immigration, as well as adapting to the changed demographics. Each of these approaches is difficult and costly in various regards. The solutions are not easy, but also it is not a crisis because demographic change is slow, allowing the society to intervene and/or adapt over time.

Another level of possible conflict, in long-term considerations, is that between population and the environment. For instance, in its 1989 annual review, the Economic Council of Canada points to problems of resource management in various areas and finds that inadequate management has reduced the organic content of soils between 36 and 49 per cent in the Prairies and by some 50 per cent in Ontario and Quebec. While ambient air quality has improved, carbon dioxide emissions are among the highest in the world on a per capita basis. The difficult question involves relating this to population growth. The population growth in the Prairie region, for example, can hardly be blamed for the deteriorating organic quality of the soil. It would be the increased demand for agricultural products at the world level, partly due to population growth, that would be to blame. One could even argue that a higher population on the Prairies, allowing for a more labour-intensive and less mechanical approach to agriculture, would involve less environmental deterioration. However, this solution would undermine the standards of living of agriculturalists.

Many have argued that the environmental problem lies less with population growth than with the level of consumption. The United States Commission on Population Growth and the American Future (1972) concluded that resource and environmental problems in the richer countries have little to do with population size or growth, but are attributable to changes in production technologies toward higher use of energy. Clearly, both population growth and standards of living are involved. Demeny (1988b) calculates that 60 per cent of the net increase in energy use in the United States over the period 1960-85 was generated by population growth. Of course, it is a bigger question to know whether this increased use of energy is a serious matter. In any case,

American population growth over the next twenty-five years is likely to be much lower, and conservation measures are likely to constrain the growth in per capita energy usage.

At some point, the degree of concern for the environment becomes a basic question of values and priorities. If one attaches a high priority to avoiding further degradation to the environment, possibly also wanting to maximize the cohabitation of the human species with the other species of the planet, then one is very likely to conclude that the population is already too large. If one feels that "small is beautiful," then again a lower population makes sense. This becomes a debate between those who see numbers of people as a problem and those who feel that more people means more ability to deal with the problems. An interesting example of this occurs in *Charting Canada's Future* (Review of Demography, 1989). When projecting population and economic growth in the long term, the authors note that per capita income is not much affected by the level of population growth. Of course, the total GNP is higher with a larger population. The authors therefore conclude that a larger population means more impact on the environment. From another point of view, one might note that a higher total size of the economy is to Canada's advantage. If Canada's population had remained at the level of 3.5 million that it had at Confederation, or the 12.3 million it had at the end of World War Two, supposedly that also would have had less impact on the environment. But would Canada be among the Group of Seven large Western industrial countries? That is, would it have as much influence in the world? Would it even be able to retain sovereign control over its large land mass?

Clearly, the issues are complex, but it does not follow that they should be ignored. In addressing these issues, this book has three purposes. First, the demographic trends are presented, in both their historical and contemporary contexts. Second, interpretations are suggested by way of putting demographic questions into a larger context. The third purpose is to discuss related policy issues. Policy outcomes never follow directly from trends or research, and I have chosen to focus on certain questions while ignoring others. Nonetheless, consideration will be given both to policies that might attempt to change demographic trends and to policies that might help to accommodate the anticipated trends. Therefore, beginning with the larger historical perspective, the discussion moves to a framework for analysing policy and then proceeds to examine each demographic component and to raise related policy issues.

1

POPULATION PROCESSES AND POLICY PROCESSES

POPULATION PROCESSES

Demography is the study of populations, their size, distribution, and composition, and the immediate factors causing population change (births, deaths, migration). We are interested in the stock and flow of population. The stock, or the population state, is a picture of the population at one point in time, including its size, its distribution over geography, and its composition along a variety of characteristics including age, sex, marital status, education, language spoken at home, occupation, income, etc. The flow, or the population processes, changes population from one point in time to another. People are born, move around, and die. Demographically, these processes are called fertility, migration, and mortality. Population states and processes are dynamically interrelated; for instance, lower births (process) produce an older population (state), and also an older population tends to have a lower birth rate.

In trying to understand how a society changes and how it compares to other societies, it is natural to start by describing its demographic profile. In effect, the study of population is closely intertwined with the study of society. One looks to the broader society to understand both the causes and the consequences of demographic phenomena. For instance, various social factors are considered when analysing the causes of variations in fertility, mortality, and migration. One also considers that certain population trends, such as the rate of growth, the distribution over space, and the composition by language, have consequences for the society.

The study of population also has a practical importance. To plan public services, it is important to know the nature of the population groups subject to these services. How many people are at retirement ages and how will this change in the future? How many single-parent families exist? What proportion of the unemployed are secondary wage earners in their families? These are among the host of questions that are important to the structuring of social programs.

The interplay between population and policy can take two forms: one can consider how policies have consequences on population dynamics, or one can consider how population dynamics have implications for policy. That is, one can consider policy questions as one of the causes of population change, or one can consider that population changes have consequences in terms of policy considerations. Some policies are aimed at influencing population processes, or they may have unintended effects on population. We will want to consider how policies influence, or might influence, mortality, fertility, and migration.

Also, demographic trends need to be considered when analysing policy issues in areas such as support services for the aged, health, education, labour force and family policy, and social security. Especially in a welfare state, where the state takes some responsibility for the welfare of individuals, detailed knowledge about the population is important for those who seek to devise appropriate policy.

Data and methods

The data used for demographic analyses come largely from the census, vital statistics, and other administrative files. In Canada, censuses are taken every five years while births and deaths are registered through vital statistics. Immigration is carefully regulated, which includes the collection of information on landed immigrants who arrive. That leaves only emigration and illegal immigration to be estimated.

The methods used basically start with proportions and rates. In the study of population states, much use is made of proportions, that is, considering how a given total population is divided into various sub-parts, each representing a certain proportion of the total. The study of population processes typically starts with rates, that is, numbers of events (especially births and deaths) per population exposed to the risk of that event.

Finally, demographic analyses often use a "cohort" approach. A cohort is a group of people who experienced a given event in a given period of time. For instance, people born in a given period (birth cohort) can be followed over their lives in terms of progression to marriage, having children, and death. Similarly, persons who finished school in a given year can be followed in terms of their entry into the labour force, career progression, and retirement. The cohort approach can be useful in studying various social and economic phenomena.

Theories on causes and consequences of population change

The points of view of Malthus, Marx, and human ecologists are useful in studying the determinants and consequences of population change. Malthus (1766-1834) is often considered to have been the first person to have developed a systematic theory of population change and its relation to economic conditions. He believed the causes of population growth were fairly natural. Because of the "passion between the sexes" and a certain urge to reproduce, there is a fairly natural tendency for the population to grow, in fact, to grow more rapidly than the available food supply. On the other hand, there are two checks on population growth. One he called "positive" (which we would now call mortality), including famine, epidemics, wars, and plagues. The other check he called "preventive" (fertility) and could take two forms: "moral restraint," that is, the deferment of marriage, and "vice," which involved prevention of births in marriage through abortion, infanticide, or what he considered to be unacceptable methods of contraception.

Malthus thought the consequences of population growth were fairly serious. Since population had a tendency to grow more rapidly than the available resources (especially food), population growth produced "poverty." Especially in his early writings, he did not see much possibility of avoiding the problem because if for some reason the food supply increased more than the population, people would probably get married earlier and have more children so that eventually there would be even more people living in poverty. He was afraid that if the conditions of the poor were improved (for instance, through a more equitable distribution of income), there would result even more population growth and thus a larger problem in the long term. He felt strongly that people had to absorb the consequences of their own actions and he preached "responsible procreation" or "moral restraint" as a way of avoiding the problem.

When we use Malthusian thought nowadays we often refer to the "Malthusian trap," that is, the population is limited by the means of subsistence, or continuous growth is not possible in a limited world. In this context, the "Malthusian solution" is to avoid having deaths increase as a "positive" solution but rather to encourage a reduction of births both through later marriage and especially through the use of contraception. In effect, the Malthusian inspiration is to consider population growth to be a serious problem causing poverty, pressure on resources, and undermining efforts to improve the society. The obvious solution is to reduce population growth by reducing births.

Marx (1818-1883) wrote extensively on the economic, political, and social relations in society, but his writing on population was mostly in opposition to Malthus. Marx thought there were various stages in human history (slavery, feudalism, capitalism, socialism) and that each stage was rather different in terms of the relations among classes or social groups in the society. Each stage had a "mode of production" – a way in which economic production was organized – and specific "relations of production," that is, relations among classes of people who have different vested interests in the production process. He also thought that each stage of human history would have its own "laws of population," that the dynamics of population growth would follow on the mode of production and the relations of production as these worked themselves out in specific economic systems.

While Marx did not specify these "laws of population" for each stage of history, he did write about the population dynamics under capitalism. He felt that the capitalist class had a tendency to become smaller but more powerful as it came to have increasing control over the means of production. In contrast, the working class had a tendency to get larger and to lose control over the product of its labour. He believed that workers were not paid the full value of their labour and that this surplus value was appropriated by the capitalist class, allowing them to invest and to become more dominant. In effect, according to Marx, the capitalist system depends on a reserve of labour. The capitalist economy has a natural tendency to have periods of strong growth and periods of recession. More workers were needed during the periods of growth, and these could be let go during periods of recession. More important, a certain surplus of labour ensured that wages be kept low in order to maximize the amount of surplus value that could be extracted.

It can be seen that Marx felt that problems of excess population were specific to the capitalist system. According to him, there were not too many people but too many poor people, and they were impoverished due to the inherent exploitation of the system. If we had a more equitable society the problem would disappear. Contrary to Malthus, who was somewhat of a pessimist, Marx was more of an optimist and felt that with the proper economic and social arrangements we would be able to produce all the food and other resources necessary to accommodate population growth. More people should be able to create more wealth and more food.

When we use Marxist thought in relation to population now, we may not necessarily follow the specific stages of human history that Marx elaborated, and we may question some of his conclusions regarding the laws of population under capitalism. The basic inspiration is that certain economic and social arrangements (or different basic structures of societies) induce certain population dynamics. If the population dynamics are to be changed, one needs first to change the economic and social arrangements. Population is not a cause of social problems, as Malthus had argued, but a consequence of socio-economic conditions.

The debate between Malthusian and Marxist thought on population takes various forms. In 1968 Ehrlich published *The Population Bomb*, which is frequently quoted to this day. He argued that the rapid population growth in the world, given limited resources, was going to tear our world apart. Several years later, Simon (1981) published *The Ultimate Resource*, where he argued that people are the ultimate resource with regard to economic growth. While Ehrlich was concerned about somewhat different problems than Malthus and Simon is not a Marxist, it can be seen that they are inspired by the different sides of this debate.

As we will see, this debate also exists in Canada, where it can take various forms. Some have argued that we need to be concerned about population growth not only because of the available resources but also because of pollution and possible climatic change. Others have argued that population growth is good for Canada since the population is small to start with and a larger population would create more markets and more economic development.

In effect, some arguments point to the disadvantages of population size and growth while others point to the advantages of numbers. This is a question to which we will frequently return. For the time being, we can probably take something from each of Malthus and Marx. From Malthus, we can take the point of view that the society needs to be concerned about its population, whether the concern be about the population growing too rapidly or not rapidly enough. That is, questions of population are important to the welfare of societies and it makes sense that certain policies be instituted to ensure that the population evolves in a way that corresponds to the social benefit. The society may want to influence people to act in ways that correspond to this aspect of social welfare. From Marx, we can take the view that population dynamics are largely a function of social arrangements, and especially of broadly defined economic structures. As the society evolves, there will be different population dynamics. To understand population trends, it is first essential to understand the underlying economic and social dynamics.

The point of view of human ecology presents a useful overarching perspective with which to conclude this discussion of theoretical orientations on population processes. The study of ecology is basically the study of organisms in their environment, how they gain their sustenance from the environment, and, in so doing, how they introduce some changes to that environment. The same is true for human ecology, except that we now add two other major considerations: in gaining their sustenance from the environment, human populations make use of organization and technology.

The interplay of these four basic considerations (population, organization, technology, and environment) presents a picture of population dynamics. For instance, population growth has largely followed new forms of organization (e.g., urban revolution) or developments in technology (e.g., agricultural revolution, industrial revolution). Changes in the environment itself can produce opportunities or hazards (e.g. stable climate or climatic change). Some have argued that population pressure on the environment or changes in organization (e.g., settlement patterns on agricultural land) or changes in technology (e.g., intensive usage of fossil fuels) can bring about changes in the environment and thus in the potential for further sustenance. Others have proposed that when a population is under pressure from its environment, this may induce it to find new forms of organization and technology to enable it to survive and prosper (necessity is the mother of invention). The perspective of human ecology enables us to put population in a very broad perspective and also to note that an organized human population will want to introduce policies to maximize its welfare in a given environment, for both the short and longer terms.

POLICY PROCESSES

The study of policy processes cannot be defined as easily as the study of population processes. Nonetheless, we need to have an understanding of the definition, theories, and determinants of policy processes. Very broadly, we can think of the study of policy as the study of "what governments do and why" (Simeon, 1976). Agencies other than governments can have policies, but we will here largely limit ourselves to government. Policies can be studied in terms of the rationales used to justify them, the means adopted, and their effects. Rationales or purposes are sometimes explicit, but some rationales are implicit. The means adopted can vary from regulation (which allows and disallows certain activities) to the distribution of the resources of the state and the redistribution from some people or groups to others.

Social policies would then be policies of government that are aimed at improving the social well-being. According to Yelaja (1978: 7) social policy is concerned with the formulation, development, and management of specific services of government at all levels, such as health, education, income maintenance, and welfare. A publication by the World Bank (1984: 9) points out that "the ultimate goal of public policy is to improve living standards, to increase individual choice, and to create conditions that enable people to realize their potential." The social well-being can be defined in terms of individual well-being (as the World Bank definition implies) or in terms of the welfare of legitimate groups within the society or of the overall organized society itself. These distinctions may be unnecessary if one assumes that what benefits the overall society will benefit the individuals within it. However, something that benefits certain groups, or even the overall society, may not benefit other specific groups. Clearly, there is room for conflict in the cost/benefit calculus around given alternatives.

It can immediately be seen that there are some links between the study of population and the study of policy. Especially if we think of social policy as attempting to improve the social well-being, it is important to know about the population whose well-being one is trying to improve. In effect, modern censuses and other forms of demographic data collection have appeared with the emergence of the welfare state. As governments took more responsibility for the welfare of citizens, they needed more knowledge about the current demographic conditions. The relationship between population and policy can go in both directions. The existing population conditions can induce policy-makers to consider certain policy approaches. In addition, social policy may have an effect on the population. Note that we are not here using the words "population" and "society" interchangeably. That a social policy would have an effect on society is almost true by definition; otherwise, the policy would be purposeless. As defined above, we are using population to refer to demographic states (size, distribution over space, composition by various characteristics) and processes (fertility, mortality, migration). Thus, our specific concern in this instance is how policy affects population states or processes.

Determinants of policy

It is important to have a broad sense of the processes of policy determination, that is, the dynamics through which policy issues are raised, given priority in relevant bodies, and adopted. These processes generally involve conflict and negotiation among relevant interest groups and across various institutions.

Figure 2: Determinants of Policy

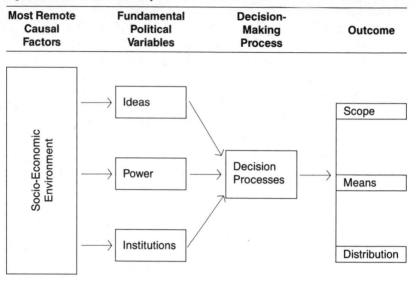

Most Remote Causal Factors	Fundamental Political Variables	Decision-Making Process	Outcome

SOURCE: Adapted from Simeon (1976).

The elaboration here will largely follow Simeon (1976) (see Figure 2), who starts by asking what we should study about policy, and then answers that the scope of policy (what governments do), the means (how governments do it), and the distribution or effect (how the costs and benefits of government action are distributed) are all significant. Policy-making involves choices and therefore conflict over alternative choices. However, at a given point in time, the range of choices is limited because of an "accepted framework" of activities that are generally taken for granted. The elements of this "accepted framework" tell us a lot about the broad determinants of policy (that is, about the scope, means, and distribution) at a given point in time. This framework also implies that policy evolves in "incremental" stages, that is, decision-makers consider a limited number of closely related alternatives that are incrementally rather than radically different (see Doern and Aucoin, 1979). There is often a limited margin of manoeuvrability. For instance, past spending constrains present spending.

According to Simeon, the elements of the accepted framework, or the broad determinants of policy, are as follows: (1) the character of the socio-economic environment, (2) political forces of power and influence, (3) social forces or dominant ideas and values of the society, as manifested through (4) the existing formal institutional structures and (5) the policy process involving given actors and the media.

The *socio-economic environment* includes such factors as the demography, geography, level of wealth, and industrialization in the country. Simeon argues that this "environment of policy" is particularly relevant to the scope of policy because it defines both the set of problems that need to be dealt with and the limits on the available resources in attacking these problems. For instance, we can argue that government actions have larger scope as a function of a larger population and more economic growth. As the society involves more exchanges (for instance, through higher urbanization and specialization) there is more need to transport people or things and to regulate the equity in the exchanges among people and groups.

The *political forces* involve the distribution of interests in the society and the resources available to those interests (that is, their power to look after their own interests). Here we pay particular attention to elite groups and powerful corporations. Simeon argues that these political forces are especially relevant to the study of the distribution of policy. That is, special interests and their political power are most relevant to understanding the distribution of benefits and burdens of policy among social groups. Obviously, inasmuch as the powerful are selfish, they will first look after their own interests. However, Simeon suggests that the self-interestedness of elites should not be taken for granted; they may also seek to serve the interests of followers. Policy may also distribute the benefits widely, especially as it involves a compromise between competing interests. Besides affecting the distribution aspects of policy, these political forces also influence its scope. In particular, as more groups have power, this proliferation of interests likely creates a wider scope to government action. A proliferation of interests would tend to promote greater expenditure to satisfy these various interests and to regulate the competition among interested parties.

The *ideas and values* of the society include the "political culture" – the dominant ideologies. There can be homogeneity (one dominant ideology) or ideological diversity. Simeon argues that ideology influences the scope, means, and distribution of policy. In effect, these ideas affect the scope of government activity (should it be large or restricted), the legitimate means to use (permissible tactics), and the desired distribution or redistribution of the costs and benefits of policy. In an article on ideas underlying Canadian social policy, Doern (1983) suggests that these ideas include redistribution of income from rich to poor, social policy rights or universal programs that are part of citizenship, and the quality of life as reflected in every area from health care to culture.

The *institutions* are the formal way the government is organized. Compared to environment, power, and ideas, institutions are the more immediate determinants of policy. The formal institutional structures in place include the federal-provincial jurisdictions, the degree of cen-

Figure 3: Institutions Involved in the Policy Process

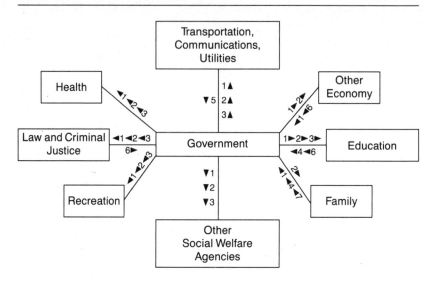

Legend
1. Financing
2. Regulations
3. Supervision
4. Labour supply
5. Energy supply
6. Information inputs
7. Client flows

SOURCE: Stone (1983: 47). Used with permission.

tralization, the role of political parties, the structure of policy planning, and the bureaucracy. The society can be thought of as a network of linked institutions, and many of these are involved in given policy processes (see Figure 3). Stone (1983) lists the following institutions, with government in the middle: utilities, health, law, recreation, other social welfare, family, education, other economy. The links among institutions have various forms, including financing, regulations, labour supply, and information and client flows. Institutions have a vested interest in maintaining or increasing their scope in the society. Policy often has ramifications in various areas and consequently the policy processes generally involve conflict and negotiation among these interlinked institutions.

Another set of immediate determinants of policy, the *process of decision-making*, involves the policy-making actors themselves, that is, the politicians, the bureaucrats, the interest group leaders, the media, and sometimes the electorate. They are the bridge through which the broader forces operate. However, these actors also have their own interests and they represent given structures; thus, they may seek to influence the outcomes in ways that would benefit these interests and structures.

This discussion of the determinants of policy highlights certain links between population processes and policy processes. As already indicated, population questions (including size, distribution over space, and composition by various characteristics) would be part of the broad environment of policy. Second, different population groups may carry different predominant ideas. For instance, it is sometimes said that the generation that lived through the depression and the baby boom generation that grew up in the 1960s carried with them certain political cultures regarding the proper role of government. Similarly, immigrant groups can bring in new ideologies. As some of these groups pass on, the ideas they represent may become less dominant in the society. In addition, different population groups may represent different interests and hold different amounts of power. One might also argue that population size is one of the elements of the power of a group. Larger groups (e.g., larger provinces or larger cohorts) may carry more weight. Similarly, the size of institutions, including the number and quality of their personnel, and the other resources at their disposal influence their relevance in the policy process.

The policy process in Canada

In their book on *The Social Policy Process in Canada*, Dobell and Mansbridge (1986) have surveyed and analysed the various agencies involved in shaping social policy. There are the central agencies (Prime Minister's Office, Treasury Board, Department of Finance, Privy Council Office), the line departments (Health, Employment, etc), provinces (with their cabinets and ministries), municipalities, and a series of nongovernmental organizations such as advisory or planning councils, business associations, labour organizations, professional associations, research institutes, service organizations, and other interest groups. It is judged that some 10,000 to 15,000 organizations have an interest in the development of social policy.

Dobell and Mansbridge argue that the social policy agencies are not as well co-ordinated as those in the economic policy area. Economic policy agencies are based on a stronger theoretical consensus and they are typically better funded. The authors speak of the two areas as "two solitudes" and argue for more integration across economic and social sectors. In particular, they suggest that both the economic and social costs and benefits should be weighted in the consideration of given alternatives. At the very least, we should not assume that social policies represent economic costs, and we should not avoid talking about the social costs of economic policy.

One component of the difficulty of social policy, as implied above, is that of conflicting jurisdictions between the municipal, provincial, and federal levels. Banting (1987a) argues that we have a "bifurcated welfare state" with the federal government dominant in the area of income security while the provinces are predominant in establishing policy in education, health, and social and community services (cited in E. Moore, 1989). Looking at the post-war era, Shifrin (1985) states that we have seen a rise of the federal role in income security, but this federal role has since "stalled."

It is worth elaborating further on the role of pressure groups or interest groups in public policy, following Pross's *Pressure Group Behaviour in Canadian Politics* (1975). While pressure groups vary considerably, from single-issue groups (e.g., anti-cruise missile testing) to institutionalized groups (e.g., Canadian Council on Social Development), Pross sees them as basically communication links between the people and the government. The advice and support of pressure groups contribute to the creation of acceptable public policy. Inasmuch as these groups, representing a broader public, are involved in the policy process, policies gain greater legitimacy as seen by the public. Given that the policy process in Canada works through the party system and the government bureaucracy, which are somewhat closed and hierarchical systems, this favours the institutionalized pressure groups over the single-issue groups. These institutionalized pressure groups can have sufficient resources (part of which often comes from government itself) to gather the necessary information, make the necessary arguments and presentations, and have continuous contact with relevant politicians and civil servants. In effect, this favours a small number of elite pressure groups (among the thousands) who consult with government regularly and work out an accommodation or consensus. It might be noted in passing that demographics are not irrelevant to pressure groups: the size of the population represented by a pressure group is often used as a justification of its weight; the composition of members often follows categories in the population (e.g., the Canadian Multicultural Council mostly involves ethnic groups other than English and French); and population regeneration is important for the maintenance of the size of a given group.

Presthus (1973) proposes that the policy process in Canada involves "elite accommodation" among the top-level legislators, civil servants, and interest group leaders. He argues that the close interaction among these three elites constitutes one of the essential mechanisms of the Canadian political-economic system. They "accommodate" in the sense that they negotiate, consult, and "hammer out an accommodation." This also implies, as Presthus suggests, that there is limited mass participation in the policy process, and in fact a limited role for the political parties in the formulation of policy. It also implies that there is little comprehensive, long-range social and economic planning. The accommodation occurs over problems as they arise. Finally, this elite accommodation implies considerable support for the status quo since it is difficult for new or weaker interests to penetrate the decision-making process. On the other hand, Presthus notes that this system of accommodation has maintained the solvency of the Canadian nation and has developed forms of resource allocation that have reasonable popular support.

We are talking about policy-making in a state that is both liberal-democratic and capitalist (Atkinson and Chandler, 1983). By liberal-democratic is meant that it seeks to provide services for the mutual benefit of all citizens. By capitalist is meant that policy-making aims to maintain the social, economic, and political stability congruent with capital accumulation. Yelaja (1978) has specified three assumptions that are implicit in a liberal-democratic approach to social policy. (1) The government has the responsibility to meet the needs of the less fortunate members of society. (2) The state has the right to intervene in areas of individual freedom and economic liberty. (3) Government intervention is necessary when existing social institutions fail to fulfil their obligations. These three assumptions need to be seen together. For instance, the government cannot meet the needs of the less fortunate unless there are some limits to individual freedom and economic liberty. The question then becomes, how much responsibility does the state have for the less fortunate and how many limits must be placed on freedom and liberty? These assumptions, which in effect define a welfare state, are very new in human history. Only in the last 100 years or so have certain states taken this kind of responsibility for the welfare of the population. As already indicated, this implies that there needs to be thorough information on the population whose welfare is at interest.

Clearly, within these broad assumptions, there is room for considerable differences of opinion or variations on the direction of social policy. Banting (1987b) argues that there is somewhat of a tension between a "universal" and a "redistributive" welfare state. In the immediate post-war period, the universal model was more dominant. Given the difficulties of the 1930s and of the war period, including the difficulty of maintaining social cohesion over the regions of the country, the dominant vision involved an attempt to counter this insecurity through a "set of universal social programs that would protect all citizens from the insecurities inherent in an industrial economy, and more generally, assist them in participating effectively in a modern society." Out of this model evolved a series of major social services in the fields of health, education, and income security: pensions, unemployment insurance, workers' compensation, family allowance, disability and sickness benefits (see also Johnson, 1987).

Banting further proposes that during the 1960s and 1970s this universal model was somewhat under question in favour of the model of a "redistributive welfare state." For instance, it was noted that the poor were not the major beneficiaries of many of the universal programs and the gap between rich and poor has not narrowed. Various proposals were made to restructure income security programs and to integrate the tax and transfer systems into a coherent redistributive mechanism. While these broad proposals for guaranteed annual income or negative income tax were not adopted, various adjustments (e.g., tax credits, income-tested supplements, selective benefits) moved the system into a more redistributive mode.

The tension between the universal and redistributive approaches also characterized the 1980s, especially in the context of a felt need to lower the national debt. Courchene (1987) notes in particular that we can no longer afford those aspects of the social policy network that serve to impede economic adjustment. He also argues for social policy that is better integrated with economic policy by supporting occupational, industrial, and geographic relocation. Nonetheless, Courchene proposes that the social security system move slowly toward a negative income tax approach. Recent developments in this direction include the greater of refundable tax credits and taxation ("clawback") of social benefits at higher incomes. "Refundable" means that the credit can be received even if income is too low for taxes to be paid, while the clawback on benefits is at a higher rate than on other income.

LINKING POPULATION PROCESSES AND POLICY PROCESSES

The discussion to this point has already raised various ways in which population and policy processes may be linked. Briefly, policy can be seen as a determinant or a consequence of population trends. Also, policy processes may partly originate in the "population environment," and they often are concerned with improving the social welfare of given demographic groups.

Demeny (1986b) argues that three conditions need to be met to justify population policy. First there needs to be a population problem, or a situation where individual decisions do not add to the recognized collective welfare. That is, because of these individual decisions (to have or not have children, to move, etc.) the population dynamics (for instance, rate of growth or decline) do not maximize the social welfare. Besides a recognized population problem, Demeny states that two further conditions must be met to justify population policy. There needs to be a sense that the population problem can be remedied, and at a cost lower than the cost of the problem itself. Finally, there needs to be a sense that the problem will not solve itself automatically. In discussions of population policy, issues are typically raised at all of these levels: Is it a problem? Can it be remedied at a cost lower than the cost of the problem itself? Will it resolve itself automatically? In regard to the problem of high population growth in developing countries, there is some consensus that it is a problem, that the problem will not resolve itself automatically, and that it can at least be alleviated within reasonable costs. As we will see, there is less consensus regarding the problem of low growth or decline. Clearly, these are core issues for a society; they relate to questions of how many people are to be added to the society, by what means, and at whose cost and benefit. It should not be surprising that these questions can generate considerable discussion and disagreement. Demeny perceives them as relating to the very "constitution of the society."

Preston (1987) specifies four ways in which population problems have been identified. At the macro-economic level, there would be a population problem if the demographic dynamics undermine the average output per worker or average productivity. At the micro-economic level, a problem occurs if one family's behaviour infringes on the welfare of other families, for instance, if large families undermine the quality of education for others or if the preference for not having children undermines the claim for secure pension benefits on the part of other families. The medical definition of a population problem pays particular attention to the health consequences of unwanted births. Finally, the environmental definition pays attention to the ways in which population dynamics may make it difficult to preserve the quality of the environment over the long term.

While we can speak of policies that might directly attempt to influence the population dynamics, clearly most population policies are implicit and are motivated by objectives that go beyond demography, by a desire to satisfy certain broad social policy objectives (Stone, 1983). For instance, questions of population size may be of concern in regard to security from military or economic invasion, or in regard to conservation of natural resources. Questions of mortality may enter into discussions about the maintenance of adequate public health. Questions of immigration may be relevant to the avoidance of perceived public disorder or the preservation of cultural values. Questions of women's roles and fertility may be relevant to the production and sharing of wealth and to opportunities for personal advancement.

Besides these ways in which policy might seek to influence population dynamics directly in order to maximize collective welfare, there are also ways in which policy in various areas needs to take into consideration the evolving demographic trends. As an example, the Economic Council of Canada (1989) points to the aging of the population as increasing the responsibilities that must be borne by future workers. The growth of the proportion at older ages will mean that "it is the 20-to-64-year olds who will be most crucial to the cohesion of Canadian society, since they will be the producers of the goods and services used by all age groups, and they will be the care givers to both elderly and children." The Economic Council goes on to argue that the rising ratio of retirees to workers will make it more difficult to achieve improvements in the living standards of working Canadians and their children. There is a "risk of a clash in priorities between future workers and retirees" and a need to "identify the policy levers available to head off this crisis."

Other examples can be given regarding the way demographic change can be involved in raising policy issues. The movement of the baby boom generation through the life cycle raised issues first in education, then in labour force entry, now with regard to promotions, and later for retirement (Kettle, 1980). The geographic distribution of the population raises questions of maintaining cohesion across regional cleavages (Breton and Breton, 1980). The linguistic composition of migration to Quebec and the patterns of language transfer raise issues regarding the preservation of the French language. The baby bust of the past two decades caused declines in school enrolment, bringing many neighbourhood groups into conflict over policies on school closures, classroom sizes, teacher salaries, and release of redundant teachers (Stone, 1983). The gap in survival rates between men and women increases the numbers of elderly women in need of pensions and health care provisions. The heavy in-migration of native peoples to western Canadian cities places pressure on social services that aid the unemployed and the poor (Stone, 1983). A higher dependence on immigration as the source of population replacement poses problems with regard to integration of people with diverse ethnic and cultural backgrounds (Priest, 1990). Population decline may accentuate problems of dislocation: as certain sectors become obsolescent, the re-absorption of associated workers may be more difficult under conditions of demographic decline.

In a review of the "Effects of Demographic Shifts on Public Policy Issues," Western Opinion Research (1986) notes that while many factors (task forces, political parties, interest groups, foreign events, the media) determine what policy issues are raised at a given time, "demographic trends will always have to be taken into consideration when determining present public policy issues and projecting future issues." The demographic trends that Western Opinion Research reviews include aging, gender differences, urban and rural distribution, family size and structure, and ethnicity (native peoples and immigration). These trends raise issues in a variety of areas, including: child benefits, day care, child support services, old age benefits, health care services, housing, social control, environment protection, immigrant services, pay equity, affirmative action, demand for education and other social services, labour market, income support, transfer payments across regions, urban renewal, and transportation.

It is important to remember that many factors besides the demographic ones highlighted here influence policy decisions. As indicated in the earlier discussion based on Simeon (1976), other important considerations are the values and priorities of the political community, as understood or promoted by decision-makers. It is not just research, empirical evidence, and analysis that dictate what we do, but also our values, what is important to us, and our vision of the future.

Preston (1987) cites an interesting example of this. Commissions based in Sweden and the United States, in the 1930s and 1960s respectively, considered the issues of population growth to the future of their societies. The Swedish commission was concerned about how to raise fertility while the American one concluded that slower growth would be better. In spite of this important difference, the two made rather similar recommendations: expand family planning services, provide equal employment opportunities for women, and expand social support for child care and child-raising. Preston concludes that the similarity in recommendations results not from the similarity in the demographic situation but because of overlap in values. Regardless of the situation, what is to be done needs to be compatible with basic cultural values. In both cases, these values probably included a wish to expand rather than restrict the domain of personal choice and a desire to reduce social inequalities rather than increase them. Clearly, organized human societies determine how population problems are defined, and these definitions delimit legitimate solutions (Preston, 1987: 641).

Therefore, social policy development does not result only from rational, objective analysis and debate (Dobell and Mansbridge, 1986: 34). Faced with difficult choices, policy-makers can be tempted to avoid taking the responsibility for these decisions by putting the onus on the researchers. Given the complexity of the real world, rare is the case where research is more than one of several input factors to a decision. Dobell and Mansbridge (1986: 41) conclude that studies based in the United States have shown that research has little direct impact on policy, but indirectly it can help to frame the issues and to cast light on various options. In order for research to be relevant to decision-makers, Fellegi (1979) proposes that researchers need to (a) identify social problems of recognized importance, (b) determine through analysis the factors related to such problems, (c) find out which of these can be influenced through decisions, and (d) effectively communicate the results.

Clearly, the policy process involves a variety of considerations. Also, the outcome often cannot be linked to the antecedents in any strictly "logical" fashion (Stone, 1983: 34). The "logic" of policy is not deductive logic ("this is true, therefore that follows"); it is not even economic logic ("maximize the benefits and minimize the costs"). Political logic includes "what will work." Of course, in justifying a policy one tries to do so in terms of deductive and economic logic, but often the logic of competing interest and power is the real underlying rationality. Stated somewhat differently, Carrothers (1977) notes that "public policies are like two-headed Janus, looking in different directions." On the one hand, values or principles are not easily compromised. On the other hand, while power, institutions, and processes are only a means to an end, they can also very much determine the end itself.

2

MORTALITY, HEALTH, AND HEALTH CARE

We have witnessed remarkable changes in longevity and health care over the course of Canadian history. At the time of Confederation, the average life expectancy at birth was forty-two years, and the leading causes of death were infectious diseases that led to mortality in infancy, childhood, and early adult life. Few reached the seventh or eighth decade of life. Health care was largely the responsibility of individuals and charities. In 1986 life expectancy reached seventy-six years, while the leading causes of death had become the chronic diseases that predominantly affect individuals in the later decades of life. Unprecedented numbers are reaching these later decades. The fastest growing age group is comprised of those aged eighty years and above. Health has become an important government priority.

The changes and adaptations foreseen for the future are equally impressive. As Stolnitz (1987: 203) has observed, "long relegated to secondary status when compared to fertility changes, foreseeable changes in death rates are again pointing to significant effects on individual planning horizons, social structures and major policy needs." The large and cumulative increases in upper-age survival chances especially may require "watershed socio-economic and even political adaptations" (p. 205). Stone and Fletcher (1986) have made similar observations: "it has been said that the second most consequential development (after the baby boom) in the recent demographic history of developed countries has been the marked decline in mortality rates at the oldest ages."

In many areas of policy, when a social problem is alleviated there is less need to allocate resources to the problem. For instance, if delinquency is declining, there is less need to spend money on delinquency. However, in the area of health and longevity it appears to be the opposite: the higher the life expectancy and the more successful the prevention of diseases, the higher the need for services and resources to cope with the health problems of survivors.

While people live longer, these extra years are not necessarily spent in good health. With longer life come longer average periods of poor health and disability. While many or most older people are healthy, it is still the case that a quarter of persons aged eighty and above are living in institutional settings and one in five persons aged eighty-five and above suffers from moderate to severe dementia (Stone, 1986a). The data from various countries would imply that 5 to 8 per cent of persons aged sixty-five and over suffer from severe dementia, and 12 to 15 per cent have some degree of cognitive impairment (Stone, 1986b). If the care-giving team for someone suffering from severe dementia involves some six to eight people per client, this clearly poses severe social health problems. With population aging, Stone (1986b) expects that care-giving for the elderly will be the single most important problem facing health care professionals.

The problems do not apply only to the elderly: half of the population aged fifteen and over cite at least one health problem, 15 per cent indicate some disability, eight out of ten visit a doctor, and there are almost two days spent in the hospital per person in the population in a given year.

In 1964, the Royal Commission on Health Services recommended that the highest possible health standards for Canadians become a primary objective of national policy. As observed by Maxwell (1987), the resulting Canada Health Act is a success: it is very popular with the public; it provides comprehensive care at reasonable cost; and it protects the elderly in particular from the burden of rising health care costs, from depletion of their financial resources, and from the threat of chronic sickness without care and from death in poverty. Yet, the chair of the Economic Council of Canada goes on to note that there are concerns: growth of health expenditures, underfunding, quality of services and access. Other concerns can be raised regarding the mix of services and preventive measures.

In order to have a better basis on which to discuss these policy issues, it is useful to review briefly the historical changes, the patterns of health and disability, the predominant causes of death, and especially the socio-demographic profile of mortality. It will be argued in particular that health policy could better take into consideration the demographics of health, morbidity, and mortality.

HISTORICAL AND ANTICIPATED CHANGE IN LIFE EXPECTANCY

The earliest estimates we have for Canada as a whole date back to 1831, when life expectancy would have been 38.3 years for men and 39.8 for women (Bourbeau and Légaré, 1982: 77). These are very low levels by today's standards. No country in the world has such high mortality, and only four now have life expectancies below forty-five years: Ethiopia, Gambia, Guinea, and Sierra Leone. The Canadian data for 1986 indicate life expectancies of 73.0 for men and 79.7 for women. According to the World Population Data Sheet of the Population Reference Bureau (1990), only Iceland and Japan, representing 2.3 per cent of the world's population, have life expectancies higher than those for Canada. These countries largely do not have the problem of providing health services over an area at all like the size of Canada.

The earlier improvements, bringing life expectancy from forty-one in 1851 to sixty-one in 1931, are largely a function of the reduction of infectious diseases like tuberculosis, pneumonia, diphtheria, scarlet fever, typhoid, and smallpox. These are diseases that struck at all ages, and often the very young were particularly vulnerable. In fact, the most important contribution to the improvements in life expectancy were due to the decline in infant mortality. One in six children did not survive their first year in 1831 compared to one in 100 in 1986. Canada's infant mortality rate is among the lowest in the world, second only to Sweden (Dumas, 1990b).

The further analysis of why infectious diseases have declined brings us to consider the standard of living as well as medical knowledge. As a component of the standard of living, improved nutrition appears to have played an important role (McKeown et al., 1972). Poor nutrition increases the susceptibility to infection, and it also increases the likelihood that the infection will be fatal. The medical improvements relevant to infectious diseases have especially involved preventive medicine, including knowledge about the importance of sanitation,

49

improvements in the care and feeding of infants, as well as the development of effective vaccines.

In spite of these improvements, infectious diseases were still an important cause of death fifty years ago. Of the potential years of life lost in 1931, 49 per cent were accounted for by diseases of the digestive or respiratory system (largely, influenza, pneumonia, and tuberculosis) and parasitic diseases, and another 23 per cent resulted from diseases of early infancy. In 1981 these causes accounted for 8 and 6 per cent, respectively, of the potential years of life lost (Nagnur, 1986: 22-23). Diseases of the circulatory system (heart) and cancer now account for 44 per cent of the potential years of life lost. In effect, the major causes of death have changed from infectious diseases to degenerative diseases that mostly affect the older population.

Consequently, the improvements over the period 1931 to 1986 have also been impressive, bringing life expectancy from sixty-one to seventy-six years. According to life expectancies in 1931, a person had a 92 per cent change of surviving to his/her first birthday; in 1981, an individual had a 93 per cent chance of surviving to his/her fiftieth birthday (Nagnur, 1986: 77-78). Between 1931 and 1981 there was a 90 per cent decline in the death rate for children under five and an 80 percent decline at ages 5-14 (Parliament, 1987).

The prospects for further improvements in life expectancy are difficult to predict. In an article "On Future Mortality" Keyfitz (1989c) notes that it is difficult to predict based on the trend. While the trend is upward, the improvements are neither faster nor slower over time. Earlier projections had expected improvements to become slower over time as further progress becomes more difficult. However, the increase in life expectancy between 1976 and 1981 was the fastest five-year progress of the sixty-year record, and the further one-year improvement to 1986 is also impressive.

Much of the uncertainty relates to the prospect for further control of diseases at older ages or for extending the length of life. Until recently, it was observed that improvements at older ages were negligible (e.g., Pollard, 1979; Dufour and Péron, 1979). It was assumed that basic aging of the body made it increasingly susceptible to one disease or the other. However, the more recent improvements in the mortality rates at older ages have brought disagreements regarding the prospective future dynamics. There has been little change in the human life span. For instance, there is no documented case of a person living beyond 113 years and 214 days, and that person died in 1928 (Manton, 1987). Yet past projections of the upper limits of average life expectancy have been underestimates and the age at which the last members of given cohorts die appears to be increasing. Interventions in basic physiological aging processes do not explain mortality changes at advanced ages. Instead, the various types of interventions that serve to delay and prevent disease may also serve to increase life expectancy at older ages (Manton, 1987). In addition, it is still possible that scientific advance will permit the arresting of specific aging processes and that the maximum human life span may reach 130 or 150 years in the next century (Guralnik and Schneider, 1987). Without stopping the aging process, Olshansky (1990) proposes that a life expectancy of eighty-five years would be a major achievement.

In the projections based on the 1986 census, Statistics Canada uses a life expectancy of 80.6 years in 2011. This would mean a progress of 0.8 years every five years. The projections are based on trends in age-sex specific causes of death. It is possible that these projections underestimate the potential for a reduction in the sex differential in life expectancy. This differential reached its highest level of 7.3 years in 1976 but had declined to 6.7 years by 1986. The Statistics Canada projections assume that the differential will still be 6.8 years in 2011. For instance, Keyfitz (1989c) suggests it would be wise to assume that the sex differential would be reduced by half due to increasing similarity in lifestyles of the sexes. But he goes on to say that "there is no science to back such a decision." Past projections have tended to underestimate the improvements in life expectancy. While this has little effect on the overall population size, small errors in forecasting mortality have a large impact on the numbers of older people and associated service needs.

HEALTH AND DISABILITY

While the improvements in life expectancy are optimistic, the depressing side is that the extra years of life are not necessarily lived in a healthy state. At the same time, there are some positive signs, especially in the explosive growth of public knowledge regarding lifestyle factors in health and in the reduction of smoking in particular.

Our knowledge of the health status of the population has been greatly increased through surveys by Statistics Canada: the 1978 Health Survey, the 1983-84 Health and Disability Survey, the 1985 Health and Social Support Survey, and the 1986-87 Health and Activity Limitation Survey. The 1978 survey, especially, has been analysed. Wilkins and Adams (1983) calculate that of the 74.6 years of life expectancy in 1978, some 13.6 years would be lived in some state of disability: 1.1 years of long-term institutionalization, 2.1 years unable to do one's major activity, 7.1 years of restriction in doing one's major activity, 1.8 years of minor activity restriction, and 1.4 years of additional short-term disability. The disability-free life expectancy was therefore sixty-one years.

Using similar approaches with the 1986 data, the disability-free period would have increased to 63.1 years out of a total life expectancy of 76.4 years (Wilkins and Adams, 1989). Since 1951, there had been a gain of nearly eight years in life expectancy but less than five years in disability-free life expectancy. That is, 36 per cent of the gain had been in disability years. While average health expectancy has increased, the burden of disability in the population has also been growing. At age fifty-five in 1986, the life expectancy with no disability would be fifteen years out of a total life expectancy of twenty-five years. This consideration of disability indicates that mixed blessings can be expected as life expectancy increases. Buck (1987) observes that the misery of old age is not due solely to heart disease and cancer but also arthritis, poor teeth, deterioration of sight and hearing, depression, senility, and Alzheimer's disease.

Some activity restriction was experienced by 14.2 per cent of the 1978 population. At ages sixty-five and over this figure rises to 40 per cent and is over half for the population aged seventy-five and over. Based on projections of population aging, Wilkins and Adams (1983) estimate that by 2051 close to 20 per cent of the population will be experiencing some activity restriction. Including all health problems, 54 per cent of the population report at least one problem and this rises to 86 per cent at ages sixty-five and over (Health and Welfare and Statistics Canada, 1981: 115). Over the year, illness reduced people's normal activity an average of 15.7 days per person, including 5.3 days spent in bed. In 1985, 81 per cent of the population aged fifteen and over had consulted a physician and 11 per cent had had ten or more consultations. These frequent consultations rise to 29 per cent in the population aged seventy-five and over (Statistics Canada, 1987: 80, 83).

From the 1986-87 Health and Activity Limitation Survey, we find that 13 per cent of the population has some disability, defined as trouble with or inability to perform one or more of seventeen daily activities (for example, walking up and down stairs or hearing what is said in a normal conversation). In the population aged fifteen and over this disability amounts to 15 per cent, and it rises to 45 per cent at ages sixty-five and over and 82 per cent at ages eighty-five and over (Statistics Canada, 1989a; Nessner, 1990). A total of 250,000 people were living in institutions because of disability. The institutionalization rate was 7.2 per cent for the population aged sixty-five and over and 32.4 per cent at ages eighty-five and over (Statistics Canada, 1989a: Table 1).

Health surveys also increase our knowledge about the lifestyle practices of the population, and here the evidence is more positive. The most positive element is the decrease in smoking, from 45 per cent of the population aged fifteen and over in 1966 to 28 per cent in 1986 (Millar, 1988). For men, there are reductions at all ages, but for women reductions have only occurred at ages 20-24 and 45-64. Based on 1978-79 data, Péron and Strohmenger (1985: 172) estimate that 21 per cent of disability days for men aged fifteen to sixty-four and 12 per cent for women are due to past or current smoking. They also estimate that smoking is responsible for 12 per cent of life lost between ages one and seventy years for men and 4 per cent of life loss for women. Smoking in the population would be responsible for 2.1 years of reduced life expectancy for men and 1.1 years for women. Collishaw (1982: 3) estimates for 1979 that 25 per cent of male deaths over age twenty-five and 9 per cent of female deaths are attributable to smoking.

For alcohol consumption there is little change, although some shift toward more moderate drinking is recognized (McKie, 1987). Péron and Strohmenger (1985: 186) estimate that alcohol is responsible for 11 per cent of male life loss between ages one and seventy, and 7 per cent of female life loss. Alcohol consumption would be responsible for 1.5 years of reduced life expectancy for men and 1.1 years for women.

Over the period 1976 to 1981 all age groups, but especially those over sixty-five, increased the proportions participating in exercise activities (Stone and Fletcher, 1986: Chart 4.2).

In the report on the Health and Social Support Survey, Statistics Canada (1987) refers to smoking, alcohol use, physical activity, and health care services as "barriers and bridges to improved health." Burke (1986) also notes that many of the major health risks facing Canadians today are socially or environmentally related: consumption of alcohol, tobacco, and other drugs, poor nutritional habits, and lack of exercise. While there is some evidence that changes in smoking are having an impact, the evidence in the other areas is less clear. Buck (1987) finds that the evidence in favour of dietary, alcohol, and exercise changes affecting mortality "is equivocal." In particular, it is hard to claim that prescriptions for lifestyle change have much impact. Probably the social and economic conditions associated with different locations in the social structure influence lifestyle, rather than individual decisions (Nathanson and Lopez, 1987). For instance, the pressure of work or various insecurities can lead people to drink or smoke as a form of relaxation, or to engage in risky behaviour. Persons of higher socioeconomic status have the advantage of various structural and cultural supports for relatively healthy behaviour. Men of higher status in particular may experience less isolation and more social support.

CAUSES OF DEATH

Since everyone dies of some cause or other, and the causes are fairly well diagnosed and reported, the analysis of causes of death provides useful insight into health questions. For instance, the significant gains in life expectancy in the period 1971-86 are partly a function of improved survival of low birth-weight babies, improved treatment of heart disease, and lower rates of accidents.

The big killers, as previously noted, are no longer infectious diseases but rather degenerative diseases, in particular cardiovascular diseases and cancer, as well as accidents. According to data from the mid-1970s, some 55 per cent of Canadians can expect to die due to heart disease, 20 per cent due to cancer, and 6 per cent due to accidents (Péron and Strohmenger, 1985: 156). According to 1981 data, the complete elimination of cardiovascular disease would add 10.9 years to life expectancy, while the elimination of cancer would add 3.4 years. In 1986, 43 per cent of all deaths were due to heart problems and 26 per cent due to cancer (Nagnur and Nagrodski, 1988).

Since cardiovascular disease is now the most prevalent cause of death, it is important to note that mortality rates, standardized for age, have been declining since 1951, especially since 1966 (Parliament, 1989b). Declines have been occurring for both sexes, across all age groups (Dumas, 1984: 86). The extent to which heart disease continues to go down will have an important impact on changes in life expectancy. In a review article, Breslow (1985) notes that cardiovascular diseases are closely related to three major factors: high blood pressure, blood cholesterol level, and cigarette smoking. In terms of reducing the risks, some countries have taken a medical approach (identifying and treating high-risk population groups) while others have taken a community approach (reducing risk factors within the whole population by emphasizing diet and lifestyle). However, comparing the experiences of various countries, Breslow concludes that early results regarding deliberate state interventions to lower cardiovascular mortality are equivocal. On the other hand, it takes some time before the results of deliberate interventions are noticeable. In the Canadian case, it is safe to conclude that the reduction in rates of cardiovascular disease are a function of both medical treatment of the disease and relevant lifestyles, especially the decrease in smoking. Weighting the relative importance of these two factors in the case of one country is not possible.

The success with regard to heart disease does not apply to cancer fatalities. Despite the medical efforts to combat this disease, the overall situation has worsened for people over fifty years of age (Dumas, 1984: 87). For all cancers, the mortality rate and especially the incidence have increased over the period 1970-86, after controlling for age. Especially for lung cancer the situation has worsened for both sexes, and this cause represents 26 per cent of cancer deaths (Gaudette and Roberts, 1988). Mortality rates by age have declined for cancers of the stomach, uterus, and cervix, have increased for lung, prostate, and melanoma, and have been rather stable for breast cancer. The increase of lung cancer is largely responsible for the overall increase in cancer mortality. While the change in smoking habits should have an impact in the opposite direction, it takes some time before this becomes visible in the mortality statistics. According to estimates by Collishaw and Tostowaryk, the number of lung cancer deaths attributable to tobacco use increased from under 4,000 in 1967 to over 8,000 in 1983 (cited in Burke, 1986: 23).

From the observation that the overall incidence of cancer has increased more than the overall mortality from this cause, one can probably draw two conclusions. The improved treatment of cancers must be having some effect. Second, there must be some reason for the overall increase in the incidence of cancer. This incidence is high: just over one in three Canadians will develop some form of cancer during his or her lifetime (Gaudette and Hill, 1990). It could be that improved diagnosis has increased the extent to which cancer is diagnosed, but there could also be some environmental reason for the increase that affects lung cancer in particular.

Accidents and violence rank third as a cause of death, but for persons between the ages of five and twenty-nine, accidents are the leading cause of death, accounting for 72 per cent of deaths (Statistics Canada, 1986a: 179). In terms of potential years of life lost, accidents were responsible for 27.6 per cent of all years of life lost in 1981 (Nagnur, 1986: 23). Traffic accidents are the largest component of accidental deaths. Traffic death rates were increasing since 1921 but declined between the early 1970s and 1984 (Millar and Last, 1988; Dumas, 1984: 89). A number of factors are responsible here, especially the greater use of seat belts, lower speed limits, better control of drinking and driving, higher costs of gasoline, and improved medical treatment of victims. Reviewing the data from various countries, especially from Japan and Britain, Chesnais (1985) concludes that interventions can clearly reduce traffic accident mortality. In Japan, there was a 50 per cent reduction in mortality following the introduction of tough laws regarding drinking and driving, speed limits, use of seat belts, and control of motorcycles. Since there are thirty-five times as many traffic injuries as traffic accident deaths, further interventions are an important priority.

Suicides are another component of the accidents and violence category, comprising about 2 per cent of all deaths (Beneteau, 1988). Rates increased especially in the 1960s and 1970s, making the rate of the 1980s double the 1920-60 rate. Eighty per cent of suicide deaths involve men. Regarding homicide, the French, British, and Italian data show that state interventions can reduce the rates, especially through the organization of the police force and legislation on gun control (Chesnais, 1985).

Without analysing all other causes of death, it is worth looking briefly at AIDS. The first eleven cases of AIDS in Canada were officially reported in 1982; by mid-1988 there had been a total of 1,765 reported deaths. Less than 2 per cent of these involved children and 94 per cent involved men. Spurgeon (1988) further estimates that the direct cost of AIDS was $130 million in 1987, and there were an additional $150 to $350 million in indirect costs, especially loss of productivity. Estimates for Switzerland, Austria, and West Germany indicate that 0.6 to 1.2 per cent of the years of potential life lost before age sixty-five are attributable to AIDS (Heilig and Wils, 1989). While deaths due to AIDS are increasing rapidly, from 525 in 1987 to 661 in 1988, this still represents a rather "minor" cause of death. For instance, AIDS deaths amounted to 17 per cent compared to deaths by suicide in 1988 (Dumas, 1990b: 36-37; Duchesne, 1989).

THE SOCIO-DEMOGRAPHIC PROFILE OF MORTALITY

In a report on *Health Status in Canada* for the period 1926-76, Wilkins (1980) concluded that there were rising life expectancy, diminishing regional differences, and persistent social disparities. The regional differences can be observed at the provincial level where the life expectancy from the highest to the lowest province has been reduced from a 7.3 year difference in 1921 to a 1.4 year difference in 1986 (Nagnur, 1986: 31; Statistics Canada, 1989b). It is worth analysing the differences over other socio-demographic characteristics, in particular age, gender, marital status, socio-economic status, and ethnic background.

Age

Mortality follows a u-curve with high levels in the first year of life, lowest rates at childhood ages, and rising rates with age. The decline in the infant mortality rate is quite spectacular, bringing the deaths per 1,000 births down from 175 in 1830 to 85 in 1921 and 7.2 in 1988 (Bourbeau and Légaré, 1982; Statistics Canada, 1989c; Dumas, 1990b: 29). The more recent decline is a function of improved survival of low birthweight infants and of a lower incidence of low birth weight.

From their analysis of mortality in Quebec over the period 1931-71, Dufour and Péron (1979) find that there have been successes in combating premature death but not in combating death at older ages. For instance, the proportion reaching their sixtieth birthday in Canada increased from 67 per cent in 1931 to 83 per cent in 1971, but life expectancy at age sixty only increased from 16.7 to 19.2 (Nagnur, 1986: 77). In terms of the risk of death, the change between 1931 and 1971 is rather spectacular: more than 80 per cent reduction between 1931 and 1971 for ages zero to fifteen in Quebec (Dufour and Péron, 1979: 52). At ages sixty to eighty-five the corresponding reduction was only 12 per cent.

As of the 1981 life tables, we can now speak of marked improvement in mortality among older age groups, especially older women (Parliament, 1987). At age sixty, life expectancy increased from 19.2 years in 1971 to 20.8 years in 1986 (Statistics Canada, 1989b). With death being postponed to later ages, we can speak of the u-curve becoming more rectangular in shape (Nagnur, 1986). In 1921, 4.1 per cent of people could expect to survive to age ninety, compared to 16.8 per cent in 1986. Among persons who were aged eighty in 1931, 18.5 per cent survived to age ninety. For persons who were eighty in 1971, the corresponding figure was 28.5 per cent (Stone, 1986a). Stone and Fletcher (1986) note the "positive health attitudes" on the part of seniors, their increased participation in exercise (in 1976 they were the group least participating; in 1981 they were surpassing the rates of age groups 25-45 and 55-64), and that seniors lead in non-smoking rates.

The reduced mortality at older ages is not necessarily linked with better health. According to the 1985 Health and Social Support Survey, 20 per cent of persons aged sixty-five to seventy-four and 29 per cent of those seventy-five and over visited a doctor ten or more times in the year (Statistics Canada, 1987). As Manton (1987: 189) concludes, given the strong linkage of morbidity, disability, and mortality at advanced ages, a large increase in life span raises serious questions about public health costs. It also appears that the same type of interventions are appropriate for younger and older people: improvements in lifestyle and in combating specific diseases. Mortality at advanced ages depends on multiple chronic degenerative disease processes similar to those that cause mortality at younger ages (Manton, 1987: 161).

Gender

Differences in mortality by gender also provide useful insight into health questions. In terms of life expectancy, this differential increased from 2.1 years in 1931 to 7.3 years in 1976. Over the period 1976-86 the differential has declined to 6.7 years. It is especially at ages 15-35 that the relative situation of men deteriorated between 1931 and 1971. Partly due to maternal mortality, in 1931 the death rate for men at these ages represented 83 per cent of that for women in Quebec. By 1971, the male rate represented 236 per cent of the female rate (Dufour and Péron, 1979: 58). Observing the trends over the period 1976-86, Gee and Veevers (1987) speak of a "middle-age turnaround" in the sex differentials. At ages 45-64 male mortality rates are now improving relative to women. However, men are still at a considerable disadvantage: the male mortality rate is still 175 per cent of the female rate at ages 45-54. The gender differences are highest at ages 20-24, where the male rate represents 350 per cent of the female rate (Dumas, 1990a).

It is clear that biology plays a role in the gender difference. Males are more likely to die before birth, and also at very young ages, which means that the differences are not simply a function of lifestyle or the stress associated with working and living conditions. In the first year of life, the male rate of mortality has been very constant relative to the female rate, representing 125 per cent of the female rate. Females are the stronger gender group from the point of view of survival.

However, the biological advantages of women would probably account for only about half of the six- to seven-year difference in life expectancy (e.g., Keyfitz, 1989c). Three other factors need to be considered. Men have the disadvantage of a higher likelihood of behaviours that are detrimental. These behaviours are particularly smoking, drinking, and a more aggressive attitude. Smoking has become more equalized by gender over time, but when we look at people aged sixty-five and over, where death is more likely to occur, we see that 21 per cent of men but 67 per cent of women have never smoked (Statistics Canada, 1987: 30). Waldron estimates, through the comparison of various studies, that two-thirds of the differential mortality at age forty is due to smoking (cited in Gee and Veevers, 1987: 443). For Canada, it is calculated that use of tobacco and alcohol can account for 3.7 years of life lost for men and 2.2 years for women (Péron and Strohmenger, 1985: 178). The more aggressive attitude of males affects the likelihood of accidental deaths. The probability of a violent death over the lifetime is 7.5 per cent for men compared to 4.3 per cent for women (Péron and Strohmenger, 1985: 156). While some men suffer from more dangerous working conditions, the differential working patterns of men and women are secondary in explaining mortality differences. Nonetheless, Gee and Veevers expect that the differences between men and women will decline as women become involved in a greater variety of activities, including more high-risk situations. This is already seen with regard to smoking, where the proportion who have never smoked is the same for men and women at ages 15-19 and higher proportions of women than men are regular smokers at ages 20-24.

While men have the disadvantage of detrimental behaviour, women appear to be socialized to admit discomfort and to solicit assistance. An interesting example of this occurred in the 1978 Health Survey (Péron and Strohmenger, 1985: 145). People were asked about their hypertension and then the actual level of hypertension was measured. For men, more had hypertension than the number who thought they had this condition. For women, more thought they had it. Other studies have shown that women are more likely to complain of symptoms and see doctors, even for diseases where it is men who have the most problems, as measured by actual mortality. In the 1985 Health and Social Support Survey, 13 per cent of women but 28 per cent of men at ages 25-44 had no consultation with a physician in the previous twelve months (Statistics Canada, 1987: 82). Women are more likely to have preventive health and dental check-ups, and practise better dental hygiene (Norman, 1986). Women are more likely to seek medical attention, have more health knowledge, and may have the habit of more regular medical visits surrounding pregnancy and children. Women typically take care of their husband's and family's health in a variety of ways. Since no one takes care of the wives, they are more likely to turn to the outside help of doctors. For men, on the contrary, the "emphasis on being strong may lead them to interpret signs of illness as signs of weakness and therefore to suppress or to ignore them as long as possible" (Gee and Veevers, 1983: 84).

Finally, certain medical advances have benefited women more than men. The deaths in childbirth have been all but eliminated. As another example, more progress has been made for breast cancer than for cancer of the prostate. Gee and Veevers (1987) note that it is possible that this phenomenon has ended as there are no improvements since 1966 in rates of breast cancer. Nonetheless, with regard to health status, women report more frequent physical and emotional health problems and have higher rates of disability (Health and Welfare and Statistics Canada, 1981: 18)

Marital status

Besides the different impact of mortality by age and gender, the differences by marital status are equally important and interesting. Here we find that married people have advantages, especially husbands. Based on data for 1981, it was estimated that, compared to those married, the single women had a three-year disadvantage and the widowed and divorced women a five-year disadvantage in life expectancy (Adams and Nagnur, 1989). For men, the single had an eight-year disadvantage and the widowed and divorced a nine-year disadvantage compared to the married men. The excess mortality for single persons has been increasing since 1960; in 1982 the mortality rate for single men at ages 25-44 represented 270 per cent of the corresponding married rate; the rate for single women was 222 per cent of the married mortality rate (Péron and Strohmenger, 1985: 223).

There are again a variety of explanations. Selectivity may play a certain role. That is, people who get married and who stay married may be partly selected on the basis of better health. However, it is likely that the differences are mostly due to variations in lifestyle. For instance, the single and divorced are more likely to suffer from cirrhosis of the liver, a disease that is clearly related to lifestyle (Beaujot and McQuillan, 1982: 46). Some authors have argued that being alone, without social support, is itself detrimental to health (Lynch, 1977). In this context, it is interesting that men profit the most from the "protective role" of marriage.

Socio-economic status

The mortality differences by income or social class are clearly more important than those by region or community size (Wilkins and Adams, 1983). With advanced medicine and medical insurance, one might expect that social differences in mortality would disappear in highly modernized countries. However, that is not the case. Using five income levels, Wilkins and Adams (1983: 98) find that those in the highest income class have a three-year advantage for women and a six-year advantage for men over the lowest income class. Comparing areas within Montreal in 1976, Wilkins (1979) found life expectancy ranging from 68.2 to 75.6 in the poorest to the richest areas. In spite of a small reduction in socio-economic inequalities, the disparities in life expectancy among twelve zones of Montreal increased between 1961 and 1976 (Guillemette, 1983). Using five median household income levels within Canada's metropolitan areas in 1971 and 1986, Wilkins and Adams (1990) find that differences have diminished, but persistent inequalities in mortality remain. In 1986, a 5.6 year difference for men and a 1.8 year difference for women existed between the five income levels.

In all likelihood, the environment plays a role in these social class differences; that is, unequal living and working conditions. However, lifestyle is also important. Attitudes and behaviour harmful to health have survived longer in underprivileged groups, especially for men. Even though medicare provides universal insurance, important differences still exist in the use of medical facilities. At ages 25-44, 23 per cent of people at the lowest income had made no consultation with a physician in the year preceding the survey, compared to 19 per cent of persons in the highest income category (Statistics Canada, 1987: 84). Persons with lower income were less likely to have dental consultations, but they had more total consultations with physicians over the year. The report on the 1978 Health Survey found that the less educated were more likely to be risking future health by current lifestyle, and the poor had more health problems (Health and Welfare and Statistics Canada, 1981: 18-19, 121). For instance, at ages 15-64, persons with secondary education or less had an average of 16.7 disability days in the year, compared to 10.9 days for persons with a degree or diploma.

Persons of higher status may be more capable of making their way through complex medical systems, and medical personnel may respond better to persons with more income. Evidence for this assertion comes from the fact that the higher mortality of lower income classes is partly a function of causes of death that are controllable, such as bronchitis, pneumonia, and cancer of the stomach (Billette, 1977). Pamuk (1985) provides an interesting analysis of social class differences in mortality for England and Wales. In the post-war period, there has been an increase in differentials, in spite of significant increases in overall affluence and in spite of socialized medicine. Pamuk suggests that the explanation of the class inequality in mortality lies in the complex interaction of two factors: available resources and behavioural patterns. For example, education determines not only a person's available resources but also her or his attitude toward health. This attitude in turn determines how effectively the available resources are used both to prevent ill health and to treat illnesses once they occur.

In reviewing the literature, Norman (1986) finds that education is the aspect of socio-economic status most correlated with mortality and that health behaviour is an important intervening variable: preventive medical check-ups, immunizations and vaccinations, use of seat belts, eating, exercise, sleep and smoking habits. In some cases there are financial considerations, for instance in the preventive use of dental services. There is also more awareness of health behaviour as a cause of illness for those with more education, while the poor may suffer from "psychological sets such as feelings of powerlessness, hopelessness, social isolation or fatalism." Surault (1979) notes that manual workers are more likely to ignore symptoms while non-manual workers have earlier recourse to health care.

In noting that the disadvantage of blue-collar compared to white-collar workers applies more to men, Nathanson and Lopez (1987) suggest that the factors are based largely on lifestyle (especially smoking) and environment (social support). They suggest it is not a matter of individual decisions but of the social and economic conditions associated with different locations in the social structure. That is, persons of higher socio-economic status, especially men, have more structural and cultural supports for relatively healthy behaviour. They may be less isolated, have more social ties, and have more alternatives to smoking as a means of reducing tension.

Ethnicity and religion

The ethnic group that suffers the most disadvantage with regard to mortality is the native peoples. Estimates for 1982-85 place the life expectancy of registered Indians at sixty-four years for men and seventy-three for women, a seven- or eight-year disadvantage compared to the overall population (Health and Welfare, 1988). By cause of death, the major difference applies to accidents, poisoning, and violence, often related to alcohol consumption (Siggner, 1986). In 1983-86 there were 378 accidental deaths for every 100,000 Indian men aged fifteen and over, compared to ninety-five such deaths per 100,000 in the total male population (Bobet, 1989). The suicide rate is twice the Canadian average. A variety of factors are responsible for the relative disadvantage of native peoples, in particular their social, economic, and cultural deprivation. Other factors include residence in remote locations with difficult access to medical services, as well as poor water, sewage, and community services.

Other differences are less striking, for instance, the life expectancy of the foreign-born does not differ much from that of the native-born (Trovato, 1986). A group showing significant advantages is the Church of Jesus Christ of Latter-day Saints, commonly known as Mormons (Jarvis, 1977). The differences are particularly striking for diseases such as cirrhosis of the liver and lung cancer. It would seem that the regulations of this church prohibiting the use of alcohol, coffee, and tobacco help to produce a lifestyle that offers to its members more protection against certain diseases.

Implications

The socio-demographic profile of mortality indicates there are significant differences in life expectancy: a seven-year difference by gender, seven years by marital status, four years by income levels, and an eight-year disadvantage for the registered Indian population. The evidence does not tend to point to "hard curative medicine" as the important factor that would reduce the differences. Equally important are questions of lifestyle, especially smoking, drinking, and driving habits, and also the effective use of preventive health consultations. Wigle and Mao (1988) recommend that we pay particular attention to educational programs to promote health and study ways to deliver existing services more effectively to the disadvantaged groups. We will return to these questions shortly because they imply that health policy should better take demographic analysis into account.

DEVELOPMENT OF HEALTH POLICY

In an article on the development of health policy in Canada, Weller and Manga (1983) note that the policy outcome needs to be seen as resulting from a variety of shifting forces: the political expansion of the role of the state in areas of welfare and regulation (sanitation, safety), questions of provincial and federal jurisdiction, the powerful medical profession as a pressure group, strong public interest (high value placed on health care), and government fiscal restraint.

Before 1945, health was largely a private matter, although the government had long been involved in the construction of hospitals, in the training of medical students, and in the care of the insane. For general health care, a mosaic of private and public insurance measures served the public unevenly.

In the period 1945-77 the main elements of state responsibility for health were put into place. The federal government took the initiative, trying to get control over this domain at a time when the provinces were in a weak position. The Hospital Insurance Diagnostic Services Act was passed in 1957 and the Medical Care Act in 1966. The purpose of these acts was to increase the supply of health personnel and facilities and to make the services available regardless of socio-economic circumstances and geography. As Badgley and Charles (1978) observe, there was certainly the positive outcome of having increased the availability and use of medical services. However, there were also continuing issues: differentials in use of services do not appear to have declined; there were some distortions of services based on what was included (focus on expensive, highly technical, curative, and individually oriented medicine) and excluded (preventive and community approaches); and there were no specific incentives for cost containment.

The period since 1977 has seen attempts to ensure cost containment at the federal level and more of the responsibility has passed to the provincial level. In 1977 the Established Programs Financing Act ensured more predictable federal increases in health and education transfers to the provinces, while also passing more of the control over to the provincial level. In subsequent years certain provinces introduced various forms of "extra billing" to cover part of the increased costs. This was stopped in 1983 through the Canada Health Act but it meant that the provinces were largely responsible for the increased costs of health care.

CONTINUING POLICY ISSUES

Improvement in longevity and health policy in particular are very much a success story for Canada: life expectancy has progressed steadily and there are only a handful of countries with better health conditions than Canada. However, certain issues remain and are subject to continued discussion.

Costs

The question of health costs is frequently raised. Clearly, personal expenditures on health are low. In 1978, family expenditure on medical and health care (insurance premiums, care, drugs, and services) amounted to 2 per cent of total family income (Ableson *et al.*, 1983: 108). As a percentage of GNP, total health costs increased from 5.5 per cent in 1960 to 7.1 in 1970, 7.5 in 1980, and 9.0 in 1987 (Health and Welfare, 1990).

No doubt this represents considerable costs. The total government expenditure for health in 1988 was $35.4 billion, which amounts to $1,365 per capita or $2,889 per employed person (Canadian Social Trends, 1989a: 35). In Ontario, for instance, the public-sector costs for health increased by 62 per cent in real terms while the real GNP growth amounted to 43 per cent in the ten-year period 1979-89. At the end of this period, health amounted to one-third of the provincial budget (Barker, 1990). While doctors received no increases in fee schedules, the greater number of billings made the total spending on medical services increase nearly 12 per cent per capita from the 1988-89 to 1989-90 fiscal years (Mickleburgh, 1991). Since 1986 the total government expenditure for health in Canada has been higher than the expenditure for education. Nonetheless, MacKenzie (1984) and Auer (1987: 188) observe that the proportion of GNP spent on health in the early 1980s was about average for the industrialized countries, as is the rate of 75 per cent of expenditures for health coming from the public sector (up from 43 per cent in 1960).

Evans (1987) has compared the health costs in Canada and the United States over the period 1950-85. He notes that there is no jump in costs in Canada following the Medical Care Act, that Canadian costs as a percentage of GNP were higher in the 1960s and the same by 1970, but by 1985 the health costs represented 10.5 per cent of GNP in the United States compared to 8.5 per cent in Canada. This would imply that public funding of health costs does not result in higher total costs. Roemer (1985) further observes that the higher costs in the United States do not translate into higher life expectancy. Other international comparisons confirm that a more socialized approach to health care has a positive impact on life expectancy. For instance, while Belgium has a higher total GNP per capita, Holland's more socialized medicine helps to give it a 2.6-year advantage in life expectancy. The more socialized approach may also be less expensive to employers who need to give their employees health care benefits. For instance, it costs Chrysler $223 per vehicle in health costs in Canada compared with $700 in the United States (MacKenzie, 1989). Conklin (1990) observes that Canada's health system is both better and cheaper.

As an important component of costs, the total number of days of hospital care have been rather stable at 42.8 million in 1985-86 compared to 41.2 million in 1971 (Riley, 1990). Age-specific rates of usage have declined for ages under sixty-five but have increased at ages sixty-five and over. The decreased usage at younger ages has more than compensated for population aging, and as a consequence the overall rates have declined from 2.80 hospital days per person in 1970 to 1.91 in 1988-89 (Mix and Gagnon, 1990: 178). Hospital stays vary considerably by age: in 1975 almost half of men over seventy-five, and more than a third of women, had been hospitalized over the year (Lefebvre *et al.*, 1979). Based on declines in the rates of use as a function of substitution by other forms of care, these authors project a mid-range figure of 84 million patient days in 2031, or 2.72 per capita. While there was under-utilization of capacity in 1975, this projection implies that by the second decade of the twenty-first century it would require all of the 1975 capacity simply to take care of older people. More recent projections suggest an increase to 55 million bed days in 1996 but 78 million in 2016 (Hamilton and Trépanier, 1989). Once again, almost all of the increase (90 per cent) is accounted for by people aged sixty-five and over. Both of these projections imply that after the turn of the century patient-days will begin to increase substantially.

Roos *et al.* (1987a) observe that dying is a much more important factor than aging per se in the high usage of hospitals. For the elderly, as for the non-elderly, a dramatic increase in use occurs in the relatively short period before death. Persons aged forty-five and over in Manitoba used an average of forty-two hospital bed days in the last year of life, while even persons aged eighty-five and over who survived the next four years had less than seven bed days per year. Projections of hospital needs might profitably take into account expected deaths as well as the population aging. For instance, the deaths per 1,000 population have decreased from 10.1 to 7.0 over the period 1941 to 1983 but have since been increasing and are expected to reach some 13.5 per 1,000 population by 2035 (Statistics Canada, 1990a: 64). The higher death rates follow on population aging because life expectancy rises to seventy-seven years for men and eighty-four for women in these projections. Close to a doubling of deaths per 1,000 population will have a significant impact on hospital usage.

The causes of growth in health care expenditures in the past two decades involve a number of factors: additional government funding, attitudes to seeking out care, medical technology, increase in life expectancy, and aging (Angus, 1984). While aging clearly plays a role, Roos and Roos (1986) estimate that a 10 per cent increase in physicians who are prone to hospitalize their patients would increase hospital costs much more than a 10 per cent increase in the population aged eighty-five and over. It is therefore the increase in consumption, including the over-consumption of medication and services, that is particularly problematic. Denton and Spencer (1983) have estimated that population aging to 2031 will require some 1.5 to 2.0 per cent more of GNP to maintain health care at current levels. Angus (1986) estimates that demographic change between 1981 and 2021 will increase health costs by 72 per cent. While these increases are significant, these authors conclude that they are not of "crisis" proportions.

Several suggestions for constraining costs have been made. Angus (1984) suggests better use of resource-saving technologies, for instance, earlier shifting from acute-care to chronic-care facilities and more use of nurse-practitioners. As possible actions, MacKenzie (1984) suggests approaches that take both a demand side (reduce risks through prevention; incentives to use the system less) and supply side (monitoring of length of hospital stay and of lab test usage; manpower controls). Roos *et al.* (1986, 1987b) observe that health care resources are especially affected by the availability of hospital beds, the increase in physician supply, and how physicians practise medicine (i.e., their proneness to place patients in hospital). As well, the cost associated with the last days or weeks of life are often excessive in relation to the benefits provided to the quality of life of the recipients, Légaré (1990a) suggests a redistribution of resources to other periods in life. Barker (1990) suggests reducing medical school enrolments, a cap on total fees per doctor, and more use of nurse-practitioners rather than general practitioners.

Alternatively, it might be argued that, rather than have health services reduced, Canadians are willing to pay for expensive health costs as an important component of their high standard of living. There would appear to be demand for more health care relative to other goods and services. In addition, government involvement in providing health facilities ensures a certain constraint on expanding services and associated costs. The experience of the United States would indicate that greater reliance on market mechanisms does not necessarily result in efficiency or cost constraint (Conklin, 1990). Barker (1990) also argues that "one of the attractions of the Canadian system has been its reputable record on expenditures" – the problem of costs has been exaggerated.

Curative and preventive approaches

Another critique that is frequently raised is that the orientation to health is overly dependent on a curative approach. This has been voiced by several quarters, including ministers of Health and Welfare. In *A New Perspective on the Health of Canadians*, Lalonde (1974) argued for less emphasis on diagnosis and treatment and greater emphasis on a holistic approach that should include lifestyle, environment, and medical care organization. Bégin (1987: 225-26) observed that our health care system is over-specialized and our approach to health is over-medicalized, at the expense of a more holistic approach. She goes on to say that there is an "urgent need to reorient the health care system in a fundamental and challenging way. This means greater emphasis on illness prevention and health promotion."

The analysis presented earlier on mortality differentials by socio-demographic characteristics of the population tends to support this conclusion. That is, the differences across social and demographic groups, which are large, appear to be less a function of differential treatment by "doctors and hospitals" but more a function of differential extent of preventive measures. It is also useful to observe that most of the overall gains in life expectancy occurred before the use of high-technology medicine. Nonetheless, medical advances are clearly playing a role, for instance in the improved survival of low birth-weight infants and in the treatment of cancer and coronary heart disease.

Some authors are more critical. For instance, Rachlis and Kushner (1989) argue that the current approach to health is wasteful: there are too many operations, too much use of drugs, and too much technology of unproven merit. They suggest lowering medical school enrolments, closing hospital beds, and reducing drug prescriptions. They also propose a redeployment of a quarter of the health care budget toward remedying the sources of illness in the wider society. At a conference on health care technology, Stoddart and Feeny (1986: 225) concluded that: technology is often accepted for general use without evaluation or before evaluation is completed; technology is often over-supplied relative to reasonable estimates of needs; evaluated technology is often used for conditions beyond those covered by the evaluation; and technology used within conditions for which it was evaluated is often used more than necessary. The basic problem is that medicine involves many uncertainties, which prompts physicians to be particularly careful and to try various alternatives.

It is no doubt difficult to resolve these issues. When someone dies waiting for an operation, because of inadequate supply of high-technology facilities, the criticism is raised that we need more of these resources. However, such facilities are often very costly without having much impact on overall longevity. For instance, organ transplants are spectacular, but they are also very expensive and their effect on the life expectancy in the population is probably too small to be measurable. Diverting budgets to preventive approaches, such as anti-smoking or drinking and driving campaigns, means that the results are hard to see in terms of specific lives saved, yet the long-term impact on life expectancy is likely larger for the same amount of expenditure. The financial incentives in the health care system doubtless have been biased in favour of institutional care and curative approaches and against the development of community approaches and preventive programs. It is hard to combat this, partly because the doctors and hospitals, which have considerable political power, have vested interests in protecting their budgets. This can become a battle between professional and political control over the health care system (Crichton, 1986).

The evidence would nonetheless suggest that decision-makers in health budgets should put more emphasis on preventive approaches: lifestyle changes (smoking, drinking, driving, exercise), attention to nutritional value of food, reduction of environmental hazards, the "counselling" role of doctors, and public education on health questions. It can be argued that our high expenditures on health care are excessively aimed at the "doctors plus hospitals" term in the equation for improved longevity.

Barker (1990) argues that a greater emphasis on preventive and community-based services probably means higher quality care but it will not in and of itself reduce costs. Mostly, these kinds of new services will complement rather than substitute for existing services. A saving will only occur if other traditional services are reduced.

Definition of health care

Questions of preventive approaches bring us to consider the wider issue of the definitions of health and illness and the extent of government responsibility. It has been observed that ill health is defined by the population and by professionals, which means that there is pressure to broaden the definition and the danger of a limitless demand for services (Stone, 1983). One can also start to ask if there is a limit to government responsibility. For instance, Stone (1983) asks if the government needs to pay the costs of care to people who abuse their bodies. What if someone goes against advice to change lifestyle in view of the onset of a specific disease – is that person's health care still a social responsibility? In effect, there are difficult questions in terms of the demarkation of the boundaries of health care, in terms of the determination of the necessity of health services, and in terms of the respective obligations of individuals, families, and the society (Evans, 1987). As longer life and an aging population increase the prevalence of various forms of disability, these questions will become particularly pressing. Stolnitz (1987: 205) concludes that the longevity gains of recent decades, which have not been accompanied by corresponding gains in disability-free years of life, will require "watershed socio-economic and even political adaptations."

These difficult questions and criticisms should not deflect from the fact that the Canadian approach to these questions has been highly successful. To quote Evans (1987: 177): "our solution to the . . . problem of funding and delivering health care narrowly defined, has been one of the most successful in the world in reconciling and striking compromises among equity, access, quality and affordability." Glaser (1987: 13) says that "the rest of the world sees little reason for Canada to make fundamental changes. When Canadian health care is noted, it is admired." Only one criticism is raised in his international comparisons – the average length of hospital stay increased in Canada in the 1970s while it was decreasing in Europe.

Surveying health conditions

While many useful statistics are gathered from doctors and hospitals on causes of death and prevalence of serious diseases, there is also a need for surveying the health conditions in the general population. Such surveys were taken in 1951 and 1978. The surveys taken since have either been part of a larger survey or have focused on specific questions. Regular periodic surveys are needed to cover the health issues in a consistent manner. Evidence from such surveys would help to determine whether we are spending our health budget appropriately and would permit a more socio-demographic rather than a medical approach to the evaluation of health. It may be partly due to the lack of such surveys that health policy does not give much importance to the reduction of the important mortality differentials that exist in the population. More systematic surveys and their demographic analysis could assist in the planning for public health through identifying the level of health and the main problems, suggesting avenues for improvement and evaluating actions that are taken (Strohmenger, 1986).

In their review of "health and inequality," Badgley and Charles (1978) conclude that the pledge of government "to ensure access to medical care to all regardless of means, pre-existing conditions, age or other circumstances" has not been fulfilled. In part, they call for a major government review of the organization, costs, and staffing of medical care. Once again, the regular surveying of health conditions would play an important role in this type of review.

Better health or prolonging life

Following on the observation that longer life does not translate itself directly into a higher level of health either for individuals or for the group, we can ask if it would not be better to orient the health system toward health improvements in old age rather than being excessively concerned about retarding death (Légaré, 1990b). The orientation toward prolonging life would put emphasis on cancer and heart disease, because they are fatal, as well as on life-extending technologies. The orientation toward health improvements in old age would emphasize diseases that cause chronic invalidity but not necessarily death: arthritis, Alzheimer's disease, osteoporosis, sensory impairment (sight, hearing), and fractures.

Légaré argues that we should spend more on research and health care for these non-fatal but debilitating diseases, while being more prepared to accept the inevitable death due to chronic diseases when it comes. He therefore advocates a shift in resources from prolonging life to making life better. This would mean trying to rectangularize not only the mortality curve but also the morbidity curve, attempting to minimize the period of incapacity before death. It may also correspond to ethical preferences as people would want to control the end of life as they now control fertility.

CONCLUSION

We have noted much change in longevity and much more government involvement in health, but health concerns remain a high priority, partly because health problems and disability affect a significant proportion of the population. Morbidity remains important in the later decades of life and more people are reaching these stages of the life cycle. In a review of the "prospects and expectations of extending life expectancy," Guralnik and Schneider (1987) note that the increase in life expectancy has not been deliberately planned. It is interesting that we plan, to a certain extent, the health budgets and the organization of health facilities but not specifically the extension of the average length of life or the reduction of disparities in life expectancy.

In reviewing the situation of less developed countries, Caldwell (1986) concludes that low mortality is within reach of all countries – it is a matter of the political and social will to attain this objective for the benefit of the entire population. One could say the same for the differentials in our own country. There is need for better analyses of the dynamics of these differences and of the potential for their reduction.

In a very significant way, the extension of life expectancy is a spin-off from the fundamental economic and social changes that produced modern industrial societies. More generally, major demographic transformations have followed on the agricultural revolution of times past and on the industrial revolution of more recent history. Since it involved a higher level of food production through deliberate planting of crops and domestication of animals, that agricultural revolution permitted significant improvements in human welfare and also population growth. Nonetheless, this agricultural revolution brought more deaths from all causes except inadequate nutrition (Muhsam, 1979: 150). Better nutrition was an important improvement that lowered mortality, but at the same time denser population settlement increased the spread of infectious diseases, the storage of food permitted rats to spread plagues, and living near stagnated water meant death from malaria. The demographic crisis brought to the native population of Canada with the arrival of Europeans provides another example of the negative effect of agricultural developments. New diseases were spreading with such disastrous results that many concluded that the Indians were "a dying breed."

Similarly, the technological and scientific advance of the industrial revolution has had significant demographic effects. Until now, the effects on mortality have been positive through improved nutrition, more surplus resources that can be used by governments to improve human welfare, and scientific advance in the control of diseases. However, the industrial revolution may be having other effects in the longer term, the results of which we have yet to experience. If the use of energy from fossil fuels produces changes in the atmosphere, including climatic instability and less protection from the sun's radiation, the ultimate consequence of the increased technological efficiency through greater use of energy may have negative consequences on mortality. Once again, it will be hard to have claimed that the changes in life expectancy were deliberately planned.

3

FERTILITY AND THE REPRODUCTION OF THE SOCIETY

Just as for mortality, there has been a substantial long-term change in fertility, from some seven births per woman in the 1850s to under two births in the 1980s. The interpretation of these changes involves a variety of considerations, including basic changes in the socio-economic structure of society and the changing role of the family in people's lives. In mortality the pattern of change has a certain uniformity, the trend being universally downward. For fertility the changes have not been so uniform, and the baby boom presented a major departure from the long-term trend. The analysis of fertility is also more complex: while everyone dies and everyone dies just once, typically of an identifiable cause, births do not have a corresponding simplicity.

Policy discussions regarding mortality also have a certain simplicity since the concern is typically to reduce mortality. For fertility, an issue of concern might be excess births, especially unwanted births, or it might be low births. Among the countries of the world, there has been consid-erably more attention paid to policies to reduce births, either to reduce population growth or to reduce unwanted births. Only recently, and in relatively few countries, have policies aimed at sustaining births been considered. While the number of children to have is in a sense an immensely personal question, it is also true that all societies, families, or human groups will try to influence people's decisions on having children in order to promote the well-being of the group or society. Some have suggested that no country should try to increase births for fear of giving a bad example to countries that need to reduce births. This is something like saying that one should not tell the thin person to eat more for fear of giving a bad example to the fat person who needs to eat less. Obviously, the optimum lies somewhere in between.

This chapter will first consider the trend in fertility and explanations that can be suggested for the fertility dynamics. Only through the understanding of these dynamics is it possible to consider policy alter-natives.

THE FERTILITY TREND AND THE DEMOGRAPHIC TRANSITION

The long-term changes in fertility are shown in Figure 4. The trend is not uniform but it does involve a decline from some seven to two births per woman. Two fertility measures are shown on the same graph. The cohort-completed fertility rate is the number of births that given birth cohorts of women had on completion of their childbearing years. In effect, the last few births for the youngest cohorts have been estimated in Figure 4, showing a level of 1.9 births for the cohort of women born in 1954 (Dumas, 1990b: 18).

The total fertility rate is called a "period" rate because it takes the rates of childbearing of various women in a given period or year and sums them to get a measure of what would be the average births per woman if these rates for one year represented the lifetime experiences of women. The period rate has the advantage of being more current, but it may misrepresent the underlying reality. For instance, if women are post-poning births but will have them later, the total fertility rate will be low compared to the ultimate completed fertility rate. The cohort approach has the advantage of better representing the underlying reality, but the measurement is incomplete until the cohort has completely passed through the childbearing years. Therefore it is important to use both measures and to appreciate the strengths and limits of each. It can be seen in the graph that in the baby boom period, say 1946 to 1966, the period rate was higher than the cohort rate. This was because the

74

Figure 4: Period Total Fertility Rate for 1871-1989, and Completed Fertility Rate for Cohorts, 1894-1954

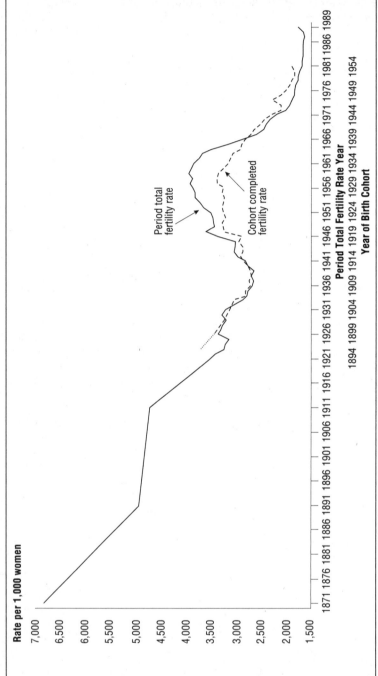

SOURCES: Romaniuc, 1984: 121-22; Beaujot and McQuillan, 1982: 54; Dumas, 1990b: 18.

timing of births in people's lives was changing toward younger ages. Since 1966, the period rate has been lower because births are being postponed to older ages. Nonetheless, it would appear that the difference between the two is no longer large, with estimates for 1989 placing the total fertility rate at 1.77 and the completed fertility rate at 1.88 births per woman.

The rate of 2.1 is traditionally used to mark replacement fertility or the replacement of one generation by the next. Two births are needed to replace the parents and 0.1 to compensate for the small number of deaths that occur before the next generation reaches reproductive age. We speak of a "population momentum" wherein the inertia of a population's past growth continues for some time after fertility declines. In effect, births continue to outnumber deaths because the demographic bulge in the population age structure is at reproductive ages. Even though they are having fewer births than are needed for replacement, this generation is sufficiently numerous to ensure more births than deaths. This momentum will continue for some time. According to projections from Statistics Canada (1990a), with fertility constant at 1.7 births per woman, births will continue to outnumber deaths until 2020.

While the long-term trend is impressive, the changes over the last twenty-five years are equally noteworthy. In 1965 the total fertility rate was 3.1 births per woman, in 1972 this rate moved below the replacement level of 2.1, and by 1985 the rate was 1.7, representing a 45 per cent decline in twenty years. Using the figure of 2.1 as representing equal sizes in the generations of parents and children, the figures of 3.1 and 1.7 can be interpreted as follows. Under 1965 conditions, the generation of children would be 48 per cent larger than that of their parents. With 1985 conditions there would be 20 per cent fewer children than parents.

Both the baby boom and the subsequent decline are partly a function of changes in the timing of childbearing. For instance, the total fertility rate reached a peak of 3.9 in 1959 but the highest cohort fertility involved women born in 1930, who had 3.4 births on average (Romaniuc, 1984: 121). During the baby boom, age at first birth was decreasing, but this trend has since reversed. The median age for women at first birth was 24.3 in 1945, 22.9 in 1965, and 25.4 in 1985. However, it is clear that the fertility trend represents much more than the effects of timing of births. Age-specific fertility rates indicate that the baby boom affected all ages except women over forty-five, while the decline has occurred in all ages except for a slight increase in rates for women aged 30-34 since 1976. Looking at numbers of births within cohorts, Needleman (1986) notes that most of the baby boom came about as a result of increases in the proportions having three to five children. An important element of the recent decline involves an increase in proportions having zero or one child, which amounted to 18 per cent of the cohort for ever-married women born in 1926-31 compared to an estimated figure of 36 per cent for the 1951-56 cohort (Needleman, 1986: 49).

In interpreting the long-term trend, demographers often make reference to the theory of a demographic transition. In the history of the more developed countries, and more recently in the Third World, mortality and fertility have moved from high to low levels over the period of the economic and industrial transformation of given countries. There is disagreement in the literature regarding the relative role of economic and cultural factors in accounting for this transformation.

In the pre-transition stage, say before 1850 for Canada, fertility tends to be uniformly high, in the order of seven births per woman. The economic explanation focuses on the role of the family in pre-industrial societies. The family was the basic economic unit in society, responsible for not only consumption but production and security. From a fairly young age, children were important as labour in family production and sustenance. The cultural explanation suggests that the very idea of planning family size was probably foreign to most people's mentalities (Van de Walle and Knodel, 1980). That is, some forms of contraception were known, especially coitus interruptus and, of course, abstinence, but the spacing of births was not much affected by the number of previous births or by the number of surviving children. Van de Walle and Knodel also suggest that there were considerable unwanted births. For instance, they refer to sayings such as "smallpox is the poor man's friend" (eliminating unwanted children) and to the high level of infant mortality, which would have partly been a function of the neglect of children who were not wanted in the first place (Boswell, 1988).

The transition in fertility, which started in Canada in the 1870s, can also be interpreted in both economic and cultural terms. With the industrial and economic transformations of society, most economic production became organized outside of the family context and the role of the family changed. Children became less valuable in family production, and the costs of children increased as they needed to be in school for a longer period. Stated differently, the economic role of children changed from that of producer to that of dependant. The movement of economic production out of the household ruptured the close link between economic production and demographic reproduction (e.g., Dickinson and Russell, 1986; Boily, 1987). In addition, social security replaced the family as the basic welfare net in the face of economic hardship, incapacity, and old age. The economic rationale for having children was reduced with the extension of state power; the family and kin groups became less important as a guarantee of security.

The cultural explanation suggests that the idea of limiting births within marriage and the use of contraception were innovations whose legitimacy spread over time. In this perspective, fertility changed as new models of the family and appropriate behaviour became prevalent. The deliberate regulation of births within marriage represented a new model of behaviour that was diffused across societies in cultural contact, first in Europe and eventually around the world. Cultural barriers have sometimes impeded the spread of the new models of behaviour. In Belgium, for example, lower fertility gained momentum sooner in the French-speaking population than in the Flemish population. Similarly, French-Canadian fertility for a long time stayed above that of English Canada. Minorities such as the native peoples can resist the "penetration" of different forms of behaviour, including the adoption of changed modes of fertility. In support of this cultural explanation, Van de Walle and Knodel (1980) note that the beginning of the fertility decline has occurred in a variety of different socio-economic conditions, and that once the decline starts the process appears to be irreversible, as if people have simply adopted to a new form of behaviour.

Earlier versions of the demographic transition theory had expected fertility in the post-transition phase to fluctuate around replacement levels as a function of changing socio-economic climates. The persistent below-replacement fertility has brought certain authors to question this aspect of the theory. Since the mid-1960s, several family-related behaviours have changed: greater propensities to cohabit, lower marriage rates, older ages at first marriage, higher divorce rates, and lower levels of childbearing. These changes are highly interrelated and have largely occurred over all the countries of European civilization, both in the market economies of the West and in the state economies of Eastern Europe (Roussel, 1989). Van de Kaa (1987) has gone so far as to call it a second demographic transition. Like the earlier transition that brought markedly lower levels of mortality and fertility to this same cultural region, these more recent demographic changes are deeply rooted in the institutional and cultural make-up of these countries, and they have profound effects on these societies.

The main effect of continued low fertility is population aging. In 1971 the average age of the Canadian population was 26.2 years, in 1986 it was 31.6 years, and by 2036 it would be around forty-five years. These are very different population profiles. The population dynamics of such a second demographic transition also imply self-reinforcing mechanisms: aging is due to low fertility, but an older population also produces fewer births. Just as population momentum has continued in spite of below-replacement fertility, so negative natural increase (more deaths than births) would tend to continue in an older population. Even if fertility were to move to above-replacement levels, the smaller numbers at reproductive ages would still imply fewer births than deaths.

Given that the larger generations of the baby boom have moved into reproductive ages, the annual number of births has not declined as much as the birth rates. Over the period 1980-88, births have been rather stable between 370,000 and 377,000 per year, with an increase to 392,000 in 1989 (Dumas, 1990b: 2). However, measured against the numbers of families, we can clearly speak of a "decline in the number of children" (Deveraux, 1990). While in 1966 some 32 per cent of husband-wife families had three or more children at home, this applied to only 14 per cent of 1986 families. Among families with husbands under thirty-five, 21 per cent had no children in 1966 compared to 36 per cent in 1986. In spite of a smaller population base, the total births were also higher in the early 1960s, at over 470,000 per year, compared to 350,000 per year in the early 1970s.

Clearly, Canada is now among the "club" of rich developed countries with persistent below-replacement fertility and significant population aging. As of 1990, only fourteen countries, representing 7.5 per cent of the world population, had total fertility rates lower than the Canadian level of 1.7: Austria, Belgium, Denmark, Greece, Hong Kong, Italy, Japan, Luxembourg, Netherlands, Portugal, South Korea, Spain, Switzerland, and West Germany (Population Reference Bureau, 1990).

EXPLANATIONS OF FERTILITY DYNAMICS

The interpretations that have been suggested for the long-term trend in fertility clearly imply that the fertility dynamics follow on a broad set of economic and cultural factors in society. In focusing further on the more recent fertility dynamics, it is useful to consider four sets of considerations: proximate, economic, cultural, and structural factors. These will provide axes on which to consider questions of influencing the level of childbearing.

Proximate factors

In interpreting fertility variation, one needs first to take into account the "proximate factors," particularly age at marriage, proportions married, divorce, and contraceptive usage. For instance, Balakrishnan (1989b: 235) calculates that under Canadian health conditions the "maximum" fecundity would be an average of some 16.4 births per woman. Of these, some 11.5 are reduced through contraceptive usage, 0.6 though induced abortions, 1.9 through non-marriage, and 0.8 through lactation, resulting in an actual fertility (excluding births outside of marriage) of 1.6 births per woman. At least in an "accounting" framework, the level of childbearing is a function of these proximate factors involving exposure to the risk of conception and successful parturition.

These immediate factors go beyond the pure mechanics of fertility. For instance, as divorce is more common, women may need to become more oriented to their own independence and self-sufficiency (Davis, 1986). Secure and efficient contraception can change the attitudes and norms toward sex, marriage, and children, as people become accustomed to the idea of sex without marriage and relationships without children (Preston, 1986).

Considering the proximate factors in more detail, the most publicized trends are those pertaining to divorce. According to the Family History Survey, the highest rates of divorce thus far have occurred in the cohort of persons who were forty to forty-nine in 1984. Of the persons who ever married, some 19 per cent had separated or divorced by 1984 (Burch, 1985: 12). Taking a period approach and projecting the 1983-84 rates of divorce by age groups over the entire marital life cycle would suggest that 28 per cent of marriages will end in divorce (Adams and Nagnur, 1989).

Other changes in nuptiality have been equally extensive. Except for a slight reversal in the 1930s, over the first six or seven decades of this century, marriages were occurring earlier and higher proportions were getting married. Around the mid-1960s these trends reversed. In 1985, 10.5 per cent of first-time brides were under twenty years of age compared to 30.8 per cent in 1965.

If we combine the 1965 age-specific marriage rates, it would imply that 95 per cent of adults could be expected to marry at some point of their lives. By 1984 this figure was down to 86 per cent (Adams and Nagnur, 1989). Not only is there a greater likelihood of leaving marriage, there is also a lower likelihood of entering it. The propensity for remarriage has also declined for the divorced and widowed, making for a higher proportion living in a post-marital single or cohabiting state (Dumas, 1985: 217).

As a consequence of marriage and divorce trends, the overall distribution by marital status has changed rather extensively over the period 1966-86, and in a direction opposite to the changes over the previous thirty-five years. At ages 25-34, 20 per cent of women and 26 per cent of men are not currently married.

Cohabitation, both pre-marital and post-marital, is another indication of family change. In 1965 it was not even measured but in 1984 some 8.7 per cent of persons aged 18-29 were in common-law unions and a total of 23.4 per cent had ever been in unions where partners live together as husband and wife without being legally married (Burch, 1985: 14). In the cohort of persons born in 1951-55, some 25 to 30 per cent of first unions involved cohabitation (Péron et al., 1987). Common-law unions tend to be short-lived as non-legal unions, but over half lead to marriage to the partner (Burch, 1989). Taken together, the trends in cohabitation and nuptiality can be read as implying considerable continuity as less formal relationships are simply substituted for marriage. Rates of formation of unions of all kinds have remained relatively constant (Burch and Madan, 1989; Grenier et al., 1987). Looking at proportions of given generations who have married by the age of fifty, Dumas (1987) observes that there has not been extensive variation: it is rare that more than 10 per cent or less than 5 per cent of a given generation stayed single to age fifty.

However, higher cohabitation does have significant consequences on childbearing. Rajulton and Balakrishnan (1990) find that cohabitation has little effect on the first birth, but subsequent births are rare in such unions. Conversely, third births are mostly restricted to women who have not cohabitated. Thus, cohabitation in place of legal marriage reduces fertility levels.

The postponement of births is another factor underlying recent fertility trends. It is found that later age at first birth is associated with lower completed family size (Rao and Balakrishnan, 1988). However, as the average family size is smaller, people who start having children later can still have time to have two or three children. The difference in completed family size between those who start early and those who start later has been reduced to about 0.5 children (Balakrishnan et al., 1988). Women who start having children later are more likely to have more education, to have higher incomes, and to have married later (Grindstaff et al., 1989). The timing of first births is more varied from person to person, but once a first birth occurs there is a high probability that a second will follow (Rajulton et al., 1990).

The proportions having no children have probably increased, although it is difficult to be certain until a cohort has moved beyond the childbearing years. Looking at women who were aged thirty in 1976, Grindstaff et al. (1989) observe that 21 per cent had no children, but five years later when they were thirty-five only 12 per cent had no children (among the ever-married). That is, 45 per cent of those with no children at age thirty had at least one child by age thirty-five. Rajulton et al. (1990) estimate that the level of childlessness for all women has moved from about 8 per cent among women who were 40-49 in 1984 to some 15 to 20 per cent among younger women. Childlessness would be related to a number of factors that are changing, such as older age at marriage, more education, and involvement in the labour force (Rao and Balakrishnan, 1986). It is also found that people who were only children or who had only one brother or sister are more likely not to have children.

The 1984 National Fertility Survey has given us an accurate picture of contraceptive usage (Balakrishnan et al., 1985). Among all women aged 18-49, some 68.4 per cent were using contraception at the time of the survey. Contraceptive usage was highest among cohabitating never-married (83.1 per cent) but it was still 50.8 per cent among never-married women who are not cohabitating. For single women who are using contraception, 71.2 per cent are using the pill. Among currently married couples using contraception, 59.4 per cent have chosen sterilization (vasectomy or tubal ligation). For all women aged 30-49, 52 per cent have either been sterilized or their husband has been sterilized (Balakrishnan et al., 1988). Once completed family size has been attained, there is a high propensity to turn to an irreversible method of contraception, to avoid unplanned births in marriage.

Abortions have increased from 3.0 per 100 live births in 1970 to 17.8 in 1987 (Balakrishnan, 1987; Wadhera, 1990). However, the rates have been relatively stable over the period 1975-87, making an average lifetime probability of thirty abortions per 100 per women. Abortions reduce fertility by about 10 per cent.

The proportion of births occurring outside of marriage has increased from 6 per cent of the total in 1965 to 22 per cent in 1988. This is affected by the level of cohabitation, and in fact, for persons over twenty, it is estimated that there is little real change once common-law unions are counted as marriages (Dumas and Boyer, 1984; see also Rajulton and Balakrishnan, 1988). Before age twenty, the increases in childbearing by non-married women are largely not occurring in cohabitation. Nonetheless, since 1960 the birth rates among teenagers have gone down. While the births to non-married teenagers have increased since 1960, the overall birth rates at ages 15-19 have declined (Romaniuc, 1984: 28, 36). Births to teenagers represented 10 per cent of all births in the 1970s compared to 6 per cent in 1988 (Grindstaff, 1990a).

This summary of the proximate factors in Canadian fertility shows that a number of factors are responsible for a change from some 3.5 births per women for those married in the 1950s to some two births for those married in the early 1970s. The decline has mostly involved lower proportions of third or subsequent births and a greater concentration at the level of two births (Péron et al., 1987). The marriage patterns (especially later marriage, more divorce, and more cohabitation) have played an important role. McDaniel (1989) speaks of the weakening of the traditional link between nuptiality and fertility. However, the greater use of contraception has been the main immediate factor. Clearly, contraception is used more because fewer births are desired.

Since there is a lower desired family size, it is useful to pay attention to people's expectations for subsequent births. In the 1984 Canadian fertility survey, the women aged eighteen to forty-nine had 1.52 children on average and they expected another 0.78 for a total of 2.30 children (Balakrishnan, 1986). In each age group, the total expected exceeded 2.0 children. If these anticipations are correct, the total fertility rate of 1.7 would be an underestimate of the ultimate completed fertility. However, it may be that not all anticipated births will material-ize. For instance, when people respond to this question they largely assume that they will be married and stay married. Comparisons to earlier surveys indicate that anticipated births tend to be revised down-ward. In the 1966-71 marriage cohort, women interviewed in Quebec in 1971 expected 3.2 births on average, but when re-interviewed in 1976 they had reduced their expectations to 2.4 children (Henripin et al., 1981). The 1956-60 birth cohort in Quebec expected an average family size of 2.9 in 1971 but of 2.0 in 1984. For Toronto, the 1944-50 birth cohort changed the average anticipated total births from 2.8 in 1968 to 2.0 in 1984 (Balakrishnan, 1986). Another useful indicator is the number who expect no more children. Among women who have two children already, 88.9 per cent expect no more children, and the figures rise to over 96 per cent for women with three or more children. Even for women with one child, 45.5 per cent expect no more children. In fact, among all women aged eighteen to forty-nine, 76.7 per cent indicated that they expected no more children. Some persons who expect births in the future may not be able to have them for reasons of natural sterility. Estimates indicate that while 91 per cent of women can become pregnant at age thirty, this is reduced to 77 per cent by age thirty-five, and 53 per cent by age forty (Rajulton et al., 1990).

Economic factors

While the proximate factors of exposure to conception provide an important part of the explanation of fertility dynamics, a more complete explanation requires the consideration of economic, cultural, and structural factors.

Explanations that focus on economic factors argue that questions of changing incomes and the costs of children are relevant to fertility. Children may be thought of as an "economic good" that adults would want, comparable to a house or a car. This explanation assumes that children are "valuable," an assumption that can be hard to defend in "economic" terms. Taking care of children may not be particularly pleasurable compared to other potential uses of adults' time, such as work and leisure (Keyfitz, 1986b). In the longer term, children may be a risky investment, as they need not return the favours.

It has been suggested that the baby boom was a function of sustained economic growth while the baby bust occurred in a period of greater economic restraint. However, the fertility trends do not relate closely to any simple economic indicator. For instance, in terms of rates the sharp-est fertility decline was over the period 1961-66, which was not a period of recession. The period 1982-84 involved the strongest recession since the 1930s, yet the total fertility rate has been basically stable.

Charles (1936) long ago pointed to the "paradox" of economic interpretations of childbearing. When real incomes have risen, fertility has declined. At the same time, inadequate means is universally given as the most potent motive for limiting the family. Charles stated it very simply: "hence arises the paradox that people limit their families for one of two reasons, because they are prosperous or because they are not" (p. 189).

Nonetheless, there is clearly some basis for an economic argument in understanding fertility trends. Romaniuc (1984: 72) observes that the income of family heads under twenty-five has deteriorated slightly relative to average family income, making a less secure environment for having children. Stafford (1987) argues that the changing levels of economic well-being are the context within which family fertility decisions are made. He notes that the fertility trends in the various regions of Canada in the post-war period have followed on the confidence that people can have regarding the future prosperity of these regions.

Attempts to analyse fertility differences though economic factors have shown mixed results. For instance, Kyriazis (1982) finds that husband's income has a positive effect on fertility at lower parities but a negative effect at higher parities. Once couples have one or two children, there would be a decreased marginal utility of children relative to other goods. Wright (1988) finds that the relationship between income and fertility is u-shaped, with higher births at both lower and higher levels of income. However, the point of inflection in the curve is rather high: only 2.3 per cent of couples are in the upper income range where fertility is positively related to income.

In effect, the values and costs of children depend on the relative priority given to various possible life pursuits. A careful economic analysis of the values and costs of children may suggest that one should not have any children (David, 1986). It may be that economic rationales are relevant to explaining why people do not have more children, but they may not explain why people have children.

Cultural factors

Economic interpretations remain incomplete. For instance, they could hardly account for the observation that, among women aged sixty-five and over at the time of the 1961 census, those of English mother tongue indicated 3.2 births on average compared to 6.4 births for those of French mother tongue (Henripin, 1974: 10). Similarly, Balakrishnan and Chen (1990) find that categories of church attendance (religiosity) involve significantly different fertility. These differences, in the order of 0.4 children after adjusting for other factors, are larger than differences by other factors such as income and education. More religious people are also less likely to have lived common-law and are more likely to have stayed in their first marriage. Chapman (1989) observes a negative relation between egalitarian gender role attitudes and desired fertility. In an analysis of the relationship between income and fertility, Krishnan (1987) finds that the effect of income varies by generation of Canadian residence, and concludes that "fertility decision making has more to do with the group norms and values rather than current or prospective economic well-being." As another example, in the Canadian fertility survey, the average expected family size of women aged 18-34 who "choose only cohabitation" is 1.4 compared to 2.3 for those who "choose only marriage." Among women who choose cohabitation but not marriage, 30 per cent expect no children (Lapierre-Adamcyk, 1987).

In a broad interpretation of fertility change in Quebec, Henripin *et al.* (1981: 351-65) speak of changes in the "social setting" and in "tastes and aspirations of the actors themselves." In his analysis of the broader issues underlying Canadian fertility, Romaniuc (1984: 83) says that "procreative behaviour may be more a matter of mores than of economics." To use Caldwell's (1985) language, cultures set limits to the kinds of cost-benefit analyses that individuals can make. In his introductory chapter to *Culture and Reproduction*, Handwerker (1986) argues that culture "specifies the content and priorities of the cost-benefit calculi in terms of which people make decisions."

Cultural explanations therefore pay attention to the norms regarding appropriate behaviour, or ideas regarding what one "should do." In particular, there may be a weakening of the normative consensus that marriage and childbearing are integral parts of the normal adult role, or conversely, non-marriage and non-childbearing have greater legitimacy. Instead, children are largely viewed as a means through which adults can receive affective gratification and blossom as individuals (Romaniuc, 1984: 64). Of course, many have concluded that children can interfere with this affective individualism.

Canada lacks a tradition of social surveys that would make it possible to analyse these types of trends in social values. For the United States, Preston (1986) shows that "marriage" and "children" bring to mind increasingly "restrictive" connotations. American survey data also indicate that behaviour is justified more in terms of its consequences for personal development and less on grounds of adhering to social values.

When voluntary childlessness was first studied, it was seen as putting into question some fundamental assumptions about adult life: parenthood is inevitable; marital happiness requires children; a family cannot really exist without children (Veevers, 1980). Now childlessness is often seen as a means of devoting energy to other pursuits. By not having children, women in particular have more possibilities of achieving social mobility. In fact, childlessness may be the easiest route to equality.

By separating sex and procreation, effective methods of contraception also support a greater freedom in relationships. As people become accustomed to the idea of relationships or marriages without children, the link between marriage and children is weakened. With the rising importance of self-gratification in relationships, people are more likely to be committed to their relationships only to the extent that these remain gratifying. This presents a problem for childbearing since having children involves a long-term commitment. People may be having fewer children in order to avoid commitments to relationships that may not last a lifetime (see Beaujot, 1986). There is some evidence that less stable relationships involve fewer children. For instance, among women married in the period 1966-81, those with no marital interruptions expect a total of 2.2 children while those with interruptions expect 1.6, a difference of 25 per cent (Lapierre-Adamcyk, 1987).

Clearly, for many people, children are a very special form of personal fulfilment. Consequently, most people have children, although it may be counter to the logic of economic rationality, and families with two children are the most popular outcome. Having more than one child allows parents to experience not only children but also relationships among their children.

Structural factors

The cultural explanations are insufficient because they do not indicate why given cultural aspirations and norms change. The analysis of structural factors looks for explanations at the level of the total political economy of the society.

Ursel (1986) has argued that labour acts in Ontario over the period 1884-1913 increasingly limited the use of child and female labour in the productive system. The manifest concern was to improve the conditions of children and women, but the laws also entrenched the distinctions between male and female labour. By putting limitations on the hours women could work, the places they could work, and the kind of work they could do, the legislation made it almost impossible for a female factory worker to earn a living wage. As women were in an economically dependent position, their livelihood was contingent on entry into reproductive relations. The resultant division of labour, often called the "breadwinner model," produced a reciprocal state of dependency between the sexes.

Especially since the 1960s, our economies have changed in ways that have produced increased demands for workers in the service areas of the labour force, traditionally dominated by women (McQuillan, 1989). The consequent change in the integration of women in the paid labour force has altered the relations between women and men and has raised the opportunity costs of children. Women have become less dependent on marriage, making divorce, cohabitation, and childlessness more feasible alternatives. Westoff (1986) also argues that the most important force underlying the weakening of marriage is the growing economic independence of women. Keyfitz (1986b) argues that low fertility is the ultimate natural outcome of gender equality, brought about by the economic roles of women. He concludes that societies that do not constrain women will contract. Davis (1984) has even questioned the extent to which societies based on an egalitarian gender role system can survive, that is, reproduce themselves.

These broad structural factors are therefore useful for understanding changes in the family, gender roles, and childbearing. With the industrial revolution, the family lost much of its function in economic production and children became economic dependants. Since women became excluded from the economic production that moved outside of the household, they also became more dependent on the extra-familial occupations of their husbands. Only more recently did women regain their roles in the labour force. Fertility first went down when children lost their economic value to parents, and again when childbearing became an opportunity cost to employed women. According to this perspective, we might expect further reductions in fertility, as labour force participation of women continues to increase. In 1986, 52.1 per cent of women and 85.2 per cent of men at ages 25-44 were "employed full-time" (Statistics Canada, 1986b: 26, 56). Therefore, there is still room for further labour force involvement on the part of women.

Traditionally there have been important fertility differences across groups, as defined by ascriptive factors such as ethnicity, language, and religion. However, these differences have all but disappeared and the differences that do remain are a function of achieved characteristics such as education and labour force participation (Beaujot and McQuillan, 1982: 75). In other words, a woman's role in society, rather than her social origin, is now the crucial factor affecting her fertility. Precisely those women who give greatest priority to their economic roles have fewer children and are most likely to opt for a life without children.

Having children presents considerable costs, especially for women. No one would be surprised to hear that women who were married or had children early in life would suffer disadvantages, but the same would appear to be true (admittedly to a lesser extent) for women who have children later. Considering women who were aged 30-44 at the time of the 1981 census, Grindstaff (1986b) found that those faring best in terms of completed education, labour force activity, and personal income were the ones without children or who had never married. Robinson (1989b) confirms that marriage increases the likelihood of labour force interruptions for women.

In another analysis of women aged thirty at the time of the 1981 census, Grindstaff (1989) observes that married women without children were at a substantive economic advantage compared to women with children. Children were found to reduce the probability of women's involvement in economic roles outside the home. Women without children were nearly twice as likely to be in professional occupations and earned nearly twice as much as their childbearing counterparts.

Analyses of fertility trends agree that the strongest predictor of fertility changes in the past twenty or thirty years is the changing labour force participation of women. Romaniuc (1984: 75) presents a graph showing the close relation between increasing labour force participation and decreasing fertility in the period since the early 1960s. A macro-economic analysis by Chaudhry and Chaudhry (1985) confirms that labour force participation is key to fertility variation over the period 1950-76. It should be noted, in anticipation of policy issues, that a different social context, such as the availability of reliable and affordable day care, may reduce this negative correlation between work force participation and fertility.

In her interpretation of fertility and family from a feminist perspective, McDaniel (1987b) argues that the distinction between production and reproduction may be artificial. Childbearing and mothering have been incorrectly seen as outside of the realm of productive activity (McDaniel, 1987c). Childbearing is a form of work that can be exploited and alienating. She focuses on the importance of structure, including gender structure as well as political economy in interpreting fertility trends and dynamics. Analysts, she argues, have a tendency to see childbearing too much in terms of choices or decisions, when it is the broader structure that is key to understanding fertility behaviour. Stafford (1987) also concludes that the political economy of Canada should be seen as the context within which to study fertility behaviour.

POLICY ISSUES REGARDING FERTILITY

The discussion of policy issues will follow the format of considering proximate, economic, cultural, and structural factors. However, it is important first to discuss the broader issue of the need and possibility for policy that would attempt to influence fertility. As was noted earlier, in order to justify a policy, it is necessary to make the case that there is a problem, that the problem can be remedied, and that the proposed remedy involves less costs than the costs of the problem itself (Demeny, 1986b). Serious questions need to be addressed at all three of these levels.

It is complex to assess whether or not continued below-replacement fertility is a serious problem. Much of the complication results from the fact that the consequences of low fertility are of a very long-term nature. These consequences are being addressed in various chapters, especially in the one on aging. However, a number of points can be raised here.

The Davis *et al.* (1986) collection, "Below-Replacement Fertility in Industrial Societies: Causes, Consequences, Policies," has some difficulty assessing consequences partly because these have yet to be experienced. The economists tend to argue that the marketplace will look after things; if children become rarer they will become more valuable and the system will correct itself (Becker and Barro, 1986; Schultz, 1986; Bernstam, 1986; see also Sharir, 1990). In effect, the economic consequences of low fertility are probably mixed. McNicoll (1986) argues that the "main economic effects" are slight, for instance, low or negative population growth should not excessively influence the labour force, technological change, investments, or consumption. However, he argues that the "distribution effects" may be more negative, producing more inequality: aging puts pressure on social security, the welfare of children may suffer, and an aging labour force would imply less mobility. Boserup (1986) also argues that an aging population means more educational costs for retraining and less efficiency and innovation. For example, if wage differentials over ages are greater than differences in productivity by age (which they probably are in systems based on seniority), then an aging labour force reduces efficiency. On the other hand, Moore (1986) argues that an aging population can mean a higher savings rate, less unemployment, more expertise, a more stable work force, and thus higher productivity. The conclusion would depend on which of these factors are given priority in an analysis of the dynamics of economic growth. As an additional complication, the factors more likely to be negative, such as efficiency and innovativeness, are particularly hard to measure.

Several contributors to "Below-Replacement Fertility" argue that the more negative consequences are political rather than economic. McNicoll (1986) speaks of the "international demographic marginalization" of the industrial countries. Bourgeois-Pichat calls it "population implosion" and Davis (1986) speaks of a "demographic vacuum." These factors are even harder to measure.

At the family level, children are no longer needed as a means of old age security. In the short term, families and adults may well be better off with few or no children. Minimizing the number of children reduces the number of dependants and maximizes the potential for adults to be in the labour force. However, in the longer term and at the level of the society, there is no escaping the need for younger generations to take care of the aged. In effect, there is a conflict between promoting the welfare of the increasingly numerous older population and maintaining a standard of living of the young working-age population in order to provide a secure basis for childbearing.

Based on data from the United States, Bernstam (1986) finds that the higher the level of inter-family transfers (in a given state), the lower the fertility. This may be because transfers tend to favour the older segments of the population at the expense of the younger, who must consequently devote themselves more to work and less to childbearing.

In a broad article on "Demographic Recruitment in Europe," Lesthaeghe (1989) concludes that there may be advantages to low fertility, but only in the short term. Low fertility, he argues, is a high-risk path: "at the present state of knowledge about the social and economic effects of future aging, it seems unwise to trivialize the demographic issues." He especially urges against moving resources from the young (who are less numerous) to the old because investment in the new generation is of paramount importance.

The reports on fertility prepared for the Canadian Review of Demography (1989) tend to argue that low fertility is a problem sufficiently serious to require attention. In its review of similar studies in other low-fertility countries, Destin (1988) concludes there is no unanimity of opinion but, nonetheless, that the most frequent conclusion is that below-replacement fertility has more disadvantages than advantages in the long term, and that it would be desirable to have fertility go back to replacement levels. Mathews (1989) noted how Canadian family policy is fairly pale in comparison to the support offered in some other European countries, particularly in what was East Germany and in France (see also Mathews, 1984). After reviewing policies in Eastern Europe, Heitlinger (1986) finds that it would be difficult to have a pro-natalist policy in Canada given the less interventionist traditions and the less centralized policy-making systems. Vlassoff (1987) points to the significance of fertility in determining Canada's demographic, social, and economic future: "in the 1990's . . . fewer young people entering the labour force and forming new households, the problems of an aging population, and the declining demand for housing and related industries, are likely to lead Canadian policy-makers to seek ways of rebuilding the nation's eroding demographic base."

While there are difficult issues in addressing the question of the extent to which low fertility is a problem, there are equally difficult questions regarding whether the problem can be remedied. The assessment of the impact of fertility policy is difficult. As we have seen, fertility is influenced by such a large array of factors that it is particularly difficult to assess the impact of one factor, namely specific policy measures. Many have concluded that the impact of policy is not evident, at least in the long term (Burch, 1986; Heitlinger, 1986). Gérard (1988) argues that, given what we know about fertility, there is not even a good theoretical basis for a pro-natalist policy.

The more convincing cases for the potential impact of pro-natalist policy involve East Germany, France, and Sweden. Comparing East Germany to West Germany and to Austria, Buttner and Lutz (1989) noted that the fertility trends are very similar over the period 1957-72, but after East Germany introduced a series of measures in 1976 that country's total fertility rate consistently involved some 0.4 to 0.5 more births per woman. Nonetheless, they conclude that the evidence is not yet available in terms of the effect on completed family size. Also looking at East Germany, Mathews (1989) concluded that the impact of the 1976 policies would involve 0.3 children for certain generations. Mathews pays particular attention to France, which once led the world in terms of low-fertility but now has a rate that is 25 per cent higher than the rest of the European Economic Community. France also has the most developed and ambitious family policy among these Western European countries. For Sweden, the policies are more recent but fertility has been increased in a context of high female labour force participation (Lesthaeghe, 1989).

Finally, the justification of policy needs to argue that the costs of the policy are lower than the costs of the low fertility problem itself. This is again a very difficult question, partly because the costs of low fertility are for the future while the costs of policies must be born today. In addition, costs may be viewed very differently in different perspectives. If the cost involves sending women back to being housewives, then surely the cost is too high and other solutions must be found.

One way to assess this question is to note that a number of countries have decided that the costs are worth entertaining. In a United Nations survey of government views on population in thirty-nine more developed countries (Europe and North America), ten countries indicate that they have implemented policies intended to raise the level of fertility and another nine intend to intervene to maintain current levels and prevent fertility from declining further (Buttner and Lutz, 1989).

The government of Quebec has arrived at a similar conclusion. A Commission de la Culture (1985) reported to the Quebec Assemblée Nationale that it is time to take actions to counter demographic trends. It proposed that the cultural, social, and economic impact of current demographic trends calls into question the very future of Quebec as a distinct society. In 1989 Premier Bourassa said that increasing the birth rate is the "most important challenge of the decade for Quebec" (cited in Picard, 1989). A number of policies have been introduced that will be reviewed later. The policies are not without their critics. For instance, Suzuki (1989) argues that "Quebec's incentives for population growth are irresponsible in an environmentally overloaded world."

Proximate factors

Obviously, it would be possible to change the level of fertility by directly intervening in the access to birth control and abortion. Such policies have occurred in some countries. For instance, in Bulgaria the access to abortion was severely restricted at a time when other methods of contraception were not readily available. McLaren and McLaren (1986) have argued in *The Bedroom and the State* that access to birth control and abortion in Canada was limited, in the period 1880-1945, by relatively deliberate state actions. As a policy direction, the reduction of access to birth control would increase the number of unwanted births, and consequently Teitelbaum and Winter (1985) quite correctly describe such approaches as "draconian." Given the weight of factors underlining the trends in marriage, it would be equally difficult to suggest policies that might increase the level of marriage in the population.

There are more supportive ways in which proximate factors can be relevant. For persons who are not able to conceive, the government support of reproductive technologies is an important factor. With a definition of infertility as one year of trying to achieve a pregnancy without success, it is estimated that as much as 15 per cent of couples have some problems in this area (Achilles, 1986). Estimates based on the Canadian Fertility Survey indicate that while 98 per cent of women can conceive at age twenty, this is reduced to 91 per cent at age thirty and 53 per cent at age forty (Rajulton *et al.*, 1990). Pepall and Sims (1986) cite evidence that some 10 per cent of variation in births is due to differences in propensities to conceive. In a review of public policies in the area, McCormack (1988) argues that these technologies should be seen first as social or reproductive services, that eligibility should not be contingent on being in a nuclear family, and that the state should see itself as facilitating rather than playing a gatekeeping role. Eichler (1988a: 280-310; 1989) suggests that much more social research needs to be done in this area, because new reproductive technologies spell a revolution for mankind "comparable to the atomic revolution."

While the problem of sub-fecundity can be devastating, the more common problem is that of unwanted conceptions and births. Thus the main issue with regard to proximate factors is reducing unwanted fertility. It is hard to estimate the number of unwanted births. Using an indirect estimation method for twelve European countries as well as the United States, Calhoun (1989) finds an average of over 0.5 unwanted births per married woman aged fifteen to forty-five, counting both births that occurred after desired family size was achieved and downward revisions of desired family size.

As indicated earlier, 22 per cent of births in Canada in 1988 occurred outside of marriage. However, a number of these are occurring in common-law relationships, especially for women aged twenty and over. It is mostly for younger women that the problem of unwanted births is serious, requiring continued efforts in education and in access to birth control (Rochon, 1989). For instance, Herold (1984) suggests that two-thirds of early sexual experiences do not involve contraception. It is not an easy task to change this because of ignorance, lack of maturity, and ideological barriers to the use of contraception among teenagers (Fisher, 1983). However, it is possible to reduce the ignorance, promote psychosexual maturity, and attack the ideological barriers.

Access to abortion is a more difficult issue since many see it as not being simply another method of contraception. Abortion policy has been criticized as not sufficiently taking into account the interests of women in controlling their bodies and their destiny (e.g., McDaniel, 1985). At the same time, most would recognize that abortion is a serious matter, representing at least a failure of contraception. Finding a solution that takes into account the interests and values of various parties has proven impossible.

Economic factors

Policies that consider economic factors would attempt to reduce the costs of children to parents. Burch (1986) speaks of removing the financial disincentives to marriage and childbearing. This approach of course assumes that people want more children and would have them if they could afford them.

Since low fertility results from fairly fundamental questions in the society, an attempt to change these would be both difficult and costly. Nonetheless, a greater involvement of the state in the economic costs of children could also be justified on other grounds, such as increasing the welfare of children, a nation's most precious resource (Hohn, 1987; Weinfeld, 1990).

The costs of children are no doubt high. Using data from the 1982 Family Expenditure Survey, Henripin and Lapierre-Adamcyk (1986) as well as Gauthier (1987) have attempted to estimate these costs. This is difficult because most of the expenditures for children are not directly identified in the survey. In effect, these authors compared families at the same standard of living (e.g., proportion of income spent on food and necessities) to see how much more income it takes with more children to achieve the same standard of living. The two studies place the average annual direct costs of the first child at slightly more than $5,000 per year. The costs vary by age of the child, with two children of pre-school ages costing a total of $2,000 but two children aged eleven and thirteen costing almost $10,000. The indirect cost, that is, revenue forgone, varies in the opposite direction: there are more costs when the children are young. For instance, at pre-school ages two children would cost some $7,000 in forgone revenue per year. The total of direct and indirect costs of three children under eight would be some $15,000 per year (Henripin, 1989: 130).

Adding these costs to age seventeen, Dionne (1989) finds that the first child costs some $83,000 for a lower-income family, $111,000 for one with medium income, and $149,000 for a higher-income family. In 1989, three children aged seventeen, twelve, and ten would cost $20,000 for one year and, after taking into account family benefits, would reduce the family's standard of living by 33 per cent, compared to a family with no children.

In this context, the family allowance, tax deductions, and tax credits for children and other transfers favouring children are very small (Mathews, 1989; Pepall and Sims, 1986). Fortin (1988a) proposes that half of the direct costs of children be carried by the state. Taking these direct costs to average $7,500 per year, he suggests that Quebec's child support budget should be doubled from its 1989 level of an average of $1,820 per child. For the province as a whole, this proposition would cost $6 billion per year (compared to a current $3.5 billion), making it equal to the old age security costs.

Calot (1990a) proposes a radically different way of thinking about taxation to take children into account. He suggests we should tax not on the basis of income but on the basis of standard of living. That is, at equal standards of living, families should pay the same tax. Since, at a given level of income a family with children has a lower standard of living than a family without children, the family with children should pay proportionately less tax. This would be a major change, but it would ensure that people are not penalized for having children. The taxes that people pay would go down proportionately to their family size, so that they would pay the same amount as others with the same standard of living. Similarly, Henripin (1989) proposes that family allowance should seek to equalize the levels of living between those with and without children, regardless of the level of income.

Considering all couples in 1987, Brouillette et al. (1990b) conclude that having children increases the risk of poverty and reduces the chances of affluence. For instance, 7.5 per cent of couples with no children fell below the low-income line, compared to 13.0 per cent of those with three or more children. Adjusting for numbers of persons in the household, they estimate that couples with two children have 16 per cent less average income than those with no children. Conversely, 37 per cent of couples with no children were 150 per cent above the median income, compared to 12 per cent of those with three children.

Certain other countries clearly have more direct transfers favouring children. In France, a family with an income of $20,000 receives a total of $4,200 in family allowance and other payments for two children and $9,000 for four children (Mathews, 1989). In Quebec, allowances have been instituted to a total of $500 for the first child, $1,000 for the second, and $6,000 for third and subsequent children (Dumas, 1990b: 22). The Child Poverty Action Group proposed in 1986 a $3,600 income credit for the first child and $3,000 for each additional child, taxed back according to total income (Callwood, 1987).

The direct payments and fiscal transfers could take the form of family allowance, tax deductions, tax credits, and other forms of support, such as housing allowances, for low-income families. Clearly, it would take a considerable amount of transfer to have an impact. While small transfers can alleviate the costs of having children, considerably more would be needed to reduce the costs to the point that fertility decisions would be affected. Deliberate pro-natalist measures would probably want to accentuate the support for the third child (Mathews, 1989). Weinfeld (1990) proposes that these not be seen primarily as pro-natalist measures but as child welfare measures, enhancing the quality of life of children and families. It makes good economic sense, he argues, to increase the human capital investment in children. Grindstaff (1990b) calls for a recognition that raising children is important enough to the society to guarantee fair economic compensation for those who are involved.

Cultural factors

One cultural approach vis-à-vis fertility would be to "attempt to make the general culture more favourable to children" (Buttner and Lutz, 1989). Hohn (1989) proposes that more attention be given to "spaces for children" in our urban landscapes and, more broadly, that more family-oriented values should be promoted. One could also argue for the importance of pronouncements by governments and other important agencies or persons about the fundamental importance of families and of reproduction to the long-term welfare of the society. To have meaning, these pronouncements would have to be backed by policy actions that manifest the importance placed on the value of children to the society. It might be argued that baby bonuses are symbolic – they reflect the government's articulated social goals (Weinfeld, 1990). Bonuses for third children at least carry the ideological message that three children is acceptable. More broadly, social support for parenthood is parenthood propaganda (Buttner and Lutz, 1990).

There could be attempts to move the normative consensus in a direction more favourable to children. This would involve building a shared consensus that children are important to the future of the society and that caring for children is an important part of normal adult roles, for both men and women. It could be that the higher fertility in France follows from a broadly shared consensus that a higher level of child-bearing is important for the society. This consensus is supported by policy measures.

Therefore, governments might try to increase the preferences for children and the extent to which men see the care of children as part of their adult roles. Such "campaigns" have been useful in mortality (anti-smoking, drinking and driving), but it would be more difficult to have a similar effect on fertility. To reduce the probability of death is a direct benefit to individuals that does not have an equivalence in fertility. Burch (1986) observes that "it is not clear if government policy can change tastes," but he nonetheless suggests that we think of ways to symbolize the social values of parenthood. It is not inconceivable that there be a resurgence in popularity of a lifestyle in which children play an integral role (Beaujot and McQuillan, 1982: 77). Grindstaff (1990b) argues that Canada is already a pro-natalist society in the sense that having children is highly valued by both women and men.

Structural factors

Recognizing that low fertility stems from structural changes in modern societies, the structural approach would attempt to correct for some of the specific ways in which these factors work against childbearing. The orientation here would especially seek to reduce the opportunity costs of children and the "work/child-care crunch."

As argued earlier, modernization has strengthened the welfare state and weakened the economic necessity for family solidarity (Hohn, 1989). In effect, a series of broad policies have had the indirect and unintended effect of depressing fertility. Policies supporting women's equality, access to education, and equal pay have made divorce easier and have broadened women's roles. Also, social security, in terms of health insurance and pensions, has implied that individuals do not need children as a means of protecting themselves against the uncertainties of health, economic incapacity, and aging. These policies are strongly supported because they promote the important ideals and objectives of more freedom, equality, personal independence, more leisure and consumption, economic growth, and social justice (Hohn, 1989).

In noting that low fertility is rooted in these very structures of social security, Demeny (1986a) offers some equally fundamental suggestions. For instance, he proposes re-linking old age security to childbearing. In the past, people took advantage from their children in terms of the social security provided by children. Now the state looks after this, and in addition, those who can most afford private pension plans are those who have no children. Demeny suggests that part of the social security contributions of children when they are in the labour force should go to supplement the public pension plans of their surviving parents. Another interesting suggestion is that of voting rights for children, exercised by their parents until the age of majority. Let one person, one vote be extended to the entire population! This is interesting in the sense that the aging population is exercising its influence to favour its own welfare, at the expense of the welfare of young adults of child-bearing ages. For instance, the budgets for pensions and health are increasing faster than those for family allowance and education. A change in the structure of the electorate, giving more say to young families, could possibly counter these trends.

Policies that would attempt to reduce the opportunity costs of children, and help to reconcile family and labour force roles, would include more publicly supported quality child-care arrangements, making the workplace more compatible with child-rearing (including parental leaves), and pension provisions for persons who are not in the labour force because of their child-care roles.

Eichler (1983: 332-33) proposes that in the case of a parent staying home to care for children, the state should pay that person's Canada Pension Plan contribution. She also suggests that there be a child-care tax credit equivalent to the average cost of day care for each child not in school and pro-rated for the hours spent in school, which parents could use for care of children or to subsidize one parent being at home. This would replace the child-care deduction, the married deduction, and subsidies to day care. The result would be to transfer incomes from families and individuals without children to those with children.

Sweden provides an example of extensive development of such policies (Ziegler, 1989; *Globe and Mail*, 1989; Moen, 1989). Mothers of young children have the right to curtail their work day to six hours. Paid leave for one parent has been extended to one year following the birth of a child, with the state paying 90 per cent of the lost income. In addition, the state pays 88 per cent of day-care costs, and a housing allowance is provided for some low-income young families based on the number of children. Adding an annual family allowance of $1,600 per child, the total budget for family support comes to $7.9 billion (or 5.4 per cent of GNP), compared to a budget of $5.7 billion for defence spending. While these policies were aimed at enhancing the options and flexibility of working parents, the total fertility rate has also increased from 1.6 in 1983 to 2.0 in 1989 (Calot, 1990b). Hoem (1990) concludes that the increase can in part be attributed to the "low-key and largely indirect pronatalism of Swedish social policies." These have consistently tried to facilitate women's presence in the labour force while also reducing the obstacles to parenthood.

In France, family allowance amounts to some $1,400 per year for two children and $1,870 for the third child. There are further allowances, based on need, for housing and for single parents. Parental leave amounts to sixteen weeks at 90 per cent of salary (twenty-six weeks if two other children are at home). Public care facilities exist as of age three, with a parent of three or more children who stays home receiving $530 per month until the youngest is aged three (Mathews, 1989; Calot, 1990a). The total support for families amounts to 16 per cent of government expenditure, or 20 per cent more than the defence budget (Calot, 1990a). Fertility rates in France have been remarkably stable at 1.8 births per woman between 1976 and 1989, which is higher than in neighbouring countries (Calot, 1990b).

In comparison to this, Canadian support is rather weak. Family allowance in 1991 amounts to $400 per year per child, taxed back. Unemployment insurance pays for twenty-five weeks after a two-week delay, making the equivalent of 56 per cent of usual earnings to a specified maximum over the twenty-seven-week period. Since it is attached to unemployment insurance, parental leaves are regulated by this program and not all working parents qualify. In 1989, there were 153,000 claims for an average amount of $4,130 each (Vaillancourt, 1990). However, these claims represented only 39 per cent of births in the year. Other programs include child tax deductions, tax deductions for child-care expenses, tax credits for low-income families, and social welfare attributable to children. Together, these programs involved about $12.1 billion in 1989, 1.9 per cent of GNP, or a per capita cost of $460 (calculation based on Fortin, 1988: 16). By comparison, the figure of $7.9 billion for Sweden amounts to $940 per capita and in France it comes to some $950 per capita.

Quebec has more programs, including higher family allowance, the baby bonuses described earlier, plus unpaid leave up to one year, including the twenty-five weeks of paid leave (Picard, 1989). Nonetheless, the total costs of federal and provincial programs for Quebec amount to $503 per capita. It is interesting that births have increased in Quebec over the period 1988-90, bringing the total fertility rate from 1.3 to 1.5 (Picard, 1991; Dionne, 1990). Age-specific rates have increased for each age up to forty and there has been a 20 per cent increase in the number of parents having three or more children. However, the average births per woman remain low compared to other provinces.

Mathews (1989) concludes that, as a beginning, priority should be given to the following: increase the coverage of parental leave and the level of support for a period of thirty-two weeks, reduce school entry to age five, subsidize day care through a tax credit, and provide a monthly allowance of $200 for the third child for the whole period before entry into school.

Battle (1988) notes that in recent budgets the total child benefits are declining. The Report of the Task Force on Child Care (Cooke, 1986) proposed free, universally accessible care arrangements for all pre-school children, which would cost some $11.2 billion per year. The Canadian Advisory Council on the Status of Women (1986) strongly supports a universal system of quality child care. Others have argued that we need not have such a heavy system, but preferably one that gives parents options between public care, private arrangements, and parental care (Ross, 1986). Vlassoff (1987) proposes better arrangements for child care, extended maternity leaves, more generous family allowance, remuneration for housewives, and more flexible working arrangements, including opportunities for part-time employment. Townson (1987) argues the policy development in the area of parental leaves should be based on the assumption that most women who will bear children will be in the work force and will want to take a relatively short leave before returning. She continues that the "lack of child care services can only be regarded as a major crisis on which public policy action is urgently required."

Given the increased labour force participation of women, the opportunity costs in the early years of a child's life probably weigh especially heavily on prospective parents. In that light, the emphasis should be on the pre-school years, including a longer parental leave period at a higher rate of compensation and better provisions for day care. In terms of parental leave, Canada compares poorly to other industrialized countries except the United States, United Kingdom, Australia, and New Zealand (Mathews, 1989). Lévesque (1988) argues for policies that would weaken the link between a woman's salary and the costs of children by rendering children less expensive in terms of the mother's time, especially through day care at low cost and leave policies. Henripin (1989) and Fortin (1988) propose that parental leave should be equally available to mothers who work and those who do not work, in order not to promote one form of care over another. Both Mathews (1989) and Henripin (1989) suggest that we subsidize child care rather than day care, giving parents a choice regarding the type of care they wish to provide for their children: one parent at home, informal arrangements, or formal arrangements.

Another structural element that could be addressed involves equalizing child care between women and men. Lévesque (1988) calls for a better division of the non-monetary costs of children between males and females. Any policy needs to take the dual roles of worker and parent into account for both women and men. We need to search for institutional support to ease the pressure arising from dual roles (Romaniuc, 1984: 111). It is of course important that parental leave policies, including leaves when children are sick, be available for either fathers or mothers. This can be justified on other grounds. Various people have noted that women now have high labour force involvement but also many interruptions associated with children and family (Kempeneers and Saint-Pierre, 1989; Robinson, 1989b). In contrast, compared to non-married men, married men have fewer work interruptions. Ways must be found to equalize these opportunity costs. As Breton (1984) concludes, only through far-sighted policies allowing males and females to share in household and family duties can greater equality in the work force be attained.

CONCLUSION

The factors underlying low fertility are extensive. They include the proximate factors of lower exposure to the risk of conception through effective contraception and lower proportions married, the economic factors of the costs of children, the cultural factors giving importance to other aspects of life, and structural factors wherein children are especially an opportunity cost to labour force participation.

Following on these approaches, it is first clear that not much can be done with regard to the proximate factors, except health and technological improvements that would benefit those who cannot conceive. In effect, the policy direction for proximate factors is to increase the availability and use of contraception to avoid unwanted births, especially on the part of teenagers.

The consideration of economic factors suggests reducing the costs of children to parents (family allowance, child tax deductions, child tax credits, baby bonuses) by having the state pay more of these costs, that is, by transfers away from families and individuals without children toward those with children. A radical suggestion along this line would be to base the taxation system on standards of living rather than income, so that families or individuals at a given standard of living would pay the same tax, ensuring that at a given level of income those without children would pay more tax.

The consideration of cultural factors would suggest ways of making our urban spaces and our culture in general more open to children. This includes promoting more family-oriented values, finding ways to symbolize the social values of parenthood, as well as attempting to build a shared consensus that children are important to the future of the society and that having and caring for children are important parts of normal adult roles for both men and women.

The structural factors would suggest facilitative social welfare measures that take into consideration the dual roles in production and reproduction, in particular, parental leave policies, flexible work time, pension plans for parents who are taking care of children, and provisions for child care. A more radical approach would involve linking old age security to past childbearing, or increasing the political weight of families with young children at the expense of the elderly. This would follow upon the observation that transfers from the working-age population to the elderly are also transfers away from children, since it is people at working ages who have or might have children.

Such provisions are based on the assumption, which is in fact supported by research evidence, that the majority of adults would desire all of the following: to have a career, to have children, to live in an intimate relationship, and to have an appropriate standard of living (Lapierre-Adamcyk, 1989; Buttner and Lutz, 1989). McQuillan (1989), for instance, suggests that the voluntary childless may be as low as 5 per cent of the total. People are not turning their backs on children but on having many children. Grindstaff *et al.* (1989) also conclude that nearly all would want to have some children, if the appropriate structural changes are forthcoming around employment equity and child care.

Needless to say, such a series of programs would be expensive. Children are an expensive form of investment in the future, but in the end they are the only investment that counts. There is also no guarantee that such approaches would in fact raise the level of fertility. Some have observed that societies with more day-care facilities and more equity laws tend to have lower fertility. For instance, as parents continue to work because they can have their children in day care, they may come to identify even less with parenthood roles and have fewer children. However, such a package of programs would probably ensure that people could have the number of children that they want, which is higher than the number they are currently having. Even if the programs only have a marginal impact on the level of fertility, a marginal difference is all that would be necessary to bring fertility closer to that needed for the society to reproduce itself into the next generation.

While this chapter has focused on fertility and consequently on the policies that might influence childbearing, it must be emphasized that the basic policies enabling people to have the children they want are best justified on non-demographic grounds, especially in terms of improving child and family welfare and working toward equality by gender. The Canadian Advisory Council on the Status of Women (1989: 17) argues that the successful integration of work and family responsibilities needs to consider child care, parental leave, flex time, benefits for part-time workers, and the broad encouragement of work environments that are supportive of employees with family responsibilities. Heitlinger (1990a) therefore concludes that pro-natalism can be coincident with progressive policies supporting women's equality, reproductive freedom, and state assistance to families with children. In the past, higher fertility has been conditional on the discriminatory treatment of women (Davis, 1984). This was done in particular through the separation of economic production and demographic reproduction. The present-day challenge is to devise policies that enhance equality in productive roles while enabling reproduction.

Another justification focuses on the interest of children. For instance, reviewing the literature in the United States, Donovan and Watts (1990) conclude that government investments in high-quality child care may produce considerable benefits in the long term by increasing children's eventual productivity. Analyses of income inequality suggest that young families with children are a group that compares poorly to others in the society. More broadly, policies can be justified by the aim of satisfying more of the needs of the population in the family domain, just as such needs have already been satisfied in the domains of health and education.

In a larger context, as Chesnais (1987) has argued, the adjustment between production and reproduction has until now mostly been made at the detriment of the latter. As we reach for higher standards of living, partly by including most adults of both sexes in the labour force, there is less and less space in our lives for reproduction. Both of these activities are clearly forms of work, as McDaniel (1987c) has emphasized. Even though reproduction has lost its importance to the economic welfare of individuals, both production and reproduction are obviously important to the long-term welfare of the society. It is a matter of how work is divided between production and reproduction, and of introducing other changes that will encourage men and women to share in both activities.

4

IMMIGRATION AND THE POPULATION OF CANADA

Canadian public policy has most explicitly attempted to influence population trends in the area of international migration. In effect, discussions of population policy in Canada often limit themselves to questions of immigration.

It is not surprising that states pay careful attention to international population movements. The movement of people across international boundaries can affect the relations between states, introducing links or sometimes conflicts. In addition, as Weiner (1985) notes, international migration can create interdependence either by "bringing the outside in" or because "a piece of you is now outside." The previous residents of other countries can have specific interests in the political processes of their new countries, and they can attempt to influence the political processes in their countries of origin. It is therefore not surprising that states pay careful attention to questions of international movement of populations, elaborating rules of entry (and sometimes of exit) to ensure the process produces a maximum of benefits. Equally understandable is the deep interest the public takes in immigration, because it affects the very society in which we live.

Immigration policy is as old as Canada itself, with the first statutes dating back to the first two years after Confederation. Given the fragile beginning of the country, the government was concerned about population growth. Particularly pressing was the need to stimulate development in the vast territory of the Canadian West and thus allow for effective sovereignty over these lands. Although committed to encouraging immigration, the attitude of the government was cautious, and it was soon made clear that not all prospective immigrants would be considered suitable. In one of its earliest pieces of legislation, restrictions were placed on immigrants by prohibiting, among other things, "the landing of pauper or destitute immigrants in all parts of Canada, until such sums of money as may be found necessary are provided and paid into the hands of one of the Canadian immigration agents" (Beaujot and McQuillan, 1982: 80).

Immigration has always presented a certain ambivalence for policymakers. On the one hand, immigration has been viewed positively, first in nation-building, then in promoting economic development, and later in building a multicultural society. On the other hand, concerns were raised about immigrants using Canada as a passage to the United States, then about immigration undermining the position of labour, and always about the different "stock of people" that arrive with "strange habits and life styles." Corbett (1957: 37) has summarized the various conflicts surrounding public policy on immigration:

> A national government dealing with immigration policy is like a ship buffeted by contrary winds. Labour blows one way and employers another, French Canadians puff up a powerful blast against the prevailing English speaking majority; various nationality associations exert their pressures; and a shrill draught of prejudice against foreigners comes from some of the old stock.

While the government policy has attempted to steer a path, sometimes rather hesitantly, between these conflicting considerations, there has also been a sense that government does not completely control the process. When agriculturalists were sought to settle the West, many in fact become unskilled labourers in Canada's early industrial development. When specialized skills were sought to fuel the urban-industrial expansion of the post-war era, many sponsored immigrants arrived as unskilled labourers (McInnis, 1980). It was widely reported in the mid-1950s that for every Italian admitted into Canada another forty-nine gained legitimate access through sponsorship (Hawkins, 1972: 51). On the refugee side, controlled arrivals appear to be a thing of the past; various refugee boards are overwhelmed with so many claimants that they cannot properly determine which claims are legitimate. Though Canada is geographically removed from the areas of the world that generate refugees, the policies permitting the landing of permanent immigrants, combined with a humanitarian attitude toward refugees, make Canada an attractive destination for refugees, both political and economic.

Consequently, Hawkins (1972: 33-35, 295) concludes that "Canada has had no settled view of immigration" and "a permanent condition of acute anxiety and nervousness obtains . . . relating to any major development in this field." In a review of policies, trends, and issues, Boyd and Taylor (1990) conclude that "future immigration will be visible, growing and increasingly spontaneous . . . the challenge will be to develop a set of criteria for the control and management of these flows."

Starting with a brief history of immigration trends and policy, this chapter will consider current policy questions from the point of view of the demographic, socio-economic, and socio-cultural impact of immigration. While the focus will be on research results, it is useful to recall that research is only part of the input to policy. In the context of a review of post-war immigration policy, Richmond (1987) observes that demographic and other research has had only a peripheral influence on policy formation.

HISTORY OF IMMIGRATION AND EMIGRATION TRENDS

It is useful to divide the history of immigration into four periods: 1861-95, 1896-1913, 1914-45, and 1946 to the present. The first period was a time of net emigration, the second saw very high arrivals, the third was somewhat of an interlude, and the post-war period has seen relatively higher levels once again.

Estimates of international migration vary for the nineteenth century, but there is agreement that the period from just before Confederation to about 1895 saw more departures than arrivals. This was a time of depression in international trade, which undermined the markets for Canadian staple products. The earlier industrialization of the American economy offered employment prospects that attracted both recent immigrants to Canada and persons born in Canada (Beaujot and McQuillan, 1982: 82-84; Lavoie, 1972). In addition, dry-farming techniques suitable for the colder climate of Canada's West were not developed until the 1880s.

The year 1896 marked the end of the long period of international economic depression and also a turnaround in net migration to Canada. While departures remained important, the gains of the decade 1901-11 more than balanced the net loss experienced in the four previous decades (Beaujot and McQuillan, 1982: 83). This followed the improved attractiveness of the Canadian West and the onset of industrialization. The years 1911 to 1913 saw record arrivals of 300,000 to 400,000 per year, which have never since been surpassed (see Figure 5). The places of origin of these arrivals largely were the British Isles, along with central and southern regions of Europe.

The onset of World War One marked an abrupt end to this wave of immigration. While immigration picked up somewhat in the 1920s, the depression of the 1930s and World War Two make the whole period 1914-45 somewhat of an "interlude" in immigration. The 1930s saw once again more departures than arrivals. Annual arrivals were under 20,000 for the whole period 1933-44. In terms of places of origin, this period was much like the previous one, with the British group being by far the largest, followed by the German and Austrian, Scandinavian and Ukrainian.

The period since 1946 can be thought of as a second wave of post-Confederation immigration. While annual arrivals fluctuated considerably, from a low of 64,000 in 1947 to a high of 282,000 in 1957, the total arrivals between 1946 and 1990 amount to 6.2 million. Although the rate of immigration compared with the total size of the Canadian population was lower than in the period 1896-1913, and while no single post-war year saw the arrival of as many as had come in each of the years from 1910 to 1913, the total arrivals of the post-war period are higher than the 2.9 million of the earlier wave.

Fluctuations have followed the path of events both inside and outside of the country. There was a spurt right after the war with the arrival of war brides and refugees. After new regulations were in place and the Department of Citizenship and Immigration was established in 1950, immigration was high for the rest of the decade. The high point in 1956-57 reflects the entry of British subjects escaping the Suez crisis and refugees from the Hungarian revolt. The dip in 1961 and again in 1983-86 coincided with downturns in the economy. The flow picked up in the latter half of the 1960s after the establishment of the Department of Manpower and Immigration and the strong economic growth of the period. The peak in 1974 is somewhat artificial since it results from an "amnesty" program whereby persons in the country without landed immigration status were admitted even if they did not meet the criteria. The increase of the period 1986-90 follows on a deliberate program of "moderate controlled growth" in immigration levels. As will be elaborated below, the places of origin of immigrants became more diversified, beginning in the 1960s.

Figure 5: *Annual Levels of Immigration and Emigration, 1900 to 1990*

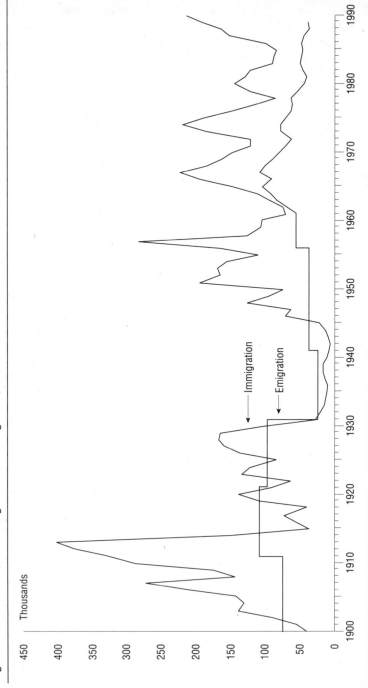

SOURCES: Dumas, 1990b: 2; Beaujot *et al.*, 1988: Figure 1.

This brief account of immigrant arrivals would be incomplete without a note on the history of refugee movements. Starting with the United Empire Loyalists around 1776, refugee arrivals continued, with various groups including Quakers, Mennonites, blacks, Doukhobors, Hutterites, Mormons, and Jews arriving in the period before World War One (Ziegler, 1988). In the period since World War Two, some of the major refugee movements have involved Hungarians, Czechs, Slovaks, United States draft dodgers and deserters, Tibetans, Ugandan expellees of Asian ancestry, Chileans, and Indochinese. Since 1978, the planning of immigration levels has explicitly taken expected refugees into account and the source countries have become considerably more diversified. The total numbers are difficult to estimate for the earlier period, but in the post-war period the total refugee arrivals have been 564,000, representing about 10 per cent of total arrivals (Nash, 1989b: 125-27, and later statistics from Employment and Immigration).

HISTORY OF IMMIGRATION POLICY

The first policy aimed at encouraging immigration was the 1868 Free Grants and Homestead Act. In subsequent years, numerous efforts were made to encourage agriculturalists to immigrate to Canada, including aggressive recruitment in the United Kingdom and Europe (Beaujot and McQuillan, 1982). The government entered into various agreements, especially with the railroad companies, for the recruitment, selection, transportation, and establishment of potential agriculturalists. In addition, mining, lumber, and especially railway interests desperately required sturdy labourers willing to accept difficult working conditions and prepared to move to areas where workers were needed. In effect the period of the mid-1880s to World War One involved a deliberate use of immigration as an instrument of industrial development and nation-building, including the settlement of the wheat-growing Prairies (Brooks, 1989). Later, the 1922 Empire Settlement Act offered assistance in settlement to British subjects. The 1925 Railway Agreement was especially conducive to the arrival of Central Europeans.

In other regards, policy attempted to restrict immigration. The 1885 Chinese Immigration Act imposed a "head tax" on prospective Chinese immigrants. At around the same time, the United States, Canada, and Australia all decided that "the Chinese were unassimilable, and they were a positive hindrance to the process of nation-building, and that with few exceptions their immigration should be stopped completely" (Rao et al., 1984: 15, citing Price, 1974: 275). This Act was updated several times to restrict the arrival of Chinese workers after the railroads had been built and was only set aside in 1947. In 1907 and 1908, measures were taken to limit immigration from Japan and India.

The Immigration Acts of 1906 and 1910 placed diseased persons as well as those advocating violent political change on the restricted categories. The 1910 Act allowed the government to introduce regulations on the volume, ethnic origin, and occupational composition of the immigrant flow. Amendments in 1919 made it possible for non-Canadian strike leaders to be deported and the prohibited classes were extended to include alcoholics, conspirators, and illiterates (Manpower and Immigration, 1974: 12). While restrictions were lifted in the 1920s, in 1933 various categories of immigration were deleted and even British subjects were discouraged (Corbett, 1957: 7). The Act was used to deport persons belonging to the Communist Party of Canada or other persons who had run into trouble with the law, often simply accused of being "public charges" (Avery, 1979: 115; Roberts, 1988).

In general, the period 1867-1946 can be seen as involving both the encouragement of immigration and attempts to restrict its flow. Encouragement was strongest in times of economic growth, particularly in the 1896-1913 period and in the 1920s, while restrictions were strongest in the 1930s. Encouragements tended to focus on British and northern European immigrants, while non-white arrivals were strongly restricted.

Following the Second World War, there was considerable uncertainty regarding the appropriate direction for future immigration. In 1944, the Quebec Legislative Assembly had indicated its opposition to mass immigration. Throughout the country, many argued that priorities should concentrate on the integration of returning soldiers. Others were concerned that Canada might return to the economic situation of the 1930s, for which immigration would be inappropriate. On the other hand, arguments were made that Canada could raise its international stature by helping to rescue persons displaced by the war in Europe (Angus, 1946). In addition, a report to the deputy minister responsible for immigration concluded that a larger population made sense from an economic point of view (Timlin, 1951).

In 1947, Prime Minister Mackenzie King set out the government's policy on immigration in a frequently quoted statement that involved a careful compromise between these divergent concerns. King called for immigration as a support for higher population growth, but cautioned that such immigration should not be in excess of the number that could be advantageously absorbed. While he recognized the obligation to humanity to help those in distress, he clearly indicated that he would not support a massive arrival that would alter the "character of our population." The "character of our population" could mean various things, but it obviously included a desire to continue receiving immigrants mainly from the traditional sources. An important administrative procedure, which was used to admit immigrants, involved the widening of eligibility for "sponsored relatives." This was an interesting political solution, since those who had argued for restricted entries could hardly oppose the arrival of relatives. This also assured that immigrants would largely be from the traditional, "preferred" sources – those who already had relatives in Canada.

The 1953 Immigration Act allowed the government to prohibit the entry of immigrants for a variety of reasons, including nationality, ethnic group, and "peculiar customs, habits, modes of life or methods of holding property." Preference was given to persons of British birth, together with those from France and the United States. Second preference went to persons from Western European countries – if they had the required economic qualifications. Persons from other countries could not enter unless sponsored by a close relative. A small exception involved an arrangement, in force between 1951 and 1962, that allowed for selected arrivals from Asian Commonwealth countries (Hawkins, 1972: 99). However, very low limits were set: a combined total of 300 people per year from India, Pakistan, and Sri Lanka.

Discrimination based on place of origin became a concern to the government of Canada in the early 1960s, and consequently the national origin restrictions to immigration were officially lifted in 1962. In 1967 a "points system" for the selection of independent immigrants was established. This reinforced the non-discriminatory aspects of immigration policy by clearly outlining the "education, training, skills and other special qualifications" under which immigrants were to be selected. The policy of multiculturalism, promulgated in 1971, underlined an open attitude to the arrival of immigrants from various parts of the world.

Immigration policy was subjected to a thorough review in the period from 1973 to 1975, culminating in the 1976 Immigration Act (Manpower and Immigration, 1974). The main change introduced by the new Act was the introduction of a target level for immigration, to be set by the minister responsible for immigration. This level is to be determined after consultation with the provinces concerning regional demographic needs and labour market considerations, and after consultation with such other persons, organizations, and institutions as the minister deems appropriate. It is an indication of the importance placed on immigration that the Act requires an annual "statement to Parliament" on the government's goals with respect to immigration. In other regards, the Act reinforced existing policy. It explicitly affirmed the fundamental objectives of Canadian immigration laws, including family reunification, non-discrimination, concerns for refugees, and the promotion of Canada's demographic, economic, and cultural goals. In effect, immigration has been administered through three "classes": the independent class is administered through the points system; the family class gains admission based on a close family connection; the refugee class is administered on the basis of humanitarian concerns.

This brief history of policy indicates that there have been considerable shifts in the admissibility of immigrants. In general, there have been more people who have wanted to come to Canada than were deemed desirable, and thus there has been a need to regulate arrivals and to select those seen as best suited to evolving conditions. However, the selection has not always produced the intended results since the actual economic activities of immigrants, once in Canada, often has diverged considerably from their intended occupations (McInnis, 1980).

Government attitude to immigration has also tended to shift rather quickly. For instance, the 1966 White Paper was very positive toward immigration: "without a substantial continuing flow of immigrants, it is doubtful that we could sustain the higher rate of economic growth and the associated cultural development which are essential to the maintenance and development of our national identity" (cited in Taylor, 1987: 3). Just eight years later, the 1974 Green Paper was much more reserved: "when all the arguments are sifted, it would probably be a not unfair assessment of our understanding of the economic consequences of higher against lower population growth rates ... to conclude that the evidence in favour of higher rates is uncertain" (Manpower and Immigration, 1974: 6).

Given that the period since 1978 has involved deliberate planning of immigration levels, it is worth taking note of the planned levels and their components (Table 1). The announced levels increased from 100,000 in 1979 to 135,000 in 1981, then declined to 85,000 in 1985 and rose to 170,000 in 1990. As can be seen, actual landings exceeded planned levels in 1978-80, then were lower than planned to 1986 and rose above planned levels in 1987-90. The major reason for the reduction in planned levels in the period 1983-85 was the economic recession, which was followed by a policy of "moderate controlled growth" in immigration levels. The reduction of the early 1980s was largely at the expense of the independent class. The family class has been rather stable since admissions are determined on the basis of the eligibility of applicants. The planning level simply represents the expected number of successful applicants. Planning for refugee arrivals has been a deliberate part of the planning activities, in co-ordination with "private" agencies that sponsor refugee arrivals. This is rather different from the situation before the 1976 Immigration Act, when refugees were accommodated on the basis of government decisions following on specific circumstances. Hawkins (1988: xi; 1989: xiv), who has carefully analysed public policy underlying immigration, concludes that the 1976

Table 1: Announced and Actual Immigration Levels, 1979-1995

Year	Announced Level	Actual Landings
1979	100,000	112,096
1980	120,000	143,117
1981	130,000-140,000	128,618
1982	130,000-135,000	121,147
1983	105,000-110,000	89,157
1984	90,000-95,000	88,239
1985	85,000-90,000	84,302
1986	105,000-115,000	99,219
1987	115,000-125,000	152,098
1988	125,000-135,000	161,900
1989	150,000-160,000	191,015
1990	165,000-175,000	212,000
1991	220,000	
1992	250,000	
1993	250,000	
1994	250,000	
1995	250,000	

SOURCES: Howith, 1988: 40; Employment and Immigration, 1989b: 2; Dumas, 1990b: 2; Employment and Immigration, 1990.

NOTE: Levels planning does not include persons already in Canada who are given refugee status.

Immigration Act "is one of the best pieces of immigration legislation to be found anywhere." It establishes "clear and liberal national objectives in immigration and refugee policy . . . and a planning process including consultation . . . leading to an annual statement to Parliament." The next section will further analyse the operation of this legislation and its impact on Canada.

POLICY ISSUES IN IMMIGRATION

Immigration policy always involves an interaction between the migration experience of the country (numbers, characteristics, their role in the economy and society) and the dominant perception regarding the value of immigration. As Kritz (1987: 950) explains:

> Immigration policy is the outcome of an interactive process at the national level that incorporates information based on a country's actual experience with immigrants, as well as the perceptions of policy making elites regarding the role of immigration and its desirability.

An advantage of the Canadian situation is that the objectives of immigration policy are clearly defined in the Act of Parliament. It is worth quoting extensively from this statement of objectives, since that will present a background on which to assess the evolving situation (Parliament of Canada, 1978: C.52, 5-6):

It is hereby declared that Canadian immigration policy ... shall be designed and administered in such a manner as to promote the domestic and international interests of Canada recognizing the need:

(a) to support the attainment of such demographic goals as may be established by the Government of Canada from time to time in respect of the size, rate of growth, structure and geographic distribution of the Canadian population;

(b) to enrich and strengthen the cultural and social fabric of Canada, taking into account the federal and bilingual character of Canada;

(c) to facilitate the reunion in Canada of Canadian citizens and permanent residents with their close relatives from abroad;

(d) to encourage and facilitate the adaptation of persons who have been granted admission as permanent residents to Canadian society by promoting cooperation between the Government of Canada and other levels of government and non-government agencies in Canada with respect thereto;

(e) to facilitate the entry of visitors into Canada for the purpose of fostering trade and commerce, tourism, cultural and scientific activities and international understanding;

(f) to ensure that any person who seeks admission to Canada on either a permanent or temporary basis is subject to standards of admission that do not discriminate on grounds of race, national or ethnic origin, colour, religion or sex;

(g) to fulfil Canada's international legal obligations with respect to refugees and to uphold its humanitarian tradition with respect to the displaced and the persecuted;

(h) to foster the development of a strong and viable economy and the prosperity of all regions in Canada;

(i) to maintain and protect the health, safety and good order of Canadian society; and

(j) to promote international order and justice by denying the use of Canadian territory to persons who are likely to engage in criminal activity.

These objectives give immigration a large mandate on issues ranging from population to social well-being and economic growth. The sections that follow will assess these questions in the context that research provides part of the basis on which to guide the implementation of policy. In effect, the main questions at any one point in time come down to three issues. (1) What should be the level of immigration? (2) What should be the composition of the immigrant stream? (3) How is the integration of immigrants to be achieved?

DEMOGRAPHIC IMPACT OF IMMIGRATION

The demographic objective is stated in the legislation quoted above, in terms of "size, rate of growth, structure and geographic distribution." The assessment of the demographic side of immigration has been difficult both because the government has not had explicit demographic goals, and because demographic objectives are often seen to be rather abstract. Nonetheless, let us treat this question first in terms of population growth, age structure, and geographic distribution. Other aspects, such as socio-economic and linguistic composition, will be left to subsequent sections.

Population growth

The basic trends in immigration have been reviewed above (see Figure 5). Recall that the two post-Confederation surges of immigration came when the rate of growth of the native-born labour force had slowed considerably. The 1896-1913 wave made up for the emigration losses of the depressed post-Confederation era, while the 1946-60 arrivals compensated for the small proportions of young adults in the 1950s that resulted from the decline of fertility in the 1930s.

The demographic impact of immigration clearly depends on the proportion of immigrants who stay in Canada. There is an important relationship between the levels of immigration and emigration, due in part to the subsequent departure of immigrants (Beaujot and Rappak, 1989). After adjusting for deaths, it is estimated that some 30 per cent of the immigrants who arrived in 1951-70 and 20 per cent of the 1971-80 arrivals had left by 1986 (Figure 6).

The estimates of departures may be slightly exaggerated if immigrants are more likely to be missed in the census, or if they are less likely to report properly their place of birth. However, it is clear that the subsequent departure of immigrants is an important aspect of international migration. In some regards, this may be surprising. Why do immigrants come if they are simply going to leave again? In other regards, one could expect that a certain proportion of people who are "on the move" will either return to their home country or re-migrate to a third country. Departures may follow a failure either on the part of the immigrant to adapt or on the part of the receiving society to integrate its newest members from abroad. However, it could also follow the successful accomplishment of the immigrant's objective and it may have been part of his/her original plan. Alternatively, the conditions may

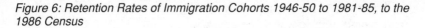

Figure 6: Retention Rates of Immigration Cohorts 1946-50 to 1981-85, to the 1986 Census

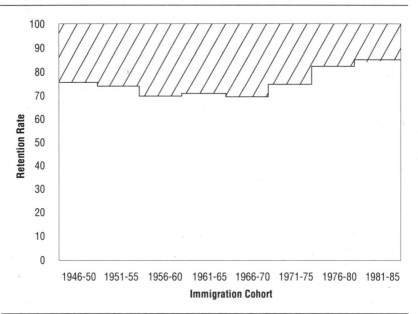

NOTE: Data adjusted for census under-enumeration.
SOURCES: Beaujot and Rappak, 1988b: 48.

change, either in the host or sending country. For instance, return migration may become more attractive when one approaches retirement. Migrants have ties to their places of origin, and modern means of communication and travel make it easier to retain these ties. As an indicator of the attachment to the home country, some 43 per cent of immigrants who arrived in the 1978-82 period and 28 per cent of the 1967-77 arrivals had not adopted Canadian citizenship by the 1986 census, even though they became eligible after three years (Jansen and Richmond, 1990). It is an outdated notion to think of immigrants as "settlers" who never look back after making a "fresh start" in their chosen country.

Demographically, the subsequent departure of immigrants accounts for some 60 per cent of total emigration from Canada (Beaujot and Rappak, 1988a). Partly for this reason, the overall relationship between immigration and emigration is positive: in general, higher levels of immigration are paired with higher levels of emigration.

The levels of immigration and emigration can best be appreciated through a comparison to the base population. In particular, it is useful to compute the average annual levels per 100 people in the Canadian population (Figure 7). In the period around the turn of the century there was an average of 2.11 annual arrivals per 100 population, compared to an average of 0.77 arrivals in the period 1951-81 and 0.52 annual arrivals per 100 population in the period 1981-90. The average figure for the whole of this century is 0.97 arrivals per 100 base population. Emigration has been more stable, with an average of 0.28 per 100 base population over the period 1951-88.

Another way of measuring the impact of immigration is to compute the proportion of population growth due to net migration. For the whole of this century, the *net* immigration of 4.5 million persons comprised 22 per cent of the total population growth. The relative contribution of immigration to population growth was highest between 1901 and 1911, when it reached 44.1 per cent. Over the period 1946-90, net migration accounted for 26 per cent of population growth.

These measures of the impact of immigration do not take into account the further impact through children born to immigrants while in Canada. At the 1971 census, the "birthplace of parents" question showed that 33.8 per cent of the entire population were first or second generation in Canada (Kalbach and McVey, 1979: 179). It is also possible to simulate population change by isolating the effect of births and deaths on the population. Applying birth and death rates observed over the 1951-81 period to the 1951 population, the population would have changed from 14.0 million in 1951 to 20.4 million in 1981 (Le Bras, 1988: 9). Since the 1981 population was 24.3 million, this implies that 38 per cent of the actual growth was a function of immigration and births to these immigrants over the period 1951-81.

Immigration and future growth

Another useful way to assess the demographic impact of immigration is through population projections for the future. In order to focus on the impact of immigration, only three projections will be analysed (Figure 8). All three projections use a constant fertility of 1.7 births per woman. They differ on immigration, which is 200,000 arrivals per year in the first projection, 140,000 in the second, and zero in the third. Emigration is introduced as a rate, which amounts to 0.25 departures per 100 population (except in the third projection, where emigration is zero). Annual net migration is approximately 120,000, 60,000, and zero in the three projection series under discussion.

In the forty-year period 1946-86, Canada's population increased by more than 100 per cent, from 12.3 to 25.4 million persons. Over the next forty years, the total increase would be much lower: 33 per cent under the high immigration assumption, 24 per cent under the low assumption, and only 10 per cent with zero net migration. The comparison to

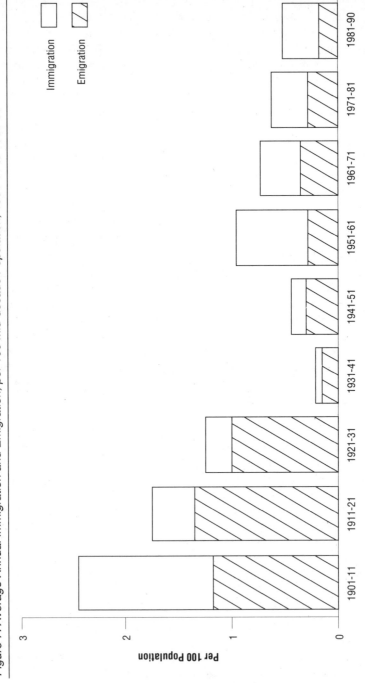

Figure 7: Average Annual Immigration and Emigration, per 100 Mid-decade Population, 1901-11 to 1981-90

SOURCES: Beaujot and Rappak, 1988b: 27; Dumas, 1990b: 2.

Figure 8: Total Population Size, 1946 to 1986, and Projections to 2036

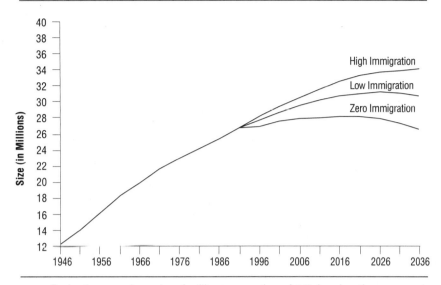

NOTE: Projections are based on fertility assumption of 1.7, immigration of 200,000, 140,000, and zero persons per year and emigration of 0.25, 0.25, and 0.0 persons per 100 population per year.
SOURCES: Statistics Canada, 1989d and 1990b.

zero migration implies that in the high projection 69 per cent of population growth from 1986 to 2026 would be a function of net migration and births to migrants. In the low projection, 55 per cent of population growth is due to migration. There are also sizable differences in the total populations. By 2026, zero net migration would give a population size of 28 million, compared to 31.4 million with low immigration and 33.8 million under high immigration. That is, the high immigration involves a population that is 5.7 million more (or 20 per cent larger) than zero net migration. Low immigration already gives a population that is 3.2 million more (or 11 per cent larger) than zero net migration.

Three turning points are particularly interesting in these projections. The first is the point at which net migration becomes equal to net natural increase. This occurs in 1999 and 2010 for the high and low assumptions respectively. After that date, more than 50 per cent of population growth is due to net migration. The next turning point is where natural increase becomes negative, after which immigration constitutes over 100 per cent of population growth. Given that the same fertility assumptions are used, this point does not vary extensively:

2018 for zero immigration, 2020 for low immigration, and 2022 for the high immigration assumption.

The final turning point is that at which population growth itself stops. This occurs in 2017 for zero migration, 2026 for low immigration, and 2034 for high immigration. After that, we must speak of population decline rather than growth. In approximate terms, each 60,000 more in net migration delays population decline by eight or nine years. Other projections have estimated that it would take an annual net migration of 163,000 (or immigration of 212,000) to prevent population decline under a fertility assumption of 1.7 births per woman (Avery and Edmonston, 1988).

While it takes some time for the growth to convert itself into a decline, the period of essentially zero growth is rather imminent. By 2000-2001, growth would be 0.8 per cent per year under high immigration, 0.6 under low immigration, and 0.3 per cent under zero net migration. In comparison, Canada's population growth was 1.2 per cent per year as recently as 1976-81.

It is in this context that some authors have argued for explicitly using immigration as a means of supporting population growth. Noting that Canada doubled its population in the post-war period with a very positive impact on national growth and development, Hawkins (1989) speaks of using immigration as a way to counter declining population. She further argues for the development of a population policy related to future political, social, and environmental needs (Hawkins, 1988: xi). Passaris (1989) notes that immigration has always been linked to economic considerations, but that now demographic considerations have gained importance, which would imply a longer-term approach to the setting of immigration levels. The Macdonald Commission also argued for long-term objectives in setting immigration levels. It made the case for demographic objectives that would use immigration to forestall population decline and stated that it would be beneficial to return to the immigration levels of the post-war period, that is, some 140,000-150,000 per year (Royal Commission on the Economic Union, 1985: 668). Analyses of European demographic trends have tended to conclude that immigration policies should be seen as a complement rather than a substitute for pro-natalist policies, partly because it takes very high immigration to compensate for low fertility (Steinmann, 1989; Wattelar and Roumans, 1988; Lesthaeghe, 1989; Hohn, 1987). The immigration solution to avoiding population decline is more palatable if fertility is also being sustained.

In Europe, the fertility of immigrants tends to be considerably higher than that of the native-born, augmenting the impact of immigration. In Canada, the foreign-born have higher fertility after arrival (A. Gauthier, 1988, 1989), but their fertility is probably lower at the time of arrival and it tends to converge with that of the Canadian-born by the end of childbearing years (Ram and George, 1990). For ever-married women, the completed family size is lower among the foreign-born (Krishnan and Krotki, 1989). The convergence is also strong in terms of mortality (Trovato, 1986).

In summary, it is unlikely that the population dynamics of the future will be the same as in the past. In particular, immigration is likely to become the only source of population growth. As we have seen, it would take a substantial level of annual immigration to compensate for the deficit in natural increase. At immigration levels comparable to the post-war average, we will no longer be talking of population growth but of population decline. While immigration is often seen as a possible compensation for low fertility, in another sense immigration may be more difficult to accommodate in an environment of population decline. When a population is growing, immigration constitutes a smaller proportion of the overall population change. Once population growth occurs through net migration rather than through natural increase, immigration will have a larger impact on the society and the structures through which it integrates new members (births and immigrants). For instance, in the period 1971-86 there were thirty-five immigrants per 100 births. At levels of immigration that would maintain population growth with low fertility, the period 2021-36 would involve sixty immigrants per 100 births. Since these population dynamics are outside of Canada's historical experience, it is difficult to anticipate their social and political consequences.

It is hard to make a policy argument based on demographic questions alone. Population per se is a fairly neutral variable in a society's socioeconomic welfare. There are both advantages and disadvantages to larger numbers compared to smaller ones. In effect, the international literature indicates a near zero correlation between population growth and economic growth (Preston, 1987). The value placed on population size also depends on which considerations are given priority: e.g., green spaces versus power in the world community. Without doubt, technology and innovations are more important than population size in promoting economic welfare. Nonetheless, it is hard to avoid the impression that numbers do count in questions of welfare and that Canada would profit by sustaining population growth. Because of the momentum of demographic phenomena, a long-term horizon must be envisaged with such a fundamental question as growth and decline. Decline cannot as easily be faced once it has started – by that point, larger numbers would be needed to introduce a correction. Policies and programs for immigration also need to be tried and tested over time. A turn-on/turn-off approach is very disruptive from a policy and institutional perspective, to say nothing of the consequence on the receptiveness of the host society.

Age structure

The impact of immigration on the age structure can best be appreciated by comparing the median age of immigrants on arrival to that of the Canadian population. The median age of immigrants has been relatively stable, averaging twenty-five years for each year between 1956 and 1976, then increasing to twenty-seven years in 1981-86. The median age of the entire Canadian population has changed much more, increasing from 26.3 in 1961 to 31.6 in 1986. In effect, the median age of arriving immigrants has been about a year younger than that of the receiving population over the period 1945-71, changing to two years younger by 1981 and four years younger by 1986.

These numbers imply that immigration has a rather minor impact on the age structure of Canadian society. In effect, simulating population change as a function only of births and deaths since 1951 produces a 1981 population with an average age that is only 0.5 years older than the actual average observed in that year. Stated differently, the 1951-81 immigration would have reduced the average age of the 1981 population by a half year (Le Bras, 1988: 12).

Similar results are obtained with projections into the future. The population projections defined earlier produce median ages in 2036 of 44.7 years under high immigration, 45.7 under low immigration, and 46.9 years under zero migration. The population aged sixty-five and over in 2036 is 24.5, 25.6, and 27.0 per cent under high, low, and zero migration assumptions. Clearly, the immigration assumptions have a rather small impact on the age structure. Nonetheless, the impact is to reduce the aging of the population. Between 1981 and 1986 the proportion over sixty-five increased from 9.7 to 10.7. In this context, the higher level of immigration would reduce this aging indicator by the equivalent of twelve years of aging.

Rappak and Rappak (1990) have projected the age composition under the assumption that there would be higher proportions of younger persons among arrivals. It is found that such scenarios would have a significant impact on the age structure, especially under higher levels of immigration.

Geographic distribution

Immigration, and to a lesser extent the subsequent internal migration of the foreign-born, has an important impact on the geographic distribution of Canada's population. In particular, these trends tend to accentuate the differences in regional population growth. Figure 9 shows that

Ontario and British Columbia have significantly higher proportions of immigrant populations than the national average.

The immigration of the post-war period has largely been to the advantage of the relative size of the populations of Ontario and British Columbia and to the disadvantage of the Atlantic Provinces and Quebec. For instance, among the Canadian-born, Ontario is only 17 per cent larger than Quebec, but adding the foreign-born makes Ontario 39 per cent larger. The foreign-born population of Ontario was four times as large as that of Quebec in 1986.

The geographic concentration of immigrants also accentuates the growth of the metropolitan areas, particularly Toronto, Montreal, and Vancouver. In the mid-1980s these three cities were the intended destination of over 60 per cent of immigrants, with Toronto alone accounting for 25 per cent of arrivals (Hersak and Thomas, 1988). The Review of Demography (1989: 34) concludes that immigrants of the post-war period for the most part have not gone to places outside of the major urban centres or to major urban centres east of Montreal. Rather than being a national phenomenon, immigration has focused on the large cities: Montreal and the large cities west of Quebec. Toronto and Vancouver, especially, have significantly higher proportions of post-war immigrants than their relative share of the Canadian-born population.

For Quebec, immigrants are highly concentrated in Montreal. Noting that 80 per cent of Quebec's arrivals settle in that one city, Termote (1988) projects that at 40,000 arrivals to the province per year, Montreal's population would increase significantly. With births, deaths, and departures taken into account, over a forty-year period this level of immigration would add 1,150,000 to Montreal's population (compared to a 1986 total population of 1,750,000).

Given that immigrants are likely to settle mostly in metropolitan areas and to follow the "pathways" established by earlier cohorts, immigration will probably continue to accentuate the inequalities in Canada's regional population distribution. For the most part, immigration cannot be seen as a means of demographic redistribution to areas of lower population concentration.

SOCIO-ECONOMIC IMPACT OF IMMIGRATION

Macro perspectives

Seward (1987d) has set the discussion of macro-economic issues within the context of the role played by immigration in labour supply and consumer demand. On the supply side, immigration can augment the productive capacity of the economy by adding to the labour force,

Figure 9: Immigrants as a Percentage of Provincial Populations, 1986

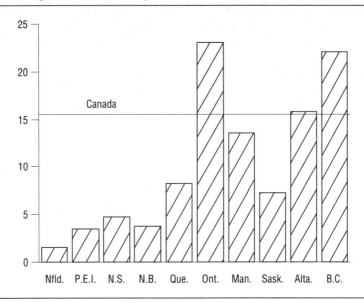

SOURCE: 1986 Census, 93-109.

especially if the new arrivals help overcome bottlenecks where skills are in short supply. Alternatively, the use of skills imported from abroad can discourage local training and the shifts in wage rates that would prompt labour force movement into areas of stronger need for skills. On the demand side, immigration can affect total consumption patterns, including government expenditure on health, education, and welfare.

Immigration played a larger role on the supply of labour in the immediate post-war era, when the skill level of the Canadian population was lower. For instance, at ages 25-64, 23.1 per cent of the 1961-69 arrivals had some university education compared to 10.5 per cent of the Canadian population in 1971. In contrast, immigrants of the 1980-85 period reflect higher proportions at both high (some university) and low (primary school or less) levels of education compared to the Canadian-born (Beaujot and Rappak, 1988b: 72-75). However, immigrants continue to have higher than average concentration in certain occupational categories and to be more likely to be self-employed (Tepper, 1988).

Seward and Tremblay (1989) have analysed the extent to which immigrants respond to the need for labour in expanding parts of the economy, thereby facilitating structural change. They find support for this structural change model in the case of male immigrants, especially those from non-traditional sources, but not among female immigrants from non-traditional sources. This suggests that immigrant women are not responding as effectively to the changing labour market. Two implications are proposed. The increasing proportion of the family and refugee classes in the early 1980s involved persons who were not selected with specific reference to their suitability for the labour force. Alternatively, there is a need to ensure that all have access to adequate labour adjustment programs: language training, skills upgrading, facilitating the recognition of foreign credentials, and removing discriminatory barriers to employment.

Another question regarding the supply of labour is the extent to which immigrants displace the native-born labour force. DeVoretz (1989a) finds that at the level of the total economy there is no evidence that the post-war stock of immigrants significantly displaced workers born in Canada. There were short-run displacements in particular industries (particularly those with strong concentrations of foreign-born or of women workers) but this was offset through job creation by immigrants across industries over time. A ten-year period was sufficient to offset this displacement.

On the demand side, Marr and Percy's (1985) summary of economic models suggests that immigration has a marginal but negative impact on per capita income and unemployment. However, as Seward (1987a) notes, these models do not take into account the human and financial capital associated with immigration flows. In the context of an aging population, immigration has the potential to facilitate adjustment by bringing in new skills at a time when flexibility in the labour force will be declining (Seward, 1987b). The foreign-born are also found to have higher peak net worth in terms of asset accumulation and to make a positive contribution to capital asset accumulation in Canada (DeVoretz, 1989b). The "business class" of immigrants is particularly relevant with regard to the transfer of capital. For instance, the 1986 arrivals from this class intended to transfer a capital value of $1.2 billion to Canada (Nash, 1988). However, this would represent only a quarter of all funds transferred by immigrants. Regarding government revenues and expenditures, Akbari (1989) estimates that immigrants, especially because of their age profile, consume less in major public services and contribute more taxes than the Canadian-born population. He concludes that immigrants clearly benefit the non-immigrants through net transfers to the public treasury.

The costs and benefits of immigration also depend on the perspective taken in the analysis. Stafford and McMillan (1986) suggest that in the neo-classical economic tradition, immigrants are beneficial because they lower wages, improve productivity, and provide a source of demand. They therefore argue that immigration is not necessarily beneficial, at least in the short term, to native workers. According to the staples theory perspective, Canada is very dependent on external trade; consequently, increasing local consumer demand and improving the skill level of the labour force are not the main "movers" of the economy (*idem*). Ternowetsky (1986) is also concerned about the costs of immigration, in terms of unemployment, poverty, inequality, and state dependency, and questions the capacity of Canada to absorb new immigrants in the current economic and social life of the country. He argues that we must "ensure that immigration does not result in the foreclosure of opportunities to resident Canadians." On the other hand, Samuel and Conyers (1987) calculate that over the period 1983-85 immigration added more jobs to the Canadian economy than the number of jobs taken by immigrants. However, this calculation largely depends on the assumed number of jobs created per immigrant arrival. The results may be different at higher levels of immigration. It has also been noted that there is generally an inverse relation between immigration levels and unemployment rates: higher immigration is associated with lower unemployment. This is probably because in periods of higher unemployment the immigration levels are likely to be lowered and there may be less interest in coming to Canada.

Given that technology and innovations are key to economic progress, it would be important to know how immigration contributes to innovation. This is obviously difficult to measure, but immigrants would appear to produce a net positive result in this regard. Being motivated to make a major change in their lives and to overcome the various barriers of migration itself, immigrants, one might surmise, are people with creativity and drive. The fact that immigrants are more likely to be self-employed might be used as an indicator of their achievement orientation. Simon (1986: 14) certainly argues that arriving at the "age of greatest physical and mental vigour," immigrants "tend to bring an unusually high degree of skill, education, self-reliance and innovative flair." McNicoll (1986: 221) suggests that "scientific prowess" in the United States "probably benefited as much from the numerically small immigration of European refugee scientists in the 1930s and 1940s as from years of natural increase."

Others have also concluded that the economic effects of immigration are positive (see Employment and Immigration, 1989d). In noting the projections under different immigration scenarios for Ontario, Simmons (1990) finds that higher levels of immigration stabilize the size of the school-age population, leading to more gradual shifts in demand for teachers and classrooms. Higher immigration also tends to stabilize the demand for new housing by stabilizing the size of the age groups most likely to be first home purchasers. Hawkins (1989: xvii) concludes that the post-war migration to Canada has had a very positive impact on national growth and development. In a broad-ranging "Canadian survey," *The Economist* (1988) suggests that Canada "could be bolder if it had a bigger and growing population, [because] it could run its economy at a fuller throttle to close a long-standing productivity gap with America." The conclusion is that "the country needs many more newcomers to create more growth, more jobs and more prosperity." Representing the largest construction trade local union in Canada, the Labourers' International Union of North America (1990) claims that much of Canada's infrastructure was built by immigrants and that Toronto clearly requires more labourers. In a broad survey of policy responses to population decline, Andorka (1989) claims that immigration has overwhelmingly positive economic effects by increasing the flexibility of the labour force and by contributing to technological development.

The macro-economic connections between economic growth and immigration are certainly complex and difficult to estimate conclusively. While the available analyses presented here largely argue for economic benefits at the level of the overall economy, this need not apply to specific sectors. For instance, non-unionized labour can suffer wage declines as they are less able to protect themselves from the greater pressure of competition brought on by the arrival of immigrants. Reviewing the evidence with respect to per capita income and unemployment, Swan (1990) and the Economic Council of Canada (1991) conclude that immigration has only small macro-economic effects. It is also important to note that most analyses would suggest that the economic connections are long-term rather than short-term. This would imply that the practice of reducing immigration during periods of recession or high unemployment does not sufficiently pay attention to the underlying nature of these interactions (see Samuel and Jansson, 1987). The Macdonald Commission argued for the consideration of long-term objectives by the admission of more young, well-qualified, and educated persons instead of people with specific occupational qualifications (Royal Commission on the Economic Union, 1985).

Micro-level economic adjustment: classes of immigrants

In analysing the socio-economic characteristics of immigrants, it is first important to appreciate the criteria through which they are admitted. Not all immigrants are admitted under the same criteria, and changes in the distribution of admissions can affect the relative status of given immigration groups. The 1976 Act specifies three classes of immigrants. The *family class* consists of close relatives of permanent residents of Canada. Such immigrants are not assessed under the points system, and their sponsoring relatives agree to provide them with lodging and care for up to ten years. The category of *independent immigrants* includes individuals who must meet all the criteria for admission according to the points system. Within this group, *assisted relatives* are people who have kin in Canada willing to support them for up to five years and who receive points because of this. The *refugee and designated classes* are admitted on the basis of humanitarian considerations.

Until about 1971, the independent immigrants selected on the basis of education, language, age, and the demand for their skills in Canada were the largest category. Over the period 1976-86 the family class was the largest category. The independent class has declined in importance, partly because there are fewer advocates in Canada calling for higher admissions in this category (Simmons, 1988). The family class and sponsored relatives have obvious advocates who wish to facilitate the admission of their close relatives. The various refugee advocacy groups ensure that we pay close attention to refugee admissions. Now that the occupational skills of the Canadian population are well developed, there is less pressure, even on the part of employers, to admit independent immigrants. The independent class includes dependants who arrive with the principal applicant. Excluding these dependants, the skill-tested independent applicants constitute only 19 per cent of total admissions for 1988. Rather than defining the major socio-economic characteristics of the immigrant flow, independent immigrants have become a "residual" category (Simmons, 1988).

Given that they are selected on the basis of skill-related criteria and the demand for their occupational skills in Canada, it is not surprising that independent immigrants have the highest level of economic adaptation. For instance, independent immigrants and assisted relatives admitted in 1979 had lower rates of unemployment and higher incomes in 1982 than those admitted in the family or refugee classes (Samuel and Woloski, 1985).

While total immigrant admissions are subject to the annual determination of immigration levels, the family class is not subject to specific limitations. As many people as meet the criteria can be admitted. Research on the family class indicates that they have a reasonable level of socio-economic integration. A survey of 1,400 family class immigrants who arrived in the period 1981-84 finds that, while the majority did not manage to enter their intended occupations and their levels of unemployment were higher than the Canadian average, their earnings and working conditions were on average better than those in their home country (Samuel, 1988a). Despite not being selected on job-related criteria, the family class immigrants have demonstrated considerable ability to penetrate the Canadian occupational structure.

The refugee class is the smallest among the three major classes. With the arrival of the Indo-Chinese "boat people," the refugee class almost equalled the independent class in 1979 and 1980. Another new feature of refugee admissions involves persons coming directly to Canada to seek asylum. Until the early 1980s refugees were almost all chosen for settlement in Canada from points of first asylum outside of the country. Since refugees are not specifically coming for economic reasons and they are consequently less likely to have transferable skills, it is understandable that their economic integration is uneven. The 1972 Asian expellees from Uganda are an example of a very successful group. After one year, their average income exceeded the Canadian average (Samuel, 1984). The Hungarian and Czechoslovakian refugees also experienced relatively rapid adjustment, having arrived when general labour market conditions were favourable (Ziegler, 1988). In contrast, the Indo-Chinese group has suffered relatively high levels of unemployment and low occupational mobility, partly because they arrived just before the recession of the early 1980s and partly because of language barriers (Neuwirth *et al.*, 1985). Especially in the first year, refugees experience serious barriers in entering their intended occupations (Abbott, 1988). On the other hand, the experience of refugees over the last quarter-century indicates that the vast majority have adjusted well economically (Samuel, 1984).

Most of the analyses of the socio-economic characteristics of immigrants are based on census data, which do not distinguish the various immigration classes. While there is much diversity among immigrants, as there is in the Canadian-born population, immigration has tended to increase the socio-economic profile of the Canadian population. In a review of the labour market adjustment of immigrants, Abbott (1988) concludes that the first three years involve lower employment, higher unemployment, barriers to entering the intended occupation, and a higher likelihood of having low-income status. However, after three to five years, the averages on these economic characteristics become very similar to those of the Canadian-born. Concentrating on the age group 25-44, Badets (1989) summarizes that the foreign-born have a 0.5 per cent higher chance of being in the labour force for men and 3.4 per cent for women. In this same age group among persons who worked full time in 1985, the average employment income of the foreign-born was 3.9 per cent higher than the Canadian-born for men and 4.2 per cent lower than the Canadian-born for women. The foreign-born have higher rates of home ownership than the Canadian-born, except those arriving in the ten years before the census (Ray and Moore, 1989). Another encouraging observation is that the second generation has shown very strong levels of economic adaptation. Richmond and Verma (1978: 34) conclude that "Canadian society has provided significant opportunities for upward mobility for children of immigrants, irrespective of ethnic origin." The analysis of a sample from Toronto also shows that the second generation has the highest level of socio-economic attainment (Rhyme, 1982).

Immigrants represent considerable diversity – in places of birth, class of entry, and length of residence in Canada. Taking the long view, it can be argued that successive waves of immigrants have improved their economic conditions and integrated into the society. Much of the disadvantage of immigrants relates to questions of language and recency of arrival.

Education

With regard to education, the relative advantage of immigrants compared to the Canadian-born was highest in the immediate post-war period, when Canadians were suffering from a poorly developed educational system. As of the 1986 census, 25.3 per cent of the foreign-born had some university education compared to 20.4 per cent of the Canadian-born population at ages 25-64 (Beaujot and Rappak, 1988b).

The educational advantages of immigrants are stronger for men. Since women are more likely to arrive as dependants, they are less "selected" on educational characteristics. In effect, women immigrants have higher proportions than the Canadian-born at both high (some university) and low (primary school or less) levels of education.

With the increased educational profile of the Canadian-born population and the greater importance of the family and refugee classes in immigration, immigrants of the early 1980s do not have such an advantage with regard to education. In the 1980-84 cohort, 17.0 per cent of immigrants at ages 25-64 had less than nine years of education compared to 14.8 per cent of the Canadian-born.

Labour force

The 1971, 1981, and 1986 censuses have documented higher rates of labour force participation on the part of immigrants than on the part of the Canadian-born. In 1981, this applied to all immigrant cohorts except those who had arrived in the year and a half preceding the census (Beaujot et al., 1988: 39). The greater labour force participation of immigrants especially applies to women. For both women and men, the labour force participation increases with a longer period of residence.

Figure 10 illustrates the 1986 data on proportions working full-time for forty or more weeks, within given age groups. Immigrant cohorts arriving before 1980 are more likely to be working full-time, especially in the case of women, than their Canadian-born counterparts. The 1980-86 cohort is a major exception to the general pattern, with lower proportions working full-time (Seward and Tremblay, 1989: 32-33).

On the whole, the unemployment rates of immigrants are compara-

Figure 10: Proportion Working Full-time, by Age, for Immigrants and Canadian-born,1986

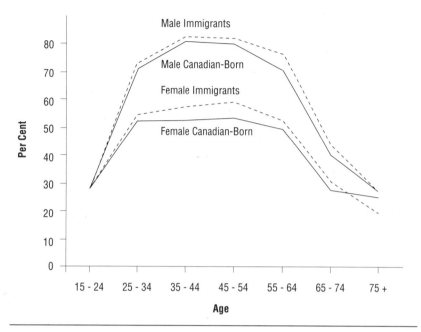

NOTE : The proportion working full-time is the proportion of a given age-sex group that worked full-time for forty or more weeks in 1985.
SOURCE : Statistics Canada, special tabulations for the 1986 census.

ble to those of the Canadian-born. In one study, the unemployment experiences of principal applicant immigrants who arrived in 1975 were followed over the period 1977-81 (Robertson, 1986). It was found that immigrants had a slightly higher "incidence" of unemployment, but the "spell frequency" and "duration" were very similar to the Canadian average. It was concluded that after a relatively short (two- to three-year) period of adjustment, unemployment patterns of immigrants are very similar to the Canadian average.

Given the strong labour force participation on the part of immigrants, it should not be surprising to find that immigration has made a rather important contribution to labour force growth. For instance, over the period 1966-86 the labour force grew by 74 per cent, or 5,547,000 persons. Of the labour force growth in these twenty years, 1,292,000, or 23 per cent, were immigrants who had arrived in the interim.

Over the next twenty years, the labour force would increase by 1,838,000 persons (12 per cent) with zero net migration and by

3,094,000 persons (25 per cent) with net migration of 100,000 per year (Denton and Spencer, 1987b: 197). With zero net migration, the labour force reaches its peak in 2006, then declines. An immigration level of 100,000 per year postpones the decline by ten years. Clearly, the labour force will expand at a much slower rate now that the baby-boom generation is past the prime ages for labour force entry.

Occupations

The occupational distribution of immigrants does not differ greatly from that of the Canadian-born labour force. Both male and female immigrants are more concentrated in the service, processing, product-fabricating, and assembling occupations. Male immigrants are also more concentrated in the managerial, professional, and technical occupations. Marr (1986) finds that the foreign-born are overrepresented in the faster growing occupations of the 1970s (Marr, 1986). However, Seward and Tremblay (1990) find that the 1981-86 immigrants are less likely to be in industries with above-average growth. The occupational distribution of immigrants in Canada contrasts sharply with the immigrant populations of most European countries, where the bulk of arrivals are labourers and unskilled workers (Dumas, 1984: 99). This generalization is somewhat less applicable to women, who are more likely to arrive as dependants rather than as principal applicant immigrants and who are disproportionately represented in the clothing industry (Seward, 1990). Nonetheless, except for some groups of immigrant women, there is little evidence of labour market segmentation by immigration status (Basavarajappa and Verma, 1990; Beaujot et al., 1988: 43).

Clearly, immigrants are involved in various parts of the economy (McInnis, 1980). After reviewing several studies on this question, Richmond and Zubrzycki (1984: 85) conclude that "the most striking feature of the distribution of the foreign-born in the labour force is the degree of similarity to the native-born." The distribution of immigrants across Canada's occupational structure facilitates their integration into the society. If they were concentrated at the top it would cause resentment, while concentration at the bottom would introduce ghettoization.

Average income

In summarizing the economic situation of immigrants, Richmond (1988: 122) writes: "while not proportionally represented in the power elites, there is growing evidence that European immigrants and their children have been economically successful and upwardly mobile in the post-Second World War period." However, Richmond continues, "although it may be premature to draw firm conclusions, the preliminary evidence concerning immigrants from Third World countries, particularly visible minorities, is not as encouraging." Let us briefly review the evidence on these questions (see also Beaujot *et al.*, 1988).

As a total group, immigrants have average levels of income that compare favourably to the Canadian-born. Among men, immigrants had average total incomes that were 7.7 per cent above the Canadian-born average in 1970, 12.0 per cent above in 1980, and 11.8 per cent above in 1985. For women, the average figures were basically identical in 1970, while immigrants were 6.7 per cent above the Canadian-born in 1981 and 5.6 per cent above in 1985 (Beaujot and Rappak, 1988b:139). These results imply that immigrants increase the average total income in Canada.

Restricting the comparison to persons working full-time for forty or more weeks in the year, average employment incomes in 1970, 1980, and 1985 indicate a 5 per cent advantage for immigrant men and a 1 per cent disadvantage for women, compared to the Canadian-born. Overall, these differences are small, especially in comparison to the difference between men and women in employment incomes for persons working full-time. For instance, among the Canadian-born, these differences amounted to a 35 per cent disadvantage for women in 1985 (Beaujot and Rappak, 1988b: 141).

Since part of these differences may be due to differences in the profile of the two groups, comparisons were made after adjusting for differences in age and education. On average employment income for persons working full-time, adjusted immigrant income averages are 3 to 5 per cent below the Canadian-born in 1980 and 1985. Thus removing their advantages in terms of age and educational profile, immigrants have a slight income disadvantage compared to the Canadian-born.

Considering the adjusted employment income situation of the different immigration cohorts, it is found that immigrant men who arrived before 1975 and women who arrived before 1970 tended to have higher average incomes in 1985 than the Canadian-born of the same age and sex groups. Immigrants who arrived later, especially the 1980-84 cohort, have average incomes below those of the Canadian-born.

After age and education, length of residence is clearly the single most important determinant of the degree of economic adaptation (Richmond, 1988: 62). However, there is also evidence that the period of adaptation is longer for more recent immigrants, especially those arriving from Third World countries.

Extensive comparisons have been made between the traditional immigrant group from Europe and the United States and the new immigrant group from other parts of the world. For instance, it is found that, in the 1975-79 cohort, the mean employment income of the traditional immigrant group represents 98.7 per cent of the Canadian-born average for men and 93.3 per cent for women (adjusting for age and education). In the new immigrant group the averages are 77.8 and 83.3 per cent of the Canadian-born for men and women respectively (see Figure 11). For men, the new immigrant group is also less likely to be working full-time than the traditional immigrant group, especially for the 1975-84 arrivals. However, women new immigrants are more likely to be working full-time (Beaujot and Rappak, 1988b).

It is important to note that Third World immigrants, who arrived in the 1960s or earlier succeeded as well or better than most other immigrants (Lanphier, 1979: 38-39). The comparison of various immigrant cohorts by period of immigration also suggests a rather encouraging account of economic adjustment since incomes rose with longer periods of residence in Canada. However, these were times of buoyant economic growth, and the Third World immigrants were smaller in number. Studies of the more recent arrivals from the Caribbean indicate that groups arriving after 1970 have had difficulty obtaining employment incomes commensurate with their educational qualifications (Richmond, 1989a). Loaiza (1989) finds that Latin American immigrants are more likely to be concentrated in peripheral industries where wages are lower. Lanphier (1979) concludes that "the chances of economic success of the newer arrivals on the same scale and within a similar time period to that of earlier cohorts is unrealistic."

A number of analyses have paid particular attention to the situation of immigrant women (Boyd, 1987; Seward and McDade; 1988, Grindstaff, 1986a; Ng and Estable, 1986). On average, immigrant women compare favourably to the Canadian-born in terms of incomes, labour force participation, and unemployment. However, this average covers much heterogeneity and the most disadvantaged are the recent arrivals from Southern Europe and Asia: "characterized by limited education and job related skills, frequently lacking knowledge of either official language, and requiring income to help support their families, these women have little option but to seek employment in ethnic-linguistic job ghettos such as the clothing industry" (Seward and McDade, 1988: 49). The policy issues here range from questions of admission through the family class to language training, skill upgrading, recognition of credentials, and child care that would provide women with more independence to pursue training or better employment options. Another particular concern involves the arrival of older widowed women in the family class who do not have access to social security (Boyd, 1989).

The immigration monograph from the 1971 census had documented interesting progress among the immediate post-war immigrants (Richmond and Kalbach, 1980: 109-18). In particular, the 1946-60 immigrant cohort tended to be below the Canadian-born average total incomes by ages and sex in 1961. However, the immigrants made greater progress over the next decade, and the 1971 census showed that these 1946-60

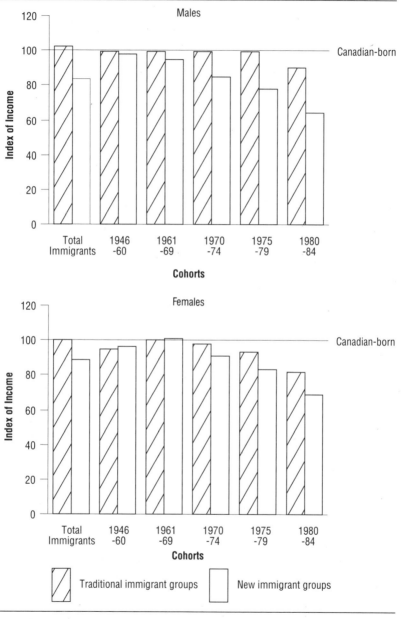

Figure 11: Average Employment Income Compared to the Canadian-born, After Adjusting for Age and Education, for Persons Aged 15-64 Working Full-time for Forty or More Weeks, by Immigration Cohorts and Sex, Showing Traditional and New Immigrant Groups, 1986

SOURCE: Beaujot and Rappak, 1988b: 141-42.

arrivals had now mostly surpassed the average incomes of their Canadian-born counterparts of the same age and sex groups. Comparing the censuses of 1971, 1981, and 1986, there are few instances of this type of progress. Particular immigrant cohorts tend to be either above or below the Canadian-born at each census. Typically, those who arrived before 1970 or 1975 are above the Canadian-born while subsequent cohorts are below the Canadian-born. The multivariate analyses done on the 1971 and 1981 censuses also confirm that recency of arrival had a more negative impact on incomes in 1980 than in 1970 (Beaujot and Rappak, 1988b). DeSilva (1989) finds that after correction for such factors as education, occupation, socio-economic status, marital status, and residence, there are no residual income differences between foreign-born and native-born. However, there is an income disadvantage for immigrants who received all of their education and some of their labour market experience in their home countries, especially in the case of recent arrivals from developing countries.

There are several possible reasons why the rate of economic adaptation (measured in terms of average differences with the Canadian-born) has become slower: the quality of immigrants may have declined (e.g., less knowledge of the official languages at arrival), the quality of the Canadian-born population may have increased (e.g., more development of education and training), economic structures may involve greater difficulty in accommodating immigrants (e.g., greater importance of seniority in wage structures, greater weight of the service sector where familiarity with the society may be more important), and more discrimination (toward immigrants who are more different from the receiving population, making it harder for employers to assess their qualifications accurately). In other words, the economic adaptation of immigrants depends on their characteristics (selectivity, age, education, language, etc.) and the nature of the receiving society (levels of skills, needs for labour, extent of closure toward outsiders).

The experience of a given cohort of immigrants will be largely a function of their quality and the economic situation at the time of their arrival. We have seen that the 1980-86 cohort was less selective, even in terms of education and labour force status. DeVoretz (1990) identifies the disadvantaged cohorts as those arriving in 1978-87. This in turn would be partly a function of the reduced relative size of the independent class and the greater importance of family and refugee classes among these arrivals. Obviously, we should not expect that persons selected on the basis of family reunification and humanitarian concerns would necessarily achieve levels of economic performance comparable to that of the receiving society. In addition, as the Canadian-born labour force achieves higher levels of education, the relative status of immigrants, especially women, would be lower (Stafford, 1990). The competition for promotions may also be stronger, given the presence of the baby-boom generations. This would lead us to expect a greater relative disadvantage for immigrants.

Low-income status

As well as comparing groups by average income, it is useful to consider variations. A particularly useful measure is the proportion of a given group that has been attributed "low income status." This status is a relative concept, based on the proportion of total income needed for the essentials of food, clothing, and shelter. Using average expenditure on these essentials, various "income cut-offs" are established depending on family size and place of residence.

In the data from the 1971 and 1981 censuses, low income was less common among immigrants than in the Canadian-born population for "economic families." However, for "unattached individuals," the foreign-born had a higher incidence of low income (Beaujot *et al.*, 1988: 79-85). In the 1986 census data, immigrants have relative disadvantages both for economic families and unattached individuals. In addition, low income status increases with recency of arrival. Compared to the traditional immigrant group, the new immigrant group arriving since 1970 tends to be at a greater disadvantage (Beaujot and Rappak, 1988b). For instance, 16.2 per cent of husband-wife economic families with a husband who arrived in the period 1975-79 had low income status – 11.9 per cent if he was born in Europe or the United States but 19.2 per cent if he was born in other parts of the world (compared to 10.2 per cent for the Canadian-born).

After reviewing studies of immigrant satisfaction, Richmond (1989b) concludes that many of the social costs of immigration have been born by the immigrants themselves: housing problems, overcoming language barriers, non-recognition of credentials, experience of racial prejudice and discrimination, obstacles to family reunion, intra-family tension, and frustrated expectations for upward mobility. Clearly, the receiving society needs to pay continual attention to the opportunity profile of its newest arrivals from abroad. Only if this profile is interpreted positively will immigration itself be seen positively both by immigrants and by the receiving society.

SOCIO-CULTURAL INTEGRATION OF IMMIGRANTS

Immigration obviously produces a population that is not completely native-born. The foreign-born have comprised 15 to 16 per cent of the total population of Canada over the period 1951-86. This proportion of foreign-born is comparable to that found in Australia (21 per cent) but considerably higher than in the United States (6 per cent). The foreign-born comprised 21.2 per cent of the metropolitan population of Canada in 1986, with Toronto having 36.3 and Vancouver 28.8 per cent foreign-born (Balakrishnan, 1988).

The long-term impact of the immigration, fertility, and mortality levels of the 1981-85 period would produce a Canadian population that is about 23 per cent foreign-born (Review of Demography, 1989: 44). An immigration level of 275,000 arrivals per year with a fertility of 1.8 produces, in the long term, a population that is about 30 per cent foreign-born (Ryder, 1985: 6).

These proportions are considerably higher than comparable data for Europe. For instance the proportions of persons from outside of Europe amount to only 2.2 per cent of the entire population of the twelve countries of the European Economic Community. The highest proportion is in Germany, with 5.5 per cent (Levy, 1988: 4). Given the low birthrates in Europe, immigration needed to keep the population from declining would produce a population where the "share of aliens and their descendants" would be some 30 to 34 per cent of the total population in the middle of the next century (Lesthaeghe *et al.*, 1988: 11). Among the major industrial countries of one million or more people, the average proportion of foreign-born was 6 per cent in the 1980s (Lachapelle, 1990).

Place of origin

The foreign-born can be divided into various categories of place of origin. Figure 12 illustrates the changing composition of the immigrant stream over the period 1946-86. Until 1970 more than half were from Europe. Since 1979 the Asian component has been the largest. The proportion from Asia, Latin America, and Africa combined increased from 8 per cent in 1961 to 65 per cent in 1980 and has since been stable around this level.

In effect, there is much diversity in the places of origin of Canada's immigrants. The annual *Immigration Statistics* lists a total of 184 countries of birth. We often pay special attention to the top ten sending countries. The nature of these top ten countries has changed substantially. In 1960-65, all but one were European; in 1980-85 all but three were in Asia and Latin America. It is interesting that in 1980-85, these top ten countries accounted for only about half of all immigrants. In 1969, twenty-two countries each sent more than 1,000 immigrants to Canada, comprising four-fifths of all arrivals. In 1988, the equivalent numbers came from thirty-seven countries (Dumas, 1990a). This is rather different from European countries, where immigrants are predominantly from one source: for example, Algerians in France, West Indians in the United Kingdom, Turkish people in Germany. Since

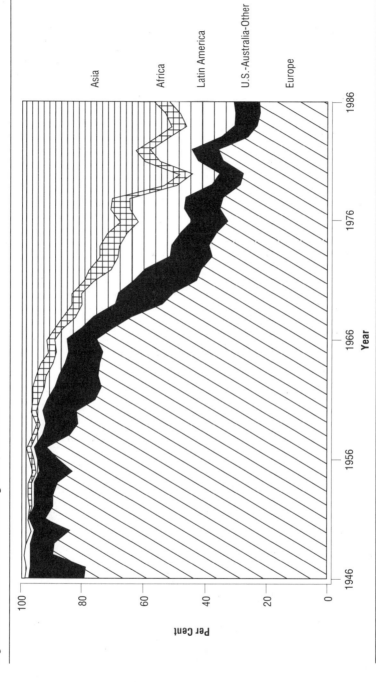

Figure 12: Place of Birth of Immigrants, 1946-86

Asia

Africa

Latin America

U.S.-Australia-Other

Europe

Per Cent

100

80

60

40

20

0

1946

1956

1966

1976

1986

Year

SOURCE: Special tabulations from Employment and Immigration.

137

racial criteria were lifted in immigrant selection, the origin of immi-grants to Canada has become very diversified. This reduces the forma-tion of "ghettos" involving persons from a given place of origin.

Nonetheless, immigrant "networks" are an important part of the migration process. Policies favouring the family class and sponsored relatives encourage a migration *chain* from a specific place of origin and often to a specific place of destination. As a consequence, the propen-sity of immigrants from various places of origin to sponsor the arrival of their relatives is a major determinant of the ethnic composition of the current flow (Simmons, 1988). In modelling the likelihood of arrivals from various parts of the world, Simmons (1989) finds that economic (level of development) and geographic (distance) variables are not very significant, but cultural variables (previous contact with English or French language, size of the ethnic community already in Canada, and sponsorship propensity) are significant in explaining the size of given arrival streams.

While the foreign-born can be divided into various places of origin, it is useful to distinguish the traditional immigrant group from Europe and the United States and the new immigrant group from other parts of the world. Among persons enumerated in the 1986 census, the new immigrants amounted to 5.0 per cent of the pre-1961 arrivals, compared to 50.3 per cent of the 1970-74 cohort and 65.1 per cent of the 1980-86 arrivals. Altogether, the new immigrant group amounted to 11.1 per cent of the total foreign-born in 1971 and 30.6 per cent in 1986.

Visible minorities

Immigration also plays the key role in terms of increasing the visible minority component of the Canadian population. Defining visible minorities as people who are neither aboriginal nor of European ethnic origin, some 4.7 per cent of the 1981 census population can be so classified (Samuel, 1987). Among these, 15 per cent were Canadian-born and 85 per cent were born abroad. As another indicator, the population born in Asia, Latin America, and Africa increased from 336,000 in 1971 to 1,152,000 in 1986, a total increase of 340 per cent. In comparison, the population born in Europe declined by 7 per cent in this period. Nonetheless, the population born in Asia, Latin America, and Africa represents only 30 per cent of the total foreign-born in 1986, or 4.6 per cent of the total population.

Based on the 1981 census, Samuel (1988c) estimated that the visible minority component would increase from 5.6 per cent of the total Canadian population in 1986 to 9 or 10 per cent by 2001. Using the 1981-85 immigration trends, the visible minority component would reach a stationary figure of about 10 per cent of the total Canadian population (Beaujot and Rappak, 1988b: 105). This is probably a maximum figure since, especially over time, persons of various visible minorities become considerably less visible. Intermarriage being strong among Canada's various ethnic groups, it can be argued that Canada is becoming a multi-ethnic society where "pluralism" rather than "visible minorities" is the more appropriate term.

The proportions of visible minorities are higher in the large cities that have received most of the recent immigrants. For all of census metropolitan areas, visible minorities comprised 8.2 per cent of the population in 1986 and 14.0 per cent in Toronto (Balakrishnan, 1988). Projecting these figures to 2001 gives 10.7 per cent visible minorities in the metropolitan population of Canada and 17.7 per cent for Toronto.

Therefore, the proportion of the population that can be classified as visible minorities is increasing, almost entirely as a function of immigration. We have also seen that the new immigrant group that has arrived over the 1970s and 1980s has not been able to take full advantage of their superior educational profile. Stated differently, the Canadian-born and the traditional immigrant group obtain greater returns for their education. As another example, recent West Indian immigrants are suffering considerable disadvantages in spite of not having a language barrier (Richmond, 1989a).

Some authors have argued that these types of observations prompt us to consider enhanced affirmative action policies for the benefit of visible minorities (e.g., Samuel, 1988b, 1990). Others have argued that the disadvantages suffered by visible minorities are not as extensive as to warrant affirmative action (e.g., Winn, 1985). Buchignani (1980) further argues that there is a danger that multiculturalism might foster social isolation by emphasizing the preservation of cultural traditions. Breton (1979: 289) also observes "that we find considerable ambivalence in our society with regard to the desirability of ethnic retention." While immigrants and their children from various places of origin need to experience the value of their traditions, and all Canadians need to appreciate the richness this brings, the emphasis on ethnic identities needs to be balanced with the importance of integrating into the larger society.

This is a question on which one's values clearly play an important role. The present author would side with those arguing against strong forms of multiculturalism and affirmative action in the case of visible minorities. The case for affirmative action could be made more easily in regard to women in Canada, the French in Quebec, and the First Nations native peoples. These are groups for whom one can document a series of structural and historical circumstances that prevented their equal access to the opportunity structure.

Arguing against strong forms of affirmative action for visible minorities does not imply an argument against other policies that attempt to achieve equality of opportunity. Clearly, such policies, along with anti-discrimination aspects of the Charter of Rights and Freedoms, are important to ensure that people have the opportunity to contribute as close as possible to their full potential to their and the society's welfare.

These arguments are also not to imply that the arrival of new immigrant groups should be further controlled. Weiner (1985) has observed that it is very unusual for a society to be open to the arrival of populations different from itself. Prime Minister Mackenzie King had also argued that immigration should "not change the basic character of our population." At the end of its discussion of immigration, the Macdonald Commission states: "The creation of a harmonious multicultural and multi-racial society will require a high degree of tolerance and civility from all Canadians, reinforced by policies aimed at preventing foreseeable conflicts" (Royal Commission on the Economic Union, 1985, II: 667). In an otherwise very positive article on the benefits of immigration for Canada, *The Economist* (1988) notes that "Canadians are just about the most tolerant people on earth, [but] even Canadian tolerance has its limits . . . the country is nearing the limits of difficult to assimilate people it is prepared to welcome." This journal concludes that the choice may be between a low level of immigration and the selection of immigrants easier to assimilate.

Nonetheless, Canada's experiment with a policy of non-discrimination in immigrant selection is relatively successful. Anderson and Frideres (1981: 328) observe that "it is already very much to the credit of Canada that it has succeeded in incorporating such human diversity into one country." In addition, Canada's commitment to non-discrimination is key to receiving political support in the international community, for immigration as well as for other forms of international relationships. While immigrants need to be selected without prejudice on questions of race or ethnicity, they also need to know they are coming to a society where the dominant structures involve English and French, and that they will need to integrate into these structures to take effective part in the society. As a discussion paper from Employment and Immigration (1989c: 13) puts it: "In the end, Canadians want immigration's economic and demographic benefits and the richness that cultural diversity can bring, but they also want to foster and strengthen Canada's national identity and culture, and to encourage immigrants to embrace certain values which define our identity as a nation." This also points to the need to avoid situations that would produce immigrant ghettos and instead to ensure that immigrants become integrated into the mainstream of society as quickly as possible. In many regards this is already the case; for instance, the foreign-born are more likely to vote than the Canadian-born (Black, 1987). In general, immigrants have a lower criminality rate than non-immigrants (Samuel and Faustino-Santos, 1991).

While integration into the broader society is to be sought, it must also be noted that ethnic enclaves can help immigrants to avoid problems of alienation and to have access to various resources that can assist in their integration to the host society. Family and personal networks play an important role in international migration, including the role of being conduits of information and of social and financial assistance (Boyd, 1990b). Ultimately, the contribution of immigrants to a host society depends not only on their human capital on arrival but on the social context in which they become incorporated (Portes, 1990). Networks, as well as the social capital of immigrant communities, affect the process of adaptation.

Questions of the absorption of "other" groups may have slightly different dynamics in Quebec from the rest of Canada. It can be argued that Quebec has a more "homogeneous" culture for which the penetration of outsiders may be more difficult. Having a less "holistic" culture, the absorption of immigrants may be less difficult for the rest of Canada. As a consequence, people who are concerned about sustaining population growth have different views in the two parts of the country. In Quebec, they are more likely to think that sustaining fertility is the key element. Births are easier to socialize into a homogeneous culture. Quebec is also more likely to see the departure of its third-language groups. In the rest of Canada, immigration is more likely seen as the easier solution. Immigration is less costly, both to the society that does not need to provide education and to adults who do not need to have more children.

This distinction between Quebec and the rest of Canada may be exaggerated. For instance, Anctil (1988) argues that the Quiet Revolution opened up Quebec to immigration, that cultural unanimity is a thing of the past, and that Quebec is moving toward a form of multiculturalism. Nonetheless, Gay (1988) disagrees, suggesting that from the point of view of most Quebec people, visible minorities do not have a real place in Quebec because they are a threat to cultural homogeneity. Both views are probably somewhat correct. For instance, the government of Quebec is taking an active role in the immigration area and most proponents of sustained population growth argue that both fertility and immigration need to be seen as part of the solution (e.g., Commission de la Culture, 1985).

Language

At the time of arrival, about a third of immigrants speak neither English nor French (Beaujot, 1990: 48). In the 1980-86 cohort, 49 per cent had home languages other than English or French according to the 1986 census. Language training in the official languages is an important priority for these newly arrived immigrants. It can be argued that the facilities available for women immigrants, especially if they are not destined for the labour force, are particularly inadequate and this accentuates their isolation and disadvantage (Boyd, 1987).

Over time the majority of immigrants have come to associate with one or the other of the official languages. To highlight this tendency, we have adopted the concept of "predominant language," which combines the responses on language spoken at home and knowledge of official languages. Persons who speak English or French at home were assigned this language as their predominant language. Persons speaking "other" languages at home were also assigned to English or French predominant language if they could speak only that language among the official languages (Figure 13). In effect, we are measuring which among the official languages is a given person's predominant language.

Using these definitions, the population outside of Quebec was 94.3 per cent English, 3.1 per cent French, and 2.5 per cent other in the 1986 census. Outside of Quebec there is less French among immigrants than in the Canadian-born population. The trends are stable over time: the overwhelming majority of immigrants and their descendants come to associate with English, among the official languages, as their main language (Beaujot and Rappak, 1988b).

The decline of the official language minority is also occurring in Quebec, but to a lesser extent. Quebec receives the majority of French-speaking immigrants to Canada. Of the foreign-born who were classified as predominantly French among the official languages, 90 per cent were in Quebec in 1986. Nevertheless, Francophones comprise less than 6 per cent of the total foreign-born in Canada. For cohorts that arrived before 1970, immigrants who stayed in Quebec contributed more to the English than to the French language. Since 1970, immigrants have been more likely to associate with the French language, especially the younger immigrants and those who do not know English at the time of arrival (Veltman, 1988). However, persons of third languages are more likely to retain these languages in Quebec.

The general linguistic trends in Canada therefore involve decreases in the official language minorities, that is English in Quebec and French in the rest of Canada. For the rest of Canada, immigration contributes to the trend as there is less French among immigrants than in the native-born population. In Quebec, immigration enhances the English minority because there is more English among immigrants than in the native-born population, and a sizable proportion of third-language migrants continue to transfer to the English language. Immigration therefore plays an important role in Canada's changing distribution by official languages. While this distribution changes very slowly over

Figure 13: Predominant Languages of Given Immigration Cohorts and Canadian-born, 1986

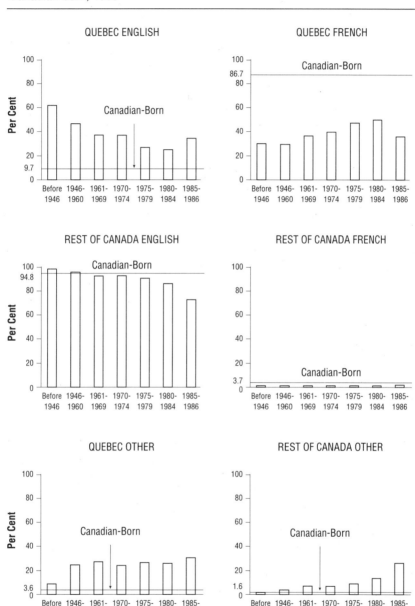

SOURCE : Beaujot and Rappak, 1988b: 71.

time, immigration is the main element producing an increase in the relative size of the English language in Canada (Lachapelle, 1988a). Partly because of Anglophone control over economic opportunity, at least in provinces other than Quebec, immigrants and their descendants are primarily oriented to the Anglophone society in Canada (Reitz, 1980).

The potential for policy to influence language use, especially at home, is clearly limited (Paillé, 1985: 61). The array of language policies in Quebec that have made French effectively the language of the society, including policies regarding language use in the schools and the Quebec government involvement in immigrant selection, is having the impact of promoting a greater association to the French language among more recent immigrants and their children (Vaillancourt, 1988). On the other hand, Paillé (1989a) observes that in Montreal there are more arriving immigrants who do not speak French than births to parents of French home language. Nonetheless, Veltman (1988) observes for Montreal that the second generation from abroad or from outside of Quebec are tending to adopt the French language as their main language spoken at home. He projects the language composition of the city to 2011 using twice the immigration level of the 1981-86 period and finds that the English language continues to decline and the French language increases.

Probably the only policy areas that would produce further strengthening of the national languages would be a more stringent use of language criteria (i.e., knowledge of official languages) in immigrant selection and further efforts of language instruction for adult immigrants who are not literate in the national languages. As we have argued in the previous section, acquiring basic linguistic skills is also key to the economic integration of immigrants.

While it can be argued that language policy in Quebec has promoted a greater association of immigrants to the French language, it must be noted that this is at the expense of departures of English and other linguistic groups. Therefore, it is at the expense of a lower total weight of Quebec in the population of Canada. Lachapelle (1988c) has put it well: it is hard to envisage scenarios that would both sustain the weight of Quebec in the Canadian total and increase the proportion of French-speakers in Quebec. The rest of Canada does not have such a problem: more of its international arrivals are English to start with, immigrants retain their languages less, and almost all transfers favour English. As Lachapelle further observes, only a higher French fertility could both increase the proportion of French and increase the weight of Quebec in Canada. This higher French fertility certainly existed in the past. The French represented 36 per cent of the total Canadian population aged 0-4 in 1941. However, by 1986, the French mother tongue amounts to only 23 per cent of the population aged 0-4 in Canada (Lachapelle, 1988c: 332).

Refugees

The socio-cultural integration of refugees deserves some additional treatment. Until 1972, refugee admissions largely involved people of European origin. As Lanphier (1988) has noted, the arrival of refugees from Tibet, Uganda, and Indochina has changed the perception with regard to the integration of refugees. In particular, it has made it possible to think that Canada can absorb "any kind of refugee" regardless of cultural background. In addition, the new Immigration Act that came into effect in 1978 has introduced refugee planning as a regular component of immigration policy planning. From the point of view of the refugees of the world, Canada is a rather ideal country because it not only has a policy on providing asylum (which many countries do) but it also has a policy to accept refugees as landed immigrants.

In his discussion paper on *International Refugee Pressures and Canadian Public Policy Response*, Nash (1989b) presents both criticisms of the government's approach and supportive comments. Critics of the government approach note, for instance, that little attention is paid to regions responsible for some 90 per cent of the world's refugees: in 1986, 31 per cent of arrivals were from Eastern Europe and 7 per cent from Afghanistan and Ethiopia. Also, over the period 1982-87, only a quarter of persons admitted under the refugee class had been designated as "convention refugees" by the United Nations and 80 per cent of entrants were men while some 75 to 80 per cent of the world's refugees are women. On the other hand, supporters of the government policy note that Canada's response has been generous by international standards: by 1986 the resettlement numbers were second only to the United States. Over the period 1980-87, refugee and other humanitarian admissions accounted for a quarter of immigrant arrivals (Ziegler, 1988). Several services are in place: transportation loan program, temporary accommodation, refugee host group program, and handicapped refugee program, along with the regular services available to all immigrants – the immigration settlement, adaptation, and language training programs.

Another issue regarding refugees involves the processing of persons who seek asylum directly in Canada. The numbers in this category rose quickly in the 1980s, faster than procedures to accommodate them could be devised. By 1989, when procedures were in place, the total backlog involved some 85,000 cases including over 100,000 people (Blackburn, 1989). The procedure involves a two-person panel deciding whether the claimant has a credible basis for refugee status. In the first two years of operation of this system, 40 per cent of these cases had been resolved. There were 21,000 accepted refugees, making an acceptance rate of 60 per cent. In the meantime, another system is dealing with the claimants who have arrived later: 21,000 in 1989 and 36,000 in 1990. Among the 50 per cent of these cases that had been resolved, 15,000, or just over half, had been found to be legitimate refugees by the end of 1990.

Clearly, questions of refugee admission are difficult to regularize. By definition, the matter is not totally under Canadian control. Nash (1989a) has suggested that refugee policy should be separated from immigration and put in the hands of an independent Refugee Commission. However, there needs to be some co-ordination between refugee and immigration policy, which is enhanced by the present arrangements.

CONCLUDING THOUGHTS

Anderson (1978: 129) has summarized well the difficulties of immigration policy: "Canada is still in the midst of hammering out an immigration policy on the anvil of public opinion. The issues are complex, informed laymen are few, and the public speaks with many voices."

This dilemma does not apply only to Canada. In a summary of population policies in Europe, Hohn (1987: 474) notes that most immigration policies do not have a demographic objective. These policies are mostly aimed at labour recruitment, but "the economic advantages of recruiting foreign labour and the social tensions resulting from immigration are clearly in conflict." Therefore, in the late 1970s and 1980s, "immigration policies have become restrictive either because of economic recession or because of social tensions, typically because of both" (*idem*: 475). European countries have especially found that sending temporary workers back home is a very difficult problem. Civil liberties have come to imply that "where you are is where you have the right to be." Therefore the distinction between temporary and permanent migration is not particularly valid (Hagmann, 1988). While not directly intended as such, immigration policy does become a demographic policy and questions of the social integration of immigrants need to be given more priority.

Immigration versus pro-natalist policy

If, as many authors have argued, low fertility is an integral part of modern society (Davis *et al.*, 1986), and if population decline has negative consequences, then the developed countries will all need to evolve a mix of policies to sustain fertility and to admit and integrate migrants (Hohn, 1987). Wattenberg (1987: 165) argues that immigration policies would be less socially disruptive, and therefore more politically feasible, if the fertility of the native-born were closer to replacement. That is, populations that are not replacing themselves may especially fear an increase in the proportion of foreigners. On the other hand, Hohn (1987) concludes that immigration policies, being less expensive than pro-natalist policies, are an easier way to increase population. Nonetheless, she points out that immigration policies are not easy, especially when the populations being admitted are very different from the native-born. As the potential for receiving immigrants from other European-based populations decreases, developed countries will increasingly face the problem of admitting and integrating "more distant foreigners." Accordingly, "the problems associated with immigration will become more not less serious in the future because of increasing cultural distance between natives and immigrants" (*idem*: 477).

While noting that immigrants enrich a society materially and culturally, Henripin (1989: 119) suggests that using immigration to compensate for a fertility deficit is giving an essential role to what should be a supportive role. He observes that the arrival of immigrants cannot be in excess of what the society can absorb, and the original society would disappear if immigrants became substitutes for births. Others have also noted that immigration is easier for a society to accommodate if fertility is at replacement levels (e.g., Andorka, 1989).

There are a variety of opinions on the issue of immigration as a means of compensating for low fertility. Recent statements on the policy implications of low fertility, based especially on the European experience, have not tended to identify immigration as a viable solution. Teitelbaum and Winter (1985) argue that "immigration as a means of retarding population decline" is not likely to be accepted by the receiving society because it changes the "cultural, racial, linguistic or ethnic composition of the national population." Noting that the levels of immigration needed to counter low fertility do not substantially affect population aging while they introduce a multi-ethnic society, Lesthaeghe et al. (1988: 22) conclude that "immigration is an inefficient counter to the problems posed by current low fertility levels" in Europe. Similarly, the various authors in the edited collection by Davis et al. (1986) do not tend to see immigration as a solution. Davis speaks of "immigrants who compete with native labour and whose contribution to the economy, many would argue, is outweighed by their driving up government welfare, educational, and medical expenditures and by the ethnic conflict that their presence generates" (p. 62). McNicoll speaks of the convergence of demographic characteristics (mortality and fertility) of immigrants with the native-born but "convergence in economic status distribution and in patterns of mobility, where cultural factors and discrimination both play a role, may be much slower" (p. 229). Espenshade notes that "the public's dissatisfaction over the presence of a large and growing immigrant community swells as the proportion of the total population growth attributable to immigration increases" so that "many writers doubt that an 'immigration solution' to allay fear of population decline will prove to be politically acceptable" (p. 258). The only exception comes from Heer, who argues that "a generous immigration policy is likely to be more economically advantageous than a pro-natalist policy" (p. 268). However, Chiswick comments that Heer's conclusion "is unfounded" (p. 270).

Several of the above statements can be questioned in the Canadian context. Many of these are based on political rather than social or economic considerations. For instance, the 1987 *Report to Parliament on Future Immigration Levels* outlines the positive economic, demographic, social, humanitarian, cultural, and international consequences of immigration. In 1990 the minister again spoke of the economic, social, cultural, and humanitarian benefits of immigration (McDougall, 1990). Canada may be unique in having a greater acceptability for variety in its population along with the policies and procedures to facilitate the arrival and integration of diverse groups.

Clearly, the absorption of immigrants, especially in the case of populations that are different from the native-born, involves a two-way adaptation process (see Samuel, 1989). As Richmond (1988: 46) concludes, the receiving society and the social systems of immigrants themselves both undergo profound changes in the process of immigrant adaptation. The receiving society must formulate policies and institutions to ensure the successful integration of the immigrants. These include policies for granting equal opportunities, for re-training (especially language acquisition), and for recognizing the value of other cultural traditions. In effect, a variety of institutions associated with socialization, public information, labour absorption, and welfare need to adapt to a changing composition of the population.

The immigrants must also adapt to their chosen society. Here, Hohn (1987: 479) suggests that "immigrants should perhaps be chosen on the basis of their readiness for integration and their (basic) knowledge of the language of the receiving countries." For this to be achieved, she further proposes that immigrant-receiving countries establish "cultural information centres" in other countries to enable people to learn about the language and culture of the country to which they are seeking admission.

Alternative immigration levels

We will conclude with reflections concerning the overall levels of immigration. It would appear that four basic alternatives are to be considered.

One alternative would be to continue with the policy of annual (or short-term) determination of levels, based in turn largely on economic and humanitarian considerations. In this framework, immigration is not really a demographic policy because demographic questions need to be viewed in the long term. The main advantages of this approach are that it has worked in the past and it allows immigration to be changed following changing circumstances. From an institutional point of view (i.e., admissions and integration), fluctuations are possibly more difficult to accommodate.

A second alternative would be to reduce immigration to a minimum, based largely on family reunification. By closing the independent class, the average quality of immigrants would be reduced. Canada could also largely abandon its responsibility for settling refugees. While such an alternative would probably have public support in certain sectors, it would not allow Canada to build policies and institutions that use immigration as a means of facing future economic, social, and demographic challenges.

A third alternative would be to hold immigration constant at a figure around the post-war average of 150,000 admissions per year. Such a strategy could be justified on the grounds that figures of this magnitude have provided beneficial results in the past. A steady state would more clearly establish immigration as a demographic policy with a long-term horizon and would enable the institutions associated with recruitment and settlement to have a more secure planning horizon. Figures of such magnitude would not greatly increase the visible minorities component of the population and the associated problems of their integration. It would also probably prompt the nation to recognize the need to sustain fertility, if population decline is to be avoided.

A fourth alternative would be to move to a substantially higher level, perhaps 250,000 arrivals per year, or some 1 per cent of the receiving population. Such levels, relative to the receiving population, have occurred in the periods 1901-31 and 1951-61. Over the long term, this level of immigration would preclude population decline. At the same time, with a fertility of around 1.7 births per woman, population growth would be well under 1 per cent per year. More immigration is probably good on economic grounds: greater supply of labour, more demand for goods and services, more competition and therefore productivity. A higher figure could also allow Canada to admit more refugees; therefore, it would have positive humanitarian implications. Given the size of the family and refugee classes, a level of 250,000 per year would permit the independent class to be a substantial proportion of the total. As "stewards" of this great land and its resources, we might be seen as managing our "endowment" for the greater benefit of humanity and less for narrow self-interests. An openness to the cultures of the world may be taken up as a socio-cultural and demographic challenge that would bring Canada into the modern international world, where European-based societies are a declining component.

The determination of an appropriate immigration level, and its composition, is clearly a political question. Research can provide some indication regarding the past, but it is for the political community to decide what it wants for its future and how immigration is to figure into that social vision. Basic to this vision is whether to intervene in population decline or to adapt the society's institutions to a declining population.

In its interim report, the Standing Committee on Labour, Employment and Immigration argued for restraining the growth of immigration in the short term (Blackburn, 1990). Noting that immigration had exceeded 200,000 in only three of the last seventy years and that there were continuing problems of social relations, concentration of immigrants and immigrant integration, the Committee proposed that we be cautious about increasing immigration beyond the level of 200,000 per year. Similarly, the Economic Council of Canada (1991: 35) suggests keeping immigration below 200,000 until 1996, then slowly increasing to 1 per cent of the population by the year 2015. However, consistent with the policy of "modest, balanced growth in immigration," the 1990 *Annual Report to Parliament* set the 1991 target at 220,000 and the anticipated level for each of 1992-95 at 250,000 (Employment and Immigration, 1990).

For the most part, there is agreement that the current Immigration Act does a good job of setting out the major objectives of immigration and the context through which it is to be handled. For instance, Hawkins (1982) describes the Act as "an innovative, liberal and effective piece of legislation." The Act specifically lets the government decide on the level and composition of the immigrant stream. Discussions regarding the level of immigration are necessarily based on visions of Canada's future. Weinfeld (1988b) suggests that there are two predominant visions inasmuch as they apply to immigration.

One view, which in its extreme version might be called "Fortress Canada," sees the country as well established and needing to protect its resources and its inheritance against destabilizing external forces. This perspective is apprehensive about a multi-ethnic society and would prefer to keep out strange elements. Tradition is preferred over change and immigration policy should be cautious. As the total number of Third World immigrants and their descendants rises, Canadian society will continue to face significant challenges in seeking ways to avoid conflict between racial, linguistic, and cultural groups (Simmons,

1988). A solution is simply to reduce the intake of immigrants. The interest in keeping out "strange elements" has been frequently expressed. In opinion surveys, the majority opinion tends to be that immigration should be lower or that it should not increase. In August, 1989, 43 per cent of respondents felt there were "too many immigrants," 13 per cent felt there were too few, and 38 per cent said there were about the right number of immigrants coming to Canada (Angus Reid Group, 1989: 4).

The alternative perspective, according to Weinfeld (1988b), views Canada as a young, rich country that has not achieved its full development. In this perspective immigration is seen as a process of "nation-building," while ethnic variety and demographic growth are interpreted positively. Using the words of an Employment and Immigration (1989c) discussion paper: "successive waves of immigrants from all over the world have successfully joined in Canada's experiment at nation-building, ... the emergence of an increasingly pluralistic society has added richness to Canadian life and has made us more open and tolerant." Passaris (1989) sees a multicultural and multi-linguistic society as a unique economic resource for trade, contacts, tourism, and technological transfer. Hawkins (1989: xx) refers to Canada's "pressing demographic needs."

In the context of the debate between these alternatives, we can say that immigration holds the key to the future of Canadian society and that enlightened discussions on immigration need to take place in policy circles and beyond. This discussion should keep in mind that societies that find ways to manage ethnicity and pluralism may well be in a stronger position to face future challenges in the interdependent world of nations (Tepper, 1987).

Clearly, questions of immigration do not involve Canada alone. Other nations can exert pressure to the effect that immigration to Canada presents for them a "brain drain" or a drain on capital. Alternatively, people from heavily populated countries can come to resent Canada's vast land and resources, arguing that we need to exercise our stewardship over these to the benefit of a humanity that goes beyond our borders. Migration pressures are generated by a world system of economic inequality and political instability. It is estimated that some 80 million people in the world are "on the move," seeking to establish themselves in a favourable country, including some 15 million refugees (Employment and Immigration, 1989d: 12). Development itself in the Third World brings various forms of dislocation (Massey, 1988). The immigration process is therefore far from being totally under Canada's policy control.

5

POPULATION DISTRIBUTION, INTERNAL MIGRATION, AND THE REGIONS

In a review of *Regional Economic Development: Canada's Search for Solutions*, Francis (1986: 29) observes that: "The ... problems of governing a country as large, as sparsely settled, and as culturally diverse as Canada are probably nowhere so evident as in policy making for regional economic development." The Macdonald Commission, which had the mandate of inquiring into "the long-term economic potential ... facing the Canadian federation and its respective regions," expressed equally bewildering concern about the problem of regional disparity:

> For a number of reasons, few of the issues in this Commission's mandate have proved more perplexing than regional development.

> There is typically, but not always, a fundamental conflict between the goals of regional economic development and those of national efficiency.

Commissioners looked at . . . often-conflicting values and concerns:
. . . freedom of movement versus community preservation; uniformity
and diversity. . . .

In a federal system . . . migration can weaken the provincial communities which federalism is designated to protect. (Royal Commission on
the Economic Union, 1985, III: 198, 217, 101, 198)

This last comment suggests that migration itself can be seen as a problem for regional development.

Starting with a brief review of the factors underlying the regions of
Canada, this chapter will focus on the distribution of the population
over space, the causes of change in this distribution, and the implications of evolving trends. The role of migration in regional disparity will
be a particular focus. In part, this becomes the issue of "bringing
people to the jobs" versus "bringing jobs to the people." Important
questions are at stake in this debate, in particular values of efficiency
versus equity and individual welfare versus community preservation.

FACTORS UNDERLYING REGIONAL DYNAMICS:
UNITY AND DIVERSITY

It is no accident that questions of regionalism are studied in a number
of social science disciplines, especially geography, economics, history,
politics, sociology, and demography. Geography plays an important
role in promoting regionalist distinctions. The populated areas of Canada essentially involve a long, thin ribbon along the border with the
United States. Even at that, the ribbon is broken twice, once by the
Canadian Shield and once by the Rocky Mountains. In a book on
Canada in the world, the French historian André Siegfried (1937: 16)
noted that, because of the narrowness of this band of habitation, Canada lacks a point of identification and is always tempted to seek a centre
of gravity from outside of itself.

The specific economic history of Canada, especially the emphasis on
the export of resources (staples) and the concentration of industrial
development in central Canada, has created further difficulties with
regard to national unity. The exploitation of various staples for export
has balkanized the nation into given economic areas; the focus of given
regions has often been on external needs rather than on national aspirations. The economic "core" of Canada, especially Toronto and Montreal
but more broadly the Windsor-Quebec axis, has established itself as the
centre of Canada, providing both a source of unity in its large population and a source of disunity due to resentment from outlying parts of

the country. For instance, it can be argued that "the Maritimes were better off before they became a satellite of Upper Canada and lost their potential for local industrialization, urbanization, economic and political independence and cultural integrity" (Gillis, 1980: 53). Other outlying areas, especially the Prairies, British Columbia, northern Ontario, and northern Quebec, have feared that they might be subject to similar "backsliding" once their specific resources (wheat, oil, wood, fish, minerals, etc.) are no longer useful or available (Stafford, 1990).

Especially in a North American context, which is the appropriate frame of reference under free trade, parts of Canada are very peripheral. However peripheral the states of Maine or Montana may be within North America, eastern Quebec, Atlantic Canada, northern Ontario, Manitoba, and Saskatchewan will always be more peripheral (Coffey and Polèse, 1987). Distance affects trade flows and diffusion of technology, as well as plant and head office location decisions. In the North American setting, southern Ontario is best suited to serve continental markets. It is the region for which communication and interaction costs are minimized.

Regional population diversity is a further barrier to social cohesion. Due to the specific settlement history of the country, the populations of various regions are rather different. For instance, Newfoundland is over 90 per cent of British origin, while Quebec is over 80 per cent of French origin and the Prairie provinces are almost half of origins other than British or French. The relative size of the populations in various regions remains unbalanced, giving weight especially to the Windsor-Quebec axis. The population movements through internal migration have largely not served to "blend" the peoples of the various regions. Movement rarely crosses Ontario going east or west (Beaujot and McQuillan, 1982: 159-65). For the most part, the peripheral regions have also failed to attract immigrants with their associated capital and skills (Anderson, 1986).

Briefly, essentially four interrelated factors underlie the persistence of regionalism in Canada: geographic questions (especially the breaks in the area of settlement imposed by the Shield and the Rocky Mountains); economic questions (inequalities of resources, especially staple products); political questions (inequalities of power, especially between centre and periphery); and demographic questions (unequal size of populations, absence of migratory exchanges spanning the country, and unequal distribution of critical ethnic groups).

POPULATION DISTRIBUTION

Before the arrival of European populations, the native peoples were concentrated in the St. Lawrence Valley and on the Pacific coast (Careless, 1963: 18-21). This is not unlike the distribution that has emerged over subsequent periods. The analysis of population distribution is an important indicator of the relative "attractiveness" of the various parts of the country and its change over time. In addition, the population distribution plays a role in the regional dynamics of the country.

As of the 1986 census, 72.0 per cent of the population lived within 150 kilometres of the United States border and 85.4 per cent lived within 300 kilometres of the border. Only 4.2 per cent lived over 600 kilometres from the United States, a line just north of Edmonton. Using another geographic axis, 70.4 per cent lived south of the 49th parallel, which delimits the southern border of the Prairie provinces, and only 0.3 per cent lived north of the 60th parallel, which delimits their northern border (Mitchell, 1989).

Looking at the population distribution by regions that run east and west, around the time of Confederation, Ontario had 43.9 per cent of the population, Quebec 32.3 per cent, and the Maritime provinces 20.8 per cent. The remaining 3.0 per cent lived west of Ontario (Beaujot and McQuillan, 1982: 147). The major changes in population distribution occurred with the immigration wave of 1896-1913. The four western provinces comprised 11.1 per cent of the population in 1901 but 23.9 per cent in 1911.

The change in population distribution since western settlement has been slower and less profound in comparison. In the period 1921-86, the Maritime provinces decreased from 11 to 7 per cent of the total, Quebec decreased from 27 to 26 per cent, Ontario increased from 33 to 36 per cent, Manitoba and Saskatchewan decreased from 15 to 8 per cent, Alberta increased from 7 to 9 per cent, and British Columbia increased from 6 to 11 per cent (Beaujot and McQuillan, 1982: 146; Mitchell, 1989: 15). Considering larger regions, the Review of Demography (1989: 30) concluded that "Canada's demographic map is fixed."

However, the changes since the period of western settlement remain significant and the distribution is hardly "fixed." Over the period 1921-86, the population of British Columbia increased five and a half times while Saskatchewan and Prince Edward Island increased by less than 50 per cent. Some of the rank orderings among provinces have even changed. In 1921, Saskatchewan was the third largest province; in 1986 it was the sixth. Conversely, British Columbia has moved from sixth to third. In 1921, Ontario was 24 per cent larger than Quebec; in 1986 it was 39 per cent larger in population.

Even considering a thirty-five-year period, 1951-86, the proportion of the total population east of Ontario declined from 40.5 per cent to 34.8 per cent of the total, while Alberta and British Columbia increased from 15.0 to 20.7 per cent of the total (Dumas, 1989). Quebec was at a high point in 1951 at 28.9 per cent of the total, compared to 25.8 per cent in

Figure 14: Population Growth, 1946-86, Canada and the Provinces

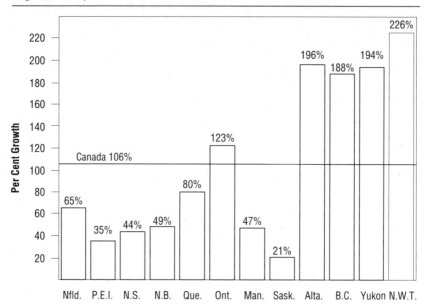

SOURCE: Statistics Canada, Cat. No. 91-210.

1986. The areas of relatively slower growth are also those of relatively low population density: Atlantic provinces to eastern Quebec, and the central prairies to northern Ontario. These areas do not include large cities, except Winnipeg (see Figure 14).

Looking at each region separately, the Atlantic provinces have declined in relative size with the decline of the importance of wood and fish as a staple base and with the establishment of the St. Lawrence Seaway, which bypassed the eastern provinces as a transportation route. The area has received few immigrants and has tended to be an area of net out-migration. As a consequence, the population is relatively homogeneous and has long-established roots in the region.

Quebec has received a considerable number of immigrants, especially to Montreal when it was "the" Canadian metropolis. However, it has not always retained its immigrants, especially the non-French, and it has lost some of its own population following on the general westward movement in North America.

Ontario has made population gains through both immigration and internal migration. With the seaway providing ocean-going transportation and the proximity to the Canadian Shield, Toronto has become established as the major Canadian metropolis. In 1951 Toronto was 18 per cent smaller than Montreal; by 1986 it was 17 per cent larger. Eight of Canada's twenty-five census metropolitan areas are located in southern Ontario, from Windsor to Ottawa. The immigration of the 1970s and 1980s has diversified the population in terms of racial origins.

The central Prairies have declined with the lowered importance of their agricultural staple base. The oil resources of Alberta have provided growth potential as long as external markets are attractive. The harsh winter climate and lack of precipitation limit the agricultural potential of the Prairies and their attractiveness for population settlement. The ethnic origins of the population are largely European but the English and French components are not much more than half of the total.

British Columbia has made continuous population gains, following on the importance of wood and mineral resources, and the agreeable climate. With the arrivals from both within and beyond the country, close to half of the population was born outside of the province.

The North represents a large part of the Canadian land mass but a small part of the population. Defining the region as including the Northwest Territories, Yukon, Labrador, and northern Quebec, the 1986 population of the region was only 140,000 people, or 0.6 per cent of Canada (Maslove and Hawkes, 1989). It is also a relatively young population and 40 per cent have aboriginal roots.

The population distribution by urban and rural areas presents another way of analysing the trends. As late as 1931, over half of the population lived in rural areas and 31.1 per cent were "rural farm"; by 1986 only 3.5 per cent lived on farms (Beyrouti and Dion, 1989). In 1871, only Montreal was a city of 100,000 or more people, and it amounted to only 3 per cent of the Canadian population. By 1986, there were twenty-five census metropolitan areas of this size, and they comprised 60 per cent of the country's population. Toronto and Montreal dominate the urban landscape, with populations of 3.4 and 2.9 million respectively, or 25 per cent of the total population (Mitchell, 1989: 26). These two metropolitan areas are larger than any province, except of course Ontario and Quebec themselves.

As a percentage of the total, the urban population increased from 62 per cent in 1951 to 76 per cent in 1971, but it has remained at essentially the same level since then. On the other hand, the twenty-five largest metropolitan areas increased from 45.7 per cent of the country's population in 1951 to 59.8 per cent in 1986 (Burke, 1987b: 14). An analysis of the inner cities of the twelve largest metropolitan areas indicates that these populations declined since 1951 and have become ethnically diversified, with 30 per cent foreign-born (Ram et al., 1989). There is a flow out of the inner cities and into the suburbs, with a replacement by immigrants (Rosenberg and Moore, 1988).

Almost half of the increase in the rural population in the period 1976-81 occurred within the boundaries of census metropolitan areas or census agglomerations (Chorayshi, 1986). Most of the growth has been in the rural non-farm component, often on the distant fringes of the large metropolitan areas (Hodge, 1986). While the total farm area is relatively stable, the number of farms is declining along with the farm population. The rural farm population declined from 1,420,000 in 1971 to 930,000 in 1986. In 1941 this figure was over three million, representing 27 per cent of the total population; it now represents less than 4 per cent of the total (McSkimmings, 1990).

CAUSES OF POPULATION REDISTRIBUTION

The immediate causes of change in population distribution involve differences in natural increase (births minus deaths), internal migration, and the extent to which international migrants go to the various regions.

Natural increase

Differences in natural increase played a role in past changes of population distribution, especially the higher fertility in Quebec in the period 1881-1961 (Beaujot and McQuillan, 1982: 151). Caldwell and Fournier (1987) point out that this "constituted a demographic investment that alone ensured the survival of French society in geographical Quebec as we know it today, despite political and economic subjugation." Compared to the relative sizes of population, the natural increase of the period 1931-61 represented advantages to the relative sizes of the provinces of Quebec, New Brunswick, Nova Scotia, and Alberta. Quebec had the largest advantage, with a natural increase 25 per cent higher than would be expected based on its relative population size (Beaujot and McQuillan, 1982: 151).

Over the more recent periods, rates of natural increase have become considerably more uniform over the provinces. With fertility and mortality becoming relatively homogeneous, and with declining natural increase, migration becomes the dominant component of differential demographic growth (Termote, 1987).

International migration

The differential arrival of immigrants to various parts of the country has a significant impact on population redistribution. It was seen in Chapter 4 that Ontario and British Columbia have significantly higher proportions of immigrant populations than the national average. The immigration of the post-war period has largely been to the advantage of the relative size of the populations of Ontario and British Columbia and to the disadvantage of the Atlantic provinces and Quebec (Beaujot and Rappak, 1988b: 52-54, 69).

International migration also accentuates the growth of the larger metropolitan areas. Of every 100 foreign-born persons, thirty-two are in Toronto, another thirty-two are in Montreal, Vancouver, Edmonton, Calgary, or Winnipeg, thirteen are in other metropolitan areas of southern Ontario, and twenty-three have settled in the rest of the country. Compared to the relative size of the Canadian-born population, especially Toronto and Vancouver, and to some extent Montreal and census metropolitan areas west of Quebec, have received disproportionately large shares of post-war immigrants (Review of Demography, 1989: 34).

Internal migration

Movement across provincial boundaries probably constitutes the main source of change in population distribution. Over the period 1981-89, the numbers of people moving across provincial boundaries averaged more than 375,000 per year, compared to international arrivals of less than 120,000 per year. At the same time, there is movement both into and out of given provinces, making the net movement considerably smaller than the total movement. For instance, in 1988-89 it took 42,400 people moving across the Nova Scotia border to make a net loss of 1,800 people. Similarly for Ontario, the gross movement was 191,800 for a net gain of 8,400 (Statistics Canada, 1990b).

The census determines people's place of residence both at census time and five years earlier. For the periods 1966-71 to 1981-86, these data imply remarkable stability in the overall patterns of change of residence (Simmons and Bourne, 1989). Some 52 to 56 per cent of people are living in the same residence as they were five years earlier. Some 24 to 26 per cent have changed residence but within the same municipality, and 13 to 17 per cent changed municipality within the province. Only 4 to 5 per cent of people are living in a different province five years later.

The overall impact of internal migration is especially visible through the lifetime migration of the Canadian-born who are still resident in the country. Of persons born in Canada and living in Canada in 1986, 15 per cent were not living in their province of birth. This figure jumps to over 25 per cent for persons born in all provinces except Quebec, Ontario, British Columbia, and Alberta.

At the 1986 census, 12.9 per cent were Canadian-born but not living in their province of birth and another 15.8 per cent were foreign-born. Here, then, international and internal migration are somewhat comparable. For most provinces the proportion born in another province was larger than the proportion of foreign-born. The exceptions are Quebec and Ontario, where the proportion foreign-born was larger than the proportion born in another province (Table 2, col. 1).

The comparison of place of birth and place of residence, for persons born in Canada and living in Canada at the time of the 1986 census, shows that only three provinces have made net gains (Table 2). In absolute numbers, the largest gains are for British Columbia, followed by Ontario and Alberta. Expressed as a percentage of the population, the net gain for British Columbia is overwhelming, at 22.0 per cent, followed by Alberta at 13.0 per cent and Ontario at 3.4 per cent of its resident population. The net losses are highest for Saskatchewan at 39.1 per cent, followed by Newfoundland, Manitoba, and Prince Edward Island at over 20 per cent of their resident populations (Table 2, col. 3).

Adding the foreign-born and the internal migration of native-born shows that only four provinces have made net gains: Ontario, British Columbia, Alberta and Quebec (Table 2, col. 6). This is a rather striking observation. While Canada is a country of immigration, having received over five million immigrants in the period 1946-86, the net impact of both international and internal migration is positive for only four provinces. In all other provinces, population movement has been to their net disadvantage. Among the provinces that have gained, it is noteworthy that the net lifetime migration represents 44.3 per cent of the resident population in British Columbia.

Considering the pattern of flows for specific provinces, the net migration has generally been from the Atlantic provinces, Quebec, Manitoba, and Saskatchewan to Ontario, British Columbia, and more recently Alberta (Burke, 1987a). Looking at specific periods since 1931, the net has been continuously positive for British Columbia. Alberta made net gains in 1951-61 and 1966-81. Manitoba and Saskatchewan had continuous losses. Ontario had gains except in 1971-81. Quebec had losses except in 1931-41, and the Atlantic provinces had losses except in 1971-76.

Analysing in detail the flows over the period 1966-85, Termote (1987) finds three reversals in the trends: (1) the Atlantic provinces make gains in 1971-76 while there are losses for Ontario; (2) in 1976-81 there is a westward shift; (3) in 1981-85 there is reduced movement to British Columbia and Alberta while Ontario gains once again. It is clearly very difficult to project trends in internal migration.

Taking a longer historical view, Dumas (1990b) observes that in both Canada and the United States, the long-term population movements have been westward and southward. In Canada, the "south" relates to the British Columbia lower mainland and southern Ontario. If freer trade brings with it a freer movement of population, this southward movement may not limit itself to the Canadian border.

Table 2: Interprovincial Lifetime Migration of Native-born and In-flow of Foreign-born, by Province, 1986

	Living in another province (1)	Born in another province (2)	Net internal lifetime migration (3 = 2–1)	Foreign-born (4)	Born out of province (5 = 2 + 4)	Total net migrants (6 = 3 + 4)
In thousands						
Newfoundland	187.3	25.0	–162.3	9.2	34.2	–153.1
Prince Edward Island	46.0	21.3	–24.7	4.5	25.8	–20.2
Nova Scotia	236.5	126.3	–110.2	41.9	168.2	–68.3
New Brunswick	204.0	94.0	–110.0	28.1	122.1	–81.9
Quebec	500.3	259.2	–241.1	532.7	791.9	291.6
Ontario	627.4	936.1	308.7	2,095.9	3,032.0	2,404.6
Manitoba	363.4	148.9	–214.5	143.9	292.8	–70.6
Saskatchewan	522.8	133.2	–389.6	73.0	206.2	–316.6
Alberta	344.5	648.0	303.5	373.2	1,021.2	676.7
British Columbia	194.2	820.9	626.7	636.1	1,457.0	1,262.8
Yukon	9.2	12.9	3.7	2.7	15.6	6.4
Northwest Territories	9.9	19.7	9.8	2.9	22.6	12.7
Total	3,245.4	3,245.4	0.0	3,943.9	7,189.3	3,943.9
Rate per 100 population						
Newfoundland	26.1	4.4	–28.8	1.6	6.0	–27.1
Prince Edward Island	31.7	17.1	–19.7	3.5	20.6	–16.1
Nova Scotia	25.4	15.3	–12.8	5.0	20.3	–7.9
New Brunswick	26.0	13.4	–15.7	4.0	17.4	–11.7
Quebec	8.1	4.0	–3.7	8.2	12.2	4.5
Ontario	9.5	10.4	3.4	23.3	33.7	26.7
Manitoba	32.4	14.2	–20.4	13.7	27.9	–6.7
Saskatchewan	39.8	13.4	–39.1	7.3	20.7	–31.8
Alberta	20.7	27.7	13.0	15.9	43.6	28.9
British Columbia	12.2	28.8	22.0	22.3	51.1	44.3
Yukon	54.4	55.1	15.8	11.5	66.7	27.4
Northwest Territories	25.1	37.9	18.8	5.6	43.5	24.4
Total	15.4	12.9	0.0	15.8	28.7	15.8

SOURCE: 1986 Census, 93-109, Table 6A and EC86B02.

NOTE: The rate per 100 population is as follows:

Col. 1: Number living in other provinces per 100 born in a given province.
Col. 2: Number born in other provinces per 100 population of a given province.
Col. 3: Net internal lifetime migration per 100 population of a given province.
Col. 4: Foreign-born per 100 population of a given province.
Col. 5: Born out of province per 100 population of a given province.
Col. 6: Total net migrants per 100 population of given province.

Dynamics of internal migration

The Canadian Charter of Rights and Freedoms recognizes the right of citizens and permanent residents "to move and take up residence in any province; and to pursue the gaining of a livelihood in any province." However, the Charter goes on to set certain limits to this broad stipulation, saying that this does "not preclude any law, program or activity that has as its objective the amelioration in a province of conditions of individuals in that province who are socially or economically disadvantaged if the rate of employment in that province is below the rate of employment in Canada." In effect, provinces that have higher than average levels of unemployment can give preference to the employment of residents of the province who are unemployed. As noted in the quotations given at the beginning of the chapter, the right of individuals to move needs to be balanced with the impact that the movement has on the communities of origin and destination.

Three general findings come from analysis of the factors underlying migration. First, it is found that migration propensities are higher for young adults as well as for persons with above average education and socio-economic status (e.g. Liaw, 1986). Second, migration is predominantly from smaller to larger places and from places with less opportunities to those with more opportunities. For instance, in moves within Manitoba in 1987-88, there were twice as many moves up the "central place hierarchy" as moves down the hierarchy (Mason and Simpson, 1988). Stafford (1990) summarizes the advantage of southern Ontario as a place of destination because of its diversity of economic opportunity, which attracts persons from other regions when their economies falter.

The third finding relates to the migration process as being disruptive in peoples lives; psychologists call it a "stressful life event." This would imply that for the most part people would prefer not to move and when they do move they will often follow others with whom they have previous connections. While there is considerable migratory interaction involving Ontario and the West, Quebec is somewhat of a "no man's land" in the sense that both in- and out-migration rates are relatively low (Termote, 1987). Except for exchanges with Ontario, Quebec appears to be disconnected from the rest of the country. Liaw (1986) calls it a "cultural barrier around Quebec," which would mean that the French-speaking population is less likely to leave the province and the English of other provinces are less likely to move to Quebec. Other data support the idea that migration is disruptive. For instance, there are always a reasonable number of return moves. For the period 1966-71, Rosenbaum (1988) estimates that some 30 per cent of moves involve returns to the province of birth or the province where people completed their highest grade of primary or secondary education. Rosenbaum calls these "failures," but the idea of returning may have been part of the migrant's original plan. Studies based in Newfoundland have found that many people seek to return to their communities if at all possible (Gmelch, 1983; House *et al.*, 1988). A survey of migrants to Winnipeg found that half were return migrants (Halli and Currie, 1986).

There is clearly often an economic motive to migration, which often acts as a pull factor. This would especially explain the choice of the place of destination. The Macdonald Commission concludes that economic incentives are the main forces shaping migration flows, particularly for Canadians in the labour force (Royal Commission on the Economic Union, 1985, III: 127). Verma and Broad (1989) estimate that most moves are either directly or indirectly generated by economic causes, with a third of 1981-86 moves being directly related to work. Asked why they had moved, close to half of migrants in Manitoba gave economic reasons (Mason and Simpson, 1988). It was also found that a quarter would move for a job that involved 25 per cent better pay.

However, there are also social factors, as people prefer not to move and as movement is often assisted by relatives and friends. For instance, the finding cited above would mean that three-quarters of people would not move, even for a job that involved 25 per cent more pay! In a study of people who moved to Hamilton and Burlington, Shulman and Drass (1979) found that over 80 per cent had pre-existing ties to the receiving community – either pre-arranged jobs or other less formal ties such as friends or relatives. This would explain the greater propensity of young adults to move, at a time when they are leaving home and thus less integrated in the community of origin. Conversely, the presence of dependants lowers the propensity to move (Liaw, 1988). Movements also follow changes in marital status and life cycle transitions (Raby, 1990; Northcott, 1988). It could be concluded that social factors are mostly involved in the decision whether or not to move: people are more prone to move when they are at stages of the life cycle that involve less integration in the community. Once the decision to move has been made, economic factors would play the major role in the choice of a place of destination. Nonetheless, close to one-fifth of moves are justified on the basis of wanting to live with or closer to families or friends (Verma and Broad, 1989).

This implies that there are restricted possibilities for policy intervention in affecting migration. The tax system supports migration through deductions for the cost of moving. The major policy that directly supports migration is the Canadian Manpower Mobility Program, which gives grants for training, looking for employment, or accepting employment to people unable to obtain a suitable job without moving.

Even if all such grants involved interprovincial movement, this program would have been responsible for only some 2 to 10 per cent of interprovincial migration over the period 1966-79 (Kosinski, 1981). Using an econometric model that estimates the impact of equalization payments, Watson (1986) finds that the higher level of equalization payments in 1977, compared to 1971, would have affected the migration of less than 10,000 people in 1977. Nonetheless, Winer and Gauthier (1982) find that the fiscal structure – government spending programs and the tax system – helps explain migration within Canada. In particular, the unemployment insurance system is one of the strongest elements in reducing the flow of migrants from the Atlantic region. Also, migration is retarded by equalization and transfer payments to persons, especially for low-income people.

In his analysis of migration flows among seventeen metropolitan areas over the periods 1956-61 to 1976-81, Shaw (1985) finds that the influence of the traditional economic variables has declined over this period. On the other hand, public-sector variables, such as federal equalization payments and unemployment insurance, have increased in importance in explaining inter-metropolitan migration. The lowered impact of traditional market forces would mean it is now harder to influence manpower mobility through measures affecting wages, job creation, and skill enhancement, while policies in the fiscal area have more impact. These fiscal structures subsidize residence in depressed regions (Shaw, 1986). Unemployment insurance benefits reduce the incentive to move in search of new job opportunities (Royal Commission on the Economic Union, 1985, III: 127).

Relative impact of demographic factors and projections for the future

The change in population distribution is a function of differences in natural increase, internal migration, and differential arrival of immigrants. The relative impact of these three factors has not been extensively analysed and it probably varies over time and space. Table 3 shows the patterns over the period 1976-86 in terms of the importance of these three factors relative to the base population.

Natural increase played to the relative advantage of Alberta, Newfoundland, Saskatchewan, and the territories. For instance, Alberta had 14.3 per cent of the country's natural increase with 9.2 per cent of the population, making for 55 per cent more natural increase than the average. International migration appears to play a larger role, especially since some provinces profit very little. The Atlantic provinces together represent 9.2 per cent of the population but their total net international migration is negative. Ontario has 35.4 per cent of the population but 45.7 per cent of net international migration. Similarly, British Columbia

Table 3: *Relative Impact of Natural Increase, Net International Migration, and Net Internal Migration, Provinces, 1976-86*

	Population distribution 1981 (1)	NATURAL INCREASE			INTERNATIONAL MIGRATION			INTERNAL MIGRATION
		Thousands (2)	Distribution (3)	Relative impact (4=3/1)	Thousands (5)	Distribution (6)	Relative impact (7=6/1)	Thousands (8)
Newfoundland	2.33	63.9	3.25	1.39	-0.6	-0.11	-0.05	-34.0
P.E.I.	0.50	9.1	0.46	0.92	0.4	0.06	0.12	-0.1
Nova Scotia	3.48	54.0	2.75	0.79	1.8	0.31	0.09	-0.2
New Brunswick	2.86	54.6	2.78	0.97	-1.8	-0.31	-0.11	-10.4
Quebec	26.45	486.7	24.75	0.94	106.8	18.61	0.70	-237.8
Ontario	35.43	620.5	31.56	0.89	262.4	45.71	1.29	63.9
Manitoba	4.22	80.3	4.08	0.97	28.9	5.03	1.19	-44.9
Saskatchewan	3.98	95.4	4.85	1.22	11.8	2.06	0.52	-12.7
Alberta	9.19	280.6	14.27	1.55	67.3	11.72	1.28	154.7
British Columbia	11.27	206.2	10.47	0.93	97.0	16.90	1.50	130.0
Yukon	0.10	3.8	0.19	1.90	0.0	0.00	0.00	-3.7
Northwest Terr.	0.19	11.2	0.57	3.00	0.1	0.01	0.05	-4.9
Total	100.00	1,966.1	100.0	1.00	574.1	100.0	1.00	0.0

SOURCE: Statistics Canada, Cat. No. 91-210, 1990.

has 50 per cent more net migration than would be expected based on relative population size. The impact of internal migration is evident from the fact that, by definition, it is positive in some provinces and negative in others. Only the three provinces of Alberta, British Columbia and Ontario showed net gain in the period 1976-86. The net departure of 237,800 from Quebec is comparable to the net gain through international migration of 262,400 for Ontario.

Since rates of natural increase are expected to decline in the future, the dynamics of population distribution will probably undergo a serious change. In the post-war period, essentially all provinces have experienced continuous growth over time. While the growth has varied from province to province, nonetheless, except for Saskatchewan in 1966-76, each province has experienced continuous growth. This is because natural increase has compensated for migration losses in the provinces that have had negative net migration. Table 2 indicated that only British Columbia, Alberta, Ontario, and Quebec had benefited from the combined lifetime migration of the Canadian and foreign-born population.

Once natural increase plays a smaller or negative role in population growth, then some regions can be expected to have declining populations. Using a total fertility rate of 1.7 and an immigration level of 140,000 per year, population decline could begin as early as 1994 in Newfoundland and 2005 in New Brunswick, compared to the period 2017-2020 in Quebec, Nova Scotia, and Prince Edward Island, 2022-2026 in Saskatchewan and Alberta, and 2030-2032 in Manitoba and Ontario. These results are based on extending the assumptions from the Statistics Canada (1990a) projections, which imply that the internal migration flow will be reduced by half over the period 1989-2011, then remain at that level. The distribution itself will continue to change very slowly. However, once some populations are declining while others are growing, the concerns over changing population distribution may become more serious.

IMPLICATIONS OF POPULATION DISTRIBUTION AND INTERNAL MIGRATION

Cities, towns, and rural areas

In an overview of "migration and the regions" Stafford (1990) argues that efforts are needed to encourage growth outside of Toronto, Montreal, and Vancouver and to deal with growth within these regions. He goes on to say that this is not easy because governments around the world have tackled this kind of problem with limited success. The problem has the additional complication in Canada that urban questions are largely under provincial or municipal jurisdiction. A Ministry of State for Urban Affairs was created at the national level in 1971 to develop federal policies and to obtain the co-operation of other levels of government. At a tri-level conference in 1973, three objectives were adopted: need for more balanced urban growth; need to redistribute urban growth to small and medium-sized towns; and need to improve the quality of the environment in large urban centres (Stone and Marceau, 1977: 62). However, since the mid-1970s the growth of the larger cities has not been as pronounced and the overall proportion of urban population has not changed. Thus the problems may have become less pressing. In addition, the conflicts over the appropriate level of jurisdiction brought the demise of the Ministry of State for Urban Affairs in 1979.

It is also noteworthy that issues of growth of the larger metropolitan areas did not draw the attention of the Review of Demography. For the first time in two decades, the largest cities grew more rapidly then smaller places in 1981-86 (Simmons and Bourne, 1989). Ram et al. (1989) find that the inner cities (i.e., central business district and the surrounding area where the earliest development occurred) of the largest metropolitan areas have declined in population over the period 1951-81 but the period 1981-86 marked a turnaround. This inner-city population of some 500,000 people also involves a concentration of young adults and elderly, non-married people, one-person households, and single-parent families. Stafford (1990) notes that in the cities of southern Ontario and Quebec, as well as British Columbia, there are problems of urban congestion and ethnic relations requiring strategies to avoid the ghettoization of ethnic minorities.

Dumas (1989) observes that the net migrants to the largest cities involve few dependants (children and older people). More generally, the census metropolitan areas have lower proportions of dependants than populations living in other areas. It is difficult to know whether this trend will continue with population aging. Two phenomena are at work. Older people are less prone to move, resulting in an "aging in place." On the other hand, those who do move go to select destinations, having a significant effect on markets and needs for services (Northcott, 1988). Okraku (1987) finds that age residential segregation is significant in cities, although somewhat lower than the levels of ethnic segregation. He expects "aging in place" to reduce this segregation in the future.

The age composition of given places is a function of the age profile of those who move as well as of those who stay. It is for this reason that the smaller towns and rural areas have higher proportions of elderly, which are not necessarily matched by the set of available services. These patterns associated with smaller places received considerable attention among studies done for the Review of Demography and Its Implications for Economic and Social Policy. MacLean *et al.* (1988) observe that the growth of the services and retail sales of small towns in Saskatchewan are sustained by the arrival of elderly populations from the rural areas. However, the supply of older people is diminishing with the reduced size of the rural population. Already, over the five-year period 1981-86, 80 per cent of rural municipalities lost population and 30 per cent lost at least 10 per cent of their population.

Another migration trend affecting small towns is the departure of the younger adult population. In a review of "Prairie Small-town Futures," Todd (1986) notes that the lack of jobs in agriculture and related service sectors means that the young move out, leaving a "relict" population in small towns and villages that is predominantly old and retired. Smaller centres have higher proportions of elderly due to the departure of the young and the reduced fertility of remaining residents. In terms of the ratio of population aged 65 + /15-64, communities of 1,000 people or less in Manitoba have double the aged ratio of the provincial average. This implies a number of needs: health, public housing, subsidized transportation, formal and informal care facilities, and recreational outlets. Todd argues that these needs of the elderly must be addressed within a broader economic context. The suggested policies involve both economics and services, in particular economic diversification and improved infrastructure to overcome isolation. An interesting case study of Chilliwack in British Columbia (B.C. Research, 1986) indicated that with an aging population, the needs for hospital facilities were first manifest. The systematic study of community needs through interviews found that the needs were "overwhelming" and they went far beyond hospital space. This again demonstrates how the changing composition of the population can have serious repercussions on the service needs in communities.

The lack of economic opportunities also applies to the rural populations. In 1986, 39 per cent of persons living on farms reported off-farm work and, in 1981, 14 per cent reported full-time off-farm work (McSkimmings, 1990; Chorayshi, 1986). For the resource industries of northern Canada, there is the increasing phenomenon of long-distance commuting, which avoids the need to build a community and supply services near a resource site (Storey and Shrimpton, 1986). As these authors observe, this could produce the result that resource development workers live in major urban centres while the North is made up of increasing proportions of native peoples and older people. For the outports of Newfoundland, House *et al.* (1988) indicate that the population has much interest in staying where they are or returning if they do leave. While the incomes from the market sphere are low, these are supplemented by unemployment insurance and by household production.

This household production includes building and maintaining their own homes and obtaining food and fuel without use of the market.

Regional economic disparity

Having studied the impact of changing population distribution among urban and rural areas, we will now turn to the interplay of population and economic disparity at the larger regional level. This question has such high priority in Canada that the commitment to furthering regional economic development to reduce disparity in opportunities is enshrined in the Constitution Act of 1982 (Review of Demography, 1989: 45).

The analyses of regional economic disparity agree that this disparity has been persistent. In an update of the earlier work by the Economic Council of Canada (1977), Coffey and Polèse (1987: 20, 23) observe that since the Great Depression the overall ranking of the provinces shows little fundamental change. Basically, Ontario and British Columbia are above average, along with Alberta since World War Two, while the Atlantic provinces, Quebec, Manitoba, and Saskatchewan are below average. They do note a slight tendency to convergence in personal income per capita over the period 1966-83, once transfer payments are included. Melvin (1987) notes that in terms of earned income per capita, the ratio of the highest to the lowest province is also very stable at 2.27 in 1961 and 2.10 in 1984. In 1989 the median family income was some 20 per cent below the national average in Prince Edward Island, Newfoundland, and New Brunswick, 10 to 15 per cent below in Nova Scotia, Saskatchewan, Quebec, and Manitoba, while it was just above the national average in Alberta and British Columbia, but 14 per cent above in Ontario (Statistics Canada, 1990c). In effect, this median income was 46 per cent higher in Ontario than in Prince Edward Island.

In 1910 Quebec represented 24.2 per cent of the national income compared to 23.6 per cent in 1989, while Ontario represented 41.3 in 1910 and 41.5 in 1989. Together, these two provinces represented 65.5 per cent of the total national income in 1910 and 65.1 in 1989. However, over this same period the three Maritime provinces declined from 10.1 to 4.7 per cent of total national income, which was mirrored by long-term growth in British Columbia's share (Polèse, 1987; Statistics Canada, 1990d).

Interpretations of disparity

In a review of explanations of regional inequality, Wein (1988) divides these explanations along three lines: staples approach, regional deficiencies, and dependence. The staples approach argues that various regions have grown and declined as external demand for their staple resources has fluctuated. This has tied regions to external markets and thus has minimized the exchanges among regions of the country.

The regional deficiencies approach is quite similar. It argues that given regions have various shortcomings, but that these go beyond staple resources *per se*. For instance, the Royal Commission on the Economic Union (1985, III: 198-220) suggests that half of the differences in earned income are a function of wage rates and the other half are due to employment rates. Wage rates reflect worker productivity, which in turn follows on capital-to-labour ratios, the educational level of the labour force, rate of adoption of new technology, quality of management, and distances that products must be shipped. Employment rates indicate the proportion of the population at labour force ages who are working, and also reflect employment opportunities for women. The greater economic diversity in central Canada means more potential for two-income families. Bryan (1988) argues that questions of market size and productivity play the predominant role, while natural resources and transportation costs have a lesser role. Melvin (1987) suggests that the different mix of occupations may be playing an important role, along with the relative endowments of the various regions (including market size). Coffey and Polèse (1986) note a definite relationship between the presence of a large urban area and the region's capacity to generate high income and employment levels. They suggest that size and density are associated with agglomeration economies through juxtaposition of firms and improved services and infrastructures.

Other authors have used dependency theory to interpret regional disparity. This approach would argue that central Canada established its dominance though tariff policies that protected its early industrial development and transportation policies that ensured links to the peripheral regions of the east and west. Matthews (1988) further argues that the immigration of central Europeans to western Canada resulted in their having few links with the centres of power in central Canada. In *Why Disunity?* Breton and Breton (1980) focus on the distribution of organizational power. Organizations of various kinds have power based on their size and the resources at their disposal. These organizations are distributed over space and the distribution is unequal in the sense that central Canada is the base of more and larger organizations. This results in a disproportionate concentration of organizational power. Breton and Breton go on to note that individuals have power on the basis of both their place within organizations and networking across organizations. Persons in central Canada have more opportunities because there are more powerful organizations and more possibilities of networking. People in the outlying regions are disadvantaged because it is difficult to establish networks over large distances.

Looking into the future, Stafford (1990) notes two forces that would contribute to increasing regional disparities. The first is the increased level of trade in the evolving world industrial system. Manufacturing will shift to low-wage areas, making peripheral parts of Canada less attractive than developing countries. Administrative corporate activities will concentrate in the largest urban centres. Regions without large cities would experience population decline, while future population growth would be concentrated in southern Ontario and Quebec and the lower Fraser Valley of British Columbia. The second force that would contribute to increasing disparities is free trade, which will emphasize the staple resources of given areas and will exercise pressure to reduce regional assistance.

Policies for reducing disparities

As can be expected, the different interpretations of regional inequality imply varying policy approaches. Coffey and Polèse (1987) state that since the 1960s, "Canada has been regarded as one of the world's leading proponents and practitioners of regional development policy." The federal government's recognition of regional economic imbalances as a policy issue dates back to the depression years (Francis, 1986). Following on the Rowell-Sirois Commission, the first programs of equalization started in 1957, but the comprehensive nature of current programs dates from 1967 (Coffey and Polèse, 1986). Unemployment insurance was revamped in 1971 to become a major player in attempts to reduce disparities.

Other conclusions are less favourable. The Department of Regional Economic Expansion was created in 1969 but disbanded thirteen years later. Lithwick (1986) has called the DREE experience an "embodiment of contradictions." These contradictions stem from the fact that issues specific to given regions can be seen to be provincial rather than federal matters. While other federal departments are based on sectors (e.g., labour, industry, health), regional development cuts across sectors. In addition, there remains an unclear sense of direction: there are persistent disparities and a consensus that public policy should try to reduce these, but the causes of the problem are neither simple nor clearly understood. Some of the functions of DREE have since been absorbed by the Department of Regional and Industrial Expansion.

The Royal Commission on the Economic Union (1985) expressed similar bewilderment: "many theories abound, but none has gained wide acceptance" ... "we have experimented with many different types of programs, policies and strategies" ... "the best that can be said is that we have prevented the less developed regions from falling further behind" ... "continuing disparity is not a crisis ... but a serious problem ... regional development must remain one of Canada's primary policy goals" ... "past policies have compensated quite adequately for disparities but have been markedly unsuccessful in promoting self-sustained economic development" (III: 198, 215, 216).

Since the DREE experience, governments appear to have limited faith in their capacity to affect regional patterns in the economy (Coffey and Polèse, 1987: 2). Looking at the persistent disparities, Polèse (1987) suggests as an "obvious conclusion" that "there are definite limits to the capacity of public policy to alter long-run patterns." That is not to say, as Polèse continues, that regional policy is of no consequence. The primary goal has become one of equity through transfer payments rather than efficiency through increased economic viability of the disadvantaged regions.

In a study for the Review of Demography, Carel et al. (1988) conclude that there is a conflict between policies designed to attain overall economic efficiency and policies designed to counteract deficiencies in regional development. They conclude that we need to resign ourselves to a degree of economic inefficiency. That also seems to be the basic conclusion of the Royal Commission on the Economic Union (1985, III: 198-201): regional development is defended in terms of equity rather than efficiency, and the Commission asks in particular "how much Canadians are willing to sacrifice, in terms of national efficiency, to guarantee . . . the maintenance of regional communities."

In its discussion of development policies, the Commission considers three approaches. The interregional market adjustment approach would maximize the free movement of factors of production (capital, labour, goods), expecting this to equalize wages across regions. As wages decline in the disadvantaged regions surplus labour will move out and industries seeking cheap labour would move in, bringing an eventual increase in wages. Compensatory policies would compensate individuals and families living in disadvantaged regions through equalization and transfer payments. Developmental policies would try to improve regional productivity and the efficiency of the labour market. This would include attempts to remove differences in worker productivity through adaptation of technology and improvement in labour skills. While the Commission supports the developmental approach, its main suggestion is that provincial governments assume the predominant role in regional development. McNiven (1987) criticizes the Commission for seeming to say that "regional development is a vexatious problem about which we know little" and states that the suggestions made are basically a "cop-out."

In effect, quite a variety of measures for dealing with regional disparity have been attempted: investments in infrastructure, human capital investments (education, training, mobility grants), rural stabilization policies, industrial assistance, mega-projects, resource and sectorial development, and compensatory or transfer policies (Wein, 1988).

The "logic" of these policies differs and sometimes is contradictory. The best example of this is that policies to improve the economic efficiency of the market would argue against transfer payments. Courchene (1981), for instance, proposes that transfer payments protect the lagging regions from the discipline of the market and in so doing lock them into a dependent state he calls "transfer dependency." This exacerbates the disparities and makes the economy less efficient. Leclerc (1989) takes an extreme view in this direction, arguing that we should "forget about rural and regional development" and invest instead in the big cities; if people refuse to move to more prosperous regions, then reduce the services to a minimum.

Matthews (1988) also criticizes regional development policies but from a rather different basis. He notes that policies encouraging outside investment in a region will not necessarily benefit the region: "when industries come from outside an underdeveloped region, the basic aim of the owners is to remove wealth from the area rather than to increase the wealth and benefit the living conditions of those who live there" (pp. 338-39). The alternative he suggests is the development of local resources and industries that will satisfy local needs. That is, taking a dependency perspective, he argues that reducing the links with the developed regions at the centre will reduce the extent to which the peripheral regions are exploited.

In effect, the priorities in the area of regional disparities are considerably a function of the value orientation used as a premise. If one takes the point of view, as Courchene (1981) does, that it is not the welfare of geographic communities that count but rather the welfare of individuals, then it would follow that one would want to maximize the national economic efficiency, eliminating barriers to trade and mobility. Breton and Breton (1980) call this the "pan-Canadian" approach because it would want to maximize everyone's right to participate in all the organizations of the country. If they are not achieving well-being where they are, the important thing is to be able to have access to opportunities elsewhere and these will be maximized if the overall economic efficiency is maximized. The alternative, which they call a "segmentalist" approach, sees each region as having its own separate organizations in order to maximize its viability as a community and to reduce the power of the centralizing organizations. In some regards, this is the debate between the Charter of Rights and Freedoms and the failed Meech Lake Accord. The Charter focuses on individuals who have rights, regardless of who they are and where they are. The Accord was conceived in terms of "special status" for Quebec and provinces that have the right to set up separate programs. One could argue that together the two constitutional developments would have represented the kind of compromise that has been important to the survival of the Canadian state.

The Macdonald Commission focused on other political aspects of the regionalist debate, arguing that there needs to be a better way of including the regions in the federal policy-making institutions. Some representation from each region in the governing party could be ensured through a form of proportionate representation based on popular vote in each region. Another alternative would be a stronger Senate with a focus on representing regional interests.

The role of population and inter-regional migration

In their study of the impact of migration on regional development, Carel *et al*. (1988) compare two lines of thought that emerge from the policy discussions presented above. The first, which is the majority view among economists, is that internal migration should be viewed as an adjustment mechanism. This neo-classical model argues that inequalities are a function of poor performance of the marketplace. If there were fewer obstacles to the free movement of the factors of production – i.e., labour, capital, and goods – then there would be higher national output and lower inequalities. Migration in particular would make for a levelling of wages over regions since there would be less unemployment in the disadvantaged regions and more competition in the more advanced regions. For instance, Courchene (1981) and Melvin (1987) would argue that transfer payments to disadvantaged regions reduce out-migration and therefore impede the marketplace adjustments that would produce more equality over regions. Courchene observes that in 1931 Saskatchewan was the largest of the four western provinces yet now it is the smallest. Saskatchewan has had more out-migration than the Atlantic provinces, which has benefited its relative economic standing compared to these provinces. We have already seen evidence to the effect that transfer and equalization payments do affect migration. Winer and Gauthier (1982) find that unemployment insurance, equalization payments, and transfers retard out-migration from lagging regions. Similarly, Shaw (1986) finds that the influence of the traditional economic variables on migration has declined while the public-sector variables have increased in importance. He concludes that "market forces that would naturally work to induce migration from low to high income regions (and thus equalize earned incomes across the country) are being short-circuited by a fiscal structure that subsidizes residence in relatively depressed regions." In reviewing this literature, Watson (1987) finds ample evidence that fiscal variables – such as tax rates, the generosity of unemployment insurance, and federal transfers – do have an effect on people's decision whether or not to leave a given region.

The second line of thought developed by Carel *et al*. (1988) is called the local development approach. This approach focuses on the broad set of factors responsible for economic development: structural changes, technological innovations, transformations of the economy. In this view, the sources of growth are largely incorporated in local populations as human capital, knowledge, and skills. As we have seen, out-migration takes the best of this human capital out of a region and therefore it redistributes the economic growth potential to the benefit of the advanced regions. Migrants not only have skills that are in demand elsewhere but they have the imagination and initiative to move (Watson, 1988). Besides bringing valuable human capital, migration brings a larger population and greater possibilities of agglomeration economies. At the same time, the regions losing population have fixed costs and even fewer benefits from economies of scale. In this view, migration will increase the disparity gap. Bryan (1988), for instance, notes that the expected "adjustment" of migration may not occur because the best leave and migrants bring with them technology, capital, and education, as well as their own labour, all of which increase the income in the receiving region. In addition, the local market of the out-migration region declines and the tax base to support services is eroded. McNiven (1987: 432) puts it well: "the problem with migration policies does not lie with the migrant so much as with the structure of the community left behind."

Although these two lines of thought appear to be in conflict, Carel *et al.* (1988) argue that they are "two complementary perspectives" whose reconciliation is nonetheless "difficult." It could be, for instance, that the development effects of migration (second line of thought) maintain the disparities in spite of its adjustment effects (first line of thought). They conclude that the long-term effect of migration on relative income and unemployment is indeterminate; it is possible that migration both reduces and increases disparities at the same time. Stated differently, we "cannot expect migration to solve Canada's regional economic problems although it must remain an essential economic adjustment mechanism" (Polèse, 1987: 24-25).

In his summary for the Review of Demography, Watson (1987) is somewhat more conclusive, suggesting that "emigration reduces per capita growth in the region left behind." He notes that migrants take aggregate demand with them, while the out-migration leaves behind the persons least able to cope with the unfavourable circumstances that led to departures. Nonetheless, Watson agrees that the evidence is "not conclusive." Similarly, Grant and Vanderkamp (1987) find that the quantitative evidence on the long-term impact of migration on sending and receiving regions "is incomplete." They suggest that, because of the multiplier and accelerator effects of migration, its role in adjustment is somewhat reduced.

It is probably necessary, as others have suggested, to admit that there is a basic conflict between attaining overall economic efficiency and counteracting deficiencies in regional development. Inasmuch as questions of equity and preservation of community remain important values, their attainment will require that we resign ourselves to a degree of economic inefficiency. Studies for the Review of Demography by House *et al.* (1988) and Irwin (1988) argue for the preservation of a way of life in the outbacks of Newfoundland and northern Canada where traditions and quality of life cannot be measured in economic terms. From this point of view, a certain amount of conflict among policies is inevitable. Stafford (1990) notes that most economic policies have reinforced the influence of the market on regional population flows. The regional development policies, equalization payments, and the various transfer payments have acted to dampen the flow of migration out of depressed regions.

Stafford (1990) concludes his discussion of "migration and the regions" with the observation that inequitable distribution of population lies at the very heart of regional problems. The wealthiest parts of the country are the urbanized, populated areas, while the poorer regions have inadequate size to permit economies of scale, and they suffer the threat of further depletion of their scarce human capital.

We can conclude with the idea of two geographic grids, one representing the distribution of resources and economic opportunity, the other representing the distribution of population. Two strategies are possible for making the two grids more symmetric: bring the people to the jobs or bring the jobs to the people. While there are many difficulties involved in taking somewhat conflicting approaches simultaneously, this may be unavoidable. The relative priority of the two approaches, along with their specific mechanisms, will be the subject of continuous debates. Where people are situated geographically will also influence their willingness to entertain one or the other alternative. In other words, sensitive national unity issues are at stake in this debate. Persons taking a pan-Canadian approach, who are more likely to be from central Canada, would argue that the overall average individual welfare will improve if we build on the strong economic areas, submit the regions to the discipline of the market, minimize the inefficiency associated with supporting the lagging regions, and therefore support migration out of these areas. After all, it is best for them if they move and everyone should be equally at home anywhere in the country. Persons taking a segmentalist approach would argue for treating each region as a separate community, ensuring its viability so that it stays within the fold, and remembering that people are attached to their communities, that they would prefer to stay where they are, and that out-migration does not necessarily improve the situation of the lagging regions.

As natural increase becomes a less important source of growth, and consequently as we can no longer think of relative growth but rather must consider that some regions will decline while others grow, this debate is not likely to lose any of its intensity.

6

CHANGING GROWTH PATTERNS
AND THEIR IMPLICATIONS

Having analysed mortality, fertility, and migration, we can now follow the overall picture of population change. This chapter will consider the growth patterns in Canada's past and the prospects for the future. We will then focus on the consequences of population growth, paying particular attention to economic, environmental, and labour force questions. The policy options to be considered include those of influencing population growth and adapting to changing growth patterns.

The impact of population growth is a complex issue. Some people take the view that population growth reduces the average well-being because the resources have to be shared by more people. According to this line of thinking, the lower the denominator the higher the average well-being. However, a larger population can also produce more resources. Therefore, the simple division of resources by population provides an inaccurate view of the impact of population change. The resources under consideration could be the overall goods and services, or available employment opportunities, or environmental resources. While population growth can mean the division of goods, jobs, or other resources among more people, it can also mean the production of more of these goods, jobs, or other resources. As was noted in Chapter 1, Ehrlich (1968) viewed population growth as a *Population Bomb*. However, this view exaggerates the impact of population growth on pollution and resource depletion, since per capita consumption plays the major role. Alternatively, Simon (1981) saw population growth as *The Ultimate Resource*, positively affecting our standard of living through economies of scale and more frequent inventions, but he did not adequately recognize that technology and quality of the labour force play a larger role than population size itself. The impact of population growth involves an interplay of environmental questions, consumption patterns, and technology, as well as population size and quality of the labour force.

PAST AND ANTICIPATED FUTURE POPULATION GROWTH

Since 1851, when the population of Canada was 2.4 million, the total has multiplied more than tenfold (see Table 4). We have already seen in the introduction that this growth has been considerably faster than that of other countries, such as England and France, or the world as a whole. Population growth has also varied considerably over Canadian history. There have been three periods when growth was close to 3 per cent per year: 1851-61, 1901-11, and 1951-56. These are rapid rates of growth indeed, surpassing the more recent figures for many Third World countries. By way of comparison, it is estimated that population growth for the total of developing countries peaked in 1965 at 2.4 per cent per year.

On the other hand, there have been three periods of population growth at or near 1 per cent per year: 1881-1901, 1931-41, and 1976-91. While growth has declined in the most recent period, it remains higher than that of the total for all developed countries, which is 0.5 per cent in the period 1985-90. According to United Nations (1989b) estimates, Australia is the only major developed country with a population growth more rapid than Canada in this period.

The higher growth in Canada as compared to most other developed countries is due both to immigration and to the after effect of the baby boom. The below-replacement fertility has until now been offset by the large numbers of young adults at childbearing ages. Even though they are having fewer than two children each, the fact that there are so many couples at childbearing ages means that there are more births than

Table 4: Population Growth, 1851-1991

Period	Population at beginning of period	Total population increase	Average annual growth rate
	(thousands)		
1851-61	2,436	793	2.9
1861-71	3,230	460	1.3
1871-81	3,689	636	1.6
1881-91	4,325	508	1.1
1891-1901	4,833	538	1.1
1901-11	5,371	1,835	3.0
1911-21	7,207	1,581	2.0
1921-31	8,788	1,589	1.7
1931-41	10,377	1,130	1.0
1941-51	11,507	2,141	1.7
1951-56	14,009	2,071	2.8
1956-61	16,081	2,157	2.5
1961-66	18,238	1,777	1.9
1966-71	20,015	1,553	1.5
1971-76	21,568	1,424	1.3
1976-81	22,993	1,349	1.1
1981-86	24,342	1,011	0.8
1986-91	25,353	1,597	1.2
1991	26,950		

SOURCE: Beaujot et al., 1988: 2; Statistics Canada, 1990b: Table 1.

deaths in the population. In terms of population growth, Canada is still living off the baby boom.

Over the five year census intervals since 1951-56, the rate of population growth has declined from 2.8 to 1.0 per cent per year. There is no doubt that the principal source of this change is the decline in births. Over the period 1961-86, immigration has also declined relative to the base population.

Projections for the future imply that the rate of population growth will continue to decline (Statistics Canada, 1990a). These projections are based on fertility assumptions of 1.2, 1.7, or 2.1 births per women in 2011, combined with immigration of 140,000 or 200,000 persons per year. The life expectancy is assumed to increase from 76.4 in 1986 to 80.6 in 2011 and emigration is assumed to be 0.25 per cent of the base population per year. The projections have a fifty-year horizon, ending in 2036.

Table 5 summarizes the basic results of these projections. In the first projection, based on fertility of 1.2 and 140,000 immigrants per year, natural increase ceases in 2007 and the population begins to decline as of 2016. The second and third projections are based on a fertility of 1.7 with immigration at 140,000 in the second and 200,000 in the third.

Table 5: Characteristics of Statistics Canada Population Projections Based on the 1986 Census

Projection No.	Total fertility rate	Annual immigration	Population in 2036	Growth 1986-2036	Last Year of Positive Natural increase	Last Year of Positive Population growth
1	1.20	140,000	27,615.4	8.9%	2007	2015
2	1.67	140,000	30,997.6	22.3%	2019	2026
3	1.67	200,000	34,153.6	34.7%	2021	2035
4	2.10	200,000	37,443.7	47.7%	–	–
0	1.67	zero net	26,819.1	5.8%	2017	2017

SOURCE: Statistics Canada, 1990a, and special tabulations.

Natural increase ceases in 2019 or 2021, and the population begins to decline as of 2027 or 2036. With a fertility of 2.1 and immigration of 200,000 per year – fourth projection – natural increase and population growth continue throughout the period (see Table 5).

In the fifty-year period 1936-86, the population of Canada increased by 125 per cent. In comparison, the next fifty years would see increases of 9 or 48 per cent under the low and high scenarios respectively. Compared to the rates of the 1970s and 1980s, the fertility rates of 1.2 and 2.1 may be seen as being outside the expected range, at least for the short-term future. Therefore, the second and third projections appear more realistic (Figure 15). These imply lower population growth that eventually becomes a decline. Over the period 1986-2036 the total increase in population size would amount to 22 or 35 per cent, depending on the level of immigration.

Compared to the past, the picture of population growth is likely to become very different in the future. While we have seen rates of growth as low as 1 per cent per year in the past, the future is likely to see markedly lower rates. Unless fertility and/or immigration increase significantly from the levels of the recent past, we are likely to see the population start to decline in absolute numbers. These are fairly uncharted grounds. There have been few experiences of population decline in the modern world.

CONSEQUENCES OF LOW OR NEGATIVE GROWTH

Economic questions: theoretical discussion

There are diverse views regarding the impact of population growth on the well-being of societies. A publication by the World Bank (1984) notes both positive and negative aspects of population growth. Population growth can promote economic growth by stimulating demand, producing economies of scale, reducing investment risks, upgrading

Figure 15: Births and Deaths, 1921 to 2035

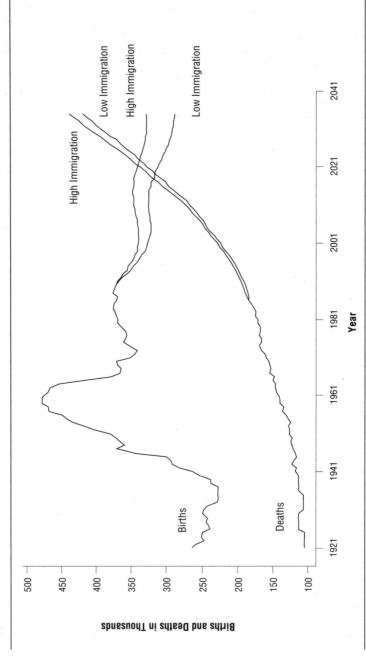

NOTE : Projections based on fertility of 1.67 and immigration of 140,000 (low) and 200,000 (high).
SOURCES : Statistics Canada, 1990a and 1990b.

the labour force, and encouraging technological innovation. On the other hand, each of these can be achieved by other means than through population growth. The World Bank goes on to note that population growth can undermine the investments per member of the labour force, can make economic adjustment more difficult, and can put pressure on natural resources. Once again, these results could occur for reasons other than population growth. This publication concludes that population pressure was probably important to the economic development of the Western world. However, this does not imply that population growth is a necessary condition for economic growth.

The conclusion may also differ depending on the level of analysis. For instance, it could well be agreed that the world would be better off with less population growth, especially in terms of pressure on resources. However, a given community may find growth beneficial. Growth of specific communities is often interpreted as meaning increasing prosperity and a larger relative importance in the total country, especially when each person's vote counts equally. The results may well differ from place to place: Ethiopia or India would probably be better off with slower growth while Australia or Canada might profit from more growth.

Whether population growth is beneficial or not may depend on the circumstances. For instance, in the context of technological progress and adequate infrastructures, population growth may be beneficial. However, without these, it may be detrimental to economic progress. Most would agree that the benefits of population growth do not require particularly high rates of growth. Similarly, lack of population growth may be particularly problematic when the population decline is strong and sustained. That is, some intermediate level may produce the benefits of population growth without introducing its detrimental aspects.

For the United States, Easterlin et al. (1978) have observed that in the period before World War Two, demographic cycles through immigration influenced aggregate demand in terms of urban development, residential building, formation of new businesses, and investment in such things as transportation, water supply, sewers, and electricity. In the post-war period, the demographic cycles have followed fertility, which influenced the labour force some twenty years later, putting a stress on unemployment and reducing the economic fortunes of young people during periods of high labour force growth.

Espenshade (1978) has reviewed the economic literature on the economic effects of zero population growth. There is considerable literature on the effects of population growth through the labour force, consumption, savings and investment, social security, and education. He concludes that the cessation of growth is not a cause for alarm: "many research questions remain unanswered, but . . . the health of a nation depends far more on the wisdom of economic policies than on underlying demographic trends, . . . on the whole, lower fertility, even at replacement level, may be economically more advantageous to society than an average family size of, say, three children." However, this review does not consider the impact of sustained below-replacement fertility.

Similar conclusions were reached by the Commission on Population Growth and the American Future. The non-demographic factors were seen as more important, and the average standard of living was expected to be higher with lower population growth:

> in the long run, no substantial benefits will result from further growth of the Nation's population, rather that the gradual stabilization of our population through voluntary means would contribute significantly to the Nation's ability to solve its problems. We have looked for, and have not found, any convincing economic argument for continued population growth. The health of our country does not depend on it, nor does the vitality of business nor the welfare of the average person. (United States, 1972: 4)

Other analyses would concur that the macro-economic effects of below-replacement fertility are not large. McNicoll (1986) suggests that the "main economic effects" are slight but the "distributional effects" may be more serious. That is, a declining population may make it difficult to redistribute resources to the disadvantaged, given the high fixed social security costs. This could especially undermine the welfare of children. There would also be slower upward mobility. Boserup (1986) argues that an older labour force will involve less efficiency and innovation, while Moore (1986) argues that the work force would be more stable with higher average expertise. An important difficulty with these types of analysis is that the factors that are particularly important to productivity, especially innovativeness and technological change, cannot easily be captured in the models. Particularly important is the question of whether an older labour force would be more or less prone to innovation and change.

Clearly, economic growth depends on a number of factors. There are economic questions, such as savings, investments, and markets, but also geographic factors, such as available natural resources, and social factors, particularly the quantity and quality of the labour force. In addition, psychological factors, such as the willingness to delay gratification by making investments, and political factors, such as basic security and confidence in the future, must be considered. Given the complexity of factors underlying economic growth, it is understandable that population growth or decline *per se* may have a limited role.

Economic questions: the Canadian case

It is often noted that periods of more rapid economic and demographic growth have tended to coincide in Canadian history. The periods of economic and demographic expansion have been especially 1851-61, 1895-1914, and 1951-66. These have corresponded to the boom preceding Confederation, the settlement of the West along with early industrialization, and the period of sustained post-war growth. On the other hand, the periods of less rapid growth have been the long depression of 1861-95, the 1930s, and early 1980s. It is difficult to arrive at an adequate interpretation of this coincidence of economic and demographic growth. Most certainly the economic climate has influenced the openness of immigration policy as well as the extent of interest in migration to Canada. The economic climate was probably a factor in the low birthrates of the 1930s and the high rates of the baby boom era.

One might also argue that population growth has had an impact on the economic climate. Slower population growth can reduce available labour supply and it can undermine investment confidence and consumer demand, especially the demand for new housing (see Barber, 1979). Given the small population of Canada and the relatively abundant resources, it could be concluded that relatively rapid population growth has been beneficial. Besides putting upward pressure on demand, growth permitted the deployment of a sufficient labour force, including the importation of skills through immigration. Nonetheless, there is not agreement here. Marsden (1972: 123) suggests: "perhaps our prosperity is dependent upon a radically slowed rate of population growth . . . we do not know." Sharir (1990: 22) states that "the relationship between population and well-being cannot be generalized."

At the regional level, population growth has been positively correlated with the relative economic growth of the various parts of the country. However, this tells us little about the nature of the underlying relationships since it is not clear which is the cause and which the effect. Nonetheless, if future growth in some localities occurs at the expense of decline in others, "some localities may be depopulated to such an extent that a process of decay will set in, and the economic well-being of the remaining population will decline" (Sharir, 1990: 22).

A number of studies undertaken for the Review of Demography have attempted to investigate the impact of population on economic well-being. Denton and Spencer (1988a) have constructed a macroeconomic model that makes it possible to analyse the impact of alternative demographic scenarios. For instance, they simulated the economic outcome of a fertility trajectory that involved a baby boom but no baby bust, finding that it would have produced a younger population but lower average per capita income. Using this model to project various alternatives for the future, Denton *et al.* (1989: 52) conclude: "perhaps the most basic point to note is that projected economic growth over the next few decades is relatively insensitive to alternatives in basic demographic assumptions . . . differences associated with alternative demographic assumptions are not negligible, but neither are they especially large." They find that growth of the economy is slower as population ages, and that growth slows down further once the labour force begins to decline. However, all the future scenarios involve increases both in total and in per capita income. In their model, an older and more experienced labour force results in higher labour productivity. Total economic growth is greater when fertility or immigration is higher; however, on a per capita basis, average incomes are lower with higher population growth (see also Review of Demography, 1989: 10-11).

In another study, Lapierre-Adamcyk *et al.* (1988) considered the contribution of socio-demographic factors to explanations of variation in productivity in Canada between 1955 and 1985. A total of fourteen parameters were estimated, of which three demographic ones were not significant: years of experience of the labour force, per cent of net immigrants per year, and level of fertility. The one demographic variable that was significant was a measure of the level of education weighted by the age-sex structure. Compared to 1955, the 1985 labour force was better educated (especially at younger ages), younger, and had a higher proportion of women. These are important qualitative changes. The results are interpreted to mean that a more educated labour force costs less in terms of productivity outcomes. Similarly, a younger labour force costs less, because workers accept lower salaries, and women cost less for a unit of productivity since they are paid less and are more likely to be working part-time. Therefore, the demographic factors that would have permitted productivity gains over the period 1955-85 would have involved a more educated, younger, and less male-dominant labour force.

These results contrast considerably with those from Denton and Spencer. A large part of the economic advantages they project for the future population of Canada results from the assumption that an older and more experienced labour force involves higher labour productivity (Denton and Spencer, 1988a). In contrast, Lapierre-Adamcyk *et al.* find that the level of experience is not significant, while a younger labour force reduces the costs of labour. It is difficult to distinguish the various factors at work: a younger labour force is probably more educated while an older one is more experienced. The problem is that salaries may not properly reflect productivity, especially if seniority is highly rewarded and younger persons, as well as women, are forced to accept lower wages. That is, as Denton and Spencer (1987a) had noted earlier, wage profiles may not properly represent relative productivity. Due to seniority arrangements, including the dominant role of older people in institutions, wage profiles may underestimate the productivity characteristics of relatively recent labour force entrants, including women, while overestimating those of older workers. This is central, because it could bring into question the optimism of the Denton and Spencer results. If they have exaggerated the productivity profile of older workers, then the advantage of an older labour force has also been exaggerated, bringing into question the advantages of slower growth in terms of per capita outcomes. In any case, the average output per worker, or productivity, is mostly a function of the quality of human capital and the technology at its disposal, thus the purely demographic factors of size and age of the labour force play a comparatively smaller role (Preston, 1987). For instance, Owen (1986) concludes that labour availability and supply will have a neutral influence because there will be fewer young workers but more experienced workers.

Other studies for the Review of Demography estimated econometric models of the Canadian economy under alternative demographic assumptions. Fortin and Fortin (1987) have tested the economic effect of changing from 1 per cent annual growth to 1 per cent decline per year. In their first estimation, the average consumption per worker is increased 13 per cent by the long-term equilibrium tendencies of this change. The advantage of population decline is that there is less need for "demographic investments," that is, less entry into the labour force and therefore less need for new investments to accommodate the new workers. This results in a better equipped labour force that can realize higher productivity. Fortin and Fortin then introduce three "corrections" to this first estimation. These corrections basically result from the fact that a declining population will necessarily be older. In the first correction, the higher proportion of older dependants among adults reduces the per capita benefit associated with the declining population from 13 to 2.6 per cent per capita. In the second correction the greater public costs of an older population change the 2.6 per cent per capita advantage to a 1.0 per cent per capita disadvantage. The third correction takes into account the reduction of net available savings that results from a lower proportion of young families in the population, which changes the net disadvantage of the declining population to 1.5 per cent per capita.

Fortin and Fortin conclude that a reduction in the standard of living, although small, could result from a demographic decline in the order of 1 per cent per year. They are cautious about the result, noting that a number of things have been left out, for instance the link of productivity and age, as well as the effect of the age structure on taxes, transfers, and entry and exit from the labour force. Some of these seem rather crucial and could bring into question the advantage of a declining population in terms of reducing the need for demographic investments. Others have argued that a younger and growing labour force involves net economic advantages. Foot (1987) points out that the young are the most flexible part of the labour force, an adaptable resource, the "new blood" with up-to-date market skills. Denton and Spencer (1987a) indicate that young labour force entrants not only add to the size of the labour force but are in large measure the vehicle for bringing in new skills and enhancing average levels of education and training. They suggest that the contribution of the young to human capital is larger than their numbers imply. The Fortin and Fortin estimates also ignore the needs for re-training that may be stronger with an older labour force.

In some subsequent work, Fortin (1989a) notes that another advantage of lower growth is a reduction in youth unemployment. He also finds that sustained below-replacement fertility, along with annual immigration of 200,000 per year, has relatively little impact on the overall level of consumption over a fifty-year period. Depending on the assumptions, the impact could range from positive 3.5 per cent per capita to negative 6.0 per cent per capita. It is concluded that below-replacement fertility is clearly not an "economic tragedy." In another summary, Fortin (1989b) emphasizes that the demographic decline will release a substantial amount of real resources by reducing the "demographic" investments required each year to equip the new workers, and he also proposes that the net impact of declining population growth on economic welfare will, if anything, be slightly favourable over the next twenty-five years.

Differences between short- and longer-term results are not well addressed by these studies. In the short term, fewer births can have a positive impact by reducing the numbers of consumers relative to producers. It is only in the longer term that lower births could have negative consequences through reduced numbers of producers. That is, the shorter time horizon picks up the costs of children but not the benefits, which can only come after these have entered the labour force.

In reviewing economic studies relating to population growth, Lapierre-Adamcyk (1986) observes that these take a relatively favourable view of the economic impact of slower population growth, but they rarely look at the consequences of population decline. The studies do not take adequate account of the adjustment costs of population decline, for instance, closing schools, busing children, and re-training teachers. Little attention is paid to the "barriers to adjustment," ranging from psychological resistance to institutional rigidity. The studies also do not tell us if reduced population size permits the maintenance and improvement of collective goods, ranging from roads to cultural institutions. They also do not address the impact of population decline on specific parts of the country. In effect, these questions from

Lapierre-Adamcyk have not been answered by the studies for the Review of Demography.

One area of agreement relates to economies of scale. The Demographic Policy Secretariat (1976) had concluded that significant economies of scale are unlikely to result from population growth alone. Marr (1987) suggests that looking at other countries for markets and supplies would be more profitable than attempting to develop economies of scale within the country. The Macdonald Commission also argued for free trade as a means of accommodating the restricted domestic market (Royal Commission on the Economic Union, 1985). Fortin (1989a) observes that differences in demand resulting from population growth are not related to average economic welfare among countries of the Organization for Economic Co-operation and Development (see also Review of Demography, 1989: 9).

Environmental impacts

Environmental perspectives on population growth pay attention to the impact on the viability of the ecosystem. Some of the early warnings concerning resource depletion have proved to be unfounded as the market and new technologies found substitutes. There is also the danger of attributing to population growth effects that relate to the level of consumption rather than the size of the population *per se*. However, there is no doubt but that broad ecological questions must be considered.

In attempting to reconcile economic and ecological thinking on population, Keyfitz (1989b) suggests that we should see the economy within the ecology. The economy influences the ecology and is limited by the ecology. For instance, in the calculation of gross national product, the depreciation of plant and equipment are netted out, but the depreciation of nature is not calculated as part of the equation. Yet the environment can stand only so much of the waste products of the economy. The Science Council of Canada (1988) also proposes the integration of environmental and economic decision-making. The Conservation Council of Ontario (1986) suggests a shift from an economically and technologically driven process to one that gives more attention to social and environmental considerations.

The Brundtland Commission argued for sustainable development, defined as development that meets present needs without compromising the ability of future generations to meet their needs (World Commission on Environment and Development, 1987). Relating specifically to population, this Commission noted that when a population exceeds the carrying capacity of the available resources, size can become a liability in efforts to improve average welfare. However, Brundtland continues, people are also a creative resource, which is an asset that societies must tap.

Therein lies the dilemma of conclusions based on environmental questions. Lesthaeghe (1989) argues that a declining population would have less possibility of investing in environmentally less damaging technology. Much of the costs to the environment stem from styles of consumption rather than population size itself.

Barrett *et al*. (1987) have proposed that the rate of population growth and of ecosystem degradation are now closely linked in Canada. For instance, forests are not replenished as quickly as they are removed. If this is related to population growth, then the future will see serious deterioration of available forests (see Review of Demography, 1989: 13). However, this does not necessarily follow. While unlikely in the context of the corporate focus on short-term profit, more people could theoretically plant more trees.

When it comes to wastes, however, there is no denying that size of the population plays a role. One can reduce the wastes per person and the ecological effects of wastes, but the number of people will continue to be part of the equation (Regier *et al*., 1973).

Energy consumption and its impact is another serious consideration. For the period 1960-85, Demeny (1988b) has calculated that 60 per cent of the increase in energy use in the United States was due to population growth. Once again, there is no necessary relation here, because larger populations could use less energy. However, this has not been happening in the developed countries. If energy use affects climatic change, then the demographic impacts are particularly relevant to the sustained human habitation of the planet (Dotto, 1988). Smil (1990) projects that, even with lower per capita use of fossil fuels in the more developed countries, the high rates of population growth in the less developed countries, along with expected increases from their low levels of per capita consumption, will involve continued global increases in carbon dioxide generation.

Observing that the average Canadian consumes ten to fifteen times more raw materials than the average world citizen, Environment Canada (1984: 8) suggests that the pursuit of unlimited economic growth has social and environmental consequences that could severely diminish the future quality of life. Nonetheless, Simon (1990) argues that larger numbers of highly trained workers would mean more inventions, including those involving resource substitution and energy sources with less negative environmental impacts. Important values are at stake in addressing these questions, including the relative value placed on the future, confidence in scientific progress, and perceptions of the appropriate relationship between people and nature.

Socio-political impacts

While economists tend to conclude that the effects of slower to negative population growth are not serious and ecologists would prefer to have smaller populations, persons who take a political stance often argue for larger populations. For instance, Legoff (1989) notes that the link between population size and political-military power is only partly attenuated by economic development: there are no powerful countries that are not also large in population. In *Below-Replacement Fertility in Industrial Societies*, several authors comment on the reduced relative size of the developed countries compared to the Third World. Bourgeois-Pichat (1986) speaks of "population implosion," Davis (1986) of a "demographic vacuum," and McNicoll (1986) of "international demographic marginalization." Wattenberg (1987) argues that the "birth dearth" spells the downfall of the "modern, industrial, free and western countries" (United States, Canada, Western Europe, Iceland, Israel, Australia, New Zealand, and Japan). In 1950 these countries comprised 22 per cent of the world population, compared to 15 per cent in the mid-1980s, 9 per cent in 2025, and 5 per cent at the end of the twenty-first century, according to the United Nations medium projections. Wattenberg is concerned not only about economic consequences but geopolitical ones: erosion of military, economic, political, and cultural influence. This may even include the lower potential for these countries to transfer capital to the less developed countries.

There is also a widespread perception in France that a disadvantage in terms of relative growth has had a long-term impact (Calot, 1990a). Two centuries ago France was more than three times the size of England and Wales; now it is about the same size. France was the first country to embark on the demographic transition. The slight fertility deficit compared to its relevant neighbours has had much impact on the relative status of France in Europe and in the world. While England managed to grow and populate other continents, ensuring its place in a colonial and post-colonial world, France hardly maintained its own. As another example, in 1950 Europe including the U.S.S.R. was twice the size of Africa; by the year 2000 they will be about the same size (United Nations, 1989a). Summarizing an OECD conference, Cliquet (1986: 40) notes that "it is feared that the decreasing demographic weight of the developed world will induce a decrease in political and cultural influence and a decline in economic competitiveness," and at the same time there will be an extraordinarily large surplus in the supply of labour from less developed countries.

It can also be argued that the century of high fertility in Quebec was a demographic investment that ensured the survival of the French society of the province (Caldwell and Fournier, 1987). The relative size of Quebec is often a point of discussion in questions relating to its viability as a "distinct society," let alone the potential for an independent status.

Teitelbaum and Winter (1985) have noted that this type of socio-political argument is based on the assumption that a smaller relative size would undermine the relative status of one's group. The argument may be seen as ethnocentric since it involves a fear that one's group will not be as strong in the future relative to others.

LABOUR FORCE GROWTH AND DECLINE

The previous section has considered the overall consequences of population growth. We will now focus on the labour force in particular. The labour force is defined as persons who are either employed or actively seeking employment (unemployed). There is a strong link between population and labour force since some 75 per cent of the change in the size of the labour force has followed demographic trends in terms of the size of the relevant age groups. As has already become evident, the labour force is also linked with economic growth since labour force growth is important to the potential growth of economic activity – the capacity to produce goods and services. We will consider the size of the labour force, its age structure, and the possible consequences of changing patterns.

Change in size

The labour force has grown rapidly in the post-war era, with a peak growth in the period 1971-76 of some 3 per cent per year. This has followed the entry of the baby boom generation into the labour force and the higher participation of women. This rate of growth was unmatched by any other Western industrialized economy (Foot, 1987). The rate of growth has since declined, to 1.6 per cent per year in the period 1981-86 (Denton and Spencer, 1987b; Denton *et al.*, 1989).

Denton *et al.* (1989) have projected the future labour force growth assuming that the recent changes in participation rates would continue, that is, increasing participation for women. Under their "standard assumption" of fertility at 1.67 and immigration at 125,000 per year, the labour force continues to grow to 2011, but at a lower rate. The total growth between 1986 and 2011 is only 21 per cent, compared to 196 per cent for the twenty-five year-period 1961-86. The decline between 2011 and 2036 amounts to 10 per cent, or most of the gain of the previous twenty years. In absolute numbers, the labour force would have declined by some 1.6 million workers. A higher level of immigration, at 200,000 per year, changes the overall patterns. The 1986-2011 growth is 30 per cent and the overall size of the labour force remains stable for the next twenty years.

Figure 16 shows how rapidly the population aged 20-64 has been growing, as the baby boomers have moved into these ages. In the ten-

Figure 16: Growth of Population Aged 20-64, 1956-2036

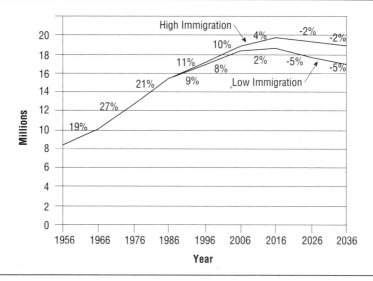

NOTE: Projections based on fertility of 1.67 and immigration of 140,000 (low) and 200,000 (high).
SOURCES: 1986 Census 93-101; Statistics Canada, 1990a.

year period 1966-76, the population of these ages grew by more than a quarter and again by 21 per cent between 1976 and 1986. While the growth of the total population has been slowing down since 1951-56, the growth of the population at labour force ages has largely continued to 1986. The future will show much less growth: about 8 to 10 per cent in the ten years around the turn of the century and becoming a decline after 2011 or 2016, depending on the level of immigration. This is a fairly secure projection because the population of these ages is not affected by the level of fertility for at least twenty years.

In effect, the slower economic growth that Denton *et al.* (1989) project for the period 2011-2035 is largely due to labour force decline. In comparing a stationary and a declining population, the most serious disadvantage that Ryder (1985) attributes to a declining population is the lower level of labour force entry. The rate of entry is some 25 per cent higher under a stationary population than under one that is declining. He sees entry into the working-age population as an indicator of the flexibility of the labour force. Low rates of entry are therefore a serious impediment in a rapidly changing environment. The renewal of the labour force means new ideas and creativity, a greater potential for research and development. In the shorter term, Seward (1987a) expects that the slower rate of labour force growth could be offset by the potential productivity gains associated with the presence of the baby boom generation. Adjustment may also be facilitated by the further entry of women. However, eventually the baby boom will be beyond the ages of greatest productivity, and the absorption of women into the labour force is a "once only" phenomenon that will necessarily come to an end.

The rapid growth of the labour force has resulted in a high proportion of the total population in the labour force. The concept of "economic dependency" takes the population not in the labour force divided by the population in the labour force (Wolfson, 1990). In 1961 there were 178.2 people not in the labour force for every 100 people in the labour force, compared to 97.0 in 1986. According to the projections by Denton *et al.* (1989), under the standard assumptions this ratio would decrease further to 89.4 in 2011, then increase to 114.9 persons not in the labour force per 100 people in the labour force by 2036. The fact that a higher proportion of the total population is in the labour force, or that there are fewer dependants per member of the labour force, plays an important role in the growth of per capita income projected by Denton and Spencer (1988a). This also holds for the period 1974-81, when the favourable change in the employment-to-population ratio was the dominant factor in growth in real income per capita (Royal Commission on the Economic Union, 1985, II: 10).

Labour force aging

While the population as a whole has been aging for some time, the population of labour force ages has in fact been getting younger on average. The average age of the population aged 20-64 declined from thirty-eight in 1971 to thirty-seven in 1986. However, the future will be rather different, showing an increase to forty-one years at the turn of the century and forty-three years in 2036.

It is also useful to compare the numbers of younger and older people through the relative size of the populations aged 25-44 and 45-64. Until the late 1980s the age group 25-44 had been growing faster than that aged 45-64, but after 1991 the opposite will occur. In 1986 there were 168 people aged 20-44 for every 100 aged 45-64. By the turn of the century, there will be 126 people aged 25-44 per 100 aged 45-64, and by 2011 there will be less people aged 25-44 than those aged 45-64 (Figure 17).

Considering the labour force itself, the 25-44 age group represented 48 per cent of the total in 1955 compared to 53 per cent in 1985 (Lapierre-Adamcyk *et al.*, 1988). By 2001 the 25-44 age group would represent 51 per cent of the labour force, and in 2011 it would be 45 per cent (Denton *et al.*, 1989). After 1996, the labour force aged 25-44 will in fact decline in absolute numbers, and by 2011 it will have been reduced by 655,000 persons, or 9 per cent of its 1996 size.

Some of the implications of an aging labour force have already been

Figure 17: Population Aged 25-44 per 100 Population Aged 45-64, 1971-2036

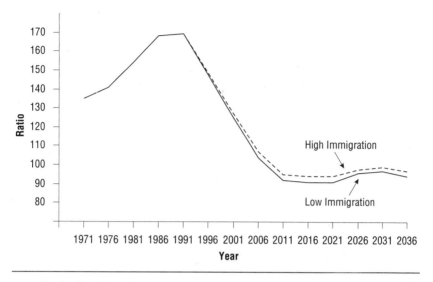

NOTE: Projections based on fertility of 1.67 and immigration of 140,000 (low) and 200,000 (high).
SOURCES: 1986 Census 93-101; Statistics Canada, 1990a.

discussed in the section on the economic impact of lower population growth. An older labour force would normally imply less recently acquired educational skills and more work experience. As we have seen, some authors imply that an older labour force is more productive (Denton and Spencer, 1988a) or reduces the "demographic overhead" associated with labour force entry (Fortin, 1989a). Given that the baby boom generation is well educated, Denton and Spencer (1987a: 10) suggest that "age-related productivity gains may act as an offset to the reduction in numbers associated with slower labour force growth." In terms of unemployment, older workers are less subject to short-term or frictional unemployment but more subject to longer-term or structural unemployment (Simpson, 1986). On the whole, the level of unemployment would be lower with an older labour force.

On the other hand, besides being more recently trained, younger workers are more flexible in terms of accommodating the need for geographic, occupational, and industrial mobility, while an older labour force can introduce obsolescence (Marr, 1987; Seward, 1987c). Foot (1987: 8) suggests that "young people ... possess up to date labour market skill, ... do not have a work history tying them to any particular organization or occupation, and can be deployed in a most efficient manner without disruptive costs to both employer and employee." Simpson (1986) suggests that as the end of working life approaches, there is less incentive to invest in one's human capital: further education, job changes, and migration become less attractive. It is interesting that labour force participation, the probability of working full time, and geographic mobility all rise to ages twenty-five to thirty. Denton and Spencer (1987a) agree that the young represent the vehicle for bringing in new skills and enhancing average levels of education and training, they are also more mobile, being less tied down by personal responsibilities, and therefore a growing labour force is likely to be more adaptable. Ryder (1985) has also expressed strong reservations about lower entries into the labour force from the bottom: "this . . . is probably the most striking and disconcerting contrast between a growing and a declining population." He goes on to say that "the work force of the future . . . will have characteristics which, under current arrangements, would prejudice productivity, vitality and flexibility, . . . we will lose a large part of the capacity to transform the economy through the vehicle of new entrants to the labour force." The problem, as Ryder sees it, is less a function of age *per se* than of recency of training. Older workers have training that dates back to an earlier time and are consequently more out of date, given the rapid growth of knowledge. An important form of adaptation is therefore to spread education over the life span rather than have it concentrated at the beginning.

Another implication that has been noted regarding the aging of the labour force relates to "crowding" and the difficulty of promotion. In France, relative cohort size does not relate strongly to unemployment rates or relative earnings (Riboud, 1988). However, this is different in Canada, given the large size of the baby boom generation. Dooley (1986) finds that cohort size has a negative effect on earnings. Fortin and Fortin (1986) estimate that the baby boom increased youth unemployment by some three percentage points over the period 1956-76 and the baby bust would reduce this unemployment by some four percentage points over 1976-90. Fortin (1989a) finds that the baby boom is not doing too badly at ages 25-34, but he expresses concern about the potential for their structural unemployment when they are aged 45-64. Denton and Spencer (1982, 1987a) find that promotion prospects are positively related to the rate of population growth and negatively related to population aging. The average age at reaching the middle rank declined by about two years in the period 1966-76 but would increase by four years over 1986-2001. In hierarchical organizational structures, this can result in "plateauing" rather than promotion, given the relative size of the older members of the labour force who "block" the mobility prospects of the younger persons (Foot and

Verne, 1990). However, it may be that the effects of cohort size are stronger in the early part of a cohort's career, diminishing over time (Murphy *et al.*, 1988).

One of the issues here regards the relative substitutability of younger and older workers. If the reduced numbers of younger workers can be substituted by older workers, then the problems are less serious. However, there may be limited possibilities for this kind of substitution. Fortin and Fortin (1986) suggest that the young and the old are not very interchangeable in the technical and social organization of economic production. The structural unemployment, with long durations, of older workers also suggests lack of substitutability. In addition, older persons do not comprise a large proportion of persons working part-time, which is another characteristic of younger workers (Wigdor and Foot, 1988: 23).

The high rates of entry into the labour force in the 1960s and 1970s will therefore contrast with an aging labour force of the 1990s and beyond. While the baby boom was moving into the labour force, there needed to be much concern about youth unemployment. While youth unemployment is still high, it has declined relative to the total. In 1975 the unemployment rate at ages 15-25 represented 74 per cent more than the average, but in 1988 it represented 58 per cent more than the average (Foot and Li, 1986). In contrast, at ages 25-34, unemployment in 1975 was 12 per cent below the average and in 1988 it was 3 per cent above the average. The Macdonald Commission noted:

> youth unemployment is a current problem which is expected gradually to disappear. An issue of potential concern for the medium to long term, however, is the prospects for the current generation of youth. Will this group become the unemployed adults of the future? . . . It would be unfortunate to have in place a range of special programs for youth at a time when the groups facing the greatest labour-market difficulties were the 25-to 34-or the 35-to 44-year-olds. (Royal Commission on the Economic Union, 1985, II: 599-600)

The labour force challenges associated with the middle-aging of the baby boom include management styles and practices as well as organization structures that involve less hierarchy (Foot, 1987).

POLICY OPTIONS

Leaving policy issues related to the labour force to Chapter 9, this section will only address issues of population growth itself. As Teitelbaum and Winter (1985) have clearly specified, there are two basic alternatives – either to try to change the population dynamics or to adapt to a changing population.

Chapter 1 noted that three things are needed to justify a direct population policy. There needs to be a sense that the population dynamics are at variance with what would produce the maximum human welfare. Second, there needs to be a sense that the problem will not resolve itself automatically. Third, the problem must be seen to be capable of remedy, at a cost lower than the cost of the problem itself. As with most hard policy questions, many things are involved and the answers are neither obvious nor easy.

Regarding the first issue, the main trends are that the rate of growth of the population and the labour force will decline, and there will be aging of the population and the labour force, and a growing proportion of elderly. The extent to which these are seen as problematic depends in part on whether one gives priority to economic, labour force, environmental, or socio-political questions.

From the discussions of Chapter 3, we can see there is more agreement regarding the second question, that the problem will not resolve itself automatically. Of course, the problem of lack of growth could be resolved by simply opening the borders to immigration, but many would not see this as a successful resolution.

On the third issue, that of costs, all alternatives have considerable costs. The alternative of adapting to a changing population has various adjustment costs: closing schools and retraining teachers; training and mobility assistance; education that is more spread out over the life cycle; equal pay legislation as well as social services such as child care (Seward, 1987a). In Chapter 7 we will note the costs of a larger elderly population, which can be accommodated through either reducing their social security benefits or increasing the taxes on workers. In the United States, this adaptation has taken the forms of anticipating a reduction in retirement benefits, an increase in taxes, and an increased age at eligibility to pensions (Teitelbaum and Winter, 1985: 118).

Chapter 3 has referred to the costs of attempting to support fertility. Teitelbaum and Winter (1985) have observed that Eastern European countries have been more prone to intervene in the support of fertility. They experienced below-replacement fertility sooner, there was no post-war baby boom, and female involvement in the labour force has been more extensive. As well, there was more acceptance of social planning as part of the activities of the state, structures were in place to achieve this planning, and immigration was not available as a solution. In Western Europe, fertility declined later, there is less of a tradition of state intervention in family matters and a wider recognition that pluralism rather than conformity was to be supported, and the higher standards of living mean that the costs of providing incentives would be higher.

Immigration presents a number of advantages, as has been noted in Chapter 4, but if it is seen as a substitute for births then there will be strong changes in the composition of the population, and the integration of multiethnic groups in the large cities will involve costs (Lesthaeghe *et al.*, 1988; Andorka, 1989). Teitelbaum and Winter (1985: 150) comment:

> Immigration as a means of retarding population decline has its own unique limitations, . . . it unavoidably leads to rapid changes in the cultural, racial, linguistic or ethnic composition of the national population. Such dramatic changes in composition appear almost always to generate widespread and often passionate opposition, based on collective fears that may well be more powerful than the fear of population decline. . . . It seems doubtful therefore whether large-scale immigration can ever serve as a politically viable response to declining population over a considerable period of years, unless the immigrant streams are considered similar in character to the receiving population.

It could be argued that one needs to work at all fronts. Adapting to a changing population is necessary in any case because aging is inevitable and slower growth is almost inevitable. These questions will be further discussed in Chapter 7. At the same time, growth could be somewhat sustained, or at least decline could be avoided, through supporting both immigration and fertility (Hohn, 1987; Lesthaeghe *et al.*, 1988: 22; Andorka, 1989).

Putting this in the context of past population policy in Canada, Marr (1987) observes that the general orientation of the period 1850-1930, as well as the 1950s to the early 1960s, was to promote growth through immigration. At other times, the policy orientation has been less clear. In *Toward a Demographic Policy for Canada*, the Demographic Policy Secretariat (1976: 25) noted that "the government of Canada has no interest in influencing the fertility rate." The 1974 Green Paper on immigration was rather ambivalent regarding the role of immigration and did not speak to the broader issue of a population policy. As noted in Chapter 4, the 1976 Immigration Act did specifically allow the government to take into account demographic questions in the determination of immigration levels. In *Charting Canada's Future*, the Review of Demography (1989) takes a rather neutral stance – if anything, it suggests that there is no crisis, that much of the change is inevitable, and policy intervention is not considered. Sharir (1990) says that since demographic change is slow, the economy and society will have enough time to adjust in a rather gradual and smooth manner.

As we have seen, in the 1970s and 1980s there was a need to accommodate the baby boom's entry into the labour force, and there was little need to further expand the labour force. While fertility has been below replacement since the early 1970s, the baby boom generation has ensured that actual births increased between 1973 and 1984. Issues of aging and population decline have arrived at a later time than in Western Europe. In Quebec the issue of sustaining population growth, and births in particular, has reached the political agenda. This is partly because the fertility has in fact been lower and immigration has not been as strong, making population decline more imminent. For instance, the Commission de la Culture (1985) concluded that in order to preserve the viability of Quebec as a distinct society there is need to work on three fronts: raise immigration, retain more of its population, and sustain births. As we have seen, a number of policies favouring fertility have been instituted, including higher tax deductions for children, higher family allowances, longer parental leaves, more day-care spaces, and baby bonuses based on family size.

Hawkins (1985) has noted that there was momentum in the mid-1970s to establish demographic policy for Canada. A Demographic Policy Steering Group of fourteen deputy ministers was established, as well as a secretariat. However, the idea received a "cool reception by the provinces" and the federal government never produced its own policy statement on population. In order to bring this issue back to the agenda, Hawkins suggests the establishment of a separate department responsible for immigration, population, citizenship, and multiculturalism, as well as a standing committee of Parliament and a task force to report on the field of immigration and population policy.

Ryder (1985, 1990) has argued for the benefits of a stationary population. He notes that a declining population presents certain disadvantages, especially in terms of renewal and flexibility of the labour force. He suggests as a primary aim in fertility the achievement of an unchanging birth cohort size, because the country has "paid a heavy price for irregular growth." However, he does not see much prospect for affecting births and thus suggests a level of immigration that would compensate for the below-replacement fertility. With a fertility of 1.8 births per women, this would require an immigration of some 175,000 persons per year (assuming 60,000 emigration). This would make the net immigration at about 25 per cent of the annual numbers of births. The proportion of foreign-born would stabilize at about 19 per cent, which is not outside of the historical experience. He suggests that levels of immigration necessary to achieve even 0.5 per cent growth per year would involve numbers, proportions of foreign-born, and immigrants per 100 births outside of the historical experience, which would imply "an unprecedented transformation of the social fabric." In effect, Ryder

(1985) makes a case for a stationary population, which would level out at some 38 million people, rather than a declining or continuously growing population. A declining population would be older and would have more dependants per worker. He also suggests other forms of adaptation, in particular the need to change the placement of education and work in the life cycle. Cliquet (1986) arrives at a similar conclusion for Western Europe: "the safest population growth model is the stationary model ... [it is] an optimum strategy for maximizing risk reductions."

While the debate certainly needs to go on, it could be proposed that Canada needs to think of a set of policies that would achieve these kinds of objectives. The fact the population changes are slow means that there is time to adjust. However, the inertia of demographic momentum means that adjustments may become more difficult at a later stage. Certainly, there is a need to adapt to an aging and slower growing population. This includes rationalized policies for education, labour, health, and pensions and social security. A case has already been made for an immigration level of some 150,000 to 250,000 per year – the mid-point of this range may be best, with a balance of independent, family, and refugee admissions. Fertility could also be encouraged, to prevent further decline or possibly to increase the rate to a level closer to 2.0. This would require a greater recognition of parenthood and childbearing as important social goals, with the corresponding policy supports, including easing of the pressure on parents arising from playing the dual roles of parents and workers.

7

POPULATION AGING

One of the key features of the changing population of Canada, resulting in effect from the long-term changes in birth and death rates, is the
transformation of the age distribution. Given their central importance,
questions of aging are discussed in several chapters. After describing
the trends in aging, this chapter will analyse ramifications on the demographic setting, the economy, and the society. The policy issues associated with aging are numerous, but the focus here will be on pensions,
health care, and support of the aged.

TRENDS AND CAUSES OF AGING

The age profile of a population can mostly be described in terms of the
population pyramid, the median age, and the proportion over age
sixty-five. In a stable demographic setting, age distributions will take

one of two forms. Under high fertility, the distribution looks like a pyramid with a wide base and an even slope to higher ages. Under stable low fertility, the distribution looks more like a vase, with very slight declines over ages until the top, where the declines are pronounced. Until about 1961, Canada's age profile looked like a pyramid and by 2036 it may well have the appearance of a vase (see Figure 18). In the interim, the shape is rather irregular, following the changing size of birth cohorts and their movement up the age profile.

Figure 19 shows how much change is occurring in the age distribution, even over a short period such as 1981 to 1988. The age structure looks somewhat like an oriental jar, narrower at the top and bottom. The relative stability in total births is visible as a rather even base, below age fifteen. In 1988, the baby boom bulge is aged about twenty-three to forty-three. The shape will gradually evolve to the one shown in Figure 18 for 2036. All persons born after 1990 are here aged under forty-five years. The baby boom will then be aged sixty-five to eighty-five, where many will have died, especially the men.

The age structure can also be described in terms of the median age and the proportion over sixty-five years of age (Table 6). The median age has increased from seventeen in 1851 and twenty-six in 1971 to thirty-two years in 1986, with projections implying a median age of some forty-five years by 2036. The proportion over sixty-five increased from 2.7 per cent in 1851 to 10.6 in 1986 with a projection of 25 per cent by 2036. These numbers imply that aging of the population is a gradual and long-term phenomenon. The period of the baby boom involved a departure from the long-term trends: the average age was younger in 1961 than 1951. Nonetheless, the speed of aging is increasing. Over the period 1946-76, the proportion over sixty-five increased by 1.6 percentage points, but between 1976 and 1986 it increased almost two percentage points. In their report on Canada's Seniors for the 1986 census, Stone and Frenken (1988) speak of the "quickening pace of the aging of Canada's population." In the period 1981-86, the population aged sixty-five and over grew at a rate three times the growth rate of the total population. The eldest of the elderly, aged eighty and over, increased four times as fast as the entire population. Stone and Frenken (1988: 35) refer to a "veritable population explosion among seniors of more advanced age" that will not end soon.

At the other end of the age profile, the number of children under five declined by 20 per cent over the period 1961-86, while the total population increased by 39 per cent. The youth population, defined as ages 15-24, declined by half a million, or some 10 per cent, between 1981 and 1986, while the whole population increased by one million (Ross, 1989).

Population aging is at a more advanced stage in Europe, where Chesnais (1989) speaks of an "inversion of the age pyramid." The proportion

Figure 18: Population Pyramids for 1961 and 2036

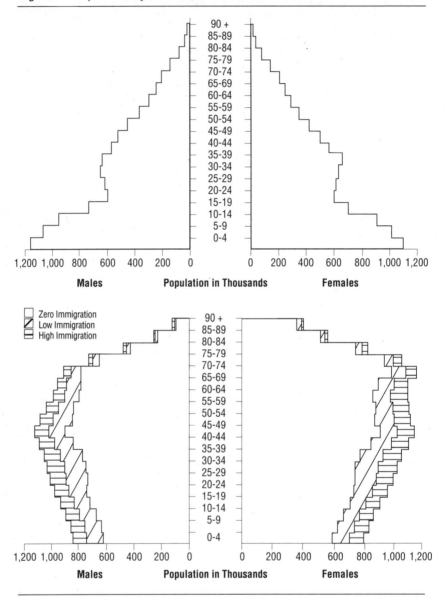

NOTE: Projections based on fertility of 1.67, immigration of 200,000 (high), 140,000 (low), and zero persons per year, and emigration of 0.25, 0.25, and 0.0 persons per 100 population per year.
SOURCES: 1961 Census Bulletin 1.2-2; Statistics Canada, 1989d.

Figure 19: Age Pyramid of the Population of Canada, 1981 and 1988

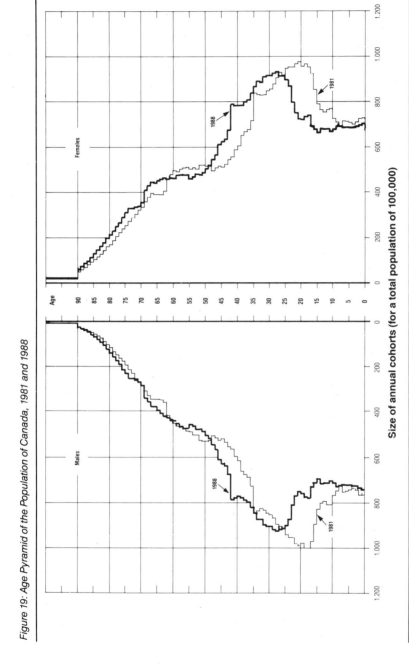

Size of annual cohorts (for a total population of 100,000)

SOURCE: Statistics Canada, Cat. No. 91-210, 1990: 12.

Table 6: Median Age and Proportion of the Population 0-14 and 65 and Over,
Canada, 1851-2036

Year	Median Age		Proportion 0-14		Proportion 65 +	
1851	17.2		44.9		2.7	
1861	18.2		42.5		3.0	
1871	18.8		41.6		3.7	
1881	20.1		38.7		4.1	
1891	21.4		36.3		4.6	
1901	22.7		34.4		5.0	
1911	23.8		32.9		4.7	
1921	24.0		34.4		4.8	
1931	24.8		31.6		5.6	
1941	27.1		27.8		6.7	
1951	27.7		30.3		7.8	
1956	27.2		32.5		7.7	
1961	26.3		34.0		7.6	
1966	25.5		32.9		7.7	
1971	26.2		29.6		8.1	
1976	28.1		25.6		8.7	
1981	29.6		22.5		9.7	
1986	31.6		21.3		10.6	
	High	Low	High	Low	High	Low
1991	33.5	33.6	20.7	20.7	11.8	11.8
1996	35.5	35.6	19.8	19.8	12.8	12.8
2001	37.5	37.7	18.6	18.6	13.5	13.7
2006	39.2	39.6	17.4	17.3	14.2	14.4
2011	40.6	41.1	16.6	16.3	15.5	15.8
2016	41.6	42.3	16.2	15.9	17.6	18.1
2021	42.6	44.0	15.9	15.6	19.8	20.4
2026	43.4	44.2	15.6	15.3	22.0	22.9
2031	44.2	45.0	15.2	14.9	23.8	24.9
2036	44.8	45.7	14.9	14.5	24.5	25.7

NOTE: Projections use total fertility rate of 1.67 and immigration of 200,000 (high)
and 140,000 (low).

SOURCES: Foot, 1982: 9; Pryor, 1984: 1; 1986 Census, 93-101; Statistics Canada,
1990a.

over sixty-five is almost 18 per cent in Sweden, a figure that Canada
would not see until about 2016 (Review of Demography, 1989: 21-22).
Nonetheless, the Canadian change is now as rapid as that of European
countries, and it will be more rapid once the larger baby boom generations move into retirement ages. While just over one in ten people was
over sixty-five in 1986, some fifty years later constant fertility would
imply almost a quarter of the population at these ages. This, along with
an average age of some forty-five years, and more than 10 per cent of the
population aged seventy-five and over, will make for a rather different
demographic profile.

The causes of population aging, as with any demographic change, inevitably involve fertility, mortality, and migration. A population that did not have any births, deaths, or migrants would age systematically by one year at a time. That is one easy thing about studying age – everyone ages at the same rate. From this perspective, Preston *et al.* (1989) speak of a "natural tendency to age." The impact of vital events and migration will depend on the age at which they occur. Because they all occur at the same age, which is at the bottom of the population distribution, births clearly counter population aging. A reduction in births therefore makes for more aging because there are fewer entries at the bottom of the age structure (see Review of Demography, 1989: 20). The impact of deaths will depend on when they typically occur. Since they are usually spread out over ages, deaths have much less impact on the age structure. A reduction in deaths that especially benefits the younger people will reduce the average age, while one that benefits the older will increase the aging. Migrants are also spread out in ages, and consequently have less impact. In a population that is closed to migration, once a set of vital rates (births and deaths) has been in place for some two generations the age structure will become fixed, reflecting these underlying rates.

The mortality decline that occurred over the period until about 1971 especially benefited the young and therefore had a slight tendency to reduce the average age. Now that there is less room for declines in mortality at younger ages, the decline is more concentrated at older ages, which therefore has a slight tendency to increase the relative weight of the top of the pyramid. International migration is concentrated at young adult ages, and it therefore tends to increase the relative size of this part of the distribution. Clearly, it is especially births, and their change over time, that have influenced the basic shape of Canada's age profile.

Grisgsby (1988) has shown that in a typical demographic transition from high to low vital rates, the effect of mortality is dominant in the first stage. The spectacular decline of infant mortality especially *reduces* the average age. After some fifty-five years, which in Canada would be about 1925, the effect of fertility decline begins to dominate. After 120 years, 25 per cent of population aging would be due to mortality and 75 per cent due to fertility. For Canada, 120 years of demographic transition would bring us to about 1990.

From this perspective, one could consider three stages of population aging. In the first stage, which is only of historical interest, the aging was slow because fertility reduction was compensated by mortality reductions at young ages. In the second stage, which lasted until about 1971, the population was aging mostly as a function of the decline in fertility. In the third stage, which has probably just begun, the aging is

Table 7: Effect of Alternative Fertility and Mortality Assumptions on Aging

	1986	Projections for 2036			
		A	B	C	D
Total fertility rate	1.67	1.67	1.67	1.40	1.40
Life expectancy	76.4	80.9	84.3	80.9	84.3
Percent 65+	10.6	25.2	27.2	27.2	29.2
Median age	32.1	45.9	47.1	48.6	49.8
0-19/20-64	0.48	0.37	0.36	0.30	0.30
65+/20-64	0.18	0.46	0.51	0.49	0.54

SOURCE: Output from MED'S using high and low mortality assumptions, and fertility of 1.67 and 1.40; immigration is 150,000.

due to both low fertility and falling mortality rates in the older population. Already by 1986, the life expectancy at age sixty was twenty-one years, which is as long as the typical period of education.

Simulations on future changes confirm that potential declines in mortality have a significant impact on the age distribution. Table 7 shows the impact by 2036 of life expectancies of 80.9 or 84.3, along with fertility of 1.67 or 1.40 births per woman. It can be seen that these mortality differences produce similar effects on the proportion over sixty-five to those introduced by the fertility differences. Taking the population sixty-five and over as a ratio to that 20-64 shows that mortality has a larger impact than fertility on this measure of aging. On the other hand, fertility has a larger impact on the population under twenty as a ratio to that 20-64. Clearly, fertility reduction makes for "population aging at the bottom" while mortality reduction contributes to "population aging at the top" (Krotki, 1990b: 32; Keyfitz, 1990; Stone, 1990).

The relative impact of fertility and mortality on population aging has been further analysed by George *et al*. (1990). Over the period 1961-86 it is found that almost all the change in the proportion of the population aged 0-19 was due to fertility change, while for the proportion sixty-five and over the mortality change was 39 per cent as important as the fertility change. Similarly, over the period 1986-2036, fertility has the largest effect in terms of the proportion under twenty, but the mortality effect is 73 per cent as large as the fertility effect for ages sixty-five and over. In fact, for the period 1986-2011, the mortality effect is larger than the fertility effect in terms of the proportion aged sixty-five and over. Using a total fertility rate of 1.7, Lachapelle (1990) finds that the proportion over sixty-five would stabilize at 23.0 per cent with a life expectancy of seventy-five and at 30.5 with a life expectancy of eighty-five.

For Quebec over the period 1986-2011, Mathews (1988) calculates that the expected mortality change explains 25 per cent of the change in the proportion sixty-five and over. As another example of simulations for the future, Manton (1987) estimates the impact of substantially higher levels of life expectancy, based on data from the United States. At a life expectancy of eighty-two with fertility of 2.1 births per woman, the proportion over sixty-five would be 24 per cent, while a life expectancy of ninety-two would raise this proportion to 33 per cent. Therefore, at these high levels, a ten-year gain in length of life increases the proportion over sixty-five from a quarter to a third of the entire population, even at replacement fertility. A life expectancy of 100 would raise the proportion to 42 per cent. In comparison, at a life expectancy of eighty-two, a rise of fertility from 1.7 to 2.1 reduces the proportion over sixty-five from 28 to 24 per cent.

Going beyond the demographic processes of births, deaths, and migration, population aging is clearly a function of improved socio-economic conditions, including higher income and education (Bourbeau et al., 1986b). Aging and income per capita are linked around the world. Putting aging in its socio-economic context, McDaniel (1987a) sees it as an indirect and unintended consequence, in an affluent and industrialized society, of successful planned parenthood. She therefore observes that aging, along with zero growth, stem from good fortune and affluence. Based on these considerations, McDaniel (1986) tends to view aging positively. It remains useful to note that out of positive causes can come negative consequences. For instance, industrialization has produced higher standards of living. However, if the associated increase in use of energy produces a significant climatic change, then industrialization also has negative consequences. Similarly, the aging associated with economic success and control over fertility might also be seen as a mixed blessing. In this context, one might ask whether it would be valuable to think of sustaining fertility to counter, in part, the extent of aging. For instance, in his conclusions on aging in Europe, Chesnais (1989) observes that aging cannot be stopped but it can be slowed by changing public expenses to the benefit of the children and young families. He argues that higher fertility is the most secure of long-term investments since it is investment in human capital and in the future labour force.

DEMOGRAPHIC RAMIFICATIONS OF AGING

Before considering the economic and social impact of aging, it is worth paying attention to the demographic impact. While aging follows on fertility and mortality rates, it also influences these vital rates. Typically, an older population will have fewer births and more deaths. As Chesnais (1989) observes, the potential for demographic decline is already inscribed in the older age distribution. There are self-reinforcing mechanisms at work: aging is due to low fertility, but an older population also produces fewer births. Just as population momentum has continued in spite of below-replacement fertility, similarly negative natural increase would tend to continue in an older population. Even if fertility were to move to above-replacement levels, the smaller numbers at reproductive ages would still imply fewer births than deaths. At the beginning of below-replacement fertility in the early 1970s, there were still almost twice as many births as deaths, and deaths per 1,000 population continued to decline to the mid-1980s. However, at constant fertility, the deaths will start to outnumber births around 2020.

It is worth emphasizing that an aging population has an influence on death rates. In the demographic projections underlying the Economic Council of Canada's (1989) *Twenty-Sixth Annual Review*, an assumption of constant deaths per 1,000 population was used. These projections assume that deaths per 1,000 population would be constant at 7.3 between 1988 and 2040, without noting that this would imply a rather heroic increase in life expectancy. In contrast, the Statistics Canada (1990a) projections imply, with life expectancy changing from 76.4 to 80.6, that the deaths per 1,000 population will increase to 13.5 by 2035.

Besides exercising a downward pressure on birthrates and an upward pressure on death rates, an aging population accentuates the predominance of women, especially at higher ages. As was observed in Chapter 2, women's advantage in life expectancy increased from some two years in 1931 to seven years in 1971. This resulted in higher numbers of surviving women, especially at older ages. At the 1986 census, the proportion over 65 was 9.1 per cent for men and 12.2 for women. Since the birthrates obviously followed the same trend for men and women, this again shows that mortality is now having an impact on aging. At particularly advanced ages, there is a very strong imbalance by sex. At ages eighty-five and over there were 44 men per 100 women in 1986 (Stone and Frenken, 1988: 33). This differential survival means a greater likelihood of older women being widowed and living alone. Given that the mortality differentials have declined slightly since 1971, the imbalance in the proportions aged by sex have stopped increasing.

As observed in Chapter 5, aging has an impact on the distribution of population over space. Three phenomena are at work: the lower propensities of older people to move produces "aging in place" ; the greater likelihood that younger people will move from the more depressed regions leaves more older people behind; and the differential choice of places of destination accentuates the proportion of older people in specific locations. Following on these trends, the proportion of elderly varies considerably over the regions and areas of the country. For instance, Prince Edward Island, Saskatchewan, Manitoba, and British Columbia had more than 12 per cent of their populations over sixty-five in 1986, compared to less than 10 per cent for Quebec, Newfoundland, Alberta, and the territories (Stone and Frenken, 1988: 27). Similarly, the proportions aged are highest in urban areas under 10,000 people and lowest in metropolitan areas as well as in rural farm areas. This distribution does not always coincide with the distribution of service facilities, especially for health, where the largest cities have the most facilities while smaller urban areas tend to have less facilities.

AGING AND DEPENDENCY

Aging has a number of demographic ramifications, including lower births, higher deaths, lower population growth, an accentuation of the imbalance between the numbers of women and men at older ages, and a regional imbalance in proportions aged. An additional demographic observation relates to what has been called "dependency," or the ratio of persons in age groups that are typically not in the labour force to those typically in the labour force.

Taking age groups 0-14 and sixty-five and over as less likely to be in the labour force, the ratio can therefore be computed to the population aged 15-64. Over this century, there has been a continuous increase in the numbers over sixty-five per 100 people at ages 15-64. In 1971 there were thirteen people at retirement ages per 100 people at labour force ages, compared to nineteen in 2001 and forty in 2036 (Statistics Canada, 1990a: 140, 177). This means that in 1971 there was one retirement-age person for every eight people at labour force ages, while in 2036 there would be one retirement-age person for every 2.5 people at the labour force ages.

While the older dependants have increased, the younger dependants have declined since 1971. Per 100 people at labour force ages, the decline has been from forty-seven in 1971 to thirty-one by 1986, and at constant fertility this would decline further to twenty-five by 2036. Taken together, the older and younger dependants are a very constant share of the total population over the period 1981 to 2011, and this represents a low level of dependency compared to past and future levels. Now that the baby boom generation has moved into the labour force, and until it begins to retire, the relative proportion of dependants in the population is at historically low levels. The present and short-term future show a very advantageous situation because the lower fertility has reduced the numbers of young dependants, and the baby boom generations are in the labour force, while the growth in the proportions of older dependants will mostly occur after the first decade of the next century.

It should be noted that this represents a relatively "gross" measure of dependency. The population aged 0-14 and sixty-five and over is not necessarily dependent, just as that aged 15-64 is not necessarily in the labour force, and if so some may be unemployed. Even employed people in the labour force often depend on public resources, while "dependent" persons often provide various support through family and other networks. In effect, most people are dependent on others in a variety of ways.

Foot (1989) has introduced a number of corrections to this calculation in order to come closer to measuring actual economic dependency. First he corrects for the fact that older dependants represent more public costs than younger dependants. The costs of pensions and health are higher than those of education, per person using the services. A number of authors conclude that the "weight" of the elderly is about two and a half to three times that of the young. Using a weight of 2.5, the "expenditure dependency" increases by 10 per cent over 1986-2001, and considerably faster after 2011. The next adjustments account for unemployment and the public costs of people in the labour force. This trend shows an increased dependency burden since 1981 but still relatively low levels until 2016. Thereafter, the burdens on the employed non-dependants rises to levels not experienced over the previous century. These computations all show that the period around 1981-86 involved historically low levels of dependency. Alternate assumptions show that the extra burden of subsequent periods could nonetheless be compensated by rising labour force participation and decreasing unemployment, at least over the rest of this century. All projections show substantial increases in dependency after 2011. Both the "expenditure dependency" and the further adjustments for unemployment costs raise the level of dependency above historical levels by 2021.

Wolfson (1990) adds the useful observation that while public costs are higher for the aged, private costs are higher for the young. The total of public and private costs may be about equal for the young and the elderly. Aging therefore involves a shift in the burden from parents to the public sector, or a growth in the public sector. More of the burden will be financed through governments rather than through intra-family transfers. In addition, he observes that lower costs to parents mean more ability to pay taxes. The expenses are nonetheless different: costs for the young are a form of investment in the future labour force, while costs for the elderly relate more directly to consumption.

ECONOMIC IMPACT OF AGING

It is clear that the early stages of aging produce net economic benefits. There are more survivors at younger ages and eventually a higher proportion of the population at labour force ages. In Canada, the labour force itself has been getting younger in spite of population aging. A somewhat older population also involves more savings because there are fewer family expenses for the young. In the short term, lower fertility means less need for family allowance and educational expenditures, along with an increase in tax revenues because there are more two-income families and fewer child deductions. Women's labour force participation advances because there is less need for their services to smaller families.

It is not so clear if these advantages persist to later stages of aging. At subsequent stages a higher proportion of the population is not at labour force ages, and there is a higher ratio of pensioners to workers and possibly more rigidity in the labour force. As noted earlier, an older labour force would probably be less geographically and occupationally mobile and therefore would be less able to accommodate to economic change. This may be compensated by a more experienced labour force, along with the potential to invest more in a smaller number of young people, which could increase productivity. A higher proportion of pensioners would mean a tendency to convert investments into consumption, which possibly could undermine economic growth. There are also higher public expenditures, which would give governments less manoeuvrability in terms of supporting the economy. As has already been noted, the aspects that have the potential of being more problematic are particularly difficult to measure: flexibility, innovativeness, and productivity of an aging labour force.

In a discussion of "some constraints and parameters" associated with Canada's demographic situation, Marr (1987) is concerned about labour force aging and slower economic growth. The lower geographical, occupational, and promotional mobility of an older labour force could mean obsolescence of the work force and its misallocation with regard to sector. For instance, there may be too many human resources in education and not enough in health, along with a difficulty in changing this allocation. A study by the Economic Council of Canada (1979) expects aging to exercise a downward pressure on potential growth of the economy, especially after the turn of the century. Tabah (1988) observes that rich countries have a "universal concern" with the structural rigidity that aging creates and exacerbates in the production apparatus. On the other hand, Habib (1988) notes that there is little correlation between economic crises, public expenditure levels, and the age structure among rich countries.

In *Canada's Aging Population*, McDaniel (1986: 48, 57) argues that the production of wealth does not decline with population aging, although there is a need to redistribute resources from the young to the old. She suggests providing "the older population with sufficient disposable income as well as consumer goods . . . so they can continue to be viable consumers." Instead of being concerned about where to find the money to meet the economic, social, and health care needs of retired people, she suggests that, even with zero population growth, better pensions would enable the economy to remain viable. However, this seems to focus on stimulating consumption without being very concerned about investments and production.

In regard to the labour force, aging initially promotes greater involvement on the part of women. However, it may eventually reduce the labour force involvement of older men. Based on data from seventeen countries, it is observed that the larger the older population, the higher the per capita pension benefits and the lower the levels of labour supply of older workers (Myles, 1981a). Thus an older population would not only promote more pension benefits but also a lower labour force participation on the part of the elderly. Among men aged 55-64, the proportion who were not in the labour force increased from 14 per cent in 1961 to 30 per cent in 1985 (Burbidge and Robb, 1986). At ages 65-69, this proportion increased from 50 to 80 per cent. The average length of the working life for men declined by 8.8 per cent over this period. Keyfitz (1989a) notes that the lower proportions of those working would not be a function of health or physically demanding work, because health and working conditions have improved. It is more likely a function of unemployment, technological change, greater pension benefits, and changing attitudes to work and leisure. Stelcner and Kyriazis (1990) find that the elderly would remain in the labour force longer if profitable job opportunities were available or if pensions and other government transfer payments were reduced.

Osberg (1988) confirms the importance of the labour market, finding that older workers who leave their jobs before age sixty-five often do so because of involuntary unemployment rather than voluntary retirement. As a consequence, a different labour market involving higher demands for older workers could increase their labour force activity. However, in reviewing studies from the United States, Breslaw and Sims (1986) conclude that poor health is by far the main reason given by workers for early retirement. While health may represent a more socially acceptable response than loss of one's job, they conclude that poor health is doubtless an important reason for early retirement. An analysis of the 1978 Canada Health Survey confirms that health is as important as potential earnings in determining the labour force behaviour of men over fifty (Breslaw and Stelcner, 1987).

There are other differences between older and younger workers. Osberg (1988) observes that older workers are less likely to have more than one job in a given year. In 1986, 20 per cent of male workers under forty-five had more than one job as contrasted with 9 per cent of workers over forty-five. If mobility across jobs is a sign of labour market flexibility, then this is reduced in an older labour force. However, part of the mobility of younger workers is associated with unemployment, which is higher for the young. Age group 15-24 accounted for over a third of the unemployed in 1986 (Statistics Canada, 1989e).

Handa (1986) argues that as workers age they acquire skills relevant to the job but sometimes relevant only to the firm in which they work. Older workers would tend to be slower to learn, thus slower at adapting to technological progress and more at risk of obsolescence of skills, and they have a harder time finding a new job if they are unemployed. Consequently, an older labour force could introduce more rigidity and a lower rate of acquisition of new skills or of upgrading of skills.

Another question relates to productivity and mobility in an aging labour force. Legoff (1989) observes that productivity does not decrease with age, at least not until age sixty-five, but age is a restraining factor with regard to mobility because of seniority, family responsibilities, home ownership, and social security related to employment. Clearly, the economic return of a change in career reduces rapidly with age. Also, while older people may not be *less* productive, seniority structures may give them more income for a given level of productivity. As an example, the median age of university professors in Canada was thirty-seven in 1970 and forty-six in 1988. While older professors may be more experienced and productive, they are certainly more expensive. In 1989-90, the average wage of 35-39-year-old professors in Ontario was $50,000 compared to $67,000 for those aged 45-49. A document by the OECD (1988b) argues that there is now too large a gap between the productivity and earnings profiles by age, which requires either an increase in productivity through retraining or a reduction in earnings at older ages.

In a broad economic context, there is always the problem of matching productive endowments and consumption needs over the life cycle. While productive endowments are stronger at certain parts of the life cycle, consumption needs are present throughout life. It can be argued that this provides insight into the very *raison d'être* of the banking system, money, and even the family (Arthur, 1988). Myles (1981b) observes that the reserves of the Canada Pension Plan have become the single most important source of borrowing for provincial governments, while private pension funds are the largest source of new investments in stock and bond markets. It will be argued in the next section that an aging population, along with the insecurity of private pensions and investments, has prompted greater development of the welfare state. While transfers to the young largely occur in families, those to the old occur through the state, giving the state a larger role in redistribution.

AGING AND SOCIETY

In his book on *The Big Generation*, Kettle (1980) has highlighted how society is affected by the movement of the baby boom generation through the life cycle. First education underwent a massive revolution, then there was concern about finding enough jobs, now about promotion prospects, and later about retirement benefits and health care. For instance, total elementary school enrolment peaked in 1960 and by 1976 it had declined by 22 per cent (Statistics Canada, 1978: 35). The labour force experienced growth in the order of 3.4 per cent per year in the period 1971-81. After 1991, this growth is likely to be around 1 per cent per year.

The family

The family is also affected, as smaller families support larger numbers of aged members. Given the irregularity in Canada's age distribution, aging has different consequences on given generations. If one considers that children would mostly be looking after parents who are some twenty-five years older, it is useful to observe that in 1986 there were fifty-two persons aged 65-79 per 100 people aged 40-54. By 2036 the ratio will be eighty-eight older people per 100 in the more supportive age group. If families are not able to accommodate this increase, there will be more dependence on other forms of support (H. Gauthier, 1989). Because of differences in age at marriage and mortality, over half of women aged seventy and over were not married in 1986. Simulating kinship and family support under various fertility conditions, Wolf (1988) finds that in a society with some 13 per cent aged sixty-five and over, only 4 per cent of the aged population are without working-age offspring. However, with a lower fertility and 23 per cent aged sixty-five and over, 17 per cent of the aged are without working-age offspring.

On the other hand, Marcil-Gratton and Légaré (1987) observe that children are far from being the only source of support for the elderly and that the lives of elderly are not much affected by their number of surviving children. Also, if one considers that people within ten years of death are in strongest need of support, that proportion is not changing as rapidly. Desjardins and Légaré (1984) estimate that the proportion of the population with a life expectancy of less than ten years would increase from 5 per cent in 1980 to 8 per cent in 2025.

The role of government and the welfare state

While there is some uncertainty regarding the impact of aging on the economy, mostly because there are both positive and negative elements, a study for the OECD observes that one of the least ambiguous consequences of aging is the potentially large increase in the role of government in transferring resources from the working age to the elderly population (Hagemann and Nicoletti, 1989: 14). Various studies have observed that the share of social outlays will rise significantly as a consequence of population aging (OECD, 1988a; Heller *et al.*, 1986). Novak (1988) concludes that as the population ages the state budget will increase in order to redistribute wealth from the young people to older people. While Denton *et al.* (1986) do not expect particularly pronounced government expenditure increases associated with population aging itself, they do expect substantial change in the composition of this expenditure, implying "major economic and political adjustments."

In a larger context, Myles (1981a) argues that the welfare state has been organized primarily around the provision of support for the elderly: "the conjunction of aging labour force and post-war political economy of advanced capitalist countries provided the historical setting for the creation of a welfare state for the elderly." It is for the elderly that the welfare state is most complete, substituting a social wage for a market wage. He argues that the retirement principle gave the welfare state its characteristic form: a welfare state for the elderly. The largest component of federal social spending is on the elderly, with Old Age Security constituting the biggest transfer program in the country (Prince, 1985).

Relative positions of young and elderly

It is often argued that an aging society will need to transfer resources from the young to the elderly. McDaniel (1986: 59) says that funds previously used for "raising children within the family could be transferred to providing pensions and health care for the older population." However, there are also unmet needs for the young that an aging society could ignore at its peril. The greater willingness to favour the aged can undermine transfers in favour of the younger dependants, and for that matter can undermine the standard of living of younger workers (who must pay the social security costs), inducing them to have fewer children. In effect, transfers from workers to elderly are transfers away from children. Consequently, transfer payments favouring children and young families continue to be important, if only as an investment in the future labour force.

Bégin (1987) observes that among the major client groups for social policy, the elderly have been the most successful and children the least successful in mobilizing support. For instance, the proportion of elderly with low-income status declined from 27.4 per cent in 1981 to 19.6 per cent in 1986, while for children aged 0-14 this proportion increased from 16.5 to 19.2 per cent (Arnoti, 1986). The declining labour force participation of the elderly may also imply a certain "luxury" not to work, while young students are working part-time in ever greater numbers. For the United States, Preston (1984) argues that on a variety of levels "young dependants" are not receiving as much support as "old dependants." For instance, education is declining as an industry, while health is increasing. In a study of eight OECD countries, including Canada, the observed trend in public policy over the period 1975-84 involved giving greater priority to pensions while according lower priority to programs directly aimed at children (O'Higgins, 1988). In 1980, the per capita Canadian family benefits were estimated at $318 U.S., compared to $5,601 U.S. for aged benefits.

There is a fairly natural tendency for an aging society to favour the elderly. Not only are there greater numbers of elderly looking after their own interests, but the age groups following them want to ensure that there are adequate structures for their own retirement. In contrast, the young have less political power: they do not vote. The number of households including children under eighteen, and consequently with a self-interest in youth, is becoming a minority. In 1986, only 39 per cent of households included children under eighteen years of age.

Pampel and Williamson (1985) have examined the determinants of spending on public pensions with a sample of forty-eight countries. The percentage of the population that is elderly and social insurance program experience were found to be of dominant importance. In addition, the impacts of the proportion of elderly are found to increase with political democracy. The authors infer that democracy permits the elderly to wield political power and to shape priorities to their advantage.

RETIREMENT AND PENSIONS

While aging affects a number of social programs, those involving retirement and pensions are most clearly affected because they are very closely linked to age. Given the provisions of access based on age, but also the provisions for spousal allowances, widows' allowances, and disability allowances, along with the contributions based on employment and income, several demographic factors are involved in the evolution of pension programs. The demographic factors of age, sex, marital status, fertility, and immigration affect both the number and types of beneficiaries and the number and types of contributors (Ducharme and Légaré, 1986).

The costs of retirement and pension benefits depend particularly on the relative numbers of contributors and beneficiaries. As Keyfitz (1988) has observed, when the population and economy are growing rapidly, no one need be much worried about equity between the generations. As long as the descendants in the labour force are more numerous and richer than their parents were, they will have little difficulty in supporting their elders, even at standards of living higher than they had when they were working. However, when demographic and economic growth slow down, the transfer of resources can become more onerous. Large retired cohorts followed by small working ones may be at a particular disadvantage. In effect, generations that do not reproduce themselves would tend to pay more than they receive in pensions (Keyfitz, 1985). Kettle (1980: 214) even suggests that the "big generation will be on its own in retirement."

History of pension programs

Public payments for retired people started in 1927, but involved only $20 per month to persons *in need* over seventy years of age (Myles, 1988a: 40). Before it became universal in 1951, less than half of persons over seventy were receiving the pension, which had risen to $40 per month. The Old Age Security Act of 1951 did not initially change the benefit rate but it now applied to all persons over seventy. By 1970 the age had been lowered to sixty-five years. In 1966 the Canada/Quebec Pension Plan was initiated to provide retirement benefits linked to past contributions while employed. In 1967 the Guaranteed Income Supplement was introduced to raise the income of those elderly who had little other income. Most provinces also administer a form of guaranteed income supplement. Thus the public pension programs include a universal program (OAS), a means-tested program (GIS), and a program based on employment contributions (C/QPP). The OAS and GIS are now linked to the cost of living, while the C/QPP increases with average wages.

While these programs started as a form of social assistance for those in need, all Western countries now have state-administered income security programs that provide a major source of income for the majority of the elderly (Myles, 1986). As indicated earlier, it is for the elderly that the welfare state is most complete in the sense of giving basic income security to all. This development of social security has been linked with the development of a concept of citizenship that confers rights and entitlements by virtue of membership in a national community rather than being a function of property, status, or market capacity. Nonetheless, there is the limitation that recipients of OAS need to have been in Canada for at least ten years after age eighteen.

When it was negotiating the C/QPP with the provinces, the federal government preferred a pure pay-as-you-go system that taxed workers in order to pay benefits to retired persons. The provinces preferred a partly funded system that collected "contributions" from workers, which would later be received as benefits. The main advantage of the "contributory route" was that it accumulated a fund of money that could be lent to the provinces for their development plans. Since the provinces spend almost all of the excess money in the plan, there is little difference between the two alternatives. It is really a new tax called a "contribution" wherein current workers pay for the retirement benefits of previous workers.

The system was very "profitable" when it was first instituted. All workers made contributions while only people who had made past contributions could receive benefits, linked to the number of years of contributions. At first this kind of a system receives much more than it gives, making it the major source of borrowing for the provinces. In this "profitable" stage, there is a tendency to increase the benefits, which in the Canadian case included widows of past contributors as well as handicapped persons and orphans.

Eventually this kind of a system has a tendency to run out of reserves, which can be solved either by increasing the contributions or by reducing the benefits (Weaver, 1986). The reserves come under pressure due to both population aging and the aging or maturing of the system itself. Since the plan started in 1966, by 1986 persons aged 65-75 were eligible for full benefits, while those 76-85 have partial benefits and persons over eighty-five have no benefits (Wolfson and Murphy, 1990). Only after 2016 will all surviving persons over sixty-five be entitled to full benefits, depending on their contributions.

As of 1985 the fund would have started to pay out more than it was receiving. Instead of returning the borrowed money, which would have increased other taxes, the provinces readily agreed to allow an increase in the level of "contributions." From 3.6 per cent of income, the rate rose to 4.6 by 1991 and will rise to 7.6 by 2011. The advantage of the profitable earlier period can be seen from the fact that the contributions will need to double to maintain the same benefits.

Another criticism made of the Canada/Quebec Pension Plan is that it is a regressive form of taxation. Workers start making "contributions" at very low income, corresponding to 10 per cent of the average wage, and contributions reach a maximum at an income equivalent to the average wage. On the other hand, the regressive nature of this plan is compensated by the progressive nature of Old Age Security and the Guaranteed Income Supplement. These two programs redistribute income from richer to poorer people (Ethier, 1985). Given the survivors' benefits, the Canada Pension Plan also redistributes money from single to married contributors.

The pension programs for the elderly represent the single largest source of government expenditure. As of 1982-83, the total cost of the three programs was equivalent to 14.2 per cent of total federal expenses (Ethier, 1985). In constant dollars, per person aged 20-64, the public-sector pension costs increased from \$573 in 1971 to \$1,282 in 1986, or at a rate of 5.5 per cent per year (Fellegi, 1988: 31). Prince (1986) calculates the additional tax breaks or "tax expenditures" that benefit the elderly and finds that this form of benefit represents 19.5 per cent of all reductions in taxes. Courchene (1987) estimates that the elderly receive \$6,500 in after-tax benefits regardless of income level.

Economic well-being of the elderly

Given these social policy developments, it should not be too surprising to find that the elderly have advanced in terms of their average standard of living compared to other population groups. Both the absolute and relative incomes of the elderly have steadily improved since the early 1970s (Fellegi, 1988: 6). The proportion of elderly persons with low-income status has declined. In 1969, 41.4 per cent of families with elderly heads were classified as having low-income status, but by 1982 the rate had fallen to 11.7 per cent (National Council on Welfare, 1988: 323). Between 1976 and 1986, Mathews (1988: 38) finds that the average income of families by age of head declined for all but persons over age sixty-five. For the United States, Duncan and Smith (1989) conclude that the elderly have had a "dramatic increase" in their standard of living over the past twenty-five years.

In spite of the improvement in overall averages, there remain disadvantaged groups among the elderly, particularly unattached individuals and families with a female head. The National Council on Welfare (1988) concludes that the economic position of elderly men and their wives has improved considerably, but the same cannot be said for the growing group of elderly women who head families or live on their own. Gee and Kimball (1987) argue that pension reform to increase survivors' benefits would improve this situation somewhat, but the problem is linked to broader issues of gender structure in society, including unequal labour force participation. In 1985, it is estimated that retiring women had been in the labour force for an average of 17.1 years compared to 42.2 years for men (Gonnot, 1990: 7). Clearly, the problem of the income level of elderly women is not a function of aging *per se*, but it is part of a larger socio-economic situation (McDaniel, 1986).

In spite of the improvements noted above, considerable pressure exists to do more for the income security of the aged. Chappell (1987) argues that income security payments are too minimal to provide an adequate standard of living, given the decreased opportunities for self-maintenance of the elderly. Gee and McDaniel (1990) make a case for better retirement benefits because so many people depend on them.

221

Similarly, Roadburg (1985: 166) argues that Canada's pension allowances are inadequate for close to half of those over sixty-five. Wolfson (1990: 16) observes that for the elderly with incomes under $20,000, that is, 53 per cent of couples and 88 per cent of persons living alone, some 70 per cent of income is from public sources. Clearly, for most elderly, public pensions are crucial to retirement income. The government paper, *Better Pensions for Canadians*, observed that while substantial improvements have been made, inadequate incomes remain too common (Health and Welfare and Department of Finance, 1982).

Costs of programs

Until now, the cost of pensions has been less affected by aging than by the increased benefits and the maturation of the pension plans. Among OECD countries, the demographic factor of growth of the aged population has accounted for slightly more than a quarter of the growth of pension costs between 1960 and 1984, while wider coverage and higher benefits are the major causes of the increases (Holzmann, 1988). For Canada between 1960 and 1981, some 34 per cent of the increase in costs would have been a function of the growth of the relevant population, 28 per cent a function of increase in the proportion of that population receiving benefits (increased coverage), and 37 per cent due to increases in average benefits (OECD, 1985). With the increased labour force participation of women, there are more contributors to the Canada/Quebec Pension Plan, which only later increases the proportion of retired women receiving benefits and the level of these benefits, corresponding to the years of contributions. Thus, considerable scope remains for further costs due to the maturation of the plan.

Several authors have projected the future costs of pension programs in the context of population aging. In constant dollars and using 1986 as representing 100, the standard assumptions from Denton *et al.* (1989: 118) show that while the population increases to 118.1, the pension costs increase to 286.1. This is based on maintaining the same level of services to an aging population. Among all government expenditures, pensions would represent 7.7 per cent of total expenditures in 1986 compared to 17.9 per cent in 2036. These "constant quality" projections do not take into account the further maturing of the Canada Pension Plan and the pressures to increase the level of benefits for the Guaranteed Income Supplement.

In addition, Denton *et al.* (1989: 38) do not analyse the potential differences based on alternate mortality assumptions, stating simply that these "would have little effect." However, Gonnot (1990) finds that an increase in life expectancy by some eight to ten years for men and four to five years for women would increase the number of retirees in Canada by some 165 per cent between 1985 and 2030, compared to a 110 per cent increase under constant mortality. Gonnot further computes the change in the level of benefits that would result if the level of contributions was held constant. Even under constant mortality, benefits for retired persons would decline by over 50 per cent if the level of contributions did not rise. For France, the change in the age distribution to 2050 would require an 80 per cent increase in contributions, a 45 per cent reduction in benefits, or a nine-year increase in the age at retirement (Chesnais, 1989).

In the projections by Fellegi (1988: 31) annual pension costs in constant dollars per person aged 20-64 would increase from $1,282 in 1986 to $3,286 in 2036, assuming no further increases in benefits. The costs to persons aged 20-64 will therefore have to increase by some 250 per cent in constant dollars over fifty years, or 1.9 per cent per year, to maintain the same level of benefits. If benefits rise as they have in the past, the increase would be to $5,336 per person aged 20-64, a fourfold increase or 2.9 per cent per year.

Projections by the OECD (1988c) are given in terms of public pensions as a percentage of GDP. In Canada, these pensions represented 2.8 per cent of GDP in 1960, compared to 5.4 per cent in 1985 and a projected 15.2 per cent in 2040. These figures are all below the OECD average, which increases to 20.2 per cent in 2040.

In terms of required increases in contributory rates, with a fertility of 1.7 births per woman, it is estimated that the levels of contributions for the Canada/Quebec Pension Plan would need to increase from 3.6 per cent of income in 1985 to 11.6 per cent in 2030 (Green et al., 1986: 215). In a report for the Ontario Economic Council, Hamilton and Whalley (1984) estimate a surcharge of 30 to 40 per cent in income tax to pay for increases in Old Age Security and Guaranteed Income Supplement.

Policy alternatives

In discussing alternative possibilities for change in pension plans, it is important to note that these are ultimately distributional policies. Since the redistribution largely is from persons in the labour force to persons retired, a sense of the appropriate level of transfer is of course needed. It is also important that any changes be made slowly and with sufficient advance warning, corresponding to the long-term nature of retirement plans. In discussing policy change, Deaton (1989: 342) observes that "reforming the pension system is a potentially volatile political issue because it involves the structurally determined interests of all major groups and institutions in a capitalist political economy: workers, unions, finance and industrial sectors, the state, and the increasing proportions of the elderly." Pension reform involves decisions about distribution of income among individuals and between different interests (Prince, 1985). In speaking of "Young and Old: Who Owes

Whom," Streib (1990) also argues that it is ultimately a political and ethical issue of how to allocate resources. Public pension plans rest on social commitments between generations and between citizens and their governments.

Myles (1984) says it is presumptuous to assume that old age will be the same in the next century. In the present environment old age is retirement, but that was not always the case and both the right to retire and the rights of the retired are the outcome of a political process. The economic well-being of the elderly is therefore best seen as the outcome of a political process. Myles (1989) concludes that "politics, not demography, determines the size of the elderly population." In this context, he notes that the broad alternatives with regard to pension plans are three: dismantle, continue, or increase. The dismantling of plans would involve a return to private and family arrangements for support in old age, with possible state social assistance in cases of destitution. The extension could go to the point of extending the idea of "citizenship in the welfare state" or "social security with a social wage" to all, thus eliminating the need to have separate programs for the elderly. A more limited extension could involve homemaker pensions, which would increase the C/QPP costs by some 36 per cent (Wolfson, 1989)

The intermediate category of continuing the programs as they are requires at least some change to make the programs sustainable. The basic alternatives here are to increase contributions and taxes, reduce benefits, or, which is somewhat the same, extend the working life. Until now, only the alternative of increasing contributions has been considered. As we have seen, this will involve a substantial increase to pay for the benefits currently promised as the number of pensioners increases. For the Canada/Quebec Pension Plan, some increase in contributions could be achieved by not "capping" the payments at a given maximum, thus making them less regressive. The alternative of reducing benefits could take either of two forms: reducing the payments overall or reducing the extent of indexing to the cost of living. The partial de-indexing of the Old Age Security payments was strongly resisted after the 1985 budget, which envisaged this change. The approach of taxing back payments for persons at higher income has reduced benefits for the persons affected. The removal of the universality of the Old Age Security would be another way of reducing benefits.

Given the difficulty associated with decreasing benefits, it is often suggested that an easier alternative would be to extend the working life. Schmahl (1987) proposes making it more expensive for workers to retire early and encouraging partial retirement. Since people live longer, it should be possible for part of this longer life to be spent working. However, there are also difficulties here. First the longer life is not necessarily spent in good health. Reviewing the evidence on this question, Duncan and Smith (1989) conclude that the elderly are experiencing steady rates of morbidity and disability. Second, the trend until now has been for earlier retirement. While one might think that older populations would have a higher proportion of their elderly in the labour force, the opposite is the case. Among ten developed countries studied by Gonnot (1990), Canada has the second lowest proportion of elderly and the oldest mean age at retirement. While Canada's mean age at retirement is sixty-three, those of Austria, Czechoslovakia, Hungary, Italy, and the Netherlands are below sixty. All these countries have higher proportions of aged than Canada.

It must also be noted that the extension of working life would not be very much affected by the elimination of mandatory retirement. Only about half of the work force is covered by some form of mandatory retirement provision, and there are more people wanting to retire before the mandatory age than the numbers who want to work longer (Gunderson and Pasando, 1988). Enticing people to work longer could be done through extending the age at eligibility to pensions. This is foreseen in the United States where the age will rise from sixty-five to sixty-seven between 2003 and 2026 (Myers, 1990). In this context, it is useful to note that Bismarck, who first established public pensions in Germany in 1889, had set the age at sixty-five (Conrad, 1990). When it established its plan in the 1930s, the United States chose sixty-five as a compromise between sixty and seventy. In 1927, Canada used the age of seventy, which was reduced to sixty-five by 1951. Most countries now have retirement ages of sixty-five or lower. For instance, it is sixty in Czechoslovakia, France, Hungary, and Italy. Besides changing the age at entitlement, extending the working life would require the dismantling of early retirement programs and altering the labour market to the benefit of older workers. This would especially involve retraining in order to maintain their productivity in the face of technological change.

Instead of increasing contributions as the population ages, some have suggested that the Canada/Quebec Pension Plan become a "funded" plan in the sense of turning it into an investment fund (Deaton, 1989). Asimakopulos (1990) finds that this "smacks of wishful thinking." In effect, this would require the provinces to raise taxes instead of borrowing from the pension plan. Ducharme and Légaré (1986) observe that a pure capital accumulation approach would involve too high a total reserve to be manageable. There is a limit to the amount of capital an economy can effectively use at one time (Keyfitz, 1988).

Another alternative is to extend private pension plans associated with employment. That was one of the proposals in the Health and Welfare and Department of Finance (1982) paper, *Better Pensions for*

Canadians. However, it proved impossible to obtain the compliance of the private sector. Among persons in the private sector, only 41 per cent were contributing to private company plans in 1979 (Tindale, 1988: 309). Especially women and persons at lower income are not part of private plans (Stafford, 1986; Gee and McDaniel, 1990). A greater reliance on private plans would inevitably increase the inequity (OECD, 1988b). Given an economy where some sectors increase while others decline, and with high labour mobility across employers, it is very difficult to provide pension security through employers (Myles, 1986: 34). Those who are in stable sectors and who remain with the same employer would do well but others would lose out. Private plans also suffer from the effect of inflation and from the problem of insolvency in the case of shutdowns, which means that workers have no assurance that they will get their entitled pension (Ethier, 1985).

The question of pensions is to a considerable extent an issue of equity over generations. Constant benefits favour smaller cohorts who pay less into the system, while constant contributions favour larger ones who receive more. Following on this observation, Keyfitz (1988) suggests that an average between these two approaches would have greater equity across generations. A partly funded plan would also ensure that generations pay more for their own retirement. In the Canadian case, this would mean raising the level of taxes while the baby boom generation is in the labour force. This would be the same as reducing the national debt during these "optimal times" while a high proportion of the population is in the labour force and before the pension plans come to full maturity. Keyfitz (1989a) also suggests that having older workers make higher contributions than younger ones would minimize tensions across generations. Given that retirement is more imminent for older workers, they would probably be more willing to increase their taxes and contributions. In contrast, younger workers have more child-rearing costs, and lower contributions toward pensions may permit them to invest more in the children of the next generation, including their numbers.

AGING AND HEALTH

Compared to pensions, health costs are more spread out over the life cycle and consequently less affected by aging. Nonetheless, costs are higher in the older ages and consequently aging increases health costs. In effect, the working population pays for improvements in health services that extend life, then it also pays for the health and pension costs of the persons who live longer. While improved health and longevity are clearly important for individuals and societies, the more improvement the higher the subsequent health and pension costs.

Fifty years ago the fight was against infectious diseases, including tuberculosis and polio. Today the main fight is against heart disease and cancer. Some authors have speculated that heart disease, cancer, and stroke will be seen as diseases of this century and that chronic-disease mortality risks are just beginning to decline (Olshansky, 1990; Manton, 1987). The social implications of the consequent life-span extensions are potentially profound because the greater the extension of life expectancy at older ages, the higher the levels of morbidity. Having been saved from death due to chronic diseases, older people are more exposed to various forms of non-fatal conditions that are often debilitating. For instance, various forms of mental disorders are prevalent and it is not clear if they are amenable to reduction. Simmons-Tropea and Osborn (1987) expect that we will consequently see an increase in non-lethal morbidity. As Olshansky indicates, the consequences of our success in achieving longevity may be that we need to think about the trade-off between additional years of life *or* improved health. As noted in Chapter 2, we may need to give more priority to health rather than longevity.

The analysis that has been made of the components of increase in health costs indicates that aging has until now played a minor role. Over the period 1960-85, health costs in Canada increased from 5.5 to 8.4 per cent of GNP (OECD, 1988a). Of this increase, 20 per cent would have been a function of population (growth and aging) and the remaining 80 per cent due to increased coverage and benefits (Fukawa, 1988: 237; OECD, 1985). Among OECD countries, the demographic factor would have contributed between one-sixth and one-quarter of the growth in expenditure between 1960 and 1984, the more important factors being increased coverage and increased intensity of care per person (Holzmann, 1988). A study of the changes in British Columbia for the period 1975-86 finds that 7 per cent of the increase in costs was due to aging, 28 per cent due to population growth, and 65 per cent due to greater use of services (Barer *et al.*, 1989). Changes in costs of health are partly a result of aging but also of a series of other factors including: alternative sources of care, extent of public funding, tolerance for pain, supply of services, and technological progress (Chesnais, 1989).

While health costs have been increasing much faster than the population has been aging, the changing age distribution will play a significant role in future costs. The rate of hospital use is almost twice as high in the population over sixty-five as in the total population and the average days of stay is almost five times as high (Stone and Fletcher, 1980: 39). Estimates for Quebec in 1980 indicate that 37.4 per cent of public health expenditures were for the population aged sixty-five and over (Desrosiers, 1987: 10). For British Columbia, 43.7 per cent of hospital days in 1986 involved persons seventy-five or over (Evans *et al.*, 1989: 446). Health surveys indicate that 85 per cent of those aged sixty-five and over have some health problem, with close to half of these reporting that the problem has curtailed their activity at least to some extent (Wigdor and Foot, 1988: 70). A small percentage of the elderly account for most of the costs. For Manitoba, 5 per cent of the elderly account for 60 per cent of hospital stays among the population aged sixty-five and over (Roos *et al.*, 1984). Persons aged 65-84 who survived the next four years had an average of 3.8 hospital bed days, compared to 1.3 days per those aged 25-64. Conversely, much of the cost is in the last year of life, where there were 23.5 bed days at ages 25-64 and 32.0 at ages 65-84 (Roos *et al.*, 1987b: 53). The increase in life expectancy reduces the costs for the time being, since fewer are dying, but eventually an aging population has a higher death rate. The health costs of dying will thus increase, possibly even more than the costs of aging. In British Columbia, 21.5 per cent of total patient days in 1986 involved persons aged seventy-five or over who were dying in the hospital (Evans *et al.*, 1989: 450). Nonetheless, the Canadian experience in controlling the growth of health care costs has been relatively good and compares favourably with that of other countries (Grenier, 1985: 259).

The projections of health costs have largely followed only the projected changes in population size and age composition. Denton *et al.* (1989) call these "constant quality" projections since they assume a constant level of service per age group. The projections imply considerable increases in costs – by 2036 the population is 18 per cent larger but health costs are 76 per cent greater than in 1986, or an average increase of 1.1 per cent per year. Assuming no economic growth of GNP, the health costs would increase from 7.6 per cent of GNP in 1981 to 12.9 per cent in 2031 (Denton *et al.*, 1987). However, with a growth of 1 or 2 per cent per year in real GNP, the constant quality health costs associated with aging would not increase the total proportion of health costs in the GNP. At the same time, constant quality health costs in a growing economy involve the difficult assumption that the economy grows but the real wages of health workers do not.

Projections by Fellegi (1988) are given in terms of costs per person aged 20-64. Holding the unit costs of medical services constant, the cost per working aged person would increase from $1,596 in 1986 to $3,241 in 2036, or by 1.4 per cent per year. Allowing unit costs of services to increase as they did over the period 1975-84, the total costs rise to $4,991 per person aged 20-64, or by 2.3 per cent per year. Results from the OECD (1988a) give a scenario similar to that of constant unit costs. In this projection, the health costs in Canada would increase from a base of 100 in 1980 to 218 in 2040. Another estimate by Woods Gordon Associates concludes that demographic change would increase health costs by 72 per cent between 1981 and 2021, without counting capital costs (Angus, 1986).

As argued in Chapter 2, a broader definition of health, with more emphases on community and social services, could decrease the expensive costs of physician and hospital services, but this would not likely reduce total costs. Adams (1990) finds that for every severely disabled person living in an institution, three are outside of institutions. This is partly a function of the severity of the disability, but it is also due to the availability of alternative sources of support, including spouses, family members, friends, and formal agencies. Costs could be reduced with less institutionalization, more out-patient treatment, and more para-physicians.

Chappell (1987) observes that no person or institution has formal responsibility for cost effectiveness or for treatment effectiveness. Since decisions on treatment are made by patients and doctors, there is a tendency to increase services that may be of marginal benefit. A. Gauthier (1990) argues that we should learn from the health experiences surrounding childbirth, where personal support is generally sufficient and medical interventions often unnecessary. There may be a certain similarity with the health care surrounding aging and dying: having a supportive person present may often be preferable to medical interventions.

AGING AND TOTAL SOCIAL EXPENDITURE

The impact of aging on total social expenditures is also worth reviewing. In general it is found that forms of expenditure apart from pension and health costs are less affected by aging and that some expenditures may decline.

Denton *et al*. (1989) present results based on seventy-five categories of expenditure at all levels of government. For each category they separate the part that would be demographically driven and the part that would be independent of the size and age composition of the population. For instance, national defence expenditure would not be a function of demographics. Using their standard set of projections, the total expenditures increase by 23 per cent between 1986 and 2036, while the population increases by 18 per cent. The main category of expenditure that declines over the period is that for education, which would be reduced by 15 per cent over period 1986-2036. Earlier projections using similar methodology had found that as long as growth of GNP per capita is in the order of 1 or 2 per cent per year, the growth of government expenditures associated with aging would not increase the overall burden on the economy (Denton and Spencer, 1985).

Four observations are useful to make on these projections. First, they are assuming "constant quality" services. In education, for instance, quality might increase as the number of students decreases. Measured in terms of student/teacher ratios, the quality of elementary and secondary education has clearly increased rather than the number of teachers decreasing in correspondence with declining student enrolments. Also, as teachers are paid more with more seniority, this also is captured as an increase in quality. Constant quality would therefore imply that the average students per teacher and the average length of service of teachers would remain constant. As the occupational group of teachers ages, it is hard to assume that average length of service remains constant. The second observation is simply that transfers from one sector to another are difficult. Continuing with the same example, the institutions associated with education, including school boards, teachers' associations, and universities, will resist having their budgets cut in favour of allocations elsewhere. Transfers across sectors can in fact have the additional complication of being transfers across levels of government. Third, in treating certain categories of expenditure as independent from the population, these projections in effect assume that there will be economies of scale in these other sectors, that is, the changes in costs will not follow on the increase in population (H. Gauthier, 1988). For this reason, in fifteen of seventeen categories, the expenses increase less quickly than the population. As a fourth observation, it might be noted that the total expenditure at all levels of government for all social programs increased by 26 per cent in constant dollars between 1981 and 1988 (Canadian Social Trends, 1989a: 35). The increase of 23 per cent projected by Denton et al. (1989) between 1986 and 2036 obviously implies considerable constraints on expenditures.

The projections by Fellegi (1988) focus only on education, health, and pensions, which comprise 31.2 per cent of government expenditure. At constant unit costs, the total expenditure for these three programs would increase by an average of 1.0 per cent per year over the period 1986-2036. With unit costs increasing as they did over the period 1975-84, the increase would average 2.3 per cent per year. In the past thirty years the GNP per working person increased by 2.1 per cent per year. Fellegi therefore concludes that if the economic growth continues as in the past, then the public expenditure claims of health, education, and pensions should represent about the same claim on the economy in fifty years as in 1986. Nonetheless, this implies a considerable reduction in the education sector, at least under the constant unit cost scenario. A real economic growth of 2 per cent per year may be a high assumption for the next fifty years. There is also the assumption that increases in costs can be constrained. Over the period 1961-85, the costs of these three programs increased by 4.4 per cent per year, close to double the rate of economic growth (Fellegi, 1988: 20).

Wolfson (1990) has made similar calculations of the costs of these three programs, but measured as a percentage of total wages and salaries. In 1984, the costs amounted to 31.3 per cent of payroll compared to a projected 46.7 per cent in 2036. He concludes that the increase is sustainable as long as taxes are allowed to increase as foreseen. Nonetheless, this implies a very substantial increase of personal income tax, and the proportions of elderly with low-income status would increase back to the levels of the early 1960s.

Projections involving other developed countries also conclude that there would not be a large increase in the relative weight of social programs on the economy as long as economic growth is in the order of 1 or 2 per cent per year. These projections also show that Canada has an advantage compared to other countries (Heller et al., 1986). In 1980, the total social expenditures were 31 per cent of GNP in France and West Germany, compared to 20 per cent in Canada, 18 per cent in the United States, and 15 per cent in Italy. Clearly, there is considerable variability in costs across countries, depending on the types of programs. Holzmann (1988) concludes that only a growth of benefits above that of productivity would lead to a burden of expenditures that could prove unsustainable. In effect, past growth of benefits has been considerably above that of productivity. Therefore, the responsibility for the increased burden lies less with population change than with an increase in "unit costs," to use Fellegi's term, or in "quality," to use that of Denton and associates. Stone and Fletcher (1990) also conclude that the affordability of social programs for an aging population is not a problem if benefit structures are not enriched strongly and labour productivity is improved. Clearly, as long as unemployment is low and labour force participation and economic growth are high, the consequences of aging in terms of social expenditures are quite manageable. Problems would occur if one or the other of these assumptions were not met, especially if average benefits continue to rise as they have in the past.

OTHER POLICY CONCERNS ASSOCIATED WITH AGING

We cannot do justice here to all the policy areas affected by aging. For the sake of completion, it may be useful simply to list some of these other areas. Questions of income security go beyond pensions and include issues of protecting incomes against inflation and dealing with serious poverty, especially for older women. In labour force questions, there are issues of opportunities for part-time work or gradual withdrawal from the labour market. In the health area, broadly defined, alternatives to institutional care and the cost and quality of nursing homes are considerations. While rates of institutionalization are decreasing for ages 65-84, they are increasing at ages eighty-five and over, and about a fifth of the population can expect to end their lives in this kind of environment (Stone and Frenken, 1988: 48-49; Connidis, 1988: 96). Regarding housing, there are issues of affordability and design, including that appropriate for the increased numbers of elderly living alone, permitting interaction with aged peers (Morin, 1986). Similarly, transportation and mobility assistance are factors of concern.

Another issue is the relative mix of formal and semi-formal services and the extent to which these can facilitate existing support of spouses, family, and friends. Connidis (1988) suggests tax deductions for parental care, along with more semi-formal services permitting elderly to remain independent, such as homemaker services, meal preparation, and elder day care. Similarly, Gee and Kimball (1987) suggest increased support for care-giving women, both elderly wives and middle-aged daughters, by providing daytime care or other services that would support home care. Driedger and Chappell (1987) remind us that the older population represents a heterogeneous group with different histories, needs, and concerns. An older population also means that educational services need to change to accommodate a changing clientele whose needs and learning styles are rather different (Wigdor and Foot, 1988).

In an Alberta survey of public opinion, Northcott (1990) finds widespread perception that Canada will face difficulty supporting its older population. Respondents tended to favour raising personal taxes, maintaining benefits paid to needy seniors, and a homemaker's pension, and a reasonable number favoured eliminating universal benefits. The option of reducing benefits was not supported, nor was that of increasing the emphasis on the family's care of their dependent elderly parents.

CONCLUSION

As we consider the various policy questions associated with aging, it is important to remember that the older population is very heterogeneous. Some need extensive services and support while others are quite independent and in fact pay more taxes than they receive in government transfers. Most elderly live on their own, report fair to excellent health, and do not report income as their greatest worry

(Wigdor and Foot, 1988: 13). The elderly make important contributions to unpaid work and even disabled persons are not necessarily non-productive (Stone and Fletcher, 1990). Also, families do not abandon their elderly and a large part of the needs of the dependent elderly are provided by spouses and children (Connidis, 1988). As aging continues, however, the proportions of older people with working-age children will decline (Wolf, 1988). If life expectancy increases dramatically, with fewer people dying of chronic diseases but larger proportions of frail and disabled elderly, then the needs of the aged will clearly surpass the support possibilities of their immediate families. Weaker familial ties, as a function of marital disruption, may also imply higher needs for formal services.

The economic ramifications of aging are difficult to disentangle. In the short term, a higher proportion of the total population is in the labour force, and there possibly is less unemployment as fewer young people are seeking employment. The dependency burdens are not initially affected because the smaller numbers of younger people compensate for the larger numbers of older people. Nonetheless, these two groups are far from being equivalent since pension costs are higher than education costs. In the longer term, there is reason to expect that aging would undermine productivity because of the reduced relative size of the 25-50 age group and the aging labour force, which in turn could reduce mobility, creativity, and motivation of workers, while increasing the cost of labour (Chesnais, 1989).

Until now the increase in health and pension costs has been less a function of aging and more a function of increased benefits, along with coverage and maturation of pension plans. However, in the future aging will play a larger role as there will be larger numbers of frail elderly needing health care, and pension costs are rather closely linked to age.

To some extent, automatic adjustments will take place and changes are slow, permitting these adjustments to occur over a long period. One major adjustment that would reduce the dependency burden would be for the working life to be extended and for education to be more spread out over the life cycle to compensate for the lower level of entry into the labour force. Stone and Fletcher (1990) propose that pension entitlement could be based on the average "years till death" of a given cohort, which would tend to extend the working life. However, this may be difficult as health is most often reported as the reason for early retirement, and the tendency has been for retirement to occur earlier as populations age. The meaning of age could also change, as health and longevity improve. Women who have spent a larger part of their adult life in the labour force will be less disadvantaged in retirement (Marcil-Gratton and Légaré, 1987). Houle and Ducharme (1987) note that the high growth in the school-age population in the 1960s is no longer viewed as a crisis but rather as an opportunity that permitted the society to put into place a variety of programs that are now highly valued. While schools were being built, medical and pension schemes were being established. Who would say that these expensive schemes, partly demographically driven, impoverished Canadian society economically or socially? They suggest that the same may well be true of the changes brought about by growth in the older population (Ducharme, 1987).

McDaniel (1987a) also reminds us that there is a tendency to attribute too much importance to aging, sometimes even seeing it as the essential force of social change, removed from its socio-economic context. At the same time, demographic parameters are "part of the material basis of all societies" (Myles, 1981a).

Tabah (1988) summarizes what he calls a "universal concern in rich countries" that takes two forms: (1) structural rigidity that aging creates and exacerbates in the economic production process, and (2) future financial viability of retirement systems. He suggests that two actions are needed: launching a lasting recovery of the birth rates and making appropriate changes in retirement arrangements. This raises the question of who is to pay for the needed adjustments. If workers pay the main costs, then it could well be at the expense of investments in children. Already, the compensation for family costs is not keeping up with pension increases, and young couples have difficulty finding room for children in their lives. Possibly the costs of aging could be divided somewhat differently between younger and older workers, along with the retired population itself (Blanchet, 1989). The retired could pay more through lower retirement benefits, for those who are not particularly disadvantaged, and delayed departure from the labour force. It may be especially the older workers, with fewer family responsibilities and with their own retirement closer at hand, who could pay more of the pension costs. If young families paid less of the social expenditure costs of aging, they could be more involved in supporting the younger generation, which is the most secure of long-term investments.

8

CHANGE IN FAMILY AND HOUSEHOLD UNITS

Although much demographic research is based on the individual as the unit of analysis, families and households are particularly relevant units for activities ranging from living arrangements and purchase of major household goods to reproduction and the socialization of children. There is much interplay between families and demographics: what is happening to families affects the population, and population change affects families.

Family behaviour influences demographics in a variety of ways. Fertility is affected by later marriage, more divorce, more cohabitation, less remarriage, more childless couples, and more single parenthood. Geographic mobility of at least one adult, and often the person's children, is affected by divorce, remarriage, cohabitation, and the end of cohabitating relationships. Morbidity and mortality are also affected by changing family patterns: divorce increases mental and physical illness for both adults and children, social support reduces the health risks of married persons, and divorced persons are more likely to engage in detrimental behaviour (Thornton and Axia, 1989).

Population change also affects family patterns. Low mortality and fertility, and the associated population aging, imply a restructuring of the individual life course and family life cycle. In analysing these trends, Matras (1989) has shown that the mortality change over the period 1921-51 especially added to the potential years of life in the working and parenting stages, while the changes over the subsequent period added especially to the post-employment and post-parenting stages. He also calculates that the change in mortality and fertility conditions between 1951 and 1981 would have reduced the proportion of an average woman's life spent as the parent of a child under fifteen from 43.0 to 25.4 per cent of her total life years. Keyfitz (1986a) finds that even the changes between 1971 and 1981 imply rather substantial differences in the parameters of family life. By age forty, under 1971 conditions, the average woman would have one living daughter compared to 0.8 under 1981 conditions. At this same age of forty she would have an average of 0.99 living sisters under 1971 conditions and 0.79 under 1981 conditions. Gee (1990) shows that people are spending less of their lives as parents of dependent children and more as adult children of possibly dependent parents. For instance, at age sixty, almost a quarter of women born in 1960 will have at least one surviving parent. At the same time, the number of children available to older parents will have decreased sharply.

Particularly in the period since the mid-1960s, the number of households has grown faster than the population. This is a function of several factors, including a higher proportion of adults (or fewer children) in the population, a lower proportion of married people among adults (more single, separated, or widowed people living alone), and a higher propensity for non-married adults to live alone. As a consequence of these factors, the slowdown of population growth has not yet affected the growth in households. Over the period 1981-86 the population grew by 4.0 per cent and households by 8.6 per cent.

Patterns of marriage and family living have undergone much change: marriage has been delayed, lower proportions are marrying, cohabitation has become a common practice, and there are more divorces, less remarriage, more single-parent families, a dominance of two-earner families, less childbearing, and more adults living alone. Authors have emphasized the increased diversity of family forms. For instance, in monographs on the family in Canada, Burch (1990) and Ram (1990) document how certain previously marginal family and living arrangements have become much more common, particularly divorce, cohabitation, and living alone. At the time of the 1986 census, one family in five involved either cohabitation or single parenthood.

After discussing family change within structural and cultural interpretations and analysing the trends in marriage and divorce patterns, this chapter will focus on specific types of household and family units. The increased plurality and instability raise a number of policy issues as societies attempt to evolve structures to support families of diverse types and to promote the welfare of individuals living inside or outside of the various family arrangements.

STRUCTURAL AND CULTURAL INTERPRETATIONS OF FAMILY CHANGE

In a broad historical perspective, the change in family patterns can be interpreted in terms of a decrease in social functions performed by families and a change in the importance of expressive activities within families.

It has been argued that in pre-industrial societies family and kin groups had a larger number of functions (e.g., Goode, 1977; Wrigley, 1977). Besides being the chief units of reproduction and socialization of the young, they were also the units of economic production, and sometimes of political action and religious observance. Family groups performed many of the essential activities of the society: production, distribution, consumption, reproduction, socialization, recreation, and protection. Individuals depended on their families to cope with problems of age, sickness, and incapacity. In effect, it was only through membership in a family that people had claim to membership in the broader society.

Industrialization and modernization brought "structural differentiation," with increasingly separate structures in society coming to play specific functions. There was a substantial increase in the role of non-family institutions such as factories, schools, medical and public health organizations, police, and commercialized leisure. The family lost many of its roles in economic production, education, social security, and care of the aged. Consequently, the long-term changes in the family are related to societal changes, especially changes in economic structures (Review of Demography, 1989: 16). In this sense, the family has become a weaker institution, less central to the organization of society and to the lives of individuals. This reduced role allows for more flexibility in family arrangements.

Other authors have focused on change within families, proposing that expressive activities have become more important (e.g., Shorter, 1975; Haraven, 1977). While in the past the family was held together because people needed each other for survival, family relations are now based more on the need for emotional gratification. Families have become centres of nurture and affection, providing individuals with emotional support as they retreat from the achievement-oriented struggles of the outside world. This places heavy demands on family relationships, which may not always fulfil people's expectations. People are more prone to abandon family ties when their emotional well-being is not satisfied.

Based on a survey of people aged 18-30 in France, Roussel (1979) observes a radical transformation of the concept of marriage. A few see marriage in traditional terms, based on established roles, expectations, and mutual obligations, where the continuation of the relationship is not dependent on the maintenance of the love that was initially experienced. But the majority feel that a continuation of strong emotional exchanges and communication is essential to the marriage. They refuse to abide by the institutionalized prerogatives – they feel that continued personal fulfilment is essential and therefore they do not make a definite commitment to a given partner.

Roussel (1989) consequently suggests that the last two decades have involved a cultural change wherein people became less interested in living up to external norms and more interested in living up to what they themselves wanted. In many areas of life it is not possible to increase the freedom from external norms. For instance, workplaces and bureaucracies must set limits on the variability of individual behaviour. On such questions as child abuse and environmental protection, we now accept a higher level of social restrictions on behaviour. However, in family-type behaviour it has become possible to live with less social constraint. Legislative changes making divorces easier and equating cohabitation with marriage also signified a greater acceptability of alternate sexual and marital arrangements. Kettle (1980) uses a similar framework: the parents of the baby boom were a "dutiful generation" committed to sacrificing themselves for groups beyond themselves, while their children are now a "me generation" with high expectations of success and personal gratification. Thornton and Axia (1989) also refer to a "substantial weakening of the norms to marry, to stay married, to refrain from sex before marriage and to have children." The emphasis on individual fulfilment can come into conflict with the very essence of raising children: the need to place the interest of children first (Bianchi, 1990). Nonetheless, most people still value marriage and family life, expecting to marry and to have children.

Consequently, family relationships have become less important on some levels and more important on others. Families have lost some of the economic, political, and religious functions they previously provided for the larger society and they have become more important as a source of emotional gratification for individuals. Nonetheless, families still perform social functions, in particular those of reproduction and early socialization. As McDaniel (1988) observes, there is the possibility of conflict between the dual functions of families as "agents of society" and "sources of emotional support to the individuals within it." Policy orientations will vary depending on the relative value placed on these two aspects.

CHANGES IN MARRIAGE AND DIVORCE RATES

Over the first six or seven decades of this century, except for a slight reversal in the 1930s, marriages were occurring earlier in people's lives and higher proportions were getting married at some point in their lives. Around the mid-1960s these trends reversed. In 1965 the median age at first marriage was 21.2 for brides and 23.7 for grooms, but by 1988 it had risen to 24.6 for brides and 26.5 years for grooms. In 1965, 30.8 per cent of first-time brides were under twenty years of age compared to 7.4 per cent in 1988.

Not only is marriage occurring later in life, but it is also happening with lessening frequency. Combining the 1965 age-specific marriage rates implied that 95 per cent of adults could be expected to marry at some point in their lives. As people wait longer to marry, there is a higher chance that the delay results in non-marriage, which increased to over 15 per cent by 1984-86 (see Table 8).

The changes at entry into first marriage are partly a function of more cohabitation before marriage. The 1984 Canadian Fertility Survey showed that, by age thirty, nine out of ten women had had a live-in relationship (either marriage or co-habitation), and 68 per cent of the most recent generation had started their marital life through legal marriage (Lapierre-Adamcyk, 1989). However, the 1986 census indicates that, especially for women under thirty-five, the combined proportion who were married or cohabiting declined appreciably (Burch, 1990: 23). For both sexes, the proportion cohabiting declined at ages 15-24. As ascribed characteristics, particularly education and occupation, play a larger role in the lives of women, the timing of the transition to marital relationships is delayed while stable work careers are being established. Women's greater economic independence allows them to have higher standards for acceptable mates and consequently to be more willing to search longer for the "right" person (Oppenheimer, 1987). For both sexes, marriage has become less central to the transition to adulthood and to the set of roles that define adult status (Goldscheider and Waite, 1986).

Not only is there less likelihood of entering marriage, there is a greater likelihood of leaving it. Making some minor extrapolations, Dumas (1990a: 39) estimates that 15.4 per cent of the 1961-62 marriage

Table 8: Summary Statistics on the Never-married, Married, Divorced, and Widowhood States, by Sex, Canada, 1970-72 and 1984-86

	MEN		WOMEN	
	1970-1972	1984-1986	1970-1972	1984-1986
Never-married				
Per cent of population never-marrying	10	17	8	14
Average time spent single (for total population)	26.3	33.2	25.0	31.8
Married				
Percentage of population marrying	90	83	92	86
Average age at first marriage	25.0	28.3	22.8	25.7
Percentage of lifetime lived as married	58	48	52	43
Number of marriages per person marrying	1.3	1.3	1.3	1.3
Average age of the married population	49.2	51.5	46.3	48.5
Divorced				
Percentage of divorced persons marrying	85	76	79	64
Average time spent divorced (for total population)	1.1	2.6	2.2	4.9
Average length of a divorce	4.9	8.3	10.0	15.8
Average age at divorce	41.5	41.6	38.6	38.8
Average age of divorced population	51.5	53.9	56.8	57.5
Average age at remarriage	42.8	43.8	40.6	41.1
Widowed				
Average time spent widowed (for total population)	2.0	1.9	9.7	8.4
Average length of a widowhood	7.8	8.1	14.5	15.4
Average age at widowhood	68.6	72.7	67.0	69.4
Percentage of widowed persons remarrying	24	14	9	5
Average age of the widowed population	72.3	75.3	73.4	75.3
Average age at remarriage	60.5	63.8	56.5	58.1

SOURCE: Adams and Nagnur, 1988: 11, 14, 15. Reproduced with permission.

cohort will experience divorce, compared to 26.7 per cent of the 1971-72 cohort. Projecting the 1984-86 divorce rates over the life cycle would imply that 28 per cent of marriages would end in divorce (Adams and Nagnur, 1988: 13). Including both death and divorce as exits from marriage, the average duration of marriage would be 31 years. For persons who divorce, the average time spent in the divorced state was

8.3 years for men and 15.8 years for women under 1984-86 conditions (Table 8).

Given the prevalence of divorce, a higher proportion of persons are marrying for the second time or living in post-marital consensual unions. For marriages occurring in 1988, 33 per cent involved at least one spouse who was previously married (Dumas, 1990b: 8). Under 1984-86 conditions, the average number of marriages per person marrying was 1.3. Nonetheless, according to the Family History Survey, of all ever-married persons, 90 per cent married only once and less than 1 per cent married three or more times (Burch, 1985: 31). The propensity of divorced persons to remarry has declined significantly, especially for women. Under 1984-86 conditions 76 per cent of divorced men and 64 per cent of divorced women could be expected to remarry (Table 8).

Goldscheider and Waite (1986) have analysed the propensities to marry in light of the relative costs and benefits of marriage for the sexes. They note that, for the United States, men are more likely to get married when they have a secure economic status. In contrast, women are more likely to use a higher personal income to "buy out of marriage." Another example of the differential costs of marriage comes from the observation that married women are more likely to suffer job interruptions (Robinson, 1986). This does not apply to men, who are less likely to have job interruptions once they are married. In terms of benefits, women tend to gain financially from marriage while men gain more in terms of non-economic benefits, including enhanced survival and mental and physical health (Goldscheider and Waite, 1986). These authors conclude that, leaving out finances, "his" marriage is more desirable than "hers" on many dimensions. Having gained other options for financial support, women would be less prone to marry. Also for men, the greater "access to wifelike social and sexual services outside of marriage ... [reduces] their incentive to make longer-term commitments of financing and support" (p. 93).

The lower proportions of remarriage, especially for women, can probably also be seen in light of these changing costs and benefits. With greater economic independence there is less need to be married, and women who have been married may be more likely to conclude that the relative "costs of marriage" are not always to their benefit. Given the age differences at marriage, especially at remarriage, and the higher mortality of men, there are also fewer potentially available mates for older women.

Widowhood can be viewed as another stage of the marital life cycle. The 1984-86 conditions imply that half of all marriages end with the death of the man while one-fifth end with the death of the woman (Adams and Nagnur, 1988: 12). The average length of widowhood would be 8.1 years for men and 15.4 years for women (Table 8). Projections for the generation of persons born in 1921-36 would imply that 60 per cent of men will be married at the time of their deaths compared to 20 per cent of women (Péron and Légaré, 1988).

The changes in nuptiality and divorce overtook a number of generations at one time. Both young people and older people suddenly become less likely to marry and more likely to divorce and to live in common-law unions. It was not only younger couples who were having fewer children; the family-size intentions of somewhat older couples were also being revised downward. These changes are clearly interrelated. Persons marrying for the second time are more likely to separate than those marrying for the first time (Dumas, 1990a: 28). People who cohabit before marriage are more likely to separate (Burch and Madan, 1986). Children of divorced parents are more likely to substitute marriage by cohabitation (Thornton and Axia, 1989). Both childless couples and those in the now longer empty-nest stage have higher risks of divorce (Rowe, 1989).

An important implication of the trends in marriage and divorce, along with population aging, is that a higher proportion of adults are not married. In the population aged twenty and over, 28.7 per cent were not married in 1971 compared to 33.4 per cent in 1986. There is also a considerable imbalance by gender among those who are not married. At younger ages women are more likely to be married or cohabitating than men, but the pattern reverses after age thirty-five (Burch 1990: 23). At ages seventy and over the proportion married is twice as high for men as for women. Taking all the non-married over twenty as those available to marry, in 1971 there were 115 available women per 100 available men, compared to 121 non-married women per 100 non-married men in 1986. Veevers (1986) speculates that this imbalance in the sex ratio among the unmarried could have a number of potential consequences including increasing women's labour force participation, increased illegitimacy and single parenthood, more tolerance for extra-marital sex, reinforcement of the double standard, less emphasis on marriage, and more emphasis on "single-blessedness."

CHANGES AMONG THE TYPES OF HOUSEHOLD AND FAMILY UNITS

The census defines a household as one or more people living in a separate dwelling. A separate dwelling is one that can be accessed either from outside or from a common hallway without having to pass through another dwelling. A family is defined as a husband and wife with or without children who have never married, or one parent with at least one never-married child, living in the same residence. In 1986, 73.8 per cent of households involved families, and 84 per cent of Canadians lived in families (Canadian Social Trends, 1989b: 27). At the same time, half of the households included only one or two people (Burch, 1990).

There are various ways of defining family and household types. We will here review the available information according to a series of definitions (Table 9). For instance, over the period 1981-86 the number of single-person households increased by 15 per cent while lone-parent families increased 20 per cent. In contrast, the number of husband-wife families with children at home increased only 2.3 per cent and the families with husband only in the labour force declined by 18 per cent. The highest increases are for non-traditional family forms. Together the common-law families and single-parent families comprised 20 per cent of families in the 1986 census.

Children living at home: the cluttered nest

Until the 1976 census, the tendency was for children to leave home at increasingly young ages, thus contributing to the length of the empty nest stage. However, the period 1976-86 saw a reversal of these trends. For instance, at age twenty-two, 48.5 per cent of young people were living with their parents in 1986, compared to 35.3 per cent in 1976 (Ram, 1990: 48). The mean years lived in the parental family increased from 22.7 to 24.2 years. Boyd and Pryor (1989) find that school attendance and low income, or unemployment, are the most important factors accounting for living with parents. They speculate that it may also be related to, or it may promote, a resurgence of family values.

Young families

While the population at young adult ages has grown, they are less likely to be married, making for a slight decline in young families with the husband or lone parent aged less than thirty-five (Rashid, 1989: 15). Nonetheless, these comprised 28 per cent of all families in 1986. Among various family types, these young families have suffered the largest decline in average income over the period 1980-85. The average income of these families, in constant dollars, declined by 11 per cent over this period. The proportion of families with low income status was 33.2 per cent for families with the husband or lone parent under twenty-five years, compared to an average of 14.1 for all families.

It is noteworthy that the proportion of young families under age thirty-five who owned their own homes increased from under half in 1971 to close to 60 per cent in 1981 (Statistics Canada, 1984b). In the period 1961-81 the proportion of young persons who were heads of households increased, but this proportion decreased in the subsequent

Table 9: Change in Various Household and Family Types, 1981-86

| | Number (thousands) | | Change (%) |
	1981	1986	1981-86
Total households (private)	8,281.5	8,991.7	8.6
Family households	6,231.5	6,635.0	6.5
Non-family households	2,050.0	2,356.7	15.0
One-person households	1,681.1	1,934.7	15.1
Total families	6,325.3	6,733.8	6.5
Husband-wife families*	5,611.5	5,880.6	4.8
Husband-wife families with children at home	3,599.1	3,676.7	2.3
Husband-wife families without children at home	2,011.4	2,202.0	9.4
Total common-law families	354.2	484.8	36.5
Common-law with children	120.2	181.8	50.7
Common-law without children	234.0	303.0	29.2
Single-parent families	713.8	853.3	19.5
Male led	124.4	151.5	21.8
Female led	589.4	701.8	19.1
Husband-wife families with			
– husband under 35	1,788.0	1,660.2	–7.1
– husband 65 or over	704.0	805.0	14.3
Husband-wife families with			
– husband only in labour force	1,962.3	1,618.0	–17.5
– wife only in labour force	138.7	186.4	34.4
– both in labour force	2,745.3	3,180.9	15.9
– neither in labour force	765.2	895.1	17.0
Total Population	24,343.2	25,309.3	4.0

*Includes common-law unions.

SOURCES: Rashid, 1989: 15; Ram, 1990: 44; Burch, 1990: 17; 1986 Census 93-107, 93-106; 1981 Census 92-935.

five-year period (Morin et al., 1988). M. Gauthier (1990) documents the various disadvantages of young adults aged twenty to twenty-four, who have the highest proportion of any age group in the labour force but rather unstable and insecure work patterns. A growing number of young people are working while they are full-time students. Rochon (1990) concludes that the families with parents under twenty-five are those most in need of programs and services.

Husband-wife families and dual careers

There are a number of reasons for the increased involvement of wives in the labour force, including family-related reasons such as lower births and more divorce. In effect, divorce has undermined the central bargain of the breadwinner-homemaker arrangement (Davis, 1984). Unable to depend on the stability of the marriage, women need to be self-sufficient. The increased independence of women also facilitates their departure from unsatisfactory marriages.

In 1967, 61 per cent of husband-wife families with at least one of the spouses under sixty-five involved only the husband in the labour force. Since 1981, the families with both husband and wife in the labour force had become the dominant category (Review of Demography, 1989: 14). Dual-earner families have therefore become "the new norm," comprising 62 per cent of all husband-wife families (M. Moore, 1989a). Dual-earner families have higher incomes, amounting to an average of almost $50,000 in 1985, of which the wives contributed 29 per cent on average. Families with the husband only in the labour force, which made up 27 per cent of families, had an average income of just under $40,000. Over the period 1973-86, Dooley (1988) finds that the "very modest" improvement in the real income of married couples was due almost entirely to growth in the earnings of wives, as well as government transfers.

Especially among the young, dual-earner families are less likely to have children at home. Only 32 per cent of dual-earner families in which the wife was under age twenty-five had children, compared to 77 per cent for comparable families where the husband was the sole earner. Among families in which the wife was 25-34, 70 per cent of dual-earner families had children, compared with 95 per cent of cases where the husband was the sole earner (M. Moore, 1989a: 26).

Stated differently, marriage and children continue to reduce women's labour force participation and to introduce work interruptions. At ages 25-44, 52 per cent of wives compared to 85 per cent of husbands were working full-time in 1985 (Statistics Canada, 1986b: 26, 56). At ages 35-49 the never-married women had the highest labour force participation rates, 79 per cent, while the continuously married had the lowest, 57 per cent (Balakrishnan and Grindstaff, 1988). Robinson (1989b) finds that marriage, just as much as children, is associated with a higher risk of employment interruption for women. Kempeneers (1989) concludes that discontinuity in employment has not changed for women who have two or more children. Among women who were aged thirty at the time of the 1981 census, the largest differences in personal income and labour force participation were between those with and without children (Grindstaff, 1990c). Married women are most likely to move to accompany a spouse and to have lower rates of labour force participation after migrating (Shihadeh, 1990).

While childless couples where both are employed have a total division of work that approaches equality, dual-earner couples with children have patterns that are far from symmetrical, with the wife spending considerably more total working hours per week (Lupri and Mills, 1987). From this point of view, one might argue that "childlessness is the easiest route to equality." Children tend to introduce a more traditional division of labour, even to marriages that started out on a relatively equal footing. Nonetheless, Harrell (1985) finds that the greater the wife's contribution to total family income, the more likely the husband was to become involved with cooking and cleaning in the house.

Although dual-earner couples can be called "the new norm," it is clear that, especially when there are young children, the involvement of wives in the labour force often remains partial and they contribute considerably less than half of the total family income while doing much more than half of the housework. For the most part, this can be seen as an adjustment that couples are making for the sake of the children. An American poll taken in 1989 that asked: "Which do you feel is more important for a family these days," 68 per cent chose "to make some financial sacrifices so that one parent can stay home to raise the children" while 27 per cent said "to have both parents working so the family can benefit from the highest possible income" (Footlick, 1990: 18). Summarizing other American data, Bumpass (1990) finds that spousal disagreements about the wife's employment are common, and they take a variety of forms involving the husband or wife thinking that the wife should work more or less than she is currently working. In spite of this ambivalence, there is much change, especially in the cases of young children. In Canada, 58.1 per cent of married women with at least one child under six were in the labour force in 1986, compared to 27.1 per cent in 1971 (Ram, 1990: 36).

Common-law unions

Cohabitation, both pre-marital and post-marital, is another indication of family change. According to the 1984 Family History Survey, almost 30 per cent of persons aged 25-29 had ever been in common-law unions (Ram, 1990: 55). Taken together, the trends in cohabitation and nuptiality can be read as implying considerable continuity as less formal relationships are simply substituted for marriage. This survey found that rates of formation of unions of all kinds had remained relatively constant (Burch and Madan, 1986).

In other regards, cohabitation is not a true substitute for marriage: common-law unions are short-lived compared to marriages, fertility rates are low for cohabiting couples, and marriages preceded by cohabitation have higher rates of dissolution. Five years after the beginning of such unions, 27 per cent of couples are still in the same union, 46 per cent have married their partner, and 27 per cent have separated (Burch and Madan, 1986: 19). The majority of persons in common-law unions thus tend either to marry their partner or to separate fairly quickly. Since cohabitation is more likely to end in marriage than in separation, it is more often a prelude rather than a substitute for marriage. This prelude does not reduce the risk of separation. After ten years of legal marriage, the rate of dissolution was 17 per cent for those preceded by cohabitation and 10 per cent for those not preceded by cohabitation (Burch and Madan, 1986: 22). Fertility is lower for women who are cohabiting. The 1984 Canadian Fertility Survey found that women aged 25-29 had an average of 0.21 children if they were single, 0.54 if they were never married but cohabiting, and 1.38 if they were married (Balakrishnan, 1989a: 35).

In the 1986 census, one out of twelve couples were living in common-law relationships, the number having increased by 38 per cent since 1981. However, as noted earlier, the propensity to live common law had declined for younger adults.

Living alone

As a consequence of the changes in the family life cycle, a larger proportion of people are living alone. Persons living alone comprise 21 per cent of households and 10 per cent of all adults (Burch and McQuillan, 1988). Living alone is particularly predominant among older women, including a full third of those over sixty-five (Ram, 1990: 45).

The analysis of income changes of persons not in families between 1980 and 1985 finds that these are consistent with those observed for families during the same time period (Rashid, 1989: 27-30). Average incomes of persons not in families decreased slightly for men and increased for women, bringing the average female income to 77.3 per cent of the average male income. For persons living alone, the average income at ages 15-64 declined by 3.2 per cent to $19,800 in 1986, while for persons sixty-five and over it increased by 8.3 per cent to $13,700. In 1985, 36.5 per cent of women and 28.1 per cent of men sixty-five and over who were not in families had low-income status, compared to 8.2 per cent of elderly families (Rashid, 1989: 38). Nonetheless, all these categories of elderly show improvement over the 1980 results.

In spite of the greater tendency to live alone, Burch and McQuillan (1988) find a strong preference for being married, or at least in some form of intimate, co-residential relationship. Persons living alone have average levels of happiness or satisfaction, although lower than those who are married or cohabiting. These authors conclude that questions of living alone have low policy priority compared, for instance, to issues affecting the care and education of children.

Single-parent families

Families involving only one parent comprised 13 per cent of all families in 1986. These families can further be differentiated according to the sex, age, and marital status of the parent. In 1971, the largest category involved a widowed parent; in 1986 those involving a separated or divorced parent made up 59.5 per cent of the total, with another 13.4 per cent involving a never-married parent (Ram, 1990: 52, 87). In 1986, 28.4 per cent involved a parent under thirty-five years of age and 17.8 per cent involved a male parent.

The growth of young female single-parent families has in fact contributed considerably to the "feminization of poverty" in Canada. In 1986, 45 per cent of female lone-parent families were classified as having low-income status (Rashid, 1989: 38). The average income in 1985 of female single-parent families was $19,200, compared to $31,300 for male single-parent families and $44,000 for husband-wife families with children (Rashid, 1989: 15; Moore, 1987: 34). Over the period 1973-86, the incomes of female single-parent families did not keep pace, producing a widening gap with other families (Dooley, 1988; Burch and McQuillan, 1988). Even the single-parent families where the mother was working full time for the full year had an average income below the low-income line (Dooley, 1990). For the most part, single-parent families do not have the option of having more than one income-earner and even having one full-time earner is often difficult (McQuillan, 1990).

Maureen Moore (1987, 1988, 1989b) has analysed female lone-parenting with the help of the 1984 Family History Survey. Compared to currently married women of the same age, female lone parents are more likely to have lived common law, to have had their children earlier, and to have less education, but they are more likely to be in the labour force. In effect, they must raise children while facing a double disadvantage of lack of support from a spouse and fewer job skills. Among women aged 18-64 in 1984 who had had children, 26 per cent had experienced lone parenthood. For about two-thirds of these, parenting alone had ended either through a new union or through the children leaving home. Among the episodes that ended, only 16 per cent ended through the children leaving home. The average duration of episodes was 5.5 years, with 10 per cent of episodes lasting less than six months and 17 per cent lasting more than ten years. Among those who experienced one episode, 12 per cent experienced two or more episodes of parenting alone.

One form of entry into single parenthood occurs through births to single women. Such births have increased over the period 1975-86, although the largest increases involved women over thirty who may in fact be in common-law unions and thus they are not becoming single-parents (Ram, 1990: 32; Dumas and Boyer, 1984). The desirability of the conjugal family is supported by the fact that over 80 per cent of women who had ex-nuptial births had married before the survey date (Moore, 1989b: 339).

Children in families

While much of the analysis of family types takes its point of reference in the adults, it is equally important to focus on how family change affects children. First, fewer families include children; in 1986, 33 per cent of families had no children living at home, including 37 per cent of husband-wife families (Table 9). Burch (1990: 39) finds that only about two-fifths of adults twenty and over live with children fifteen or under, including half of adults aged 20-39 and one-third of those aged 40-59. The immediate experience of young children therefore involves a minority of the adult population.

Couples with young children at home are more likely to be dissatisfied with their marriages, compared to childless couples or those whose children have left home (Lupri and Frideres, 1981). Eichler (1988: 181) argues that the strain involved in raising children may have increased because they are dependent for a longer time while there are fewer adults per household, along with fewer children who can occupy each other.

While the experience of orphanhood has clearly declined, children have experienced other forms of family instability. On the average, they have experienced a shift toward living in mother-only and reconstituted families. In 1961, 93.6 per cent of children under twenty-five living at home were in husband-wife families, 5.0 per cent in female lone-parent families, and 1.4 per cent in male lone-parent families. By 1986, 85.6 per cent were in husband-wife families, with 11.9 and 2.5 per cent in female and male lone-parent families respectively (Burch and McQuillan, 1988). The 1986 census also found that 3.8 per cent of the children living at home were in families involving common-law unions. The Family History Survey showed that 2.1 per cent of women and 4.4 per cent of men had at some point in their lives raised stepchildren (Burch, 1985: 31).

Not only does this mean greater diversity in the lives of children, there is evidence that "relationships in remarried families" can be rather different (Hobart, 1988). Fathers in particular tend to reduce their attachments to their children once these are in reconstituted families. Data from the United States suggest that most fathers become marginal in the lives of their children within a few years of separation (Bumpass, 1990). Compared to those still married, separated mothers also have less contact with their adult children who have left home. Kantrowitz and Wingert (1990: 27) conclude that stepchildren have more developmental, emotional, and behavioural problems than children in intact families. The increased proportion in non-traditional family settings therefore increases the proportion of disadvantaged children. In 1984, 36.5 per cent of low-income children were in lone-parent families. Since these largely involve mother-led families, the trends also contribute to the feminization of poverty.

Besides the high incidence of low income for single-parent families, husband-wife families have a higher incidence of low income if there are children present. In 1985, 8.6 per cent of husband-wife families with no children had low income, compared to 15.8 per cent of those with two children under six (Rashid, 1989: 16, 39). Over the period 1981-85, the proportion of given age groups with low income declined or remained stable for most groups, but it increased for children fifteen and under (Arnoti, 1986). These low incomes generally mean poorer housing, health care, recreation, and education (Burch, 1990: 38). As a function of variability in family types and in numbers of family members in the labour force, the inequality in the material well-being of children appears to be widening (Dooley, 1989b; McQuillan, 1990).

Dooley (1989b) finds that the presence of children under eighteen invariably raises the incidence of low income for families. Families with children experienced no increases in after-tax real income between 1981 and 1987. Taxes and transfers reduce the proportion of low income by some 75 per cent for elderly families but by only 16 per cent for husband-wife families with children and by 6 per cent for single-parent families (Brouillette *et al.*, 1990a).

Using data from the 1984 Family History Survey, Marcil-Gratton (1988) has provided interesting insights into how low fertility, higher labour force participation, and increased separation and divorce are relevant to the family lives of children. In the early 1960s, 25 per cent of births were first births compared to 44 per cent in the early 1980s. This means that children have more "inexperienced" parents. They also have fewer older brothers and sisters: half of the generation born in the early 1960s had two older brothers or sisters, compared to one-fifth for those born twenty years later. One in five had a brother or sister ten or more years older, compared to one in twenty for the later generation. Because of lower fertility and its concentration over a short time in the lives of adults, children have less opportunity to interact with and learn from siblings. In fact, one in ten children born in the early 1970s was an only child at the age of ten.

The work lives of mothers also affects children's lives as part of their early socialization is transferred to others at an increasingly young age. In the early 1960s, 90 per cent of mothers stopped working at the birth of a first child, compared to 50 per cent in the early 1980s. The proportion working soon after the birth in the early 1980s would be comparable to the proportion working twenty years earlier when children were twelve years old.

The diversity of marriage behaviour is also relevant. In the early

1960s, 5 per cent of children were not born in a marriage, compared to 14 per cent twenty years later. Among children born in the early 1960s, 13 per cent saw the separation of their parents by age ten, compared to 23 per cent for those born in the early 1970s. Among the latter, half had been in reconstituted families, 20 per cent saw a second episode of single parenthood, and 10 per cent had seen a second reconstituted family, all before age ten. Among children born in 1961-63, 8 per cent lived in a single-parent family by age six, compared to 18 per cent for those born in 1975-77 (Marcil-Gratton, 1988).

In speculating on how these kinds of changes affect the well-being of children, Burch (1990: 38) suggests:

Only a child is absolutely dependent on its family for survival and well-being. Adults can typically support themselves, and can seek to meet their social and emotional needs in many ways. They do not have to be married or to have children. But children, especially infants and young children, have to live in a family or family substitute. Moreover, in most of the family changes discussed in this report, some elements of individual choice are involved – people choose to divorce, to live alone, to have a child, always, of course, in the face of constraints, including choices of others. But the young child has no choice. He or she must simply live with what society and his or her parents offer.

The elderly and families

Families with a husband aged sixty-five or over comprise 14 per cent of all husband-wife families. Their average family incomes are lower than all but those with the husband under twenty-five, but they are the only age group to have made gains in average income over the period 1980-85 (Rashid, 1989: 15). They are also the group with the lowest incidence of low income: 8.2 per cent of families where the husband or lone parent is sixty-five or over had low income, compared to 33.3 per cent at age group 15-24 (*idem*: 38). Over the period 1973-86, elderly couples experienced the highest income growth rate of any type of family (Dooley, 1988). Since elderly families depend heavily on government transfers and their average incomes are low, they need to be concerned about the effect that inflation can have on pension benefits. However, those elderly living in families have clearly made gains relative to other groups.

The same does not apply to the elderly who are not living in families. In 1986, 13.6 per cent of men and 33.6 per cent of women aged sixty-five and over were living alone (Ram, 1990: 45). Since women have less pension income related to previous employment and since pension-splitting between spouses often does not occur, widowed women suffer economic disadvantages. The greater importance of family roles for women, along with greater longevity, means that women as widows are more often impoverished than men. While the incomes of the elderly in general have increased, women living alone have fallen behind and this has contributed to the "feminization of poverty" (Gee and Kimball, 1987).

While many elderly are living alone, this does not mean they are isolated. Stone (1988) finds that, for the elderly in private dwellings, relatives and close friends are more important than formal support. Only some 7 to 10 per cent of the elderly have no surviving children (Péron and Légaré, 1988). Most elderly who have never married have family and friends with whom they are engaged in exchanges (Strain, 1990). The evidence would indicate that while co-residence of elderly persons with their children has declined, families do not abandon their elderly. Contact between siblings in later life is also important, especially for women, those who are not married, and the childless (Connidis, 1989).

FAMILY-ORIENTED POLICIES

Because families are valued, many policies are legitimated in terms of their support for families and/or criticized for not supporting families. Given the diversity of family types and the diverse goals and needs of individuals both inside and outside of families, it is very difficult to develop a consistent set of programs and services to satisfy these diverse orientations. For instance, given the importance that family relations play in the welfare of most people, one would want to support the stability of family units. On the other hand, sometimes individuals are suffering in their families and one would want to support their departure. In effect, the divorce legislation has made it increasingly easy for adults to separate from their families while attempting to ensure that separated parents continue to be responsible for dependent children. Mirabelli (1989: 10) sees a "real tension between the desire to support families with policies and programs and the trend toward individualism as the principle defining relationships between persons and the state."

The orientation toward family policy will depend on the "model of the family" to which one subscribes. In a sense, family policy may have been easier in the days when the breadwinner model was dominant. Policies could support the income of husbands and treat wives and children as dependants. But such orientations promote the continuation of male-dominant gender relations both inside and outside of families, and they play against the independence of women. Unless they are barred from working, it is peculiar to treat wives as dependants, although one may want to support mothers looking after their children. In effect, parents have a variety of orientations regarding the care of their children, with some preferring at least partial withdrawal from the labour force when the children are young and others favouring a true dual-earner arrangement.

For instance, the Royal Commission on Taxation recommended in 1966 that families be used as the basis for income tax. Instead, income tax has been based on individual income, although various adjustments have been introduced to take into account the family situation. Treating the spouses separately presents advantages to families with two incomes. Given that income taxes are based on individual income, whatever adjustments are made to take into account the family in effect tend especially to benefit richer people, as well as married people, while undermining women's orientation to have a separate income (see Péron and Morissette, 1986).

If the family becomes the only unit of reference, it can prompt people to live separately in order to have the greater needs and more deductions associated with separate units. This already happens with welfare payments, which reduce or eliminate the support to mothers when there is a "man in the house." The same applies to subsidized day care where the fewer the adults in the family, producing a lower family income, the greater the established need on which to base the subsidy. Similarly, older people will have a higher total Guaranteed Income Supplement if they live separately. This is what Eichler (1988: 395-97) has called the "familism-individualism flip-flop": policies that are aimed at helping families can end up disadvantaging at least some families or discouraging people from living in families.

Family policies are necessarily based on an understanding of what the family is. But we have seen that there is much diversity of family types, and the society is in a transition from one dominant model (breadwinner) to another (dual-career). Policies that treat wives as dependants support one model while those that promote universal day care support another. But both co-exist: mothers who stay at home may not want their husband's incomes to be taxed for the benefit of subsidizing day care. Similarly, dual-career families are not able to profit from "married deductions." For the elderly, spouse's allowance and Canada/Quebec Pension Plan survivor benefits largely do not benefit women who have their own pensions based on continued work history.

Given the diversity that exists, there is a need to be flexible. It cannot be expected that all contradictions will be resolved. There is need to support such programs as spousal allowance and survivor benefits for those who have lived, or wish to live, their lives under the assumptions of the breadwinner model. Similarly, there is a need to support benefits related to work roles (day care, parental leave, flex-time) for those adopting the two-earner model.

Besides being flexible, it could also be argued that family policies should be based less on the needs of adults and more on promoting the welfare of children in families. As indicated earlier, children have the least choice in family matters and the society needs to ensure that the changing family behaviour of adults is not detrimental to children. Marcil-Gratton (1988) concludes that parents tend to forget their children's interest in the transformation of their lives and thus recommends that the society should give greater priority to the interest of the child. Similarly, in concluding his wide-ranging discussion on "What's Happening to the Family?" Bumpass (1990) finds that shifting attitudes mean more individual freedom for adults but that the well-being of children is undermined and there is insufficient investment in children. Noting that the elderly have made much progress since 1971 while families with children have experienced little improvement, Brouillette *et al*. (1990a) suggest fewer benefits to the elderly in order to finance more family benefits.

In a broad ranging article discussing policy issues associated with "poor children in Canada," Roseman (1990) argues:

> To finance better programs for the poor, Canadians will have to accept a redistribution of income from the childless to the child-rearing. This may sound unfair, but everyone has a stake in other people's children. They are the future labor force, the workers who will be creating the goods and services we will consume during our retirement years. As fertility rates remain low and children become relatively scarce, it makes good economic sense to invest in their welfare.

She goes on to observe that children are poor because their parents are poor, which requires that we attack unemployment and low wages, and/or provide better transfers to the poor. Education, job training, and upgrading programs, including a "training savings plan," are suggested as the main means of attacking the problems of the working poor. Mothers, and single-parent mothers in particular, need better access to child care, along with pay equity and affirmative action, better salaries and benefits for part-time work, and leave programs when children are sick. To guarantee a minimum floor, Roseman further suggests enriching the child tax credit:

> But payments substantial enough to lift families out of poverty – on the order of $4,000 to $5,000 a year for each child – cannot be achieved without cuts in benefits to other groups, such as the elderly.
> In Canada, the old are benefiting at the expense of the young. . . .
> Almost 25 years ago, the federal government decided to guarantee a minimum income for Canada's oldest citizens. There is a desperate

need for a similar guarantee for the country's youngest citizens, giving them a social floor through which they cannot fall into poverty and dead-end jobs.

It is an investment in human capital, an investment in our own future standard of living.

Clearly, the discussion of family policy includes issues that span the various chapters of this book, including in particular fertility, aging, gender differences, and income inequality.

We have noted that the particularly disadvantaged families are those involving lone parents and young parents. In both cases, much of the disadvantage results from the presence of young children. We also noted that families with children tend to be economically disadvantaged compared to those without children. More generally, it can be argued that various orientations toward the family could agree on the need to provide "relief for parents." This relief could take various forms, ranging from more broadly available child-care facilities to facilitating one parent staying home with young children or paying another family member to take care of the children. In concluding the discussion on "changing patterns in child care," Eichler (1988: 337-38) argues for a set of policies that would support parental leaves, financial assistance to parents, day care, days off, and alternate workloads with better part-time benefits.

Questions surrounding the elderly inside or outside of families have been treated in the previous chapter. Here again, there is need to be flexible and to accommodate change. Gee (1990) observes that more of the weight of supporting frail elderly is likely to fall on adult children, who will be less numerous to share the burden. Persons born in the 1930s will have the advantage of having several surviving children, but those born in the 1960s will be disadvantaged in terms of the availability of children to provide care. Gee suggests that there is a need to enhance independent living regardless of family membership status and to enhance accessibility to formal services without assuming a model of family responsibility for the aged. She also proposes various forms of relief for those adult children, especially daughters, who are caring for elderly parents: elder day care, tax deductions for dependent parents, and provisions in the Canada/Quebec Pension Plan that would not penalize persons who withdraw from the labour force to care for elderly parents.

CONCLUSION

Changing patterns of fertility and mortality, with associated population aging, change the parameters of family life. In particular, a lower proportion of people's lives is spent as parents of dependent children and a higher proportion as adult children of dependent parents (Gee, 1990). In concluding his monograph on "families in Canada," Burch (1990) writes that fundamental demographic changes such as longer lives, delayed marriage, and less childbearing have made marriage and the family a smaller part of people's lives. This also follows on the long-term structural changes in society that have reduced the number of roles filled by families in the society. However, family relations continue to be very important to people's emotional gratification and fulfilment. In spite of higher proportions living alone, adults have a strong preference for living in an intimate relationship. While there is much change, it is also useful to note that the 1984 Family History Survey found seven out of ten women with children still living in their first nuclear families by the survey date. This survey also indicated that 90 per cent of the ever-married did so only once.

Families have become increasingly diversified. This diversification, especially the trends toward two-earner and single-parent families, brings more disparity across families. Children are less numerous, but when they are there they tend to restrict women's labour force activity and to disrupt income-earning continuity. But children can also be ignored as adults change their family, work, and living patterns to maximize their own fulfilment.

This leads us to suggest that the policy emphasis regarding families should focus more on the support of children. Families with children appear to be in greatest need, especially lone-parent families and young families. There are diverse orientations regarding the type of family that should be promoted. A greater focus on the welfare of children could suggest initiatives that need not be biased toward one or the other model of family living.

9

POPULATION AND SOCIO-ECONOMIC CHANGE

Many analyses of socio-economic welfare take their point of reference in the population, often divided into relevant groups. Especially in a welfare state, where a main objective of public policy is to improve the well-being of the population, there is need for extensive knowledge on the population whose welfare one is trying to improve. Stated differently, the focus is on the composition of the population along various relevant characteristics. The policy questions at this stage generally do not focus on changing the population but on adapting to the demographic situation.

Among the various questions that could be raised on this topic, this chapter will focus on education, labour force, gender, and distribution of income. The main underlying policy issue is that of income security, which at the societal level is largely achieved through employment and government transfers.

EDUCATION: TRENDS AND DIRECTIONS

In the immediate post-war period, Canada's educational system was poorly developed. In 1951, the total post-secondary students numbered about 95,000 (Vanderkamp, 1988: 5), and there were five university students per 1,000 population in Canada compared to 15 per 1,000 in the United States (Pike, 1988: 266). There followed a period of considerable reform in education, especially of increased funding that eventually brought Canada into line with other industrial countries. In 1985 the total post-secondary students had risen to 1,075,000. While the population had not quite doubled in size since 1951, the number of post-secondary students had increased elevenfold. The ratio of total enrolment to the population aged 20-24 was second only to the United States among eight major industrial countries (Pike, 1988: 269).

Expenditures for education rose especially in the 1960s. In 1971, education represented 22 per cent of all government expenditures, compared to 14 per cent in 1961 (Pike, 1988: 266). With the growth of other programs, especially those for health and pensions, and the narrower population base at prime ages for educational participation, government expenditures for education were down to 12 per cent of total government expenditures in 1988 (Canadian Social Trends, 1990: 34). Since 1986, the total government expenditures for health have been higher than for education.

Primary and secondary levels

At the elementary and secondary levels, the number of students followed closely the movement of the baby boom through the corresponding ages. In addition, the participation rate for secondary education increased substantially over the 1960s (Beaujot and McQuillan, 1982: 124). The proportion of the population aged 14-17 in school increased from 76 per cent in 1962 and 84 per cent in 1981 to 90 per cent in 1985 (Gilbert and Guppy, 1988). As a function of the enrolment rates, but especially the changing age distribution, the total number of students at both levels combined increased substantially until 1970, but by 1985 it had declined by 18 per cent. The peak enrolment was in 1968 for elementary and 1972 for secondary education (Wilkinson, 1986: 537). In the period 1985-88 the total enrolment increased slightly, by 2 per cent over three years.

In spite of the 18 per cent decline in enrolment in the period 1970-85, the total costs of elementary and secondary education increased by 47 per cent in constant dollars (Wilkinson, 1986: 537). The increased costs would largely be a function of lower student/teacher ratios as well as better educated and more experienced teachers. The number of teachers was basically the same in 1982-83 as in 1971-72, but they had some five years more teaching experience on average.

With the higher participation in secondary education, the proportion of the 1986 population who were high school graduates reached 57 per cent for age groups 20-25 and 25-34, compared to 25 per cent in age group 55-64 (Mori and Burke, 1989: 26). This publication also shows higher levels of labour force participation, lower unemployment, and higher incomes for persons with secondary school graduation compared to those without graduation. For instance, among persons working full-time, the graduates have a 24 per cent income advantage.

Post-secondary level

Starting from a much lower level, the post-secondary enrolment increased at a faster rate. At universities, the average annual rate of growth for full-time students over the period 1951-85 was 5.5 per cent at the undergraduate level and 8.9 per cent at the graduate level (Vanderkamp, 1988: 5). For instance, the number of full-time university students doubled between 1960 and 1967. For part-time university attendance, the growth rates were 14.1 and 9.3 per cent per year at the undergraduate and graduate levels, respectively. The college post-secondary sector was largely established in the mid- to late 1960s and by 1985 it represented 40 per cent of the total post-secondary enrolment. Since 1968 the growth has been 6.4 per cent per year for the career programs and 7.7 per cent for the university transfer programs.

In analysing the factors behind the change in enrolment levels, Vanderkamp (1988) notes the importance of population trends, labour market needs, institutional innovation, and public policies. The policy instruments would include tuition fees, financial aid to students, and, especially, operating grants to post-secondary institutions. In constant dollars, the average university fees declined by 33 per cent between 1971 and 1981, then increased by 6 per cent to 1985 (Vanderkamp, 1988: 41). University operating expenditure per student, in constant dollars, doubled between 1960 and 1977, then declined by 16 per cent to 1985 (Vanderkamp, 1988: 48). The college sector followed a similar path, with a peak year of operating expenditure per student in 1978 and a subsequent decline by 28 per cent to 1985. The total government outlay for post-secondary education, including operating grants, sponsored research, capital grants, and student aid, almost doubled in constant dollars between 1960 and 1978, then declined by 18 per cent to 1985 (*idem*: 54). One consequence of these trends is that student/faculty ratios increased over the period 1978-85 (Vanderkamp, 1988: 50).

The enrolment and funding of post-secondary education have therefore involved a major contrast to primary and secondary education since the mid-1970s. Primary and secondary enrolment declined by 18 per cent between 1970 and 1985, while total funding increased 47 per cent. At the post-secondary level, the total full-time equivalent enrolment has continued to increase, in fact by 28 per cent between 1978 and 1985, during which period the total funding declined by 18 per cent.

Part of the difficulty has involved rather inaccurate projections of post-secondary enrolment. The movement of the baby boom would have implied a peak year for post-secondary enrolment around 1982. Projections made in the 1970s also noted that the participation rates had been rather constant in the later part of the decade, especially for men. For instance, the projections from Statistics Canada put the total full-time enrolment for 1986-87 at 551,400, which turned out to be 31 per cent short of the mark (Zsigmond et al., 1978: 126; Canadian Social Trends, 1990: 34). Picot (1980: 18) had projected that the rate of post-secondary participation would decline over the period 1976-86 while the rate began to increase as of 1980 (Mori and Burke, 1989: 23). Between 1980 and 1988, the proportion of persons aged 18-21 at university increased from 11 to 16 per cent, while those aged 22-24 increased from 7 to 9 per cent (Potts, 1989: 29). This was more than sufficient to counter the 13 per cent decline in the population aged 18-24, resulting in a 30 per cent increase in full-time university enrolment.

Subsequent analyses have shown that the demographic factor of movement of given cohorts through the age structure plays a less significant role in the case of post-secondary enrolment (Vanderkamp, 1988: 7). In addition, the age catchment of education, especially for the university sector, has become broader, particularly when part-time students are considered. Foot and Pervin (1983) have shown that enrolment is positively influenced by operating grants, which keep tuition low, by rising per capita incomes, which make education a valuable investment, by higher unemployment, which reduces the opportunity costs of spending time in school, and by smaller cohort sizes, which reduce the competition and hence increase the expected returns to education. This last consideration of cohort size implies a counterbalancing factor wherein larger cohorts would be less likely to pursue higher education, other things being equal. Besides the reduced competition, smaller cohorts may have less difficulty obtaining equivalent per capita investments both from parents and from the society for their education. Foot and Pervin therefore expect that enrolment will continue to be counter to the demographic trends, at least for the university sector. Vanderkamp (1988: 86) also demonstrates that enrolments are an important driving force behind the levels of operating grants.

In addition, it can be expected that "whole life education" will continue to grow. According to Hobbs and Kirk (1987) this would follow on the demographic shifts involving fewer young people, social changes, and structural changes in the economy that give a premium to knowledge. Wigdor and Foot (1988: 50) also expect that post-secondary students will be older on average. Already, the proportion of university enrolment under age twenty-five declined from 62.8 per cent in 1976 to 56.1 per cent in 1986. Among part-time undergraduates, those under twenty-five comprise only a quarter of the total.

As a result of changing enrolment, the level of education of the population has increased substantially. In 1961 some 2.3 per cent of the population aged twenty-five and over had a university degree, but by 1986 this figure had increased to 11.1 per cent, with another 30.0 per cent having some post-secondary education (Mori and Burke, 1989). The total with some post-secondary education or degrees increased from 21.3 per cent of the population aged twenty-five and over in 1971 to 41.1 in 1986. More than half of persons aged 25-34 have some post-secondary education.

Economic returns are considerably higher with more education. For instance, the unemployment rates in July, 1990, were 5.9 for those with a college diploma and 4.1 with a university degree, compared to an overall rate of 7.6 per cent.

Issues

While levels of education have increased, substantial numbers still have inadequate education, especially as measured by literacy. According to a survey taken in 1987, Southam (1990) finds that 24 per cent of the population aged eighteen and over "cannot read, write or use numbers well enough to meet the literacy demands of today's society." Among these, one-third are high school graduates, and only one in ten would consider taking remedial classes. Based on a 1989 survey, Statistics Canada estimates that 15 per cent of Canadians cannot read English or French well enough to deal with most written material encountered in everyday life. Besides these, another 22 per cent have some difficulty and basically avoid reading (Montigny, 1990). The Conference Board (1989) estimates that 11 per cent of the labour force lacks basic literacy and numeracy skills.

The Royal Commission on the Economic Union (1985, II: 760-61) suggested that more priority should be given to the training needs for those who leave school early or who wish to return to school later. For those who return, a Registered Education Leave Savings Plan would permit a transfer of income from periods of employment to those of education. Greater flexibility in moving back and forth from employment to education could be advantageous on a number of grounds. For those who leave school early, there is the consequence that they have received a deficient "educational subsidy" compared to others. For instance, at age seventeen only 72 per cent are in school in Canada, compared to 78 per cent in Sweden, 87 for the United States, 89 for Germany, and 94 for Japan (OECD, cited in *Globe and Mail*, 1990). In addition, close to half of young people never attend a post-secondary institution. The Macdonald Commission recommends that the first years of employment for these people be thought of as an apprentice-ship. A wage subsidy could be justified on the grounds that their early work experience is partly a training stage.

Another issue involves funding. The total government expenditure for education was some $32.5 billion in 1988, or $2,660 per employed person (Canadian Social Trends, 1990: 34). The federal government is involved at the post-secondary level, and that involvement has changed over time. In the period 1951-66, the federal government pro-vided direct subsidies to universities, based on the population of the province. During 1967-76 there were transfers to the provinces, partly through tax points, to cover half of the operating expenses of universi-ties. Since 1977, the transfer has occurred through the Establish Pro-grams Funding formula, which is linked to population size and change of the GNP. In effect, the direct federal involvement has declined and transfers to the provinces have increased at slower rates. Some have argued that the partial withdrawal of the federal level has given the provinces more flexibility to use transfer funds for sectors other than education. As a consequence, the Royal Commission on the Economic Union (1985, II: 748-55) suggested either that the federal government fund students instead of provinces or that it return to covering half of operating expenses. The first approach, paired with higher tuition, would have the advantage of forcing more change in the system, follow-ing on student demand for given programs. The second approach would prompt higher total subsidies for the post-secondary sector.

The broader case of underfunding has been made in several reports and commissions. For instance, in Ontario the Bovey Commission (1984) argued that one cannot have quality and universal access with-out paying a higher price. By not paying a higher price, it can be argued that quality has suffered, especially through increased student/teacher ratios and larger class sizes. Campbell (1989) observes that "provincial governments have chosen to throw big money at the health-care system because the political fallout from crowded emergency wards is so much more intense than the risk of cramming one more student into a first-year psychology class." A background paper by Employment and Immigration (1989a) expects rising educational and skill requirements. While 22.4 per cent of current jobs involve seventeen or more years of education, it is expected that close to half of new jobs created over the period 1986-2000 would have such requirements.

Gender differences are another important issue. Men have more variability in education, being both more likely to drop out of school early and more likely to advance to the highest levels of education (Gilbert and Guppy, 1988). Another generalization is that there has been considerable progress toward a more equal distribution of educational opportunity by sex. It was largely because of inaccurate projections of women's post-secondary enrolment that the enrolment projections made in the 1970s were short of the mark. In 1951 there were twice as many men as women enrolled but by 1985 slightly more than half (55 per cent) of bachelor and first professional degrees were granted to women (Vanderkamp, 1988: 6, 28; CAUT, 1990: 6). In the period 1980-88, the growth of undergraduate enrolment was twice as high for women, 44 per cent, than men, 18 per cent (Potts, 1989). As of 1986, among the top ten fields of study, women outnumbered men in seven fields: commerce, management and business administration, arts, humanities, health, education, recreation and counselling. Men outnumbered women in engineering, mathematics, and applied sciences (Ross, 1989: 7). Women's enrolment has also increased faster than men's at the graduate level, but there remains considerable imbalance: for every 100 master degrees awarded to men in 1988 there were eighty-three degrees awarded to women, and there were forty-nine doctorates to women for every 100 to men (CAUT, 1990: 6).

LABOUR FORCE TRENDS

Labour force questions have been treated in the chapters on population growth and on aging. We have seen that labour force growth has rather closely followed the changing size of the young adult population, making for annual growth in the order of 3.2 per cent per year in the 1970s and 1.9 per cent in the 1980s (Parliament, 1990). Since almost all persons enter the labour force at some point of their lives, these trends are more closely linked to demographics than trends in post-secondary education. Nonetheless, here again there are important variations in participation rates, particularly the larger involvement of women. In the period 1975-88 women entering or returning to the labour force comprised two-thirds of the total growth (Parliament, 1989a). While labour force growth will likely be lower in the future, becoming a decline after 2011 or 2016, the anticipated growth may be underestimated if women's participation becomes closer than expected to that of men.

Marriage and children continue to suppress women's labour force participation, and it is difficult to estimate how much this will change in the future. For the single, there is not much difference between men and women. However, at ages 25-44 over 96 per cent of men but 71 per

Table 10: Labour Force Participation Rates, 1985

Age	Total	Single		Married		Widowed and Divorced	
		M	F	M	F	M	F
15-19	51.0	52.0	49.0	74.1	63.0	55.1	41.5
20-24	85.5	88.5	85.0	95.2	75.3	87.7	67.8
25-34	83.9	89.1	84.8	96.8	70.5	91.9	76.2
35-44	83.3	81.4	80.4	96.4	70.7	89.5	77.3
45-54	76.8	71.0	72.5	93.5	60.9	82.2	67.8
55-64	52.7	51.7	51.6	73.3	33.7	59.3	39.1
65+	8.2	14.1	7.9	14.8	4.6	8.0	3.2
Total	66.0	72.6	65.9	81.0	57.4	53.4	29.4

SOURCE: 1986 Census 93-111: Table 1.

cent of married women were in the labour force in 1985 (see Table 10). The differences are still there, though less marked, for the widowed and divorced. While the job interruptions of married women are becoming shorter, there is little evidence that they are less numerous (Le Bourdais and Desrosiers, 1988). However, Jones *et al.* (1990: 141, 143) estimate that if all women participated in the labour force like the highly educated women do now, that would increase their total participation by some 16 per cent. Alternatively, if the marital status suppressor was removed, women's total labour force contribution would increase by 42 per cent.

For the older population, the chapter on aging has documented the trends toward lower labour force involvement, at least for men. Combined with greater longevity, this means that the proportion of adult life spent in the labour force is declining for men. In 1951, 80.8 per cent of life years at ages fifteen and over were spent in the labour force, compared to 75.7 per cent in 1981 (Matras, 1990: 149, 153). For women, the trends involve an increase from 22.1 in 1951 to 43.6 per cent of life years at ages fifteen and over spent in the labour force in 1981. Nonetheless, the gender differences remain strong, implying that under 1981 conditions the life years spent in the labour force would be 68 per cent higher for men than for women.

For the young population, the labour force involvement is strong and increasing, in spite of higher educational participation (see Table 11). Combining the sexes, age group 20-24 has the highest rate at 87 per cent in the labour force in 1990. They are also the group most likely to have had two or more jobs over the year (M. Gauthier, 1990). In 1986, persons under twenty-five comprised one-fifth of all workers in Canada (Ross, 1990). Krahn and Lowe (1990) find that recent high school graduates have a very limited range of work opportunities and are concentrated in consumer service occupations. University graduates do better,

Table 11: Labour Force Participation and Unemployment Rates, by Age,
1975, 1980, 1985, 1990

	Labour Force Participation				Unemployment			
	1975	1980	1985	1990	1975	1980	1985	1990
15-19	41.7	71.1	70.1	74.7	12.0	13.2	16.5	12.3
20-24	75.2	84.4	85.4	86.6	–	–	–	–
25-34	73.1	78.6	82.8	85.7	6.1	6.6	10.8	7.7
35-44	73.1	78.3	82.1	86.3	4.4	5.0	7.8	5.9
45-54	62.0	72.8	75.8	79.9	4.5	4.9	7.2	5.7
55-64	62.0	54.0	51.2	49.8	4.3	4.5	8.2	4.9
65+	10.1	8.7	7.7	6.7	5.0	–	2.0	–
Total	58.8	66.4	67.6	69.2	6.9	7.5	10.5	7.6

NOTE: The 1975 participation rate is for ages 25-44 and 45-64. The unemployment rate shown for 15-19 applies to ages 15-24.

SOURCE: Statistics Canada Cat. No. 71-001 (July).

at least if they find entry-level employment in professional and managerial occupations. While youth have improved their relative situation with respect to unemployment, it would appear that their job entry status and employment income have not benefited from the lower competition associated with smaller cohort size.

Other analyses confirm that young people were inordinately affected by the recession of the early 1980s and that many of the jobs created in the period since that time have been low-level jobs (Myles et al., 1988). As a consequence, average wages have declined 17 per cent at ages 16-24 in the period 1981-86 (Wannell, 1989).

More generally, there has been a decline in middle-level jobs, with increases in bottom and upper middle-level employment. The Economic Council of Canada (1990) speaks of a polarization between "good jobs" involving high skills, high pay, and relative security and "bad jobs" with low pay, little security, and much part-time or temporary status. Half of new jobs created in the period 1981-86 are what they call "non-standard," including part-time, short-term, temporary, and self-employment with no employees. Women, as well young and older workers and the poorly educated, are overrepresented in the bad jobs category.

LABOUR POLICY ISSUES

One of the issues surrounding employment involves a debate between job creation and training. In the 1970s there was widespread development of direct employment programs. While this provides for welfare in the sense of giving income to those not otherwise employed, doubts arose regarding the extent to which this helped the long-term employability of the persons involved. The focus since the early 1980s has been on training programs or on merging job creation and training to prepare people for the perceived demands of the labour market. There is also more focus on skill development for persons who have been unemployed over a long term, and on the needs of certain disadvantaged groups like youth and women (Prince and Rice, 1989). However, the total budgets for "job strategy" have been reduced and there is an expectation that the private sector will become more active in the broad area of "labour force development strategy" (Employment and Immigration, 1989a).

In reviewing policy surrounding youth employment, Lowe (1986) argues for a set of programs that would ease transition into gainful employment, combining general education, vocational training, and work experience. He notes that Sweden has all but eliminated youth unemployment by ensuring that persons under age twenty are entitled to education, vocational training, or a special youth job. As indicated in the section on education, it can be argued that strategies are needed to enhance the employment prospects of those youth who leave school early.

There is also need for strategies to accommodate the growing numbers who are combining parenting and working. Along with combining school and work, as well as various forms of part-time, part-year, temporary, or multiple job strategies, the combination of parenting and work might also be considered to be a "non-standard work form." In the latter case, the labour market adjustment implications include parental leave, movement between part-time and full-time work, flex time, and day care (Boyd and McQuillan, 1990).

The labour force includes persons who are unemployed and actively seeking employment. In the period 1971-86 the total numbers employed increased by 3,580,000 while the unemployed increased by 650,000. While unemployment is a serious problem, the majority of the increase in the labour force has clearly been in the employed category.

The unemployment insurance system was established in 1940, following recommendations of the Royal Commission on Dominion-Provincial Relations. The system grew dramatically in the early 1970s and by 1988 involved a total expenditure of $10.6 billion in 1987-88 (Health and Welfare, 1989: 61). A small amount of this is used for other purposes. For instance, maternity leaves account for 3.9 per cent of total beneficiaries. In its analysis, the Royal Commission on the Economic Union (1985, II: 587-618) noted that the system contributes to an increase in the duration of unemployment since it permits people to search longer for alternative employment. It also increases the volume of temporary lay-offs as people enter into "implicit contracts" that involve employment only for sufficient time as to be able to receive unemployment insurance benefits. For similar reasons, it increases the work-force participation rates of women and youths. Finally, it tends to subsidize depressed regions and industries with unstable employment patterns, thus slowing labour market adjustments.

In its suggested reforms, the Macdonald Commission proposed that the focus of the Unemployment Insurance Commission should be on two specific goals: insurance against loss of employment and facilitating labour market adjustment by permitting a longer job search. However, they suggest that regional redistribution should not be handled through this system. In particular, they suggest that regional differentiation in the operation of the system should be abolished. They also suggest reducing the benefit rate and raising the minimum weeks of work required to qualify. In 1989, workers in some regions could qualify, after ten weeks, for forty-two weeks of benefits at 60 per cent of their earnings. This would mean that benefits could equal 250 per cent of their total earnings. Reducing this ratio would reduce the extent to which the system can be used as an "implicit contract."

Other inquiries and studies, particularly the Forget Commission of Inquiry on Unemployment Insurance and the House Royal Commission on Employment and Unemployment in Newfoundland, have arrived at similar conclusions, especially that the system should be used for insurance rather than to supplement income for seasonal workers and that it should not undermine the incentive to work (see also Courchene, 1987: 77-80). Reforms introduced in 1990 changed the minimum weeks needed to qualify from 10-14 weeks to 10-20 weeks, depending on the level of unemployment in the region, and made the duration of benefits more dependent on the duration of work (Employment and Immigration, 1989a). However, the regional differentiation has been kept intact. A proper reform of the system would require a reform of the social security system itself, to which we will return at the end of the chapter.

GENDER DIFFERENCES

The question of differentials between women and men is a large issue that also merits separate treatment. Much demographic data are presented separately by sex, permitting analyses of the broader issues of persistence and change in differences across gender. We have already noted the importance of these questions in such areas as morbidity and mortality, fertility dynamics, family patterns, and the impact of aging. The focus here will be on socio-economic questions, in particular labour force participation, income differences, and associated policy matters relating especially to equal opportunity.

The broad understanding of gender differences is a complex matter in which questions of biology, socialization, family dynamics, social structures, and cultural norms all play important roles. The key questions appear to be identified in the subtitle of a book by Hamilton (1978), *The Liberation of Women: A Study of Patriarchy and Capitalism*. The change and stability of differences are mostly a function of economic questions, i.e., the place of the sexes in relations of production, and cultural questions, i.e., definitions of appropriate roles. The ways in which men and women play different economic roles, both outside and inside of households, along with the value placed on these roles, help in understanding the overall differences. For instance, Ursel (1986) has shown how the regulation of female wage labour around the turn of the century in Ontario restricted women's ability to earn a living wage and helped to entrench the mutual dependence of the breadwinner-homemaker family and gender model. As another example, in economic terms women can be called "junior partners" since on average working women contribute about a third of total husband-wife family income (Grindstaff and Trovato, 1990).

Besides these economic questions, the cultural importance given to the male role, or patriarchy, inherited in various ways over generations, interprets the persistence of many differences as a "natural part of life." For instance, the 1950s have been referred to as the "golden age of the family," when women were encouraged to fulfil themselves through their roles as wives and mothers. As another example, when the rules of a children's game are written in sexist terms, "the first player does this, then he does that," it is telling girls that this game is really a boys' game where they do not fully belong. In various ways our language defines the statuses of the sexes and undermines women's claim to a mature and equal adult status.

Eichler (1978: 145) has posed the question well: "Why . . . is it that in spite of . . . legal changes the improvement in the social, economic and political position of women is very small." In terms of policy questions, Cook (1976: 1) has set the stage as follows:

Suppose you were asked to create the traditions and institutions defining the rights and responsibilities of women and men in a new society. Suppose, in addition, that you had an equal probability of being born into that new society as a male or female. Would you create a society and an economy in which the opportunities, responsibilities, and rewards associated with the family, the educational system, and the labour market were shared by women and men in the same manner as they are today?

Labour force participation

Clearly, there has been much change in women's labour force participation. In 1951, only 24 per cent of women aged fifteen and over were in the labour force compared to 84 per cent of men, while 58 per cent of women and 77 per cent of men were in the 1989 labour force (Connelly and MacDonald, 1990; Parliament, 1990). This is a very significant social change, to the point that essentially all women are now part of the labour force at least for some parts of their lives. Among women aged 25-34 in 1986, only 19.3 per cent had not been in the labour force in either 1985 or 1986. For all married women with children at home, the proportion working full-year full-time more than doubled between 1973 and 1986, from 15.8 to 32.9 per cent (Dooley, 1989a: 5).

However, this broad change masks the persistence of important differences associated with women's higher likelihood of working part-time and their more frequent work interruptions. Though women comprised 44 per cent of all employed people in 1989, they included 72 per cent of persons working part-time (Parliament, 1989a, 1990). At ages 25-44, 59.2 and 87.8 per cent of women and men respectively were working full-time in July, 1990. In 1985, 44.9 per cent of men compared to 23.8 per cent of women aged fifteen and over had worked full-time for forty-nine or more weeks. The 1984 Family History Survey showed that work interruptions are frequent for women and that some two-thirds of these interruptions are associated with childbearing, marriage, or the geographic mobility of the spouse. Less than 1 per cent of men's work interruptions were for these reasons (Burch, 1985: 27). While younger women have experienced shorter interruptions, there is even more discontinuity because they are more likely to have worked and to work again after a shorter interruption. Le Bourdais and Desrosiers (1988) conclude that the matrimonial and professional trajectories of women are increasingly marked by discontinuity and that the attachment of women to the labour force is limited, showing little sign of becoming more continuous. One significant change is noted: women under thirty-five are less likely to have interrupted their work after a first birth.

Observing rather similar phenomena, Jones *et al.* (1990) interpret the results rather differently, in terms of the "individuation of women's life course paths." They see women having more varied work lives, changing their labour force status more frequently and easily than in the past, less concentrated in particular jobs or sectors of the economy, and consequently having more "lives of their own." They note that most women working part-time are doing so by choice and that women now have more alternatives. Jones *et al.* also refer to the "fragmentation" of women's lives; while women are involved in more activities than men, they have less choice about when and where they will spend their time. Consequently, there is now more variation across women in their work, marital, and parenting experiences, which can be interpreted as more variety or less need to be continuously employed full-time.

Along with the greater involvement in a number of disciplines of study, women have also entered a number of occupations that were traditionally dominated by males. Between 1971 and 1981 women made up more than half of the growth in the following professional categories: pharmacists, university teaching and related occupations (non-tenured), mathematicians, statisticians and actuaries, management occupations in the social sciences and related fields, optometrists, and chemists (Marshell, 1987: 8). Focusing on specific skills, Boyd (1990a) observes some convergence in the gender gap, but within blue-collar and service occupations women remain concentrated in the less skilled categories.

Income differences

The changes in the relative labour force participation of the sexes have not been marked with equivalent changes in relative employment incomes. As a percentage of male incomes, the average earnings of female workers changed from 48.7 per cent in 1970 to 55.6 per cent in 1985 (Gunderson, 1989). These differences are partly a function of part-time work. While the proportion of employed men working part-time increased from 11.6 per cent in 1970 to 12.8 per cent in 1985, the corresponding proportions for women increased from 28.9 to 32.6 per cent (Connelly and MacDonald, 1990: 27). Considering only persons working full-time, the employment incomes of women represented 45.9 per cent of men's income in 1951, compared to 52.3 per cent in 1971 and 65.3 per cent in 1988 (Fillmore, 1990: 281). The analyses that have attempted to account for these differences have considered productivity-related factors, occupational segregation, and wage discrimination (Royal Commission on the Economic Union, 1985, II: 624-30).

Productivity-related factors, or human capital – differences in education, training, and experience – probably account for more than half of the difference. Although education has become less differentiated by sex, considering the entire labour force, 14.2 per cent of men compared to 12.5 per cent of women had a university degree in 1990. It is particularly difficult to account for past work history since most surveys do not ask the extensive questions needed to differentiate employment experience. Even though persons may be working full-time in the year under observation, there may be considerable differences in their past work histories. Le Bourdais and Desrosiers (1988) nonetheless conclude that job interruptions are very costly to women in terms of revenue and professional status. They note that interruptions and part-time work are frequent at ages 25-35, precisely when acquiring experience is crucial to a person's career. Using the data from the 1973 Canada Mobility Survey, which does have information on employment history, Goyder (1981) finds that sex differences in work histories are more important than education and occupation in explaining income inequalities.

Occupational segregation is probably the second most important factor in employment income differences. Gender segregation is substantial: in 1981, over 60 per cent of men or women would have to change occupational category in order to have the same occupational distribution (Fox and Fox, 1987: 390). Looking at the period 1931-81, Fox and Fox find that segregation remained very high, though there was some decline in the 1960s and 1970s. The chief reason for the decline involved entry of women into occupations previously almost exclusively male. Looking at the more recent period, Parliament (1989a) finds that the range of jobs women are doing has grown but the majority are still concentrated in a narrow range of traditional female occupations: 73 per cent of women, compared to 30 per cent of men, are in clerical, sales, service, teaching, or health occupations. While women have become more numerous in professional and managerial categories, their concentration has also increased in such occupations as community, business, and personal services and clerical, sales, and service (Connelly and MacDonald, 1990: 22-23; Shea, 1990). This is partly because of the greater number of women in the labour force. Connelly and MacDonald (p. 33) find that the occupations with the largest increase in numbers of women are those where employment incomes are low. Maxwell (1990) adds that women are overrepresented in what the Economic Council of Canada calls "bad jobs" where wages are low, benefits are poor, and there is much part-time or temporary employment. An analysis of trends in Germany points to occupational segregation, rather than gender differences in education or wage discrimination by employers within the same job, as being primarily responsible for wage differences (Hannan *et al.*, 1990).

This occupational segregation is obviously related to the division of labour within households (Shapiro and Stelcner, 1987). It could be said that women choose jobs that are less demanding, that permit part-time work, and where one does not suffer so much from intermittent work patterns in order to accommodate their parental and household activities. This means that they are more concentrated in jobs where human capital, or education and experience, are not particularly important. However, one could equally say that women have little choice and that the nature of women's work in the home and in the labour force reinforces and perpetuates the broader gender differences. Family circumstances in particular, including questions of power and inequality within families, condition women's paid and unpaid work (Armstrong and Armstrong, 1984).

The relative importance of discrimination in explaining gender income inequalities depends on the breadth of definition given to this concept. Inasmuch as one argues that segregation is not a function of choice, one would conclude that it is due to discrimination in a broad sense: the structural divisions in society discriminate against the potential for equal opportunity. Even in a narrower sense, there clearly are ways in which women suffer discrimination just because they are women, for instance, as victims of rape and spousal violence.

Partly because of these differences in definition and partly because wage discrimination is generally measured as a residual when other factors have been taken into account, there is considerable disagreement about its relative importance. Reviewing the various studies, the Royal Commission on the Economic Union (1985, II: 626) observes that wage discrimination within given occupations and establishments is responsible for some 5 to 10 per cent of income differences. Overt discrimination of the "door-slamming variety" is surely rare, but there can be more subtle hiring and job assignment practices that bar women from access to employment and promotion opportunities (Calzavara, 1988). Especially if persons making personnel decisions are mostly men, there is the possibility that they will evaluate women and men differently. Nonetheless, Anselm (1990: 21) can make the following claim:

> It is profoundly unlikely that women's relatively low wages are a function of discrimination. If discrimination exists, the collusion in discriminatory hiring by firms has also to be possible. Yet no empirical evidence for such a possibility exists.

In effect, once careful controls are made for other characteristics, the wage differences are sometimes found to be rather small. Parliament (1989a) finds "almost no difference between average earnings of comparable, never married, women and men." Using data from the social science faculty at one university, Swartzman et al. (1991) find that after controlling for experience and education, there are basically no remaining salary differences by gender. Nonetheless, there remain other important differences, with women representing only 19.5 per cent of faculty. As another example, while average female wages of persons working full-time in 1981 represented 68.9 per cent of male wages, for secondary school teachers this rises to 86.8 per cent and for graduate nurses to 95.4 per cent (Fillmore, 1990: 281).

The policies considered for reducing the inequalities by gender follow on the above interpretations. Inasmuch as human capital is the issue, one would want to work toward a more equal distribution of the sexes across programs of study, and especially to reduce discontinuities in women's work lives (Wilson, 1988). Questions of job interruptions are particularly difficult to address because they often follow on other household and family decisions. To the extent that change and variety are seen as improving the quality of life for women and their families, then one cannot also expect people with differing work experiences to have equivalent incomes. Some withdrawals from the labour force result from inadequate child-care facilities, pointing once again to the importance of supporting parenting roles and re-entry to the labour force after an interruption.

Questions of discrimination are addressed through policies on equal pay. This proved inadequate since the onus was on the employee to prove that her/his salary disadvantage followed on discrimination while doing the same job. The policies for equal pay for work of equal value, which have been introduced at the federal level and in several provinces, permit a more systematic look at pay policies among the job classes of a given establishment. There remains the possibility that work done by women will be undervalued even when a systematic review takes place. The larger difficulty is that many establishments are too small or do not have sufficient numbers of men to permit a systematic evaluation.

Policies of affirmative action or employment equity attempt to increase women's presence in more senior positions and consequently to reduce occupational segregation. In so doing, the policies would help correct past injustices in hiring practices. The federal public service has the most experience with this policy, which was implemented in 1983. The policy requires the gathering of data to document that the employer has treated the specified groups equally. Swimmer and Gollesch (1986) observe that a major finding of this data-gathering is that the staffing process in government departments has largely not involved systematic biases: the proportion of women winning job competitions is comparable to the proportions applying, and the promotions of women are at least as large as their share in the occupational categories from which the promotions take place. Consequently, the system is basically equitable, although it probably was not so in the past. The problem is that hiring and promoting more women to compensate for past injustices depends on job vacancies, which are not numerous given budget restraints.

Instead of pursuing "assimilation to a man's world" Heitlinger (1990b) argues that gender policy should not ignore the family side or devalue women's traditional unpaid work in the home. She argues in particular that the recognition of childbearing brings us to consider "a more flexible conception of gender equality, which can locate the significance of pregnancy in the network of relationships and contexts in which men and women find themselves." The challenge is to "take into account the reproductive difference, without defining women primarily in terms of their difference from men." She therefore proposes that we need to acknowledge the different needs of women who have opted for different life courses in relation to the family and work. Those who have primarily done unpaid family work need better pension plans, career women need equal rights with respect to work, while those who mix the two need benefits for part-time work and opportunities for re-entry into the labour force.

Clearly, the reduction of differentials by gender requires intervention on a number of fronts. This includes the more legalistic approaches of equal pay and employment equity, but also diversifying women's skills in terms of programs of study, child-care policies permitting less job interruptions along with less loss of status when interruptions occur, achieving more equal divisions of domestic work, and reducing gender biases in our language and culture (Abella, 1985; Anselm, 1990).

INCOME DISTRIBUTION

The Canadian economy has grown rapidly in the post-war period. While growth has been slower since the mid-1970s, real income per capita more than doubled between 1963 and 1988 (Economic Council of Canada, 1988: 1). On the other hand, real wages for some categories of workers declined between 1977 and 1988, and various analyses indicate an increased polarization of employment income (Economic Council of Canada, 1990). The growth of consumer service occupations has helped produce a bifurcated post-industrial labour market (Myles, 1988b). In constant dollars, average family income increased 16 per cent between 1973 and 1980, then declined by 6 per cent to 1984 and increased by 11 per cent to 1989. Over the period 1980-85, average earnings of all males with employment income declined by 4 per cent while those of females increased 3 per cent (Gunderson, 1989). Even for persons working full-year full-time, men showed no average change while women's employment income increased 2 per cent.

In spite of economic growth, as well as various other substantial economic changes such as the transformation to a service economy and the massive arrival of women in the labour force, the distribution of income has remained remarkably stable over the past three decades (Statistics Canada, 1984a). This distribution is most often measured in terms of the share of total income received by given proportions of individuals or families. Basically, the bottom fifth of the population has about 4 per cent while the top fifth has 40 per cent of total income.

Through the analysis of trends by age, family type, effective labour force participation, and the composition of income, Wolfson (1986a) shows that this overall stability is partly a function of "offsetting factors." In particular, family trends are producing more inequality: lower fertility means more variation between families with and without children; increased labour force participation makes for differences between families based on number of earners; more separation and divorce result in more disadvantaged single-parent families; and more baby boom children leaving home makes for more young individuals or families with low income. The equalizing forces compensating for these changes are especially the decline in the role of employment income and the increasing role of investment and government transfers in total income. Wolfson shows that even during the recession period of the early 1980s, the social safety nets with their automatic responses to a weaker economy were producing more equality.

Other analyses have confirmed these basic tendencies. Burch and McQuillan (1988) note how the increase both in two-earner families and in single-parent families has prompted more inequality in the employment earnings of families following on differences in the number of earners. In 1951, 57.0 per cent of families had one income recipient and 29.7 per cent had two; by 1981 the proportions were basically reversed, with 57.2 per cent of families having two income recipients and 20.9 per cent having one (Hunter, 1988: 87). Increasingly, the single-earner families are single parents who do not have the option of having more than one person in the labour force. In the United States, Treas (1987) shows that the increased involvement of women in the labour force has produced greater equality among husband-wife families but more disparity across family types.

Analysing income distributions before and after taxes in 1988, shows that the lowest fifth of families have only 2.7 per cent of total income before transfers, but after transfers and taxes this rises to 7.7 per cent (Statistics Canada, 1990e; Vaillancourt, 1985). Banting concludes that there are clear movements toward greater inequality in market incomes, which are largely neutralized by the tax and transfer system. While Banting (1987c: 310, 331) finds that "the vast edifice of modern social policy is at best only mildly redistributive," the redistributive role of the state has at least maintained stability in income distribution. The proportion of government transfers increased from 7.0 per cent of average total incomes in 1948 to 14.9 per cent in 1985 (Matras, 1990).

Other analyses of income distribution focus on the proportions of given groups defined as having low income. Statistics Canada defined low income in 1969 to focus on income levels where most spend 62 per cent or more for food, shelter, and clothing. These were revised in 1978 on the basis of 58.5 per cent of income for these necessities (Méthot,

1987: 7). Family size and the nature of the area of residence are also taken into account. In effect, this means that in 1989 a four-person family with income below $26,800 or an unattached individual with income below $13,500 living in a city of 500,000 or more people would be defined as having low-income status.

Using the 1969 base, the proportion of families with low income declined from 18.3 per cent of all families in 1971 to 7.4 per cent in 1989. For individuals not in families, the proportion with low income declined from 43.1 per cent in 1971 to 19.4 per cent. These data show an increased incidence of low income between 1980 and 1985 for families and for non-family persons under sixty-five years of age (Rashid, 1989: 38). There has also been an increase in the share of government transfers in the income of low-income families and individuals. Fortin (1985: 178) documents a near doubling of the share of government transfers in the total income of low-income families in the 1960s and 1970s.

Little is known about the extent to which families and individuals retain their low-income status over time. For the United States, the Panel Study of Income Dynamics documents considerable change over a ten-year period (Duncan, 1984). While 6.8 per cent were classified as having low income in 1978, only 2.6 per cent were so classified in eight out of the ten years, and almost a quarter of individuals had spent one year out of ten in a family defined as poor. Only about half of persons classified as poor were also poor the following year. Speculating on the Canadian case, Le Bourdais (1987) expects that low income is often not constant for individuals. For women, it would mostly follow on family questions, particularly marriage and separation or divorce. For men it would mostly follow on their labour market situation, especially employment and unemployment. Since the young do not tend to have long-term unemployment and younger lone-parent women tend to remarry, this would also mean that low-income status would often be temporary. This conclusion coincides as well with the observation that low income increasingly affects the young and non-married women.

THE INCOME SECURITY SYSTEM

Social welfare has been defined as both an ideal where basic welfare is equated with the rights of citizenship and an array of social services through which certain goods and services are provided by the collectivity (Drover and Moscovitch, 1981; Djao, 1983). As such, social services cover the range of questions from education and health to pensions and assistance to those unable to work. The post-war period, especially the 1960s, saw the establishment of Canada's basic social welfare structures, including the various pension plans, national health care, the

Canada Assistance Plan, as well as substantial revisions to unemployment insurance and family allowance.

The programs differ considerably. Some are universal, such as Old Age Security, family allowance, and health care. Others are means tested, for example, social assistance through the Canada Assistance Plan and the Guaranteed Income Supplement for the elderly. Other programs are funded jointly by workers and employers, particularly unemployment insurance and the Canada/Quebec Pension Plan. Other policies, often at the provincial level, are also relevant: workers' compensation, minimum wages, housing, correctional services, child welfare, day care, legal aid, employment, and job creation strategies. The income security system overlaps with the income tax system through such measures as deductions for children and the elderly, married deductions, and the child tax credit (see Table 12). All of these measures are at least partly justified in terms of providing social security or reducing inequalities.

It is difficult to make comparisons with other countries because the accounting practices differ. Nonetheless, analyses across comparable countries of the Organization for Economic Co-operation and Development would imply that Canada is not far from the average (OECD, 1985: 21). According to these statistics, Canada spent 12.1 per cent of GDP on social programs in 1960 and 21.7 per cent in 1981. This puts Canada slightly below the OECD average of 25.2 per cent. Canada's social expenditure as a proportion of GDP is above that of the United States, Japan, Australia, New Zealand, Switzerland, and Greece, but below other comparable European countries (Figure 20).

Observers have noted that Canada's social security system advanced considerably until the early 1970s, but subsequently changed little. In effect, the subsequent period was one of slower economic growth, combined with concern about the size of the national debt. Analyses and proposals for improvement have therefore assumed that changes or adjustments should not substantially increase the total level of expenditure. The more fundamental proposals regarding changing the system have involved guaranteed annual income or negative income tax (Johnson, 1987). On the other side of the debate is the questioning of universality and the proposals to target more specifically those in need. According to Mansbridge (1987: 77) the main "unmet needs" are: single-parent families, children in poverty, older non-married women, and the working poor, with particular reference to larger families.

The Royal Commission on the Economic Union (1985, II: 769-803) provides a thorough discussion of proposals for income security reform, which is worth summarizing. This Commission suggests that the system should meet six main criteria. It should: be effective, be fair, provide incentives, discourage abuse, respect the dignity of benefi-

Table 12: Estimates of Government Social Security Programs in Canada, 1984-85

Target Group	Cost in billions $		No. of Persons ('000)
	Federal	**Provincial**	
Poor			
Canada Assistance Plan	4.1	4.1	3,000
Provincial Tax Credits	–	1.6	107
Veterans' Allowance	0.5	–	–
Social Assistance to on-reserve Indians	0.2	–	–
Guaranteed Income Supplement & Spouses' Allowance	3.1	–	1,440
Child Tax Credit	1.1	–	5,000
Social Housing	1.1	–	–
Total	**10.1**	**5.7**	
Families			
Child Care Expense Deduction	0.1	0.0	370
Family Allowance	2.4	–	370
Child Tax Exemption	0.9	0.5	6,600
Married & Equivalent to Married	1.4	0.6	3,230
Total	**4.8**	**1.1**	
Employment Assistance			
Unemployment Insurance	11.6	–	3,200
Training Allowance	0.1	0.1	64
Workers' Compensation	–	1.6	620
Employment Expense Deduction	0.8	0.4	–
Total	**12.5**	**2.1**	
Elderly			
C/QPP	4.4(CPP)	1.6	2,330
OAS	8.3	–	2,700
Tax Assistance RRSP, C/QPP	4.7	2.3	–
Age Exemption	0.3	0.2	0
Pension deduction	0.1	–	903
Veterans' Pensions	0.7	–	655
Total	**18.5**	**4.1**	
Total income security	**45.9**	**13.0**	
Grand Total	– 61.6 –		

SOURCE: Royal Commission on the Economic Union, 1985, II: 772. Reproduced with the permission of the Minister of Supply and Services Canada.

ciaries, and be easy to administer. It should be effective in providing at least a basic level of security, but in spite of extensive spending, substantial numbers still live in poverty. It should provide for equity in terms of progressive taxation and redistribution, but on the whole it redistributes very little while some parts of the system are regressive. For instance, tax deductions provide no benefit to those without taxable income while they benefit most those with highest incomes. The sys-

Figure 20: Total Social Expenditure as a Percentage of GDP, OECD Countries, 1981

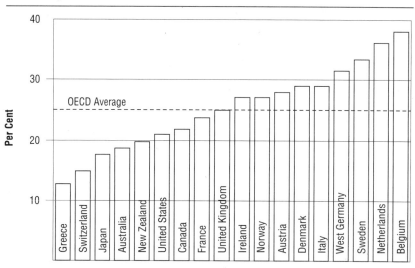

SOURCE: Banting, 1987c: 312.

tem should create incentives and opportunities to work and improve one's own situation, but it does not when social assistance is higher than minimum wage or when employment income is subject to a marginal effective tax rate of more than 100 per cent for some people receiving social assistance. The system should also discourage abuse, but this is not seen as a particularly serious problem, the main abuse probably being that of undeclared income. In terms of administrative ease, the system is judged to be particularly complex for both users and administrators. The Commission therefore concludes that the system is "badly flawed," partly because it has been put into place "piecemeal" over a sixty-year period: "the issue is not whether reform is necessary but rather how deep and rapid that reform should be."

The Macdonald Commission reviews the two basic delivery methods of universality and selectivity in terms of the above criteria. Universality means payments to all persons who are in given categories, then taxing back those with higher incomes, as occurs for family allowance and pensions. Selectivity means first testing the need of prospective recipients, as occurs for guaranteed income supplement and social assistance. Macdonald suggests that universality is preferable in terms of respecting the dignity of beneficiaries and possibly administrative ease, but there is no obvious preference for one or the other system in terms of the main criteria of effectiveness, equity, and creating incentives.

The comprehensive reform that is proposed is a universal program involving guaranteed income. This would involve no increase in total social expenditure, partly by eliminating a series of programs and tax measures: guaranteed income supplement, family allowance, federal contributions to social assistance, tax deductions for children, child tax credit, and married exemptions. They argue that this proposal is better than the current system on all criteria. In particular, one universal system can more easily be progressive, and it can provide incentives by taxing back the guaranteed income only slowly as employment incomes rise. Various authors have supported these proposals, especially when noting that they satisfy a basic need in terms of a program for the working poor (Hum, 1987; Kennedy, 1989; Woodley, 1989). Wolfson (1986b) has provided proposed adjustments in order to better integrate guaranteed income with the income tax system.

A major impetus for this type of universal system comes from analyses of deficiencies in the unemployment insurance program. In particular, many have argued that unemployment insurance has become a type of guaranteed income for certain categories of intermittent workers. In so doing, it discourages economic adjustments. It is argued that unemployment insurance could be more strictly an insurance system if basic income security was provided through guaranteed income (Forget, 1986).

Other analyses are more critical of the guaranteed income approach. A large universal system would give the government less room to manoeuvre. In effect, it would give ministers and administrators less to do, which could also be seen as a saving. It may provide more redistribution than the middle class is willing to accept (McCullum, 1985). Courchene (1987) argues that guaranteed income is too expensive for now but that we should continue moving in that direction through refundable tax credits and clawback of social security benefits. Fortin (1985: 180) notes that there is an inevitable trade-off between equity and efficiency in the sense that achieving a more equal distribution of incomes means accepting a reduction in the average standard of living. Nonetheless, he proposes that, by providing a closer integration of taxation and transfers, a negative income tax would reduce the variability of marginal tax rates. Mendelson (1987) argues that the Macdonald Commission focused too much on income security and insufficiently on training and jobs. Seward and Iacobacci (1987) also pose the debate as one between guaranteed income and labour market assistance for full employment. Inasmuch as one wants to focus on those who are not employable, selective programs can provide more total support to the poor (Hum, 1987).

The analysis of the social security system is therefore very difficult. The extent of equity can be judged differently depending on where one places oneself. For instance, income from the Canada Pension Plan is taxable and thus the program is progressive. On the other hand, more educated people may contribute for a shorter period since they begin working later and they may benefit more since they live longer. Unemployment insurance redistributes toward those with unstable work patterns, yet it provides nothing for the poorest elements who do not work or who work insufficiently to qualify. Tax deductions for dependent children benefit those with children as contrasted to those without, but it provides no benefit to those without income. Public expenditures for higher education are partly justified in terms of improving opportunities of the more disadvantaged, yet middle-class children profit by higher participation. More generally, the income security program is criticized because poverty has not disappeared and because the existing programs sometimes contribute to the problem (Mendelson, 1987). For instance, unemployment insurance adds to the total amount of unemployment and it may reduce incentives to relocate to areas of the economy that are more stable, while social assistance may reduce the incentive to work.

For these reasons Mendelson (1987) observes that, contrary to the situation in the 1960s, there is "no shared view on further development and reform of our social programs." Of course, it does not follow that searches for reform should be abandoned. We must not lose sight of the fact that the current system of transfers and taxes does redistribute toward the disadvantaged. We must remember, too, that the large numbers who consider themselves part of the "middle class" need to feel that the system is also for them. If people do not feel that they benefit, at least in terms of a security net, or that the net is much too expensive for the type of security that is provided them, then the support for the system itself will be seriously undermined. But, in effect, people's situation does change considerably from year to year. Those with low income one year are not necessarily the same the next year. Being disadvantaged because of youth or age occurs to most at one or two points of their lives. In addition, being without the security of family or employment is not an insignificant risk, in view of the changing marital trajectories and the changing viability of given enterprises or sectors of the economy.

10

POPULATION AND SOCIO-CULTURAL COMPOSITION

Besides studying the population composition by socio-economic characteristics such as education, labour force status, and gender and income groups, demography considers the composition along socio-cultural lines, such as ethnicity and language. The focus here will be on native peoples, language, and ethnic and visible minorities. Policy issues raised in the discussion of such questions bring into consideration the definition of Canadian society and how it accommodates the changing aspirations of its constituent groups.

FIRST NATIONS PEOPLES

Demographic and socio-economic conditions

It is difficult to estimate the size of the aboriginal population at the time of first European settlement of this part of the continent. Clearly, various distinct groups were established across the land. As is typically the case in a largely gathering and hunting economy, the population density was low and size was relatively stable, with a pattern of slow growth over the long term. It can be suggested that the population was in a certain equilibrium with its environment, given the economic and political conditions (Normandeau and Piché, 1984: 18). Charbonneau (1984: 32) places the total size at about 300,000 people. This is an insecure estimate because it is based on very approximate indications on the part of various explorers. The approximations inevitably followed initial encounters with arriving Europeans. These encounters can well have disturbed the original population either through promoting displacements or by introducing new diseases. It would also appear that the demographic density was highest along the lowlands of the St. Lawrence, in the region above the Great Lakes, and on the Pacific coast (Careless, 1963: 18-21). Although based on a fairly different economic system, the population distribution over space would have had certain similarities to the current patterns.

European arrivals clearly upset the previous demographic equilibriums. This occurred especially as a consequence of epidemics involving new diseases, particularly smallpox, for which the native peoples lacked resistance. Warfare, including the introduction of more destructive weapons, and the confrontation of economic systems also brought death and undermined the previous subsistence patterns. In particular, the original inhabitants were displaced toward the more remote and less valuable geographic areas. Using the population figure of about 100,000 for 1900, Charbonneau (1984) speaks of three centuries of depopulation. He also notes that over a 300-year period a growth rate of -0.37 per cent per year is sufficient to reduce a population to one-third of its original size.

Over the present century, demographic growth became positive once again, taking some fifty years to re-establish the size estimated for 1600. The peak growth was in the 1960s, reaching a natural increase of 3.3 per cent per year for the Indian and 4.2 per cent for the Inuit populations (Robitaille and Choinière, 1987: 27). This was a function of declines in mortality, which were then followed by fertility declines. Nonetheless, the growth remains rapid, with a natural increase of 2.3 for the Indian and 3.0 for the Inuit over 1971-81, compared to the figure of 0.8 for all of Canada.

In presenting the population size of the First Nations peoples, it is necessary to introduce a number of classifications based on administrative practices and census definitions. Following on the 1876 Indian Act, registered or status Indians were defined as persons registered as Indians or entitled to register as Indians (Frideres, 1988: 7). Essentially, they were members of legally recognized bands. The definition was based

Table 13: Census Count of Aboriginal Population, 1986

	Indian	Métis	Inuit	Total
Single origins	286,230	59,745	27,290	373,260
Multiple origins	239,395	58,895	6,175	338,460
Single and multiple combined	531,445	128,640	33,465	711,725

NOTE: Excludes an estimated 45,000 persons in incompletely enumerated Indian reserves or settlements. Also excludes inmates.

SOURCE: Norris, 1990: 37.

on the legal status of the husband and male lines of descent, except for illegitimate children, and as a consequence various persons lost the status and have been referred to as non-status Indians. As of 1985 the definition was changed to allow for the reinstatement of persons who had lost their status due to marriages to non-Indian men. In effect, registered Indians are those for whom the various programs of the Department of Indian and Northern Affairs are administered. As a consequence of this registration and of the corresponding administrative procedures, various administrative data are more complete on this population. A third group is the Métis who are defined as having mixed ancestry. Initially, this title was confined to those with French and Indian blood, but it is now seen as an ethnic group including most people with partial Indian ancestry (Frideres, 1988: 15-16). Finally, the Inuit of the far North are generally treated separately and are those people known as Inuit, Eskimos, or Inuvialuit. The 1981 census enumerated 292,700 status indians, 75,100 non-status, 98,300 Métis, and 25,400 Inuit (Statistics Canada, 1984c). Since some 86,000 non-status Indians were in the process of registering for Indian status (Loh, 1990: 13), the 1986 census did not separate the two categories, but it did invite people to state a number of ethnic origins. Counting the total of single and multiple origins, the population amounted to 711,700 persons with aboriginal ancestry, not counting some 45,000 persons on reserves who were incompletely enumerated due to lack of co-operation with the census (Table 13).

The figure of 750,000 represents 3.0 per cent of the 1986 population of Canada. Available projections indicate that the aboriginal population will continue to grow at a faster rate than the total population. Loh (1990) projects that the registered Indian population will increase from 403,000 in 1986 to about 720,000 by 2011. Bourbeau et al. (1986a) project that the Inuit population will increase by 60 per cent between 1981 and 2000, reaching a total size of 41,000. Hagey et al. (1989) place the total aboriginal population at 1,145,000 in the year 2001, which would mean 3.9 per cent of the population of the country.

It is also important to recognize the diversity in the native population. Besides the status diversity indicated above, there are almost 600 Indian bands and some 2,300 reserves (Ponting, 1988: 621). They are diverse ethnically and have long thought of themselves as quite different peoples. They are spread out over the country, and there are eleven major language families (Burnaby and Beaujot, 1986). Nonetheless, at the 1986 census, only 97,280 persons indicated an aboriginal language as that spoken most often at home. The Inuit are most likely to speak their language at home, and while they are small in numbers, they represent over 75 per cent of the population on 30 per cent of the total area of Canada (Bourbeau *et al.*, 1986a).

The native peoples are undergoing a demographic transition from high to lower mortality and fertility. Mortality declined first but remains relatively high, with a life expectancy of 64.0 for men and 72.8 for women in 1982-85 for registered Indians (Norris, 1990: 49). The differential is seven or eight years compared to the total population, and this difference has not changed much since 1961 (Robitaille and Choinière, 1987: 24). The major causes of death are "accidents, poisoning and violence," with many of these deaths being alcohol-related (Siggner, 1986: 5-6). In 1986, there were 175 such deaths per 100,000 population. This was down from 321 in 1978 but still represented three times the average for the whole country (Bobet, 1989). The rate of suicides is twice the national average. The infant mortality rate was 17.2 per 1,000 births in 1981, close to twice the national average, but this was down from 79.0 per 1,000 in 1960. For the Inuit, life expectancy would have been as low as thirty in the period 1941-51, rising to sixty-five in 1971-81 (Robitaille and Choinière, 1987: 24).

The fertility transition for the registered Indian population took place essentially since the late 1960s (Romaniuc, 1987). The total fertility rate was 6.1 in 1968 compared to 3.2 births per woman in 1982 (Norris, 1990: 45). Inuit fertility is higher, at 4.1 in 1983.

Besides the reductions in fertility and mortality, and rapid growth, the aboriginal population is characterized by geographic movements that involve a certain exodus from reserves. In 1966, 16 per cent of the registered Indian population were living off reserves, compared to 29 per cent in 1984 (Siggner, 1986: 4). Those not on reserves are mostly in the larger metropolitan areas, where they often have disadvantages compared to other internal or international migrants to the larger cities (Frideres, 1988: 208). The Inuit population has undergone considerable change in residence from isolated areas to small settlements that have more services (Irwin, 1988).

This demographic profile of a relatively small and diverse population, with dispersed settlement across the country but especially in remote locations, and rapid growth, sets certain constraints on the opportunity profile of native peoples. Various other characteristics also indicate relative disadvantages compared to the averages for the entire population of the country. In terms of education, the retention rate of registered Indians to grade 12, compared to the numbers in grade 2 ten years earlier, was 31 per cent in 1984-85. While this is higher than the 18 per cent for 1975-76, it remains very low compared to the national average (Siggner, 1986: 9). In 1981, 19 per cent of the out-of-school population had some post-secondary education, compared to 36 per cent for the entire population. For employment, 31 per cent of the status Indians aged fifteen and over were employed in 1986, compared to 60 per cent for the overall Canadian population (Hagey, 1989). The 1980 income averaged 60 per cent of the average for the general population, and 35 per cent of income was from transfer payments, compared to 16 per cent for the entire population. In constant dollars, social assistance increased 90 per cent between 1971 and 1981 (Siggner, 1986). In 1984, 47 per cent of dwelling units failed to meet basic standards of physical construction and 36 per cent were seriously overcrowded. In general, there are improvements in living conditions, but these continue to lag significantly behind the average. For the Inuit, 60 per cent have not attended high school, less than 40 per cent of the population aged fifteen and over are employed, and for those with income the average is 60 per cent of the Canadian average (Siggner, 1989). The average family income for all aboriginals was 57 per cent of that for the entire population in 1985 (Hagey, et al., 1989).

In effect, as Frideres (1988: 322) summarizes, the native people occupy a marginal position in modern Canadian society. They have benefited little from economic development and are still forced to devote most of their energies to providing their basic needs. A high degree of isolation from the mainstream society has maintained a traditional way of life. Nonetheless, there is change, in particular with regard to education and urbanization. In addition, native organizations are becoming more active, and there is a stronger articulation of political and social goals.

Policy issues

Clearly, the aboriginal population has been and will continue to grow rapidly. This is likely to have an impact on a variety of areas, including housing, needs for economic development and social services on reserves, and political and social influence (Hagey et al., 1989). The growth will be especially rapid at young adult ages, putting pressure on education and labour force expansion. Between 1981 and 2001 the number of those aged sixty-five and over will double, requiring more facilities for the elderly.

There are a number of other policy concerns regarding First Nations people, including health, education, social services, housing, and employment. In reviewing the situation of Inuit, Irwin (1988) speaks of the problems of high population growth, high unemployment, low levels of education, decline of traditional language and culture, increased social breakdown, and, ultimately, welfare dependence. As a consequence, the "Lords of the Arctic" have become the "wards of the state." Irwin argues for "imaginative social programs to give Inuit the opportunity to help themselves through education, training, community service, and participation in the subsistence economy. He cites the Cree hunters' assistance program and the homeowners' assistance program as examples of approaches through which self-sufficiency has been increased.

The immediate issues facing native people are increasingly seen within the broader concerns of native rights, land claims, and self-government or sovereignty. Over most of Canadian history, there has been a tension between the policy alternatives of promoting assimilation and of maintaining separate structures. Until 1960, when they received the right to vote in federal elections, it was necessary to give up registered Indian status to gain full citizenship. One could not have the benefits of Indian status at the same time as those of full citizenship. In 1969, a White Paper proposed a number of further changes to reduce the separate treatment of the native peoples in federal policy. This was seen as being oriented to assimilation and was soundly rejected by native organizations. It has been argued that this White Paper, and especially the reaction to it, represented a significant turning point (Weaver, 1981). Although the native peoples are a small and diverse population, making it difficult to have separate structures, it is clear that assimilation is unlikely in the foreseeable future. There is also considerable political support for some form of self-government (Patterson, 1978).

Frideres (1988: 359) defines self-government as involving greater self-determination and social justice, economic development to end dependency, protection and retention of aboriginal culture, and social vitality. To achieve these objectives, Frideres argues that political institutions, a territorial base, control over group membership, and continuing fiscal support are needed. Thus, self-determination in both the political and economic sense would be necessary to break the cycle of welfare dependency. To be able to play a larger role in their own future, native peoples clearly need a more solid economic base; hence the importance of claims for rights over lands and resources. As Ponting (1988: 624) notes, "land is at the heart of the conflict between aboriginal people and colonizing populations." Land is not only important to economic self-sufficiency, but it is also seen as a basis for culture, lifestyle, and identity. Ponting (1988: 625) further observes that "most Canadian Native peoples have never explicitly given up their sovereignty or title to land through conquests, annexation or treaty." While greater self-government might be seen as providing more cultural separateness and persistence, Frideres (1990) expects that the associated incorporation and economic development will lead instead to the elimination of administrative, political, legal, and economic arrangements that set Indians aside from other Canadians.

Although the principle of some form of self-government receives considerable support, there is much difficulty in negotiating its exact meaning and in bringing it about (Platiel, 1987). For instance, some favour the constitutional declaration of an "inherent right" that would subsequently be defined by the courts, while others favour a "contingent right" whose exact meaning is first negotiated. This also raises questions regarding the relative importance of individual and group rights. Traditional liberal individualism, as enacted for instance in the Charter of Rights and Freedoms, refers especially to individual rights, while self-government involves the recognition of group rights or of some kind of "distinct society." In effect, self-government and associated land rights raise difficult political and economic issues. However, it is probably also true that there is now a considerable element of good will in the society to support the resolution of these difficulties. Speaking of the situation in the 1920s, Jenness (1954) noted prejudice against Indians across the country: the average person looked down on Indians as inferior and undesirable. There has since developed a greater recognition that much of the fault lies with historical injustices perpetuated by the colonizing peoples, and that a wealthy society should be able to accommodate better the needs and rights of the original inhabitants of the land. Patterson (1978: 185) concludes:

> Canada's Native peoples are not a "problem" which can yield a "solution." They constitute a distinctive, varied, and on-going part of Canadian culture, population and life. As such, they will continue to occupy a place in Canada's social policy.

LANGUAGE

After the First Nations peoples, the French constitute the distinctive minority that has special status and whose presence helps define the nature of Canadian society. Here the focus is much more on language than on ethnic origin. We will consequently focus on the national languages of English and French, their relative magnitude, and the dynamics of change. In 1986, 7.0 per cent of the population spoke languages other than English or French at home and 1.2 per cent knew neither of the official languages. The largest component of the latter is recent immigrants who are likely to learn one of the languages, as well as native peoples in remote regions. Most issues relating to language groups other than English and French can be treated in the next section, on ethnicity.

Recent censuses have included three language questions. Mother tongue is the language first spoken and still understood. Home language is the language used most often in the home. Knowledge of official languages asks if people know either or both of English and French sufficiently to be able to carry on a conversation. The comparisons of mother tongue and home language provide a measure of language retention or transfer.

Demographic trends

In 1760, the French population of the current territory of Canada amounted to at least 80 per cent of the total non-native population (Lachapelle and Henripin, 1980: 10-11). It is estimated that by around 1805 the English group attained the majority. By 1850 the French group had fallen to 30 per cent of the total, a level that would remain almost constant for the next 100 years. By 1986, the French group comprised 25 per cent of the Canadian population.

Issues of English-French relations have been a recurring theme in Canada. More than a question of language and communication, these relations involve "recurrent power struggles for the control of the means required for society building in its economic, cultural and linguistic dimensions" (Breton, 1988: 557). In effect, there is competition for resources and for control of institutions, along with the opportunities that these provide. Breton further observes that new rounds of competition have been triggered by changes in relative size of the groups, political mobilization, and unresolved contradictions. The development of policies of accommodation between English and French has been a constant challenge (Cartwright, 1988b).

In the period 1850-1950 a fairly stable balance was maintained, with approximately 60 per cent English and 30 per cent French (Review of Demography, 1989: 6). This relative balance followed mostly on underlying demographics: higher French fertility compensated for immigration, which largely supported the English group. The underlying dynamic was broken in the 1960s, when all factors played against the relative size of the French group. Most importantly, the French lost their fertility advantage while the English maintained their immigration advantage, and language transfer favoured English over French, especially outside of Quebec. As a result of the operation of these factors, 23.3 per cent of the population spoke mostly French at home by 1986, while 69.2 per cent spoke mostly English, with another 1.6 per cent declaring both as the language spoken most often at home

Table 14: Distributions by Mother Tongue, Home Language, and Official Languages, 1986

	Canada	Quebec	Rest of Canada
Mother Tongue			
English	62.7	9.3	81.2
French	24.5	81.9	4.5
Both English and French	1.5	2.8	1.1
Other	11.3	6.0	13.2
Total	**100.0**	**100.0**	**100.0**
Home Language			
English	69.2	11.2	89.3
French	23.3	81.5	3.1
Both English and French	1.6	3.0	1.1
Other	5.9	4.2	6.5
Total	**100.0**	**100.0**	**100.0**
Official Languages			
English only	66.8	5.7	88.0
French only	15.8	59.0	0.8
Both English and French	16.2	34.5	9.9
Neither English nor French	1.2	0.8	1.3
Total	**100.0**	**100.0**	**100.0**

NOTE: Multiple responses including English, French, and other languages have been included with English and French.

SOURCE: 1986 Census special tabulations; 1986 Census MT86A01A.

(Table 14). Assessing the relative importance of the various factors, Lachapelle (1988a, 1988b) concludes that international immigration plays the largest role in the relative decline of the French group in Canada. Fertility and mortality differences are small. Linguistic transfers are not that common: the net transmission of French from mother to child is rather constant at about 95 per cent in recent decades. In contrast, international migration reinforces the English group. For instance, in the population aged 0-4 in 1941, who were 45-49 in 1986, the proportion whose mother tongue was French fell from 36 per cent to 26 per cent. Three-quarters of this observed difference is due to international migration. Besides international migration, the differences in fertility and mortality, along with language shifts, all play against the French group for the country as a whole (Lachapelle, 1987). In terms of births, those of French mother tongue represented 36 per cent of the total in 1941, compared to 29 per cent in 1961 and 23 per cent in 1986 (Lachapelle, 1988c: 332).

The French-language minorities outside of Quebec and New Brunswick have typically undergone considerable erosion. As long as they could maintain a certain isolation, often in rural areas or in extractive industries, and maintain communities around religious affiliations, there was considerable persistence of these minorities. However, with the broader scale of social interaction and the reduced role of religion in defining communities, the French minorities have been undermined (Beaujot and McQuillan, 1982: 193-96). Thériault (1989) maintains little hope for the French-speaking communities outside of Quebec and Acadia. The rural isolation, often based on a parish identity, is no longer available. The groups no longer have the necessary "compact relationships" that would assure their long-term existence as language communities. Intermarriage has also played a significant role, since in most cases English is adopted as the home language (Castonguay, 1979; Robinson, 1989a). As a result of these factors, Cartwright (1988a) speaks of the bilingual "belt" around Quebec having become a series of "pockets." For all persons of French mother tongue outside of Quebec, 30 per cent do not cite it as the language used most often at home (Bourbeau, 1989: 25). Beyond New Brunswick and Ontario, this figure rises to 50 per cent.

While the proportion with French mother tongue or home language has continued to decline, Lachapelle (1989a) notes other data suggesting that French has improved in status since the early 1970s. There is an increase in the extent to which parents pass the French language on to their children. Outside of Quebec, the knowledge of French has increased, especially among younger cohorts. French has increased as a proportion of the population of Quebec due to the departure of other groups and due to the increased rate at which other groups who remain in Quebec transfer to French. The proportion of the non-French mother tongue group of Quebec who can speak French increased from 33 per cent in 1961 to 62 per cent in 1986. As a result of these various factors, the proportion of the Canadian population able to speak French has remained stable, measuring 32 per cent both in 1951 and 1986 (Grenier and Lachapelle, 1988). While French is declining as a language spoken at home, it is increasing as a second language.

Another important generalization is that in the period since 1961, and especially since 1971, the linguistic duality has increasingly involved a territorial duality. The French majority has increased in Quebec while the English majority has increased outside of Quebec. Official languages are increasing where they are in the majority and decreasing where they are in the minority. In terms of mother tongue, nearly 90 per cent of Francophones lived in Quebec in 1986, where they account for 83 per cent of the population. In contrast, 95 per cent of Anglophones lived in other provinces, accounting for 80 per cent of the population (Review of Demography, 1989: 6).

The main positive result for the French language in Quebec is that its proportion has increased, especially since 1966. The 1986 level of 83 per cent French mother tongue is the highest level in a century and a half

(Lachapelle, 1989b). However, a major component of the changing proportions results from net departures of non-French groups. In the period 1966-86, the departures of English from Quebec were more than sufficient to compensate for the transfers to English from French and other groups (Lachapelle, 1988c: 338). Persons who transfer to English are also more likely to leave the province. In effect, this has meant that the increasing French predominance in Quebec has been at the expense of a decreasing relative size of the Quebec population in Canada (Lachapelle, 1988c).

Factors other than migration have played less significant roles in affecting the French majority in Quebec. Language transfer produces a result that is basically neutral for the French language: there are about as many people whose mother tongue is French who speak other languages at home as there are people of other mother tongues who speak French at home. However, at ages under thirty, the transfers involve a net deficit for the French language (Bourbeau, 1988: 238). Veltman (1988) also observes that Anglicization has not stopped for the French-born of Quebec.

While recent international migrants are more likely to associate with the French than the English group, the English group continues to gain more immigrants than its relative share in the base population (Termote and Gauvreau, 1988: 149). The geographic concentration of immigration in Montreal also presents a problem with regard to the assimilation to the French language. Most immigrant groups, except Haitians and Portuguese, are in residential locations of English concentration. Veltman (1986, 1988) finds that even if the schools are French, English is used extensively and the children continue to identify with the English language. Only when the children go to schools with high proportions of French, as in the case of the Portuguese, do the recent immigrant children adopt French as their main language of interaction. Veltman also observes that the older immigrants are less likely to switch languages. When they do transfer, those who know French, or neither English or French, are more likely to transfer to French. Those who know English on arrival are more likely to integrate into the English group or leave the province. It can be seen that a variety of factors are important in the linguistic choices of immigrants: age at arrival, knowledge of official languages at arrival, linguistic concentration of the chosen residential location, language of instruction in the schools, and linguistic composition of the school population itself. Nonetheless, Veltman (1988) finds that those of the second generation from abroad or from outside Quebec are tending to adopt French as their home language.

Paillé (1989a) expresses concern about the potential for the French language to maintain its own on the island of Montreal. Representing

60 per cent of the population of the metropolitan area, it is here that immigrants are most likely to arrive initially. High non-French immigration, combined with low French fertility, is expected to reduce the French mother tongue concentration below the 60 per cent level it maintained over the period 1976-86. For instance, in the school population, the French mother tongue represented 63.8 per cent of the total in 1971 compared to 54.2 per cent in 1986. As of 1987, there were more non-French mother tongue immigrants than births to French home language mothers on Montreal Island.

The English mother tongue group has been declining as a proportion of the total Quebec population for more than a century. In 1844 they comprised a quarter of the population, compared to 11 per cent in 1986 (Caldwell, 1988). Since 1971, the English mother tongue group has also declined in absolute numbers and is increasingly concentrated in Montreal. Fertility is very low, measured at 1.2 births per women in 1981, barely half of the replacement level (Tremblay and Bourbeau, 1985). Compared to the past, the English group is now benefiting less from language transfers and it continues to suffer substantial departures to other provinces. Given other factors, such as aging and internal ethnic diversity, Caldwell expresses concern about the viability of what was once an important community in the province.

It is noteworthy how internal migration is selective of English and other languages in leaving Quebec and of French in going to Quebec. In the period 1976-81, the rates of out-migration for Quebec were 1.7 per 1,000 for French, 7 per 1,000 for other, and 39 per 1,000 for English home language (Termote and Gauvreau, 1985: 43). Thus the English out-migration rate was twenty-three times that of the French, and close to 20 per cent of the English home language persons left the province in the five-year period. The rates of out-migration from the rest of Canada (to Quebec) were: 13.1 for French, 0.4 for other, and 0.5 per 1,000 for English. Here the French rate is twenty-six times as high as the English rate. There is little migratory exchange between the French of Quebec and the English of the rest of the country.

National policy issues

Language policy issues are particularly complex because there is more diversity at the national than at provincial levels, and there is a tension between alternative orientations. Breton and Breton (1980) refer to the contrast between the pan-Canadian and segmentalist perspectives. The pan-Canadian approach argues for promoting the two languages across the country, while the segmentalist view argues for building on the strength of majority languages in given areas. Clearly, more than just language is at stake; basic conceptions of the society, including approaches to maintaining unity in the face of diversity or for creating a different form of association across the two major parts of the country, are reflected and determined by these two approaches.

The federal policy has largely adopted a pan-Canadian approach, especially through ensuring that the national level civil service operates in the two languages and by supporting official-language minorities and second-language education. The proportion of those in the civil service whose mother tongue is French in effect increased from 21.5 per cent in 1965 to 27.0 per cent in 1986 (Brooks, 1989). Official bilingualism increased the value of French language proficiency for entry and mobility within the federal bureaucracy.

Policies promoting immersion education in French have increased the knowledge of the French language. Enrolment in French immersion programs increased from 38,000 in 1977-78 to 224,000 in 1987-88 (Grenier, 1989: 43). More than 5 per cent of eligible students are enrolled in such programs (Bourbeau, 1989). More generally, official-language bilingualism has increased from 13.5 per cent in 1971 to 16.2 per cent in 1986, and knowledge of French has increased in the English mother tongue population. In Quebec about half of the non-French are bilingual compared to 30 per cent of those with French mother tongue. Outside of Quebec, the French are most bilingual, at almost 80 per cent compared to 6 per cent for the non-French (Albert, 1989). Overall, bilingualism is four times as high in the French than in the English mother tongue population of Canada, but Anglophones have made progress especially in Quebec and the contact regions (Grenier and Lachapelle, 1988). The rise in the status of the French language has pushed a greater number of non-Francophones to learn the language.

Other discussions are less supportive of the thrust of federal language policy. Cartwright (1988a) is concerned that the bilingual zone that provides for a transition between English and French Canada "has withered." Canada could be becoming more like Belgium in terms of the geography of language, with Ottawa and Montreal being somewhat equivalent to Brussels as the only area where the two languages effectively coexist. Reflecting in general on languages in geographic contact, Cartwright (1989) further observes that "in the war of languages, contact and interaction will eventually lead to unilingualism." Possibly a minority language can withstand the assimilative pressures only if it has control of government or a linguistic boundary. Laponce (1988) suggests that in order to assure the survival of French in North America, one should favour the concentration of the population and give it control over its boundaries.

Guidon (1988: 90) observes that federal language policy is "a political irritation for English Canada which is entirely irrelevant to a modernizing Quebec." McRoberts (1989) argues that the Royal Commission on Bilingualism and Biculturalism (1968) made a serious mistake in not adopting the territorial principle as a basic underlying approach to language policy. The idea of promoting the two languages across the country worked counter to the aspirations of Quebec and made little sense in most parts of English Canada. Two attempts to establish "bilingual districts," as suggested by the Royal Commission and adopted as part of the 1969 Official Languages Act, were doomed to failure because there was no clear social consensus supporting this approach. Polèse (1990) argues for a territorially based bilingualism if Canada is to survive as a bilingual nation. Fortier (1988), as Official Languages Commissioner, can nonetheless make a strong plea for the present policy:

> Most Canadians remain firmly opposed to a straight territorial solution to Canada's special linguistic dilemma, as being, in the end, a recipe for national suicide. With all its imperfections, some form of official bilingualism is the only answer that does not point toward a progressive dismemberment of Canada.

Provincial issues

There have also been substantial developments in Quebec language policy, and these have been aimed at supporting the French language. In the late 1960s, the Royal Commission on Bilingualism and Biculturalism had observed that Francophones controlled little of the economic activity in Quebec. The better-educated French population who were upwardly mobile had little opportunity to work in French in the private sector. In terms of public institutions, Quebec had developed into "two solitudes," each with control over its own education systems, hospitals, and social service agencies (Coleman, 1983). In addition, most immigrant children were going to English schools. The aim of policies adopted in 1974 (Bill 22) and 1977 (Bill 101, Chartre de la langue française) was to reverse these trends. In particular, the policies sought to expand the use of French as the language of work at middle and senior levels of management in the private sector. Second, there was an attempt to integrate the linguistically separate education, hospital and social service agencies. Finally, immigrant children were required to go to French schools. Besides these specific objectives, these policies in effect went a considerable distance to improving the social mobility prospects of the new Francophone middle class that had emerged during the Quiet Revolution (Brooks, 1989: 287). Francophones gained greater access to economic structures and almost exclusive control over state agencies.

In further assessing the demographic impact of language legislation, Paillé (1989b) notes first that the trends in the language of education have been reversed. In 1976-77, 38 per cent of the foreign-born students were in French schools compared to 78 per cent in 1985-86. The proportion of the population with no knowledge of French was reduced from 11.6 per cent in 1971 to 6.5 per cent in 1986. Policies promoting the French language as the language of work and as the language of education for immigrants to Quebec have reversed previous trends, which involved a decline in the proportion of French-speakers in the province over the period 1951-71. Raynauld (1989) concludes that French in Quebec is less at risk today than ever before, except for the risk posed by Francophones themselves in failing to learn it well. Nonetheless, Dion (1989) is not convinced that the French language laws have achieved the intended goals and he argues in particular that the English language in Quebec does not need support, except in education. Vaillancourt (1989) sees the economic advantages of having several languages and argues for an openness to the world in order to profit from this human capital.

New Brunswick and Ontario are the main other provinces that have adopted special language provisions. These are also the provinces bordering on Quebec, for which, along with Quebec, the Royal Commission on Bilingualism and Biculturalism had suggested an official bilingual status. New Brunswick did in effect adopt official bilingualism, but it has been the only province to do so. The linguistic composition in Acadia (northern and eastern New Brunswick) is very stable, with 58 to 59 per cent of the population of French mother tongue over the period 1951-86 (Lachapelle, 1989a: 13). For Ontario, the orientation has been to increase services in French, focusing on an area of northeastern Ontario where 65 per cent of Francophone Ontarians live. The proportion of French in this small region ranges from 25 to 75 per cent of given counties (Cartwright, 1988b).

Clearly, the politics of language do not simply involve language as a means of communication. It is an aspect of personal identity and institutional affiliation, and it sets certain parameters to collective aspirations as a society. Constitutionally, it involves a search for a means to reflect the dualistic nature of the country. The increasing territorial duality means that most people live in regions where their language is in the majority. This is the case for 89 per cent of the French mother tongue and 95 per cent of the English mother tongue. There is reduced potential for the minorities – English in Quebec and French in the rest of Canada – to provide a real presence and a viable community that would help to define the nature of the country. In terms of home language, these minorities comprise only some 5 to 7 per cent of the population of the whole country. Consequently, Bastarache (1989) argues that "there is now a consensus in favour of developing a distinct society in Quebec, as against building a bilingual country." Polèse (1990) also proposes that the growing disequilibrium between Canada's two language communities, more than any other factor, may eventually contribute to the demise of a bilingual Canada and to the political separation of Quebec.

If the minorities are to hold an institutionally bilingual country together, this glue is becoming weak. However, increased individual bilingualism in the official languages, from 12 per cent in 1961 to 16 per cent in 1986, may provide a substitute. Ultimately, it is a question of values, aspirations, and economic potential for defining the society in which people want to live.

ETHNIC ORIGINS

Ethnicity is another significant socio-cultural dimension on which to study the composition of the Canadian population. It refers to membership in a group marked off from others by its origins. The concept is used here in its broad sense, including a focus on visible minority groups and on policy issues regarding multiculturalism.

At the time of Confederation, the non-aboriginal population of Canada involved basically two groups. Persons of British and French origin comprised more than 90 per cent of the total. At the level of languages, English and French have continued to dominate, but at the level of ethnicity Canada gradually became a more diverse multicultural society during the twentieth century. By 1986, almost 40 per cent indicated that their ancestry or cultural origin was other than totally British or French. The explicit recognition of this dimension of Canadian society is often placed in the fourth volume of the report of the Royal Commission on Bilingualism and Biculturalism (1968), where it was emphasized that "biculturalism" is an incomplete reflection of Canadian reality. A more explicit recognition came in the 1971 Multiculturalism Act.

The concept of ethnicity involves a variety of meanings. As defined by the census, it refers to the origin of one's ancestors who first arrived on this continent. For some, this is an important aspect of identity but for others it is a rather irrelevant consideration. It is generally recognized that the concept of ethnicity has lost some importance vis-à-vis the concept of language (Krotki, 1990a). At the same time, the measurement of ethnicity has had to capture a changing social reality, making comparisons over time difficult. The 1986 census was the first explicitly to encourage people to list a variety of ethnic origins, following both paternal and maternal lines of descent. Some 28 per cent of respondents indicated more than one ethnic origin. This could be interpreted to mean that multiculturalism is becoming an important phenomenon, even at the individual level where people identify with a variety of cultures. On the other hand, it could well be that the whole concept of ethnicity is rather meaningless, especially for people who are of mixed origin or whose ancestors have been in Canada for some time, and who would prefer to simply call themselves "Canadian."

The profile on ethnicity in the 1986 census emphasizes increased diversity and the importance of immigration in creating this ethnic diversity (White, 1990). It is suggested that Canada contains over 100 different ethnic and cultural communities. As a consequence, no single ethnic or cultural group is dominant. Focusing on British and French as the most numerous, 34 per cent indicated only British origins, 24 per cent French, 5 per cent were British and French, and another 13 per cent were of multiple origin including British and/or French and other. That leaves a quarter of the population with neither British nor French origins and almost 40 per cent indicating at least some origins other than British or French. All provinces west of Ontario, plus the territories, had more than half of respondents who included origins other than British and French (Figure 21). In Quebec, 78 per cent were of French single origin and an additional 5 per cent were French and other. Among the Canadian population who indicated neither British nor French origins, 63 per cent were of European origin, 16 per cent of Asian origin, 6 per cent were aboriginal, 3 per cent were black, and 12 per cent were of other origins (White, 1990: 17).

Visible minorities

Based on the 1981 census, a classification of visible minorities was established, using the questions on ethnic origin, birthplace, religion, and mother tongue. In effect, this identified the persons who were non-white, non-Caucasian, and non-aboriginal. The major categories of visible minorities were black, Far East Asian, Southeast Asian, Pacific Islanders, West Asians and Arabs, and Latin Americans. A total of 4.7 per cent of the 1981 population were classified as visible minorities, with 85 per cent of these being of foreign birth (Samuel, 1987). In Toronto and Vancouver, the visible minorities comprised one-seventh of the population.

With a similar definition but based only on the ethnic origin question, 6.1 per cent of the 1986 census population can be classified as visible minorities (Beaujot and Rappak, 1988b: 101). This includes persons who are of Asian, Pacific Island, or African origins, including blacks (92 per cent of the total), and persons of Latin American origin, including Caribbean and West Indian blacks (8 per cent of the total). All multiple origins that included the above were here included with the visible minority population. In this total, 66.9 per cent were foreign-born. For the census metropolitan areas, the visible minorities comprised 8.2 per

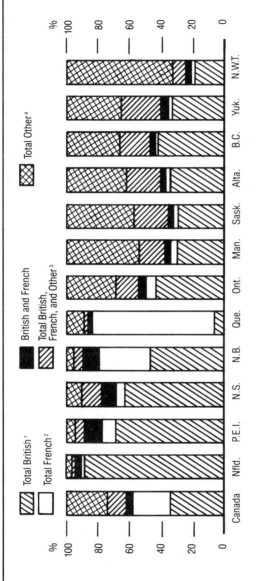

Figure 21: Proportion of Population Giving Total British, French, British and French, British, French, and Other Ethnic Origins, Canada, Provinces, and Territories, 1986

Legend: Total British[1] | Total French[2] | British and French | Total British, French, and Other[3] | Total Other[4]

1. Total British: includes single origins English, Irish, Scottish, Welsh, British, n.i.e., Other British, and the British Only multiple.
2. Total French: includes single origins French, Acadian, French Canadian, Québécois, and the French Only multiple.
3. Total British, French, and Other: includes British and Other, French and Other, and British, French, and Other.
4. Total Other: includes single origins other than British and French, and multiple origins that exclude British and French.

SOURCE: Statistics Canada, *The Daily*, 3 December 1987, p. 33.

cent of the 1986 population, including 14.0 per cent in Toronto (Bala-krishnan, 1988).

Clearly, the visible minority population is growing as a function of immigration. Among the arrivals for 1975-86, some 56 per cent are in the visible minority category. Fertility would also appear to be slightly higher for persons born in Asia and Latin America (A. Gauthier, 1988). Compared to the overall rate of 1.7 births per woman, the 1986 total fertility rate was 2.2 for persons born in Asia and Latin America. However, this could be partly a function of timing, as immigrants may delay births until after arriving in Canada, thus inflating a period measure such as the total fertility rate.

It should also be noted that while persons of non-European origin may be quite "visible" in the few years after arrival, or in the first generation, this visibility decreases as styles of clothing, speaking, and living become adapted to the majority population. Once ethnicity becomes unimportant in marriage selection, the concept of ethnicity takes on a rather different meaning (Krotki and Odynak, 1990). In this sense, the visible minority category is probably an upper limit of the number that might be defined as really visible.

Socio-economic profiles and their determinants

There is also considerable research on the socio-economic profile of ethnic and visible minority groups. The 1981 census data indicated that those classified as visible minorities had on average more education, higher labour force participation, and lower unemployment, but they earned slightly less than the Canadian average (Samuel, 1987). Part of the difference in earnings would be a function of recency of arrival. Beaujot and Rappak (1988b) found that persons born in Asia, Africa, and Latin America who arrived before 1970 had an average socio-economic profile that compared very favourably to the Canadian average.

Kalbach and Richard (1988) find that persons who identify less strongly with ethnic origins have higher levels of socio-economic achievement. For instance, foreign-born persons from a given background who identify with a mainline Canadian church or who have no religious preferences have higher average levels of socio-economic status. Also, persons who had intermarried across ethnic groups had higher levels of education and superior occupational attainment (Kalbach and Richard, 1989). They conclude that persistence of ethno-religious characteristics presents an obstacle to economic mobility (Kalbach and Richard, 1990). Assimilation tends to enhance the chances of achieving a higher level of integration and socio-economic status (Kalbach, 1987). Nonetheless, Breton et al. (1990: 256) conclude on the basis of the analysis of ethnic identity in Toronto that "although ethnicity appears to impede incorporation in the larger society, it some-times provides the social resources that can facilitate it." That is, ethnic retention and social incorporation are not necessarily two ends of a continuum but may be distinct phenomena.

Considering the period 1931-71, Lautard and Loree (1984) find that occupational differentiation over ethnic groups had declined but remained substantial. They conclude that the ethnic mosaic remains a vertical one. However, considering the intergenerational mobility on the basis of a 1973 survey, Boyd *et al*. (1985) discovered that the differen-tiation over the traditional European origin groups has declined signifi-cantly and that the opportunity structure, especially through educa-tion, has enabled these various groups to achieve social mobility. In *Immigration and Ethnic Conflict*, Richmond (1988) concludes that Euro-pean immigrants and their children have been economically successful and upwardly mobile. However, he continues, "although it may be premature to draw firm conclusions, the preliminary evidence concern-ing the immigrants from Third World countries, particularly visible minorities, is not as encouraging."

Several other authors have pointed to problems faced by visible minorities. Patel (1980) places the origin of the difficulties in European colonial expansion, which justified the domination of other peoples in terms of racial inferiority. Bolaria and Li (1985) observe that by defining certain visible groups as inferior, majority groups can and have excluded them from equal participation. The resulting exclusion forced certain groups, the Chinese and blacks in particular, to accept lower wages. Thus, employers could benefit from their cheap labour. Wein-feld (1988a: 593) observes that discrimination was either perpetuated or tolerated by the government well into the latter half of the twentieth century.

As a contemporary example, Henry and Ginzberg (1988) performed experiments with white and West Indian black applicants for employ-ment in Toronto. By sending matched white and black applicants to respond to the same "help wanted" advertisements, they found that the white applicant was offered the job in twenty-seven out of 191 cases, compared to nine out of the 191 cases for blacks. In 700 telephone applications, whites received positive responses in 87 per cent of cases compared to 60 per cent for blacks. Studies of minority groups them-selves find that people report widespread experiences of prejudice and discrimination against them (Patel, 1980: 13). For instance, the two visible groups in a Toronto sample were more likely to report having experienced discrimination when trying to find a job and to see dis-crimination as a serious problem (Breton, 1990: 209). Jansen and Rich-mond (1990) observe that while outward expressions of racial attitudes are generally covert or polite, there is overwhelming evidence that discrimination does occur: disadvantages on the labour market, sometimes hate literature, and police harassment. It is always difficult to know whether a person's difficulty is really a function of his/her ethnic origin or if it is simply attributed to this factor. Most people will experience certain cases of exclusion, and race becomes an easy explanation through which people may account for the experience. In their overview of the evidence, Anderson and Frideres (1981: 229, 327) note that the position of minorities in Canada has been improving but that racism remains a "virulent ideology ... justifying invidious distinctions and behaviours," and that the society has a long way to go to eradicate racism and prejudice against non-whites. Li (1988) concludes that important disparities in education and income are associated with ethnic origin and that these disparities imply there is not equal opportunity. However, a review by the Economic Council of Canada (1991) finds diminishing levels of prejudice and that after standardizing for other factors there is no systematic discrimination against immigrants, as a whole, or against visible minority immigrants, with respect to income.

Other interpretations of the data involve different conclusions. Winn (1988) observes that there is much variation in income within ethnic groups and that certain groups, such as the Japanese and Koreans, have high income following on their strong propensities for post-secondary education. The main income problem, according to Winn, results from low rates of return for investments in higher education obtained abroad. This may be due to various factors, including language difficulties or the unsuitability of the training to Canadian conditions. On the basis of a regression analysis, deSilva (1989) finds no strong evidence for the view that visible minority immigrants earn less than comparable native-born because of discrimination. Weinfeld (1988a) also observes that the economic achievement of children and grandchildren of immigrants suggests that the foundations for realizing equality have been laid. However, he observes continuing problems regarding visible minorities.

Policy discussions

The policy discussions surrounding the ethnic aspects of Canadian society are even more varied than the interpretations of the data. The Special Parliamentary Committee on Visible Minorities in Canadian Society specifically defined integration as meaning participation while retaining as much cultural heritage as desired without being denied equality of opportunity.

On certain things there is considerable agreement. For instance, there is widespread consensus on the importance of equal opportunity and on attacking the barriers that prohibit equal participation, especially in employment and in the economy. Since Canada is becoming a more socially diverse country, laws, policies, and programs have been needed in a variety of areas ranging from settlement services for immigrants to human rights codes prohibiting discrimination. Both the 1961 Bill of Rights and the 1977 Human Rights Act prohibit discrimination. Kalbach (1987) notes that certain other avenues for reducing differences have long been recognized, in particular job training and specialized education in official-language skills for immigrants.

Other avenues present more disagreement, as for instance affirmative action, which is often called employment equity in Canada. The 1982 Charter of Rights and Freedoms specifically prohibits discrimination while permitting affirmative action to overcome the disadvantage experienced by given groups. Tepper (1989) calls for enhancing these programs, which have weak enforcement mechanisms and largely apply only in the federal civil service, federally regulated business, and federal contractors. A 1986 report from the Public Service Commission notes that visible minorities comprise 4.3 per cent of the labour force but 1.7 per cent of the federal civil service (Brooks, 1989: 195). On the other hand, Winn (1988) argues that strong forms of affirmative action such as quota hiring will mostly benefit the best educated or those members of visible minority groups who are not suffering distinct disadvantages. Breton et al. (1974: 20) had proposed that "the stronger the minority-group effort to achieve political representation, the more negative will be the response of the majority."

Reitz (1988) observes that while racial discrimination exists, racial conflict in Canada has been moderated due to a number of factors, including multi-ethnic political structures and culture. The high proportion of the first generation among visible minorities means that they are less organized. The socio-economic status of these minorities has not been as negative as in other countries. Immigration policy would also have contributed to reducing the conflict by being selective and thus enhancing the socio-economic status of racial minorities, and through its support of such broad goals as economic expansion and nation-building. Kalbach (1987) points to the importance of immigration selection criteria that would reduce ethnic concentrations or enclaves associated with social and economic inequality.

The policy on multiculturalism is also seen within the context of Canada's evolving ethnic composition. Here again there is disagreement, with some arguing it contributes to ethnic and racial peace and others saying it contributes little to the real cultural life of the country (Krotki, 1990a). The multicultural policy enacted in 1971, and enhanced in 1988, specifies four areas of activity: assistance to cultural groups, overcoming barriers to full participation, cultural interchanges to enhance national unity, and assistance in official-language education. As reviewed by the Standing Committee on Multiculturalism (1987), the policy has developed from one dedicated to cultural preservation to one that seeks to ensure social, economic, and political equality for Canadians from all cultural and racial origins. In effect, the areas of cultural interchanges for national unity and of assistance in official-language training have more to do with Canada's bilingual nature. The Secretary of State spends seven times as much on bilingualism as on multiculturalism (Stasiulis, 1988: 87).

It can be argued that multiculturalism is problematic because it fosters ethnic distinctiveness when equal participation would require a focus on integration in the society. Kallen (1988) argues, for instance, that the concept is inherently problematic for three reasons: it favours particularism rather than universal social values; there is difficulty in having many cultures along with two languages; and as an ethno-political movement it is not necessarily representative. Brooks (1989) also observes that the main beneficiaries of multicultural policy have been ethnic organizations that received status and state funding. It is unclear to what extent these organizations represent the interests of the various ethnic groups. Kalbach and Richard (1990) observe a contradiction between the maintenance of distinctiveness and the fact that persistence of ethno-religious characteristics presents an obstacle to social and economic mobility. Kalbach (1987: 9) argues that "too much emphasis on the virtues of maintaining and preserving the uniqueness of Canada's diverse ethnic populations will make the task of reducing ethnic inequalities in the labour force more difficult." Multiculturalism, he argues, should not be at the expense of a more equitable economic integration and the assimilation that this may require.

In his report for the Macdonald Commission, Breton (1986: 47-48) argues that "research results do not indicate a strong and widespread demand for state intervention in the ethno-cultural field." Initiatives and demand for multiculturalism, he argues, come mostly from ethnic organizational elites and their supporters, government agencies involved with multiculturalism, and political authorities seeking voters. Weinfeld (1986) observes that we lack a comprehensive evaluation of the effects of ethnic organizations. Multiculturalism has enhanced the power of ethnic community leaders and their organizations, while most persons they represent are not particularly informed or involved. He notes, however, that this is not that different from other areas of policy, where few Canadians are actively involved.

Nonetheless, Samuel (1990) and others have argued that the recognition of the distinctiveness of various groups was necessary once the principle of respect for French and aboriginal minorities was accepted as an inherent part of Canadian society. While the policies arouse anxieties and uncertainty, Hawkins (1982: 78) concludes that they are also a "civilized and civilizing factor in national and community development." In effect, while it is difficult, policies would be best if they met a delicate balance between the enhancement and respect for cultural richness and variety *and* the integration that is necessary to ensure equal participation.

In *Ethnic Demography*, Halli *et al.* (1990) observe that "the French fact, the aboriginals of the northlands, recent visible minorities, bilingual and multicultural policies . . . have made Canada into a plural mosaic." Tepper (1987) welcomes a more diverse Canada for various reasons, including sustained economic growth through contact with various countries, and enhanced cultural richness. He argues that societies that are best able to manage ethnicity will be in an advantageous position in the evolving international arena. Anctil (1988) also sees immigrants bringing in modernity and keeping Canadians in touch with the rest of the world. Taking a long historical view, McNeill (1986) sees poly-ethnicity as the normal state of affairs in civilized societies.

A variety of institutions need to respond to the changing clientele and the changing work force (Parekh, 1988). This requires efforts not only to ensure equal opportunity, but also "reformulating the official definitions of the state" (Tepper, 1987). In effect, the greater ethnic diversity in the population brings a number of changes and requires various adaptations. Breton (1979: 289) concludes that "it is not surprising that we find considerable ambivalence in our society with regard to the desirability of ethnic retention." Bibby (1990) is concerned that in trying to accommodate such diversity, Canadians have ended up with a "mosaic madness" . . . "no single vision of their society, no glue that holds their nation together." Clearly, the emphasis on ethnic identities needs to be balanced with the importance of integration into the larger society.

CONCLUSIONS

While births, deaths, and changes of residence are very personal events, together they delimit the life of societies over history. Fertility and immigration are the fundamental mechanisms through which populations, countries, or societies are regenerated in the face of departures through death and emigration. These regeneration processes not only determine the number of people, they also change the character of the population and thus of the society. The characteristics of the population are changed in terms of age and sex structure, socio-economic composition, cultural make-up, and regional distribution.

Given the importance of the evolution of demographic events to societies, it is natural that considerable importance is attached to understanding the changes, and their implications, as well as to ensuring that these operate in the best interests of the society. The political orientations to evolving demographics can take two forms, either attempting to influence the course of demographic events or ensuring that the society makes the necessary adjustments to accommodate the population change.

DEMOGRAPHIC TRENDS AND ISSUES

The main components of Canada's shifting demographic situation involve lower fertility, lower growth, and population aging. These are setting parameters that are in many regards different from those that have operated in the past. Over the forty-five-year period since 1946, Canada's population more than doubled, growing from 12.3 to 26.9 million. Most would interpret this past change positively, noting that the baby boom and the immigration boom of the post-war period have permitted Canada to move in unprecedented directions. The country would be rather different if it had basically stood still at its 1946 population. Projections made at the time did not foresee these fertility and immigration changes, proposing instead that the population would reach a maximum of about 15 million. It could be argued that the actual evolution ensured more domestic control over resources, increased the status of the country among the nations of the world, and contributed to economic growth and social development.

Over the forty-five-year period 1991-2036, current projections indicate that, unless there is a substantial increase in fertility, population growth will stop completely, with immigration becoming the only component of growth after about 2020. The average age of the population would increase from thirty-two to forty-five years, while the proportion aged sixty-five and over would change from one person in ten to one in four. These are rather different scenarios than those we have known in the past, making it difficult to anticipate the impact on the society.

The issues that arise from a population that is aging and growing more slowly include economic, family, and social considerations. At the economic level, concern can be raised regarding productivity, savings, changing types of consumption, more needs for tax revenue, and consequently a greater role of government in the economy (Cliquet, 1986). At the family level, there is the implication of more isolation, including higher proportions widowed and more people without children, which is compounded by higher numbers of single-parent families. At the social level, questions arise regarding social security systems, and there is the possibility of less intergenerational solidarity and support. That is, different sectors of the population, especially the young and the elderly, may have fewer overlapping and more conflicting concerns.

The impact of changes may also vary over time. For instance, aging may have largely positive implications in the short term, through fewer family demands made on adults and a higher proportion of the population at labour force ages. However, the longer-term impact of aging may be more negative, with higher proportions at retirement ages and associated social security costs. Chesnais (1989) observes that the major negative consequences of the transformation of the age structure will occur after the year 2000, presenting "the largest challenge of the 21st century" for the countries of the Western world.

The demographic trends ultimately have consequences on the relative sizes of given countries. For instance, the unification of East and West Germany makes it substantially larger than other Western European countries, such as France and the United Kingdom. In that light, it is interesting to observe that, should united Germany adopt the fertility pattern of the western part of the country, by the year 2030 the whole country would be smaller, 60.6 million, than West Germany itself was at unification, 63.2 million (Buttner and Lutz, 1990).

THE POLICY PROCESS

In discussing policy questions, it is always important to recognize that information and research comprise only one of the relevant factors.

Ryder (1985) observes that "population issues have a necessary place on our social agenda, but it is a limited place." Among the determinants of policy, besides the role of the decision-makers themselves, four other factors can usefully be distinguished (Simeon, 1976). First is the distribution of ideas and values in the society regarding the type of society we want and the means to use in achieving the necessary objectives. Second is relative power of competing groups, along with the resources they have for promoting their interests. Third, institutions are often interrelated or in situations of conflict with regard to their interests in a given policy question. Finally, the socio-economic environment, defined broadly, and its change over time contribute to the definition of the issues that gain priority along with the resources available to address these problems.

It is mostly at the level of the socio-economic environment that demographic questions may become determinants of policy. As a consequence, research is important for understanding the evolving demographics and their implications. However, demographic phenomena can be important in the evolution of ideas and values, since given generations, age groups, or new arrivals from outside can bring their own ideas regarding the preferable future of the society. Immigrants, for example, bring a strong interest in promoting multiculturalism. In addition, questions of numbers and of composition, thus demographic questions, can have an impact on the relative power of the various groups in competition or on the relative impact of given institutions.

Several examples can be suggested regarding the role of these various determinants of policy. At the level of ideas or values, there are contrasting views regarding optimizing for the present or the future, or optimizing for economic or environmental concerns. A report by Environment Canada (1984), for instance, argues that the pursuit of unlimited economic growth has social and environmental consequences that could seriously diminish the future quality of life. There are also values about the relative importance placed on nature or people and the interplay between humanity and nature. This can bring us back to the conflict between Malthusian orientations, where more people mean more problems, as contrasted with Marxist views suggesting that, with the proper social arrangements, more people means more resources to solve the problems.

With institutions, there are different stakes in immigration between federal and provincial levels of government, since the federal level is responsible for admissions while specific communities and provinces must accommodate the new arrivals. As another example, public institutions may gain greater scope in an aging society, which can be to the disadvantage of private-sector institutions. Regarding questions of power, an example would be the relative strength of groups arguing for more public facilities for child care in contrast to those proposing that the family is the proper setting for early childhood.

THE MAIN ALTERNATIVES

Before considering in more detail the trends and issues in given domains, it is useful to review the basic alternatives and their relative strengths and weaknesses.

One alternative is to make various adaptations to accommodate the evolving or anticipated demographic trends. Adaptations are necessary in any case, since a continuation of the aging process is inevitable. It would take a return to four or five births per woman to stop the aging process (George *et al.*, 1990). The main forms of adaptation involve resource transfers for the benefit of the elderly and restructuring aspects of the labour force. The resource transfers refer particularly to pensions and health, which are affected by the age structure. Given the slower growth and aging of the labour force, there is need to ensure its continued flexibility by putting more emphasis on training and retraining, as well as on attempting to extend the productive work life of older persons. All these adaptations are difficult. More resource transfers involve higher taxes and a greater role of the public sector in the economy. Retraining may pose problems for persons who would resist making changes later in life, while health questions may make it difficult to work longer.

Equally difficult are the alternatives that would attempt to change or influence demographic trends. The immigration approach sustains demographic and labour force growth and provides a slight counter to population and labour force aging. However, immigration requires strong planning in a long-term context, appropriate integration programs for the new arrivals, and maximizing the distribution of immigrants over space, as well as various efforts to build a harmonious multicultural society. The "immigration solution" therefore requires a number of services and various adaptations, especially in education. Chesnais (1989) contrasts these "desiderata" to what is often, instead, largely unorganized arrivals to select large cities, which follow on short-term labour force needs or on pressure from the world outside.

The "fertility solution" is also costly, both to parents and to the society. At the level of the society, there is a need to deal with the incongruities between individual and social interests (Cliquet, 1986). At the level of individuals, there is the competition between parenthood and other work and lifestyle options. It is also necessary to support families that may be very different in terms of size, structure, and needs. The fertility approach therefore requires resource transfers to the benefit of children, thus posing conflicts with the needs of the elderly.

Given this balance of costs, a case can be made for entertaining all three major alternatives. The various adaptations to an aging society are necessary in any case, although the need for them would be somewhat reduced if labour force growth can be sustained and if aging can be minimized. The immigration solution presents advantages in terms of sustaining population growth and maintaining flexibility in the labour force. At the same time, arrivals from the outside can be more easily accommodated if fertility is sustained, thereby ensuring that immigration does not change the basic socio-cultural character of the population more than is considered acceptable. Children are costly in a variety of ways and require various kinds of sacrifices, but they are ultimately the most important investment in the long-term future of the society. If the immigration approach has economic benefits with social and political costs, the fertility solution could be said to have economic costs with social and political benefits.

MORTALITY AND HEALTH

Much progress has been made in terms of mortality. Life expectancy was only thirty-eight to forty years a century and a half ago; now it is over seventy-five years. Until about 1971, the reduced mortality benefited especially the young, and women more than men. Since that time, there have also been reductions in the mortality levels of older people and the gender differential has begun to decline. It was commonly said that mortality did not play a substantial role in aging since the improvements especially benefited the young or were spread out over the life cycle. Now that the improvements occur at older ages, the extension of life expectancy contributes to population aging.

Biological factors clearly play a role in mortality, as evidenced by the different survival prospects by gender and age. However, the analysis of differences by gender, marital status, and socio-economic status indicates that the lifestyle factor plays a significant role. Men have long been greater abusers of alcohol and tobacco, and their more aggressive tendencies contribute to their higher accident mortality rates. Women are less likely to take risks and are more prone to admit a health problem and to seek assistance. For instance, the 1985 Health Survey found that, at ages 25-44, twice as many men as women had not seen a doctor over the previous year.

Progress in life expectancy does not necessarily reduce the burdens, since the medical costs of looking after the survivors continue to increase. With an aging population, the levels of poor health and disability are both substantial and rising. Morbidity remains important in the later decades of life, and this becomes problematic as more people reach advanced ages. The increased numbers of "frail elderly," sometimes with seriously debilitating but non-fatal diseases, pose various burdens on the health care system.

An important component of health costs occurs in the last months or days of life. Various analyses conclude that aging is not the most significant factor with regard to increasing health costs. For instance, health costs are much more sensitive to an increase in the number of physicians who are prone to hospitalize their patients than to an increase in aging (Roos and Roos, 1986). However, there is a tendency to ignore the impact of death itself on the costs. Until the mid-1980s, the deaths per 1,000 population were declining slowly. But with an older population, there are eventually more deaths. Projections indicate that by the year 2036 there would be almost twice as many deaths per 1,000 population. If aging does not have a significant role in health costs, death does have an impact because of the concentration of costs in the last months of life.

Other health issues include the debate between preventive and curative approaches. Curative medicine has clearly played a role in more recent mortality improvements, for instance, in the cases of accident victims and low-birthweight infants. However, differentials over population groups and surveys of health conditions indicate the importance of preventive interventions. It might well be argued that the "counselling" role of medical practitioners, in terms of improving health habits, is more important than the curative role. Prevention is not as spectacular, but it can have a larger impact at the level of population aggregates. It should be possible to reduce the mortality prospects for men, persons who are not married, lower-income groups, and native peoples. It is partly a question of giving sufficient priority to these objectives.

FERTILITY AND REPRODUCTION

Fertility also has changed considerably from a time when average births per woman were over seven, around the time of Confederation, to the level of 1.7 in the 1980s. The baby boom of the period 1946-66 was a significant departure from the long-term trend, introducing uncertainty in terms of projecting the future. However, it is now largely agreed that the baby boom resulted from a series of specific circumstances that are unlikely to repeat themselves. This was a period of sustained economic growth, with associated optimism about the future and societal focus on family roles, especially for women. The changes over the past twenty-five years have also been substantial. The total fertility rate for 1965 implied that the generation of children was 48 per cent larger than the generation of parents. Under 1985 conditions, there would be 20 per cent fewer children than parents.

It is sometimes difficult to appreciate the fertility trends because the total fertility rate has been below the "replacement level" of 2.1 births per woman since 1972, but births are likely to outnumber deaths until about 2020. As with other industrialized countries, Canada is basically in a phase of demographic decline. The increase only continues as a function of the growth potential accumulated in the age structure during the past period of demographic expansion. If present trends continue, "this potential will inevitably exhaust itself, just as a sum of capital disappears when not renewed" (United Nations, 1989a: 2).

Explanations of fertility change can usefully distinguish proximate, economic, cultural, and structural factors. Proximate factors include the lower propensity for adults to be married or living as couples, along with higher contraceptive usage. Economic factors focus on the increased costs of children to parents. Available data would indicate that three children aged ten, twelve, and seventeen cost some $20,000 for one year and reduce the standard of living of the family by 33 per cent compared to a family without children (Dionne, 1989). Cultural factors have promoted a greater concern for self-gratification and a greater freedom of choice in family-related matters, including the greater acceptability of divorce, cohabitation, and not having children. Structural factors point to the broad changes in the political economy, which have increased women's roles in the paid labour force and thus increased the opportunity cost of children and changed the economic aspects of the relations between men and women. Presser (1986: 199) observes that a further postponement of childbearing on the part of women would increase their relative power, both because they would become more economically independent and because a longer child-free context would make them more aware of gender inequalities. Women could then use their greater power to negotiate a more equal deal with their husbands, as well as with the workplace and the broader society, on sharing the costs of child-rearing.

These same factors can be analysed in terms of possible policy concerns, including reducing unwanted births and sustaining the level of reproduction. Reducing unwanted births needs to focus on the larger numbers of unmarried young adults, along with the factors that would promote usage of contraception.

In regard to sustaining fertility, the proximate factors are not particularly relevant, except possibly in terms of health and technological improvements that would benefit those who cannot conceive. The consideration of economic factors suggests reducing the costs of children to parents by having the state pay more of these costs in the form of family allowance, child tax deductions, child tax credits, and baby bonuses. In effect, this means transfers away from families and individuals without children toward those with children.

Cultural factors point to making our culture more open to children, promoting more family-oriented values, finding ways to symbolize the social values of parenthood, and attempting to build a shared consensus that children are important to the future of the society. This would include a greater sense that having and caring for children are important parts of normal adult roles, for both men and women. Structural considerations suggest measures that account for the dual roles of adults in production and reproduction. In particular, this would include parental leave policies, flexible work time, pension plans for parents who are taking care of children, and provisions for child care.

Such a series of programs would be expensive. Anyone who has cared for children knows that children are expensive in a variety of ways. But ultimately this is the only form of investment in the future that really counts. Programs can be justified on a number of grounds, especially improving child and family welfare, investing in children as a "scarce resource," and working toward equality by gender.

INTERNATIONAL MIGRATION

In contrast to many other advanced industrial countries, Canada has a long history of policies and programs through which immigration has contributed significantly to population change. Over this century, net international migration has accounted for some 22 per cent of total population growth. This does not count the further impact through births to immigrants. Simulating the change over the period 1951-81 implies that 38 per cent of the growth was a function of immigration and births to these immigrants over the period. In 1986, 16 per cent of the population of Canada was foreign-born, which is higher than the major industrial countries except Australia and Israel. Immigration has little impact on the age structure and it reinforces the trends in growth of the largest cities, but it also counters the trends toward slower population growth.

While the demographic side of immigration is relatively easy to assess, the economic implications are harder to delineate. In a summary of economic impacts of immigration to Canada, Employment and Immigration (1989d) cites a number of positive results, including the importation of capital, job creation through higher consumption and business formation, economic stimulation through expenditures on food and shelter, and asset accumulation. The foreign-born have more labour force activity, less unemployment, and higher incomes on average. This report sees the main costs as being short term, specifically initial settlement and adjustment. Other summaries are less optimistic. Seward and Tremblay (1990) observe that the more recent immigration is going largely to the part of the labour force where there is the least security, particularly the low-paying jobs of the service sector. Women in the garment industry are another example of immigrants in jobs with little opportunity for mobility; in addition, they are working under the threat of displacement due to the removal of international trade barriers. Richmond (1988) finds that immigrants from Europe and their descendants have done well in Canada, but he doubts that the trends will be as favourable for the more recent arrivals from Third World countries.

Although specific economic concerns can be raised, properly controlled immigration is likely to present a net economic benefit, if only because the majority arrive at the most productive stages of the life cycle. Without having to invest in their education, the receiving country benefits from their various talents and abilities. The receiving society is probably best served if immigrants have a socio-economic profile not too different from that of the society to which they are arriving. If they arrive with superior profiles it may cause resentment; if they arrive at the bottom of the economic ladder there is the possibility of forming ghettos. In effect, we have seen that the socio-economic profile of the foreign-born is not that different from the Canadian-born. The 1980-85 cohort may have been an exception due to the lower proportion of the independent class. It would appear that a balance among the family, independent, and refugee classes is more likely to present an average profile that, at least after a few years, is not that different from the Canadian-born.

While immigration is likely to present net economic benefits, the social impact may not be as positive (Bourbeau et al., 1986b). Immigration changes the regional distribution and the linguistic composition in ways that can be interpreted negatively. Termote (1988) finds that an immigration of 40,000 per year to the province of Quebec would increase the size of Montreal by some 1,150,000 over forty years. Lachapelle (1988a) concludes that immigration has been the main factor reducing the relative weight of the French in Canada, while Paillé (1989a) is concerned about the relative impact of immigration and fertility on the future linguistic composition of Montreal Island. With such social impacts in view, the Parliamentary Standing Committee recommended slower immigration growth over the period 1991-93 (Blackburn, 1990). This committee expressed concerns with respect to social relations, concentration of immigrants, and immigrant integration.

After questions of national unity, few public policy questions in Canada are subject to as much debate as immigration. Immigration is blamed for ethnic tensions, housing shortages, unemployment, and whatever major ills are facing the country at a given time. But immigration also represents mobility, opportunity, challenge, diversity, contact with other cultures, openness to the world, and a dynamic approach to the future. Immigration has made a substantial contribution to the sense of national identity and purpose.

The question is always to know how to control the size and composition of immigration – and how to organize the economic and social integration of immigrants to assure that the society is not changed more than is deemed acceptable. It must also be appreciated that immigration helps the society to develop and retain vital contacts with the outside world.

INTERNAL MIGRATION AND DISTRIBUTION

Internal migration is best considered within the discussion of regional diversity in Canada. The net movement within the country, along with the differential arrivals from abroad, is largely responsible for the slow changes in the relative demographic sizes of the provinces and regions. This change has largely involved a net movement westward and to southern Ontario. Dumas (1990b) observes that similar patterns of movement to the south and west are occurring in the United States. In addition, if free trade implies a freer movement of people, as it already does within the European Economic Community, the southern movement on the continent would clearly involve departures from Canada.

Policy questions concerning regionalism and migration come down to the question of "moving people to the jobs" or "jobs to the people." Given the lack of fit between the geographic grids of economic opportunity and of demographic distribution, the problem becomes a matter of determining which factor to try to influence. In many ways it is easier to move people, and certain policies, such as tax deductions for moving expenses and the Manpower Mobility Program, encourage departures out of the more depressed areas. However, there are also costs associated with this "solution," in particular the further undermining of the economic potential of regions through the departure of some of their more productive elements. As a consequence, simultaneous attempts are made to encourage growth and to discourage departures from the more depressed regions. This occurs especially through equalization payments, regional differences in unemployment insurance benefits, and policies for regional economic expansion.

As the country moves toward demographic dynamics wherein the difference between births and deaths is small or negative, the differential impact of internal and international migration will become even more visible. No longer will we be talking of relative growth but of some regions growing while others are declining. The continued movement toward inequality in the demographic size of the various regions of the country puts stress on a constitutional system that attempts to treat the provinces equally.

DEMOGRAPHIC GROWTH AND AGE STRUCTURE

The three principal traits of contemporary demographic evolution in Canada are closely related: reduced fertility, aging, and lower growth. For the past, it can be observed that periods of more rapid economic and demographic growth have tended to coincide. This is also true at the provincial level, where there is a positive relation between economic and demographic growth. However, the causal relations are not well established and it could be that these relationships would be different in the future, with economic change being less dependent on labour force growth. It is also possible that aging has had a positive impact in the past through the relative growth of the population at labour force ages, but that its impact may be more negative in the future through the relative growth of persons at retirement ages.

Even though the demographic growth has been slowing down for some thirty-five years and aging has occurred for almost a century, the labour force has not been subject to these factors until very recently. Thanks to the baby boom and to the entry of women into the paid labour force, the labour force has been growing rapidly and actually getting slightly younger. An important question is to know what might be the impact of a labour force population that is both aging and growing much more slowly or declining. Among the studies done for the Review of Demography, two take a relatively optimistic attitude on this question, while two others are more pessimistic.

Denton and Spencer (1988a) emphasize the fact that an older labour force will be more experienced. In their model, the productivity of age groups is measured by income. Since incomes rise with age, an older labour force increases per capita incomes. Fortin (1987) considers that a labour force that is growing less rapidly will need less new investments to accommodate new workers. This would permit "capital deepening" or more investments per worker and a higher quality labour force. It will be necessary to ensure improvement in the quality of the labour force, through emphasis on education, training, and retraining.

Foot (1987) speaks especially of the disadvantages of an aging labour force in terms of reduced flexibility. There would be less geographic mobility, less mobility across sectors of the economy, and consequently less possibility to accommodate changes in the relative growth of the various sectors. An older worker has less to gain in terms of increased lifetime earnings and more to lose in terms of seniority through any movement, training, or change of occupation. Similarly, Ryder (1985) is concerned that a declining population would imply less entry into the labour force from below. He suggests that the future labour force will have characteristics that, in current arrangements, would imply less productivity, vitality, and flexibility. We would lose a large part of the capacity to transform the economy by means of new entrants to the labour force.

Lapierre-Adamcyk *et al.* (1988) observe that the only demographic element that has enhanced productivity over the period 1955-85 has been a measure of level of education weighted by the age-sex structure. That is, the productivity of the economy has benefited from a higher level of education, especially for the young, and from a labour force that became younger and less male-dominant. This could be interpreted by suggesting that younger workers and women, including those working part-time, are exploited in that they receive less income than their productivity would justify, while older male workers receive more income for given levels of productivity. An older labour force would consequently cost more for a given unit of productivity. If the Denton and Spencer (1988a) simulations have overestimated the productivity of older workers, this brings into question the results showing that slower demographic growth brings higher per capita incomes.

Equally important to know is the possibility of extending the work life. It is often suggested that more labour force participation on the part of older persons could make up for the lack of young persons. In effect, Osberg (1988) finds that many of the retirements of persons aged fifty-five to sixty-five are due to lack of opportunity to work rather than a desire to stop working. On the other hand, studies in the United States emphasize health questions, and Simpson (1986) notes that older workers have less to gain through further training investments. Equally interesting is the observation that the older a population the younger the average age at retirement (Myles, 1981a; Gonnot, 1990). In order to make people work longer, it would be necessary to reduce substantially the retirement benefits – and there would still be the problems of poor health and of training that may no longer be up to date.

There remain important unanswered questions regarding the economic and labour force implications of lower growth and aging. There are studies of the impact of higher or lower demographic growth but not on the impact of demographic decline. In addition, insufficient attention has been paid to the adjustment costs of decline, for instance, in terms of school closures, psychological resistance to further training on the part of older workers, and various institutional rigidities, including seniority systems.

More work has been done on the costs of aging in terms of existing social programs. The projections by Fellegi (1988) measure the costs in constant dollars, per person aged 20-64. Allowing for increases in the unit costs comparable to the increases of the 1975-84 period, the demographic aging between 1986 and 2036 would imply a fourfold increase in the constant dollar cost of pensions and a threefold increase for health, relative to the population at labour force ages. While some savings are envisioned for education, the education sector may well argue for more expenditures to enhance quality and to service the retraining needs of older persons.

FAMILIES AND HOUSEHOLDS

Several studies have documented the increased diversity of family and household types, including the growth of single-person households, single-parent families, consensual unions, families without children, two-income families, and reconstituted families. The study by Marcil-Gratton (1988) is unique in analysing the changes from the point of view of children. Lower fertility, higher female labour force participation, and more divorce have markedly changed the early life experiences of children. A higher proportion of births are first births, implying that the average child has parents who have less experience at parenting. Children are also less likely to have a brother or sister ten or more years older who could be a guide in life, and they also have less opportunity to interact with siblings. In the early 1960s, only 10 per cent of mothers did not stop work after the first birth compared to half of mothers in the early 1980s. The proportion returning to work soon after a birth is similar to the proportion twenty years ago who were working when the child was twelve years old. For children born in the early 1960s, 13 per cent saw the separation of their parents before age ten, compared to 23 per cent among those born in the early 1970s. Among the latter, half have lived in reconstituted families, 20 per cent lived a second period of lone parenthood, and 10 per cent have seen a second reconstituted family, all before age ten.

The greater diversity and flexibility in family types are, for the most part, advantageous for adults – at least it is mostly their choice. However, one can ask how the welfare of children is affected by these choices (Burch, 1990; Bumpass, 1990). The child has no choice and must be content with what the parents or the society provides. Being fewer in number, one might think that children would have more resources, since these can be divided among a smaller number of recipients. While this is certainly true in some regards, there is also a tendency, as Preston (1984) has noted, for an aging society to give more attention to the elderly among the two main demographic categories of dependants. Péron and Légaré (1988) are concerned about older persons who have no surviving children, but we must also be concerned about children who lack the presence or the time of their parents.

On the other hand, it would appear that many parents consider that two persons working full time when the children are young is not the ideal situation for children and families. An American poll found that twice as many respondents would prefer making financial sacrifices so that one parent can stay home compared to the alternative of maximizing family income by having both parents working (Footlick, 1990). One cannot expect that the parent who interrupts her/his work for the sake of the children and family will have the same income opportunities at a later stage in life. This may be one of our most serious social dilemmas. The main problem is that there are major differences between two alternate solutions to this dilemma. Certain people and pressure groups want the society to pay the costs so that parents, especially mothers, do not have to make such high personal sacrifices. But others prefer not to put their children in the care of others and, at the same time, do not want to have to pay the taxes that would enable other parents to have highly subsidized child care. These two competing models of family and gender roles pose a serious policy dilemma.

It might be concluded that children should be subsidized rather than a specific model of the family. For instance, might one not subsidize the care of children instead of only the care of children in day-care settings. This would allow parents to make a choice: one parent who stays home, possibly putting the funds in a retirement or educational savings plan for that parent, informal arrangements through relatives, or formal day-care arrangements. There are consequences of such choices, especially for the parent who decides to stay home. But who is to judge the relative value of two jobs pursued without interruption compared to what could be a higher quality of life for children or for a family? It might be noted that this choice was not left open when it came to the education system. That is, parents were not subsidized in order to allow them the alternative of using these funds to pay for their children's schooling. But on schooling it is fairly clear that the school setting is best for most children, while the same cannot necessarily be said for day care.

One might alternatively argue that the state should mostly promote community-level services for child care. That would maximize women's involvement in the labour force, which may be particularly important in the contexts of both slower population growth and the push for gender equality (Lapierre-Adamcyk, 1990). It would also minimize women's vulnerability to the problems of family breakdown and single-parenthood.

More generally, the increased diversity of family types makes family policy difficult. Some families are in considerable need, especially lone mothers with young children, while others are much more independent, particularly dual-career couples with no children. Given this diversity, family policy must be flexible, and one might argue that there will be less contradiction if more focus is given to the needs of children.

SOCIO-ECONOMIC AND SOCIO-CULTURAL COMPOSITION

Demographic analysis permits focused attention on sub-groups of the population as defined by such characteristics as education, labour force status, gender, income, ethnicity, and language. The "welfare state" requires detailed knowledge on the welfare of the various sub-groups of the population, in order to be able to plan policies that can improve ·this welfare. Consequently, the collection of detailed information through censuses and surveys and analysis of these data along demographic parameters form an essential component in the governing of modern societies.

The education system has been subject to the movement of the baby boom and baby bust through the various age classes. Other aspects of the system have not specifically followed these demographic patterns. In particular, the university enrolment did not decline as expected, and expenditures increased more at primary and secondary levels even though enrolments were declining. This points to the relative underfunding of the post-secondary sector. Given the smaller number of new entrants to the labour force, there is even more need to pay attention to the quality of their education and to provide structures for return to school or retraining. For those who leave the education system early or who lack basic skills, there is need to invest in their early work experiences to make these an "apprenticeship-like" learning environment.

Labour force participation has increased for younger people, especially women, and declined for older persons, especially men. However, even at ages 25-44 only 87.9 per cent of men and 59.2 per cent of women worked full-time in 1990. Training, job creation, and labour mobility, along with unemployment insurance, are the main policy areas that specifically concern the labour force. Unemployment insurance provides an important form of security and subsidizes the income of workers. However, many have argued that unemployment insurance has become a form of general social security for depressed regions and that the system would work better if it were more purely an insurance scheme, leaving broader social security to other structures.

Analyses show basic persistence of gender differences in income. An important part of the income difference would appear to follow on occupational segregation, which itself is related to various factors, including women's greater involvement in family roles. Due to lack of data, very little information is available regarding the impact of different levels of experience on the relative income of men and women. We do know that job interruptions remain very high for women and are often associated with their primary care-giving role within the family. While men have job interruptions as well, these are rarely related to family demands. Two specific attempts to ensure more gender equality are only slowly having an impact. Pay equity has been instituted in various jurisdictions to enhance equal pay for work of equal value. Employment equity tries to ensure equal opportunity in the competition for employment and promotion, in part by attempting to redress the impact of past discrimination. Another challenge is for policy to recognize both productive and reproductive roles, along with the different options that people may choose with regard to family and child-rearing responsibilities (Heitlinger, 1990b).

The analysis of the income distribution over sectors of the population shows remarkable stability in spite of much economic change and the introduction of several social security programs. The more disadvantaged groups are single parents and elderly women living alone. The growth of both of these demographic groups has contributed to the feminization of poverty. Over the period 1980-85, young families, especially those with children, suffered relative disadvantages, while older families made more gains. Many have argued that the income security system is in need of a major overhaul. An approach like that of guaranteed annual income would reduce the contradictions in the system and its administrative complexity, while ensuring more equitable transfers toward the working poor and their dependent children. Osberg (1990) reminds us that it is our social programs that give meaning to the Canadian community: "the social democratic vision of a broadly based welfare state" has become "the institutional embodiment of the ideal of community." At any one time most people are self-sufficient and consequently not dependent on the social security network, and they may complain about the tax costs, but social programs are also important to most people at least over parts of the life cycle.

Turning to factors of socio-cultural composition, the native peoples suffer a number of disadvantages, some of which are related to demographics, such as much geographic dispersion and ethnic or linguistic diversity in the context of a relatively small total size. In spite of high mortality, there is also high natural increase, which means a young population with large numbers trying to enter the labour force. Several policy issues emerge, in areas ranging from health and housing to employment and social security. While native people have in the past been subject to much outright discrimination, including policy discrimination that took a very "paternalistic" attitude, it is probably fair to say that there is now much more good will in the society to support the resolution of these difficulties. There has developed a greater recognition that much of the fault lies with historical injustices perpetrated by the colonizing peoples and that a wealthy society should be able to better accommodate the needs and rights of the original inhabitants of the land. These needs and rights are increasingly articulated within the broad umbrella of land claims and some form of self-government.

On language, the basic national trend has involved the growing relative size of the population who mostly speak English. This is especially the case in western Canada and in Atlantic Canada east of New Brunswick. However, there are also trends favourable to the French language, in particular its greater majority in Quebec. There is also more bilingualism in the official languages, with noticeable increases among people whose first language is English. The likelihood of parents to pass the French language on to their children has also increased. French-language immersion has become popular, amounting to some 5 per cent of eligible students. Although changes are slow, language policy has clearly had an impact. In Quebec, it has made an increasingly Francophone province. In the rest of the country, the greater importance given to the French language has prompted more learning of the language. However, the linguistic composition of the provinces remains very different, making it difficult to co-ordinate the aspirations of the various groups and to hold the country together. In particular, the linguistic minorities have become very small, giving most people the everyday experience of only one of the official languages. This undermines bilingualism as a means of uniting the country and suggests placing greater importance on accommodating the linguistic makeup of the populations of given provinces or regions.

In terms of ethnic origin, Canada is increasingly diverse and immigration plays a major role in this diversity. Much attention has been placed on visible minorities, although it is not a concept on which it is easy to obtain census data. As Canada becomes more diverse, it could be argued that the "visibility" of given groups will decline, especially as styles of behaviour become less distinguishable over generations. There is considerable consensus on the importance of equal opportunity as a means of reducing differences. There can be some difficulty with affirmative action approaches that would set quotas for employment and promotion. Contrary to the case of gender, it is hard to claim that recent immigrants have suffered from systematic discrimination over history that now needs to be corrected. Policies on multiculturalism need to pay attention to both ethnic distinctiveness and integration through equal participation. In effect, a delicate balance is needed between the enhancement and respect for cultural richness and variety and the integration necessary to ensure mobility and equal opportunity. Clearly, the greater ethnic diversity in the population brings a number of changes and requires various adaptations. The successful management of ethnicity can play a significant role both internally and in terms of a country's place in the world community (Tepper, 1987).

Lord Maynard Keynes, the father of modern economics, frequently said that big historical events are often caused by slow demographic processes (United Nations, 1989a: 1-2). Today, he would surely pay attention to the rift that separates the rapidly growing and young Third World populations from the aging and slow-growing or declining populations of the more developed countries. In the long term, these different demographic dynamics will surely bring changes in the relations among nations. The changes within Canada are no less striking, especially in comparison to the recent past. While demographic changes are slow, continued attention is required to understand their impact and to meet the challenges of adaptation.

REFERENCES

Abbott, Michael G. 1988. "Immigration and Labour Market Adjustment," in C.M. Beach and A.G. Green, eds., *Policy Forum on the Role of Immigration in Canada's Future*. Kingston: John Deutsch.

Abella, Rosalie. 1985. "Equality at Work and at Home," *Policy Options*, 6,10: 27-32.

Ableson, Janet, Peter Paddan, and Claude Strohmenger. 1983. *Perspectives on Health*. Ottawa: Statistics Canada Cat. No. 82-540.

Achilles, Rona. 1986. "The Social Implications of Artificial Reproductive Technologies." Ottawa: Report for Review of Demography, Health and Welfare.

Adams, Owen. 1990. "Profile of the Institutionalized Population of Canada: Findings from the Health and Activity Survey," paper presented at the meetings of the Canadian Population Society, Victoria, June, 1990.

Adams, O.B., and D.N. Nagnur. 1988. *Marriage, Divorce and Mortality*. Ottawa: Statistics Canada Catalogue No. 84-536.

Adams, O.B., and D.N. Nagnur. 1989. "Marriage, Divorce and Mortality: A Life Table Analysis for Canada and Regions," in J. Légaré, T.R. Balakrishnan, and R. Beaujot, eds., *The Family in Crisis: A Population Crisis?* Ottawa: Royal Society of Canada.

Akbari, Ather H. 1989. "The Benefits of Immigrants to Canada: Evidence on Tax and Public Services," *Canadian Public Policy*, 15, 4: 424-35.

Albert, Luc. 1989. "Language in Canada," *Canadian Social Trends*, 12: 9-12.

Anctil, Pierre. 1988. "Modernity at our Doorstep: The Immigrants in Canadian Society," paper presented at the meetings of the Canadian Population Society, Windsor, June, 1988.

Anderson, Alan B., and James S. Frideres. 1981. *Ethnicity in Canada: Theoretical Perspectives*. Toronto: Butterworths.

Anderson, Grace M. 1978. "Immigration and Social Policy," in S.A. Yelaja, ed., *Canadian Social Policy*. Waterloo, Ont.: Wilfrid Laurier University Press.

Anderson, William P. 1986. "Demographic Trends and Economic Development in Canada's Peripheral Regions." Ottawa: Report for Review of Demography, Health and Welfare.

Andorka, Rudolf. 1989. "Policy Responses to Population Decline in the 21st Century: Pronatalism, Migration Policy, Growing Labour Force Participation or Other Alternatives," *International Population Conference, New Delhi*. Liège: International Union for the Scientific Study of Population, Vol. 3: 303-12.

Angus, Douglas. 1984. "The Long-term Budgetary Problem," in *Report of the Policy Forum on Medicare in an Age of Restraint*. Kingston: John Deutsch.

Angus, Douglas E. 1986. "Vieillissement et coûts des soins de santé: y a-t-il un problème," *Cahiers Québécois de Démographie*, 15, 1: 11-26.

Angus, H.F. 1946. "The Future of Immigration into Canada," *Canadian Journal of Economics and Political Science*, 12: 379-86.

Angus Reid Group. 1989. *Immigration to Canada: Aspects of Public Opinion*. Ottawa: Employment and Immigration.

Anselm, Mercy. 1990. "Why Women's Wages Stay Low," *Policy Options*, 11, 4: 19-22.

Armstrong, Pat, and Hugh Armstrong. 1984. *The Double Ghetto: Canadian Women and their Segregated Work*. Toronto: McClelland and Stewart.

Arnoti, Brigitta. 1986. "Children in Low-income Families," *Canadian Social Trends*, 3: 18-20.

Arthur, W. Brian. 1988. "Intergenerational Relations," in R. Lee, ed., *Economics of Changing Age Distributions in Developed Countries*. Oxford: Clarendon Press.

Asimakopulos, A. 1990. "Review of the Political Economy of Pensions," *Canadian Public Policy*, 16, 1: 109.

Atkinson, Michael M., and Marsha A. Chandler, eds. 1983. *The Politics of Canadian Public Policy*. Toronto: University of Toronto Press.

Auer, L. 1987. "Some Statistical Background Material," in *Aging with Limited Health Resources*. Ottawa: Economic Council of Canada.

Avery, Don. 1979. *"Dangerous Foreigners": European Immigrant Workers and Labour Radicalism in Canada, 1896-1932*. Toronto: McClelland and Stewart.

Avery, Roger, and Barry Edmonston. 1988. "Canada's Stationary Population Equivalent: The Effect of Variations in Population Conditions," paper presented at the meetings of the Population Association of America, New Orleans, April, 1988.

B.C. Research. 1986. "Community Reactions to Changes in the Structure of its Population." Ottawa: Report for Review of Demography, Health and Welfare.

Badets, Jane. 1989. "Canada's Immigrant Population," *Canadian Social Trends*, 14: 2-6.

Badgley Robin F., and Catherine A. Charles. 1978. "Health and Inequality: Unresolved Policy Issues," in S.A. Yelaja, ed., *Canadian Social Policy*. Waterloo, Ont.: Wilfrid Laurier University Press.

Balakrishnan, T.R. 1986. "Current and Expected Fertility," manuscript.

Balakrishnan, T.R. 1987. "Therapeutic Abortions in Canada and their Impact on Fertility," in *Contributions to Demography*. Edmonton: Population Research Laboratory.

Balakrishnan, T.R. 1988. "Immigration and the Changing Ethnic Mosaic of Canadian Cities." Ottawa: Report for Review of Demography, Health and Welfare.

Balakrishnan, T.R. 1989a. "Recent Trends in Cohabitation in Canada and its Demographic Implications," manuscript.

Balakrishnan, T.R. 1989b. "Changing Nuptiality Patterns and their Fertility Implications in Canada," in J. Légaré, T.R. Balakrishnan, and R. Beaujot, eds., *The Family in Crisis: A Population Crisis?* Ottawa: Royal Society of Canada.

Balakrishnan, T.R., *et al.* 1988. "Age at First Birth and Lifetime Fertility," *Journal of Biosocial Science*: 167-74.

Balakrishnan, T.R., and Jiajian Chen. 1990. "Religiosity, Nuptiality and Repro-duction in Canada," *Canadian Review of Sociology and Anthropology*, 27, 3: 316-40.

Balakrishnan, T.R., and Carl Grindstaff. 1988. "Early Adulthood Behaviour and Later Life Course Paths." Ottawa: Report for Review of Demography, Health and Welfare.

Balakrishnan, T.R., K.J. Krotki, and E. Lapierre-Adamcyk. 1985. "Contracep-tive Use in Canada, 1984," *Family Planning Perspectives*, 17, 5: 209-15.

Banting, Keith G. 1987a. *The Welfare State and Canadian Federalism*. Kingston and Montreal: McGill-Queen's University Press.

Banting, Keith G. 1987b. "Visions of the Welfare State," in S. Seward, ed., *The Future of Social Welfare Systems in Canada and the United Kingdom*. Ottawa: Institute for Research on Public Policy.

Banting, Keith G. 1987c. "The Welfare State and Inequality in the 1980's," *Canadian Review of Sociology and Anthropology*, 24, 3: 309-38.

Barber, Clarence. 1979. "Some Implications of Declining Birth Rates in Devel-oped Countries," paper presented to the Royal Society of Canada, Saska-toon, May, 1979.

Barer, M.L., *et al.* 1989. "Trends in Use of Medical Services by the Elderly in British Columbia," *Canadian Medical Association Journal*, 141: 39-45.

Barker, Paul. 1990. "An Assessment of Ontario's Health Strategy," *Canadian Public Policy*, 16, 4: 432-44.

Barrett, Michael, *et al.* 1987. "Potential Environmental Impact of Changes in Population Size, Age and Geographic Distribution," *Canadian Studies in Popu-lation*, 14, 2: 261-77.

Barrett, Michael, and Chris Taylor. 1977. *Population and Canada*. University of Toronto: Faculty of Education.

Basavarajappa, K.G., and Ravi B.P. Verma. 1990. "Occupational Composition of Immigrant Women," in S. Halli *et al.*, eds., *Ethnic Demography*. Ottawa: Carleton University Press.

Bastarache, Michel. 1989. "Will Current Demographic Trends Jeopardize Cana-da's Evolution Towards Official Languages Equality?" *Demolinguistic Trends and the Evolution of Canadian Institutions*. Ottawa: Secretary of State.

Battle, Ken. 1988. "Child Benefits in Decline," *Policy Options*, 9, 1: 3-6.

Beaujot, Roderic. 1985. "Population Policy Development in Canadian Demog-raphy," *Canadian Studies in Population*, 12, 2: 203-19.

Beaujot, Roderic. 1986. "Dwindling Families," *Policy Options*, 7, 7: 3-7.

Beaujot, Roderic. 1990. "Immigration and the Population of Canada." Ottawa: Employment and Immigration Discussion Paper.

Beaujot, Roderic P., K.G. Basavarajappa, and Ravi B.P. Verma. 1988. *Income of Immigrants in Canada*. Ottawa: Statistics Canada Cat. No. 91-527.

Beaujot, Roderic P., and Kevin McQuillan. 1982. *Growth and Dualism: The Demo-graphic Development of Canadian Society*. Toronto: Gage.

Beaujot, Roderic, and J. Peter Rappak. 1988a. "Emigration From Canada: Its Importance and Interpretation," *Population Working Paper No. 4*. Ottawa: Employment and Immigration.

Beaujot, Roderic, and J. Peter Rappak. 1988b. "The Role of Immigration in Changing Socio-demographic Structures." Ottawa: Report for Review of Demography, Health and Welfare.

Beaujot, Roderic, and J. Peter Rappak. 1989. "The Link Between Immigration and Emigration in Canada, 1945-1986," *Canadian Studies in Population*, 16, 2: 201-16.

Becker Gary S., and Robert J. Barro. 1986. "Altruism and the Economic Theory of Fertility," *Population and Development Review*, 12, suppl.: 69-76.

Bégin, Monique. 1987. "Demographic Change and Social Policy: Implications and Possible Alternatives," in S. Seward, ed., *The Future of Social Welfare Systems in Canada and the United Kingdom*. Ottawa: Institute for Research on Public Policy.

Beneteau, Renée. 1988. "Trends in Suicide," *Canadian Social Trends*, 11: 22-24.

Bernstam, Mikhail S. 1986. "Competitive Human Markets, Interfamily Transfers, and Below-replacement Fertility," *Population and Development Review*, 12, suppl.: 111-37.

Beyrouti, Monique, and Marcelle Dion. 1989. *Canada's Farm Population*. Ottawa: Statistics Canada Cat. No. 98-133.

Bianchi, Suzanne M. 1990. "America's Children: Mixed Prospects," *Population Bulletin*, 45, 1: 1-40.

Bibby, Reginald W. 1990. *Mosaic Madness: The Poverty and Potential of Life in Canada*. Stoddart.

Billette, A. 1977. "Les inégalités sociales de mortalité au Québec," *Recherches sociographiques*, 18: 415-30.

Black, Jerome H. 1987. "Study of the Impact of Immigrant Political Behaviour." Ottawa: Report for Review of Demography, Health and Welfare.

Blackburn, Jean-Pierre. 1989. "Refugee Claimant Backlog Clearance," Report of the Standing Committee on Labour, Employment and Immigration. Ottawa: House of Commons.

Blackburn, Jean-Pierre. 1990. "Interim Report on Demography and Immigration Levels," Report of the Standing Committee on Labour, Employment and Immigration, Issue No. 40. Ottawa: House of Commons.

Blanchet, Dider. 1989. "Qui supportera les conséquences? Effets des évolutions démographiques sur la protection sociale et le marché du travail," *International Population Conference, New Delhi*. Liège: International Union for the Scientific Study of Population, Vol. 3: 289-301.

Bobet, Ellen. 1989. "Indian Mortality," *Canadian Social Trends*, 15: 11-14.

Boily, Nicole. 1987. "Dénatalité, immigration et politique familiale: la point de vue des femmes," paper presented at the meetings of the Association des Démographes du Québec, Ottawa, May, 1987.

Bolaria, B. Singh, and Peter S. Li. 1985. *Racial Oppression in Canada*. Toronto: Garamond.

Boserup, Ester. 1986. "Comment," *Population and Development Review*, 12, suppl.: 238-42.

Boswell, John. 1988. *The Kindness of Strangers: The Abandonment of Children in Western Europe from Late Antiquity to the Renaissance*. New York: Pantheon.

Bourbeau, Robert. 1988. "Trends in Language Mobility between English and French," in J. Curtis *et al.*, eds., *Social Inequality in Canada: Patterns, Problems, Policies*. Scarborough: Prentice-Hall.

Bourbeau, Robert. 1989. *Canada: A Linguistic Profile*. Ottawa: Statistics Canada Cat. No. 98-131.

Bourbeau, Robert, Robert Choinière, and Norbert Robitaille. 1986a. "Impact de la croissance prévue de la population inuit sur les programmes fédéraux." Ottawa: Report for Review of Demography, Health and Welfare.

Bourbeau, Robert, Robert Choinière, and Norbert Robitaille. 1986b. "Vieillissement des groupes ethniques au Canada et développement socio-économique." Ottawa: Report for Review of Demography, Health and Welfare.

Bourbeau, Robert, and Jacques Légaré. 1982. *Evolution de la mortalité au Canada et au Québec, 1831-1931*. Montréal: Presses de l'Université de Montréal.

Bourgeois-Pichat, Jean. 1986. "The Unprecedented Shortage of Births in Europe," *Population and Development Review*, 12, suppl.: 3-25.

Bovey, Edmond C., J. Fraser Mustard, and Ronald L. Watts. 1984. "Ontario Universities: Options and Futures." Toronto: The Commission on the Future Development of the Universities of Ontario.

Boyd, Monica. 1987. "Migrant Women in Canada: Profiles and Policies," *Immigration Research Working Paper No. 2*. Ottawa: Employment and Immigration.

Boyd, Monica. 1989. "Immigration and Income Security Policies in Canada: Implications for Elderly Women," *Population Research and Policy Review*, 8: 5-24.

Boyd, Monica. 1990a. "Sex Differences in Occupational Skill: Canada, 1961-1986," *Canadian Review of Sociology and Anthropology*, 27, 3: 285-315.

Boyd, Monica. 1990b. "Family and Personal Network in International Migration: Recent Developments and New Agendas," *International Migration Review*, 23, 3: 638-70.

Boyd, Monica, et al. 1985. *Ascription and Achievement: Studies in Mobility and Status Attainment in Canada*. Ottawa: Carleton University Press.

Boyd, Monica, and Kevin McQuillan. 1990. "Conditions of Work and the Redistribution of Work-time," in R. Beaujot, ed., *Facing the Demographic Future*. Ottawa: Royal Society of Canada.

Boyd, Monica, and Edward T. Pryor. 1989. "The Cluttered Nest: The Living Arrangements of Young Canadian Adults," *Canadian Journal of Sociology*, 14, 4: 461-77.

Boyd, Monica, and Chris Taylor. 1990. "Canada: International Migration Policies, Trends and Issues," in W.J. Serow et al., eds., *International Handbook on International Migration*. New York: Greenwood Press.

Breslaw, J.A., and W.A. Sims. 1986. "The Effect of Health on the Labour Force Behaviour of the Elderly in Canada." Ottawa: Report for Review of Demography, Health and Welfare.

Breslaw, Jon A., and Morton Stelcner. 1987. "The Effect of Health on Labour Force Behaviour of Elderly Men in Canada," *Journal of Human Resources*, 22, 4: 490-517.

Breslow, Lester. 1985. "The Case of Cardiovascular Diseases," in J. Vallin and A.D. Lopez, eds., *Health Policy, Social Policy and Mortality Prospects*. Ordina: IUSSP.

Breton, Albert. 1984. *Marriage, Population and the Labour Force Participation of Women*. Ottawa: Economic Council of Canada.

Breton, Albert, and Raymond Breton. 1980. *Why Disunity? An Analysis of Linguistic and Regional Cleavages in Canada*. Montreal: Institute for Research on Public Policy.

Breton, Raymond. 1979. "Ethnic Stratification Viewed From Three Theoretical Perspectives," in J.E. Curtis and W.G. Scott, eds., *Social Stratification in Canada*. Toronto: Prentice-Hall.

Breton, Raymond. 1986. "Multiculturalism and Canadian Nation-Building," in A. Cairns and C. Williams, eds., *The Politics of Gender, Ethnicity and Language in Canada*. Toronto: University of Toronto Press.

Breton, Raymond. 1988. "French-English Relations," in J. Curtis and L. Tepperman, eds., *Understanding Canadian Society*. Toronto: McGraw-Hill.

Breton, Raymond. 1990. "The Ethnic Group as a Political Resource in Relation to Problems of Incorporation," in R. Breton *et al.*, eds., *Ethnic Identity and Equality: Varieties of Experience in a Canadian City*. Toronto: University of Toronto Press.

Breton, Raymond, *et al.* 1990. *Ethnic Identity and Equality: Varieties of Experience in a Canadian City*. Toronto: University of Toronto Press.

Breton, Raymond, Jill Armstrong, and Les Kennedy. 1974. *The Social Impact of Changes in Population Size and Composition: Reactions to Patterns of Immigration*. Ottawa: Manpower and Immigration.

Brooks, Stephen. 1989. *Public Policy in Canada: An Introduction*. Toronto: McClelland & Stewart.

Brouillette, Liliane, *et al.* 1990a. "L'évolution de la situation économique des familles avec enfants au Canada et au Québec depuis 15 ans," manuscript.

Brouillette, Liliane, *et al.* 1990b. "Les couples avec enfants ou sans enfants: opulence ou pauvreté," Cahier de recherche No. 43, CERPE, Université du Québec à Montréal.

Bryan, Ingrid. 1988. "Regional Inequalities and Economic Policy," in J. Curtis *et al.*, eds., *Social Inequality in Canada: Patterns, Problems, Policies*. Scarborough: Prentice-Hall.

Buchignani, N.L. 1980. "Accommodation, Adaptation and Policy: Dimensions of the South Asian Experience in Canada," in K.V. Ujimoto and G. Hirabayashi, eds., *Visible Minorities and Multiculturalism: Asians in Canada*. Toronto: Butterworths.

Buck, Carol. 1987. "How Direct is the Path," in *Aging with Limited Health Resources*. Ottawa: Economic Council of Canada.

Bumpass, Larry L. 1990. "What's Happening to the Family?" Presidential Address to the meetings of the Population Association of America, Toronto, June, 1990.

Burbidge, J.B., and A.L. Robb. 1986. "Consumption and Labour Supply Late in the Life Cycle." Ottawa: Report for Review of Demography, Health and Welfare.

Burch, Thomas K. 1985. *Family History Survey: Preliminary Findings*. Ottawa: Statistics Canada Cat. No. 99-955.

Burch, Thomas K. 1986. "Pronatalist Policies: An Appraisal with Special Reference to the Canadian Situation." Ottawa: Report for Review of Demography, Health and Welfare.

Burch, Thomas K. 1989. "Common-law Unions in Canada: A Portrait from the 1984 Family History Survey," in J. Légaré, T.R. Balakrishnan, and R. Beaujot, eds., *The Family in Crisis: A Population Crisis?* Ottawa: Royal Society of Canada.

Burch, Thomas K. 1990. *Families in Canada*. Ottawa: Statistics Canada Catalogue No. 98-127.

Burch, Thomas K., and Ashok Madan. 1986. *Union Formation and Dissolution*. Ottawa: Statistics Canada Cat. No. 99-963.

Burch, Thomas K., and Kevin McQuillan. 1988. "One-Adult and Two-Earner Households and Families: Trends, Determinants and Consequences." Ottawa: Report for Review of Demography, Health and Welfare.

Burke, Mary Anne. 1986. "Changing Health Risks," *Canadian Social Trends*, 1: 22-26.

Burke, Mary Anne. 1987a. "Interregional Migration of the Canadian Population," *Canadian Social Trends*, 6: 17-25.

Burke, Mary Anne. 1987b. "Urban Canada," *Canadian Social Trends*, 7: 12-18.

Burnaby, Barbara, and Roderic Beaujot. 1986. "The Use of Aboriginal Languages in Canada: An Analysis of the 1981 Census." Ottawa: Supply and Services Canada.

Buttner, Thomas, and Wolfgang Lutz. 1989. "Estimating Fertility Responses to Policy Measures in the German Democratic Republic," *Population and Development Review*, 16, 3: 539-55.

Buttner, Thomas, and Wolfgang Lutz. 1990. "Measuring Fertility Responses to Policy Measures in the German Democratic Republic," paper presented at the meetings of the Population Association of America, Toronto, April, 1990.

Caldwell, Gary. 1988. "L'avenir de la communauté anglophone du Québec," *L'Action Nationale*, 78, 5: 359-65.

Caldwell, Gary, and Daniel Fournier. 1987. "The Quebec Question: A Matter of Population," *Canadian Journal of Sociology*, 12, 1-2: 16-41.

Caldwell, John C. 1985. "Strengths and Limitations of the Survey Approach for Measuring and Understanding Fertility Change: Alternate Possibilities," in J. Cleland and J. Hobcraft, eds., *Reproductive Changes in Developing Countries*. Oxford: Oxford University Press.

Caldwell, John. 1986. "Routes to Low Mortality in Poor Countries," *Population and Development Review*, 12, 2: 171-220.

Calhoun, Charles A. 1989. "Desired Family Size and Excess Fertility in Europe and the United States," *Popnet*, 16: 1-4.

Callwood, June. 1987. "The Playgrounds of Canada, Poverty is the Hidden Bully," *Globe and Mail*, 16 September 1987, A2.

Calot, Gérard. 1990a. "La politique démographique d'autres pays," in R. Beaujot, ed., *Faire Face au Changement Démographique*. Ottawa: Royal Society of Canada.

Calot, Gérard. 1990b. "Fécondité du moment, fécondité des générations: Comparaisons franco-suédoises," *Population et Sociétés*, 245: 1-4.

Calzavara, Liviana. 1988. "Trends and Policy in Employment Opportunities for Women," in J. Curtis *et al.*, eds., *Social Inequality in Canada: Patterns, Problems, Policies*. Scarborough: Prentice-Hall.

Campbell, Murray. 1989. "Crunch for Universities," *Globe and Mail*, 24 May 1989: A1, A3.

Canadian Advisory Council on the Status of Women. 1986. "Caring for our Children." Brief presented to Special Parliamentary Committee on Child Care.

Canadian Advisory Council on the Status of Women. 1989. "Dimensions of Equality: An Update of the Federal Government Work Plan for Women." Ottawa: Status of Women Canada.

Canadian Social Trends. 1989a. "Social Indicators," *Canadian Social Trends*, 15: 35.

Canadian Social Trends. 1989b. "Changes in Living Arrangements," *Canadian Social Trends*, 12: 27-29.

Canadian Social Trends. 1990. "Social Indicators," *Canadian Social Trends*, 18: 35.

Carel, Geneviève, William Coffey, and Mario Polèse. 1988. "L'impact de la migration sur le développement régional: la confrontation de deux courants de pensée." Ottawa: Report for Review of Demography, Health and Welfare.

Careless, J.M.S. 1963. *Canada: A Story of Challenge*. Toronto: Macmillan.

Carrothers, A.W.R. 1977. "Foreword," in R. Breton, *The Canadian Condition: A Guide to Research on Public Policy*. Montreal: Institute for Research on Public Policy.

Cartwright, Don. 1988a. "Linguistic Territorialization: Is Canada Approaching the Belgian Model?" *Journal of Cultural Geography*, 8: 115-34.

Cartwright, Don. 1988b. "Language Policy and Internal Geopolitics: The Canadian Situation," in C.H. Williams, ed., *Language in Geographic Context*. Clevedon: Multilingual Matters.

Cartwright, Don. 1989. "Languages in Contact: Is Conflict Inevitable?" *Journal of Canadian Studies*, 23, 4: 130-35.

Castonguay, Charles. 1979. "Exogamie et anglicisation chez les minorités canadiennes-française," *Canadian Review of Sociology and Anthropology*, 16, 1: 21-31.

CAUT (Canadian Association of University Teachers). 1990. "A Statistical Glance at the Changing Status of Women in Universities," *CAUT Bulletin*, December, 1990.

Chapman, Beatrice E. 1989. "Equalitarian Sex Roles and Fertility in Canada," in J. Légaré, T.R. Balakrishnan, and R. Beaujot, eds., *The Family in Crisis: A Population Crisis?* Ottawa: Royal Society of Canada.

Chappell, Neena L. 1987. "Canadian Income and Health-care Policy: Implications for the Elderly," in V.W. Marshall, ed., *Aging in Canada*. Toronto: Fitzhenry & Whiteside.

Charbonneau, Hubert. 1984. "Trois siècles de dépopulation amérindienne," in L. Normandeau and V. Piché, eds., *Les populations amérindiennes et inuit du Canada*. Montréal: Presses de l'Université de Montréal.

Charles, Enid. 1936. *The Menace of Under-population*. London: Watts.

Chaudhry, Mahinder D., and Nanda K. Chaudhry. 1985. "The Fertility Rate in Canada, 1950-1976: A Socio-economic Analysis," *Canadian Studies in Population*, 12, 1: 1-30.

Chesnais, Jean-Claude. 1985. "The Prevention of Deaths from Violence," in J. Vallin and A.D. Lopez, eds., *Health Policy, Social Policy and Mortality Prospects*. Ordina: IUSSP.

Chesnais, Jean-Claude. 1987. "Population Trends in the European Community 1968-1986," *European Journal of Population*, 3, 3-4: 281-96.

Chesnais, Jean-Claude. 1989. "L'inversion de la pyramide des âges en Europe: perspectives et problèmes," *International Population Conference, New Delhi*. Liège: International Union for the Scientific Study of Population, Vol. 3: 53-68.

Chiswick, Barry R. 1986. "Comment," *Population and Development Review*, 12, suppl.: 269-72.

Chorayshi, Parvin. 1986. "Modern Agriculture and its Impact on Farm and Rural Communities: Rural Canada, Persistence and Change." Ottawa: Report for Review of Demography, Health and Welfare.

Cliquet, R.L. 1986. "Economic and Social Consequences of Current Demographic Developments on OECD Countries: Clarifying the Issues," manuscript, Population and Family Study Centre, Brussels.

Coffey, William J., and Mario Polèse. 1986. "Demographic Evolution and Regional Development: Issues and Implications." Ottawa: Report for Review of Demography, Health and Welfare.

Coffey, William J., and Mario Polèse. 1987. "Introduction: Still Living Together," in W.J. Coffey and M. Polèse, eds., *Still Living Together*. Ottawa: Institute for Research on Public Policy.

Coleman, William D. 1983. "A Comparative Study of Language Policy in Quebec: A Political Economy Approach," in M.M. Atkinson and M.A. Chandler, eds., *The Politics of Canadian Public Policy*. Toronto: University of Toronto Press.

Collishaw, Neil. 1982. "Deaths Attributable to Smoking, 1979," *Chronic Disease in Canada*, 3, 1: 1-5.

Commission de la culture. 1985. *Étude de l'impact culturel, social et économique des tendances démographiques actuelles sur l'avenir du Québec comme société distincte*. Québec: Hôtel du Parlement.

Conference Board of Canada. 1989. "Employee Literacy in Canadian Business." Ottawa: The Conference Board of Canada, Human Resource Development Centre.

Conklin, David W. 1990. "U.S. Health Care: Why Canada's System is Better and Cheaper," *Policy Options*, 11, 4: 15-18.

Connelly, M. Patricia, and Martha MacDonald. 1990. *Women in the Labour Force*. Ottawa: Statistics Canada Cat. No. 98-125.

Connidis, Ingrid Arnet. 1988. *Family Ties and Aging*. Toronto: Butterworths.

Connidis, Ingrid. 1989. "Contact Between Siblings in Later Life," *Canadian Journal of Sociology*, 14, 4: 429-42.

Conrad, Christop. 1990. "La naissance de la retraite moderne: L'Allemagne dans une comparaisons internationale, 1850-1960," *Population*, 45, 3: 531-63.

Conservation Council of Ontario. 1986. "Toward a Conservation Strategy for Ontario." Toronto: Conservation Council of Ontario.

Conservation Council of Ontario and Family Planning Federation of Canada. 1973. *A Population Policy for Canada?* Toronto: Conservation Council of Ontario and Family Planning Federation of Canada.

Cook, Gail C.A. 1976. "Opportunity for Choice: A Criterion," in G.C.A. Cook, ed., *Opportunity for Choice: A Goal for Women in Canada*. Ottawa: Information Canada.

Cooke, K. 1986. *Report of the Task Force on Child Care*. Ottawa: Status of Women Canada.

Corbett, D.C. 1957. *Canada's Immigration Policy: A Critique*. Toronto: University of Toronto Press.

Courchene, Thomas J. 1981. "A Market Perspective on Regional Disparities," *Canadian Public Policy*, 7, 4: 506-18.

Courchene, Thomas J. 1987. *Social Policy in the 1990s: Agenda for Reform*. Toronto: C.D. Howe Institute.

Crichton, Anne. 1986. "Healing Ourselves," *Policy Options*, 7, 9: 14-17.

David, Paul A. 1986. "Comment," *Population and Development Review*, 12, suppl.: 77-86.

Davis, Kingsley. 1984. "Wives and Work: Consequences of the Sex Role Revolution," *Population and Development Review*, 10, 3: 397-417.

Davis, Kingsley. 1986. "Low Fertility in Evolutionary Perspective," *Population and Development Review*, 12, suppl.: 48-67.

Davis, Kingsley, Mikhael S. Bernstam, and Rita Ricardo-Campbell. 1986. "Below-Replacement Fertility in Industrialized Societies: Causes, Consequences, Policies," *Population and Development Review*, 12, suppl.

Deaton, Richard Lee. 1989. *The Political Economy of Pensions: Power, Politics and Social Change in Canada, Britain and the United States*. Vancouver: University of British Columbia Press.

Demeny, Paul. 1986a. "Pronatalist Policies in Low-fertility Countries: Patterns, Performance and Prospects," *Population and Development Review*, 12, suppl.: 335-58.

Demeny, Paul. 1986b. "Population and the Invisible Hand," *Demography*, 23, 4: 473-88.

Demeny, Paul. 1988a. "Social Science and Population Policy." New York: The Population Council Working Paper 138.

Demeny, Paul. 1988b. "Demography and the Limits to Growth," *Population and Development Review*, 14, Suppl.: 213-44.

Demographic Policy Secretariat. 1976. "Toward a Demographic Policy for Canada." Ottawa: Employment and Immigration.

Denton, Frank T., and Byron G. Spencer. 1982. "Population Aging, Labour Force Change and Promotion Prospects." Hamilton, Ont.: McMaster University, QSEP Report No. 3.

Denton, Frank T., and Byron G. Spencer. 1983. "Population Aging and Future Health Care Costs in Canada," *Canadian Public Policy*, 9, 2: 155-63.

Denton, Frank T., and Byron G. Spencer. 1985. "Prospective Changes in Population and their Implications for Government Expenditures," in T.J. Courchene *et al.*, eds., *Ottawa and the Provinces: The Distribution of Money and Power*. Toronto: Ontario Economic Council.

Denton, Frank T., and Byron G. Spencer. 1987a. "Population Change and the Canadian Economy: A Survey of the Issues." Institute for Research on Public Policy Discussion Paper 87.A.2.

Denton, Frank T., and Byron G. Spencer. 1987b. "Changes in the Canadian Population and Labour Force: Prospects and Implications," *Canadian Studies in Population*, 14, 2: 187-208.

Denton, Frank T., and Byron G. Spencer. 1988a. "The Macroeconomic and Demographic Consequences of Alternative Life Cycle Choices." Ottawa: Report for Review of Demography, Health and Welfare.

Denton, Frank T., and Byron G. Spencer. 1988b. "Endogenous versus Exogenous Fertility: What Difference for the Macroeconomy," in R. Lee, ed., *Economics of Changing Age Distributions in Developed Countries*. Oxford: Clarendon Press

Denton, Frank T., Christine H. Feaver, and Byron G. Spencer. 1986. "Prospective Aging of the Population and its Implications for the Labour Force and Government Expenditure," *Canadian Journal on Aging*, 5, 2: 75-98.

Denton, Frank T., Christine H. Feaver, and Byron G. Spencer. 1989. "MEDS-Models of the Economic-demographic System: A Report of the Project and some Preliminary Analysis." Ottawa: Report for Review of Demography, Health and Welfare.

Denton, Frank T., S. Neno Li, and Byron G. Spencer. 1987. "How Will Population Aging Affect the Future Costs of Maintaining Health-care Standards," in V.W. Marshall, ed, *Aging in Canada*. Toronto: Fitzhenry & Whiteside.

DeSilva, A. 1989. "The Economic Destiny of Immigrants," manuscript of research monograph for Economic Council of Canada.

Desjardins, Bertrand, and Jacques Légaré. 1984. "Le seuil de la vieillesse: quelques réflexions de démographes," *Sociologie et sociétés*, 16, 2: 37-48.

Desrosiers, Hélène. 1987. "Impact du vieillissement sur les coûts du système de santé et des services sociaux: les véritables enjeux." Québec: Commission d'enquête sur les services de santé et les services sociaux.

Destin. 1988. "Étude de l'impact de l'évolution démographique sur la politique économique et sociale: l'expérience d'autres gouvernements dans l'élaboration de projets similaires." Ottawa: Report for Review of Demography, Health and Welfare.

Deveraux, Sue. 1990. "Decline in the Number of Children," *Canadian Social Trends*, 18: 32-34.

DeVoretz, Don. 1989a. "Immigration and Employment Effects." Ottawa: Institute for Research on Public Policy, Discussion Paper 89.B.3.

DeVoretz, Don. 1989b. "Immigrant Asset Performance." Ottawa: Employment and Immigration, Discussion Paper.

DeVoretz, Don. 1990. "Economic Impacts of Immigration Forces in Canada's Labour Market," manuscript.

Dickinson, James, and Bob Russell. 1986. "The Structure of Reproduction in Capitalist Society," in J. Dickinson and B. Russell, eds., *Family, Economy and State*. Toronto: Garamond.

Dion, Léon. 1989. "The Impact of Demolinguistic Trends on Canadian Institutions," in *Demolinguistic Trends and the Evolution of Canadian Institutions*. Ottawa: Secretary of State.

Dionne, Claude. 1989. "Le choix d'avoir un enfant," paper presented to ASDEQ conference, April, 1989.

Dionne, Claude. 1990. "Workshop presentation." Montreal: Département de démographie, 25th Anniversary Conference.

Djao, Angela Wei. 1983. *Inequality and Social Policy*. Toronto: Wiley.

Dobell, A.R., and S.H. Mansbridge. 1986. *The Social Policy Process in Canada*. Montreal: Institute for Research on Public Policy.

Doern, G. Bruce. 1983. "The Liberals and the Opposition: Ideas, Priorities and the Imperatives of Governing Canada in the 1980s," in G.B. Doern, ed., *How Ottawa Spends*. Toronto: Lorimer.

Doern, G. Bruce, and Peter Aucoin, eds. 1979. *Public Policy in Canada*. Toronto: Gage.

Donovan, Suzanne, and Harold Watts. 1990. "What Can Child Care Do for Human Capital," *Population Research and Policy Review*, 9, 1: 5-24.

Dooley, Martin. 1986. "The Over-educated Canadian? Changes in the Relationship among Earnings, Education and Age for Canadian Men 1971-81," *Canadian Journal of Economics*, 19: 142-59.

Dooley, Martin D. 1988. "An Analysis of Changes in Family Incomes and Family Structure in Canada between 1973 and 1986 with Emphasis on Poverty among Children." Hamilton, Ont.: McMaster University, QSEP Research Report No. 238.

Dooley, Martin. 1989a. "Changes in the Market Work of Married Women and Lone Mothers with Children, 1973-1986." Hamilton, Ont.: McMaster University, QSEP Research Report No. 254.

Dooley, Martin. 1989b. "The Demography of Child Poverty in Canada, 1973-1986." Hamilton, Ont.: McMaster University, QSEP Research Report No. 251.

Dooley, Martin. 1990. "Recent Changes in the Economic Welfare of Lone Mother Families," paper presented at the meetings of the Canadian Population Society, Victoria, June, 1990.

Dotto, Lydia. 1988. *Thinking the Unthinkable: Civilization and Rapid Climate Change*. Waterloo, Ont.: Wilfrid Laurier University Press.

Driedger, Leo, and Neena Chappell. 1987. *Aging and Ethnicity*. Toronto: Butterworths.

Drover, Glenn, and Allan Moscovitch. 1981. "Inequality and Social Welfare," in A. Moscovitch and G. Drover, eds., *Inequality: Essays on the Political Economy of Social Welfare*. Toronto: University of Toronto Press.

Ducharme, Pierre. 1987. "Démographie et sécurité sociale: le cas des régimes publics de pensions," *Perception*, 10, 5: 18-21.

Ducharme, Pierre, and Jacques Légaré. 1986. "Stagnation démographique et impacts sur le nombre et les caractéristiques des bénéficiaires des régimes publics de pensions." Ottawa: Report for Review of Demography, Health and Welfare.

Duchesne, Louis. 1989. "L'obésité, le SIDA et la grippe: trois causes de décès au Québec de 1983 à 1987," *Cahiers Québécois de Démographie*, 18, 2: 405-14.

Dufour, Desmond, and Yves Péron. 1979. *Vingt ans de mortalité au Québec*. Montréal: Presses de l'Université de Montréal.

Dumas, Jean. 1984. *Report on the Demographic Situation in Canada 1983*. Ottawa: Statistics Canada Cat. No. 91-209.

Dumas, Jean. 1985. "Mariages et remariages au Canada," *Cahiers Québécois de Démographie*, 14, 2: 209-30.

Dumas, Jean. 1987. "L'évolution des premiers mariages au Canada," *Cahiers Québécois de Démographie*, 16, 2: 237-65.

Dumas, Jean. 1989. "Le rôle des migrations dans le développement économique," paper presented at ASDEQ, April, 1989.

Dumas, Jean. 1990a. *Report on the Demographic Situation in Canada 1988*. Ottawa: Statistics Canada Cat. No. 91-209.

Dumas, Jean. 1990b. *Rapport sur l'état de la population du Canada 1990*. Ottawa: Statistics Canada Cat. No. 91-209.

Dumas, Jean, and Louise Boyer. 1984. "Mise au point sur l'accroissement récent de la fécondité des célibataires au Canada," *Cahiers Québécois de Démographie*, 13, 2: 311-22.

Duncan, Greg J. 1984. *Years of Poverty, Years of Plenty*. Ann Arbor, Mich.: Institute for Social Research.

Duncan, Greg J., and Ken R. Smith. 1989. "The Rising Affluence of the Elderly: How Far, How Fair and How Frail?" *Annual Review of Sociology*, 15: 261-89.

Easterlin, Richard A., Michael L. Wachter, and Susan M. Wachter. 1978. "Demographic Influences on Economic Stability: The United States Experience," *Population and Development Review*, 4, 1: 1-22.

Economic Council of Canada. 1977. *Living Together: A Study of Regional Disparities*. Ottawa: Economic Council of Canada.

Economic Council of Canada. 1979. *One in Three: Pensions for Canadians to 2030*. Ottawa: Economic Council of Canada.

Economic Council of Canada. 1988. *Twenty-Fifth Annual Review*. Ottawa: Economic Council of Canada.

Economic Council of Canada. 1989. *Twenty-Sixth Annual Review*. Ottawa: Economic Council of Canada.

Economic Council of Canada. 1990. *Good Jobs, Bad Jobs*. Ottawa: Economic Council of Canada, Study No. 22-164.

Economic Council of Canada. 1991. *New Faces in the Crowd: Economic and Social Impacts of Immigration*. Ottawa: Economic Council of Canada, Study No. 22-171.

Ehrlich, Paul. 1968. *The Population Bomb*. New York: Ballantine Books.

Eichler, Margrit. 1978. "Social Policy Concerning Women," in S.A. Yelaja, ed., *Canadian Social Policy*. Waterloo, Ont.: Wilfrid Laurier University Press.

Eichler, Margrit. 1983. *Families in Canada Today*. Toronto: Gage.

Eichler, Margrit. 1988. *Families in Canada Today*. Toronto: Gage.

Eichler, Margrit. 1989. "Reflections on Motherhood, Apple Pie, the New Reproductive Technologies and the Role of Sociologists in Society," *Society/Société*, 13, 1: 1-4.

Employment and Immigration. 1989a. *Success in the Works*. Ottawa: Employment and Immigration.

Employment and Immigration. 1989b. *Annual Report to Parliament on Future Immigration Levels*. Ottawa: Employment and Immigration.

Employment and Immigration. 1989c. *Immigration to Canada: Issues for Discussion*. Ottawa: Employment and Immigration.

Employment and Immigration. 1989d. *Immigration to Canada: Economic Impacts*. Ottawa: Employment and Immigration.

Employment and Immigration. 1990. *Annual Report to Parliament, Immigration Plan for 1991-1995*. Ottawa: Employment and Immigration.

Environment Canada. 1984. "Sustainable Development: A Submission to the Royal Commission on the Economic Union." Ottawa: Environment Canada.

Espenshade, Thomas J. 1978. "Zero Population Growth and the Economies of Developed Nations," *Population and Development Review*, 4, 4: 645-80.

Espenshade, Thomas J. 1986. "Population Dynamics with Immigration and Low Fertility," *Population and Development Review*, 12, suppl.: 248-61.

Ethier, Mireille. 1985. "Survey of Pension Issues," in F. Vaillancourt, ed., *Income*

Distribution and Economic Security in Canada. Toronto: University of Toronto Press.

Evans, Robert G. 1987. "Hang Together or Hang Separately: The Viability of a Universal Health Care System in an Aging Society," *Canadian Public Policy*, 13, 2: 165-80.

Evans, Robert G., *et al.* 1989. "The Long Good-bye: The Great Transformation of the British Columbia Hospital System," *Health Services Research*, 24, 4: 435-60.

Fellegi, Ivan P. 1979. "Data, Statistics and Information: Some Issues in the Canadian Social Statistics Scene," paper presented at a joint session of the Canadian Sociology and Anthropology Association and the Canadian Population Society, Saskatoon, May, 1979.

Fellegi, Ivan P. 1988. "Can We Afford an Aging Society?" *Canadian Economic Observer*, 1, 10: 4.1-34.

Fillmore, Catherine. 1990. "Gender Differences in Earnings: A Re-analysis and Prognosis for Canadian Women," *Canadian Journal of Sociology*, 15, 3: 275-99.

Fisher, William A. 1983. "Adolescent Contraception: Summary and Recommendations," in D. Byrne and W. Fisher, eds., *Adolescents, Sex and Contraception*. Hillsdale: Lawrence Erlbaum.

Foot, David K. 1982. *Canada's Population Outlook*. Toronto: Lorimer.

Foot, David K. 1987. "Population Aging and the Canadian Labour Force." Institute for Research on Public Policy Discussion Paper 87.A.5.

Foot, David K. 1989. "Public Expenditures, Population Aging and Economic Dependency in Canada, 1921-2021," *Population Research and Policy Review*, 8, 1: 97-117.

Foot, David K., and J.C. Li. 1986. "Youth Unemployment in Canada: A Misplaced Priority?" *Canadian Public Policy*, 12, 3: 499-506.

Foot, David K., and Barry Pervin. 1983. "The Determinants of Post-secondary Enrolment Rates in Ontario," *Canadian Journal of Higher Education*, 13, 3: 1-22.

Foot, David K., and Rosemary A. Verne. 1990. "Population Pyramids and Promotion Prospects," *Canadian Public Policy*, 16, 4: 387-98.

Footlick, Jerrold K. 1990. "What Happened to the Family? The 21st Century Family," *Newsweek*, Special Edition, Winter/Spring, 1990: 14-20.

Forget, Claude. 1986. *Report of Commission of Inquiry on Unemployment Insurance*. Ottawa: Supply and Services.

Fortier, D'Iberville. 1988. *Annual Report*. Ottawa: Commissioner of Official Languages.

Fortin, Bernard. 1985. "Income Security in Canada," in F. Vaillancourt, ed., *Income Distribution and Economic Security in Canada*. Toronto: University of Toronto Press.

Fortin, Bernard, and Pierre Fortin. 1986a. "Le déclin démographique et l'évolution des coûts du secteur publique." Ottawa: Report for Review of Demography, Health and Welfare.

Fortin, Bernard, and Pierre Fortin. 1986b. "Le déclin démographique et la situation économique des jeunes: résultats préliminaires et conjectures." Ottawa: Report for Review of Demography, Health and Welfare.

Fortin, Bernard, and Pierre Fortin. 1987. "Croissance économique et décroissance démographique à long terme: l'optimisme du modèle néoclassique pur est-il justifié?" *Canadian Studies in Population*, 14, 2: 171-86.

Fortin, Pierre. 1988. "Les allocations pour enfants et la politique des naissances au Québec," paper presented to Colloque international sur les politiques familiales, Québec, June, 1988.

Fortin, Pierre. 1989a. "L'impact du choc démographique sur le niveau de vie à long terme." Montréal: Université de Montréal, CERPE Cahier No. 18.

Fortin, Pierre. 1989b. "Ten Observations on the Macroeconomic Implications of the Demographic Decline." Ottawa: Report for Review of Demography, Health and Welfare.

Fox, Bonnie J., and John Fox. 1987. "Occupational Gender Segregation of the Canadian Labour Force, 1931-1981," *Canadian Review of Sociology and Anthropology*, 24, 3: 374-97.

Francis, Jack. 1986. "Don't Wait for Utopia," *Policy Options*, 7, 8: 29-30.

Frideres, James S. 1988. *Native Peoples in Canada: Contemporary Conflicts*. Toronto: Prentice-Hall.

Frideres, James S. 1990. "Policies on Indian People in Canada," in P.S. Li, ed., *Race and Ethnic Relations in Canada*. Toronto: Oxford University Press.

Fukawa, Tetsuo. 1988. "Population Change and Social Expenditure," in *Economic and Social Implications of Population Aging*. New York: United Nations.

Gaudette, Leslie A., and Gerry B. Hill. 1990. "Canadian Cancer Statistics," *Health Reports*, 2, 2: 103-26.

Gaudette, Leslie, and Georgia Roberts. 1988. "Trends in Cancer since 1970," *Canadian Social Trends*, 8: 8-13.

Gauthier, Anne. 1987. "Nouvelles estimations du coût de l'enfant au Canada," *Cahiers Québécois de Démographie*, 16, 2: 187-208.

Gauthier, Anne. 1988. "Quand les différences sont négligées," paper presented at the meetings of AIDELF, Montréal, June, 1988.

Gauthier, Anne. 1989. "A propos de la différence de fécondité entre le Québec et l'Ontario," *Cahiers Québécois de Démographie*, 18, 1: 185-94.

Gauthier, Anne. 1990. "Coûts et vieillissement: une question démographique ou une question de médicalisation?" paper presented at ACFAS, May, 1990.

Gauthier, Hervé. 1988. "Vieillissement et dépenses de l'état," *L'Action Nationale*, 78, 5: 282-300.

Gauthier, Hervé. 1989. "Incidences du vieillissement sur les dépenses sociales," paper presented at ASDEQ meetings, April, 1989.

Gauthier, Madeleine. 1990. "Valeurs et genres de vie des jeunes d'aujourd'hui," in R. Beaujot, ed., *Facing the Demographic Future*. Ottawa: Royal Society of Canada.

Gay, Daniel. 1988. "The Situation of Visible Minorities and the Future of Canadian Society," paper presented at the meetings of the Canadian Population Society, Windsor, June, 1988.

Gee, Ellen M. 1990. "Demographic Change and Intergenerational Relations in Canadian Families: Findings and Social Policy Implications," *Canadian Public Policy*, 16, 2: 191-99.

Gee, E.M., and J.E. Veevers. 1983. "Accelerating Sex Differentials in Mortality: An Analysis of Contributing Factors," *Social Biology*, 30: 75-85.

Gee, Ellen M., and Jean E. Veevers. 1987. "Recent Trends in Canadian Sex Differentials in Mortality: The Middle-Age Turnaround," in *Contributions to Demography*. Edmonton: Population Research Laboratory.

Gee, Ellen M., and Meredith M. Kimball. 1987. *Women and Aging*. Toronto: Butterworths.

Gee, Ellen, and Susan McDaniel. 1990. "Pension Politics and Pension Challenges: Retirement Implications," paper presented at the meetings of the Canadian Sociology and Anthropology Association, Victoria, May, 1990.

George, M.V., A. Romaniuc, and F. Nault. 1990. "Effects of Fertility and International Migration on the changing Age Composition in Canada," paper presented at the Conference of European Statisticians, Ottawa, September, 1990.

Gérard, Hubert. 1988. "Possibilités et limites des politiques natalistes en Occident," *Cahiers Québécois de Démographie*, 17, 1: 7-20.

Gilbert, Sid, and Neil Guppy. 1988. "Trends in Participation in Higher Education by Gender," in J. Curtis *et al.*, eds., *Social Inequality in Canada: Patterns, Problems, Policies*. Scarborough: Prentice-Hall.

Gillis, A.R. 1980. "Urbanization and Urbanism," in R. Hagedorn, ed., *Sociology*. Toronto: Holt.

Glaser, William A. 1987. "International Perspectives," in *Aging with Limited Health Resources*. Ottawa: Economic Council of Canada.

Globe and Mail. 1989. "Swedish Mothers, Fathers Earn One and a Half Year Paid Leave," *Globe and Mail*, 11 June 1989: A1.

Globe and Mail. 1990. "Assessing our Educational Weakness," *Globe and Mail*, editorial, 22 January 1990.

Gmelch, George. 1983. "Who Returns and Why: Return Migration Behavior in Two North Atlantic Societies," *Human Organization*, 42, 1: 46-54.

Goldscheider, Frances Kobrin, and Linda J. Waite. 1986. "Sex Differences in the Entry into Marriage," *American Journal of Sociology*, 92, 1: 91-109.

Gonnot, Jean-Pierre. 1990. "Demographic, Social and Economic Aspects of the Pension Problem: Evidence from 12 Countries," *Popnet*, 17: 3-10.

Goode, William J. 1977. "World Revolution and Family Patterns," in A.S. Skolnick and J.H. Skolnick, eds., *Family in Transition*. Boston: Little, Brown.

Goyder, John C. 1981. "Income Differences Between the Sexes: Findings from a National Canadian Survey," *Canadian Review of Sociology and Anthropology*, 18, 3: 321-42.

Grant, E. Kenneth, and John Vanderkamp. 1987. "The Role of Migration in Balancing Regional Supply and Demand Discrepancies." Institute for Research on Public Policy Discussion Paper 87.A.16.

Green, Douglas, Judith Gold, and John Sargent. 1986. "A Note on Demographic Projections for Canada," in J. Sargent, ed., *Economic Growth: Prospects and Determinants*. Toronto: University of Toronto Press.

Grenier, Gilles. 1985. "Health Care Costs in Canada: Past and Future Trends," in F. Vaillancourt, ed., *Income Distribution and Economic Security in Canada*. Toronto: University of Toronto Press.

Grenier, Gilles. 1989. "Bilingualism among Anglophones and Francophones in Canada," in *Demolinguistic Trends and the Evolution of Canadian Institutions*. Ottawa: Secretary of State.

Grenier, Gilles, David E. Bloom, and D. Juliet Howland. 1987. "An Analysis of the First Marriage Patterns of Canadian Women," *Canadian Studies in Population*, 14, 1: 47-68.

Grenier, Gilles, and Réjean Lachapelle. 1988. "Aspects linguistiques de l'évolution démographique." Ottawa: Report for Review of Demography, Health and Welfare.

Grindstaff, Carl F. 1986a. "A Socio-Demographic Profile of Immigrant Women in Canada, by Age at Immigration, Women Age 30-44." Ottawa: Report for Review of Demography, Health and Welfare.

Grindstaff, Carl F. 1986b. "The High Cost of Childbearing: The Fertility of Women Age 30-44, Canada, 1981." Ottawa: Report for Review of Demography, Health and Welfare.

Grindstaff, Carl F. 1989. "Socio-economic Associations with Fertility: A Profile of Women at Age 30," *Canadian Studies in Population*, 16, 1: 43-60.

Grindstaff, Carl F. 1990a. "A Vanishing Breed: Women with Large Families: Canada in the 1980s," manuscript.

Grindstaff, Carl F. 1990b. "Canada as a Pro-natal Society," manuscript.

Grindstaff, Carl F. 1990c. "Long-term Consequences of Adolescent Marriage and Fertility," in *Report on the Demographic Situation in Canada 1988*. Ottawa: Statistics Canada Cat. No. 91-209.

Grindstaff, Carl F., T.R. Balakrishnan, and Paul S. Maxim. 1989. "Life Course Alternatives: Factors Associated with Differential Timing Patterns in Fertility among Women Recently Completing Childbearing, Canada 1981," *Canadian Journal of Sociology*, 14, 4: 443-60.

Grindstaff, Carl F., and Frank Trovato. 1990. "Junior Partners: Women's Contribution to Family Income in Canada," *Social Indicators Research*, 22, 3: 229-53.

Grisgsby, Jill S. 1988. "The Demographic Components of Population Aging." University of Michigan, Population Studies Centre Research Report No. 88-124.

Guidon, Hubert. 1988. *Quebec Society: Tradition, Modernity and Nationhood*. Toronto: University of Toronto Press.

Guillemette, André. 1983. "L'évolution de la mortalité différentielle selon le statut socio-économique sur l'Ile de Montréal, 1961-1976," *Cahiers Québécois de Démographie*, 12, 1: 29-48.

Gunderson, M. 1989. *Employment Income*. Ottawa: Statistics Canada Cat. No. 998-129.

Gunderson, Morley, and James Pasando. 1988. "The Case for Allowing Mandatory Retirement," *Canadian Public Policy*, 14, 1: 32-39.

Guralnik, Jack, and Edward Schneider. 1987. "Prospects and Expectations of Extending Life Expectancy," in T.J. Espenshade and G.T. Stolnitz, eds., *Technological Prospects and Population Trends*. Boulder, Colorado: Westview Press.

Habib, Jack. 1988. "Aging Population: Structure and Support for the Elderly," in *Economic and Social Implications of Population Aging*. New York: United Nations.

Hagemann, Robert P., and Giuseppe Nicoletti. 1989. "Ageing Populations: Economic Effects and Implications for Public Finance." OECD Working Papers No. 61.

Hagey, N. Janet, Gilles Larocque, and Catherine McBride. 1989. "Faits saillants des conditions des autochtones 1981-2001." Ottawa: Indian and Northern Affairs.

Hagmann, Hermann-Michel. 1988. "L'efficacité des politiques migratoires: un essai d'évaluation," in AIDELF, *Les migrations internationales*. Paris: AIDELF.

Halli, Shiva S., and Raymond Currie. 1986. "Toward an Understanding of Migration Patterns in Urban Prairies: A Comparative Approach." Ottawa: Report for Review of Demography, Health and Welfare.

Halli, Shiva, Frank Trovato, and Leo Driedger. 1990. "The Social Demography of Ethnic Groups," in S. Halli et al., eds., Ethnic Demography. Ottawa: Carleton University Press.

Hamilton, Coleen, and John Whalley. 1984. "Reforming Public Pensions in Canada: Issues and Options," in D.W. Conklin, ed., Pensions Today and Tomorrow. Toronto: Ontario Economic Council.

Hamilton, Kirk, and Hélène Trépanier. 1989. "Hospital Care in the 21st Century," Canadian Social Trends, 15: 31-34.

Hamilton, Roberta. 1978. The Liberation of Women: A Study of Patriarchy and Capitalism. London: George Allen and Unwin.

Handa, Jagdish. 1986. "Wage and Occupational Structure in an Economy with an Aging Population: The Canadian Case in the Years Ahead." Ottawa: Report for Review of Demography, Health and Welfare.

Handwerker, W. Penn. 1986. Culture and Reproduction. Boulder, Colorado: Westview Press.

Hannan, Michael T., Klaus Schomann, and Hans-Peter Blossfeld. 1990. "Sex Differences in the Dynamics of Wage Growth in the Federal Republic of Germany," American Sociological Review, 55, 5: 694-713.

Haraven, Tamara K. 1977. "Family Time and Historical Time," Daedalus, Spring, 1977: 57-70.

Harrell, W. Andrew. 1985. "Husband's Involvement in Housework: The Effects of Relative Earnings Power and Masculine Orientation." University of Alberta: Edmonton Area Series Report No. 39.

Hawkins, Freda. 1972. Canada and Immigration: Public Policy and Public Concern. Montreal and Kingston: McGill-Queen's University Press.

Hawkins, Freda. 1982. "Multiculturalism in Two Countries: The Canadian and Australian Experience," Journal of Canadian Studies, 17, 1: 64-80.

Hawkins, Freda. 1985. "Towards a Population Policy for Canada," paper presented at the meetings of the Canadian Population Society, Montreal, June, 1985.

Hawkins, Freda. 1988. Canada and Immigration: Public Policy and Public Concern. Second Edition. Montreal and Kingston: McGill-Queen's University Press.

Hawkins, Freda. 1989. Critical Years in Immigration: Canada and Australia Compared. Montreal and Kingston: McGill-Queen's University Press.

Health and Welfare. 1988. "Health Indicators Derived from Vital Statistics for Status Indian and Canadian Populations 1978-1986." Ottawa: Health and Welfare.

Health and Welfare. 1989. Basic Facts on Social Security Programs. Ottawa: Health and Welfare.

Health and Welfare. 1990. National Health Expenditure in Canada, 1975-1987. Ottawa: Health and Welfare.

Health and Welfare and Department of Finance. 1982. Better Pensions for Canadians. Ottawa: Supply and Services.

Health and Welfare and Statistics Canada. 1981. The Health of Canadians: Report of the Canada Health Survey. Ottawa: Statistics Canada Cat. No. 82-538.

Heer, David M. 1986. "Immigration as a Counter to Below-Replacement Fertility in the United States," *Population and Development Review*, 12, suppl.: 262-67.

Heilig, Gerard, and Anna Wils. 1989. "AIDS Costs More Years of Potential Life," *Popnet*, No. 15.

Heitlinger, Alena. 1986. "Overview Report on Eastern European Population Policies." Ottawa: Report for Review of Demography, Health and Welfare.

Heitlinger, Alena. 1990a. "Changing Meanings of Pronatalism: From Reproductive Coercion to Women's Equality," manuscript.

Heitlinger, Alena. 1990b. "From Equal Treatment to Positive Action," paper presented at the meeting of the Canadian Sociology and Anthropology Association, Victoria, May, 1990.

Heller, Peter S., Richard Hemming, and Peter W. Kohnert. 1986. *Aging and Social Expenditure in the Major Industrial Countries, 1980-2025*. Washington: IMF.

Henripin, Jacques. 1974. *Immigration and Language Imbalance*. Ottawa: Manpower and Immigration.

Henripin, Jacques. 1989. *Naître ou ne pas être*. Québec: Institut québécois de recherche sur la culture.

Henripin, Jacques, *et al.* 1981. *Les enfants qu'on n'a plus au Québec*. Montréal: Presses de l'Université de Montréal.

Henripin, Jacques, and Evelyne Lapierre-Adamcyk. 1986. "Essai d'évaluation du coût de l'enfant." Report to Bureau de la statistique du Québec.

Henry, Frances, and Effie Ginzberg. 1988. "Racial Discrimination in Employment," in J. Curtis *et al.*, eds., *Social Inequality in Canada: Patterns, Problems, Policies*. Scarborough: Prentice-Hall.

Herold, Edward S. 1984. *Sexual Behaviour of Canadian Young People*. Toronto: Fitzhenry & Whiteside.

Hersak, Gene, and Derrik Thomas. 1988. "Recent Canadian Developments Arising from International Immigration." Ottawa: Employment and Immigration, Discussion Paper.

Hobart, Charles. 1988. "Relationships in Remarried Families," *Canadian Journal of Sociology*, 13, 3: 261-82.

Hobbs, C.F., and F. Kirk. 1987. "Issues in Education, Leisure and Labour Force Participation." Ottawa: Report for Review of Demography, Health and Welfare.

Hodge, Gerald. 1986. "Need for a Rural Perspective on Demographic Tendencies." Ottawa: Report for Review of Demography, Health and Welfare.

Hoem, Jan M. 1990. "Social Policy and Recent Fertility Change in Sweden," *Population and Development Review*, 16, 4: 735-48.

Hohn, Charlotte. 1987. "Population Policies in Advanced Societies: Pronatalist and Migration Strategies," *European Journal of Population*, 3: 459-81.

Hohn, Charlotte. 1989. "Policies Affecting Families and the Population," in J. Légaré, T.R. Balakrishnan, and R. Beaujot, eds., *The Family in Crisis: A Population Crisis?* Ottawa: Royal Society of Canada.

Holzmann, Robert. 1988. "Ageing and Social-security Programs," *European Journal of Population*, 3, 3/4: 411-37.

Houle, René, and Pierre Ducharme. 1987. "La nouvelle transition démographique au Canada: le vieillissement de la population." Ottawa: Report for Review of Demography, Health and Welfare.

House, J.D., *et al.* 1988. "Going Away and Coming Back: Economic Life and Migration in Bird Cove and Anchor Point." Ottawa: Report for Review of Demography, Health and Welfare.

Howith, H.G. 1988. "Immigration Levels Planning: the First Decade." Ottawa: Employment and Immigration Canada.

Hum, Derek P.J. 1987. "The Working Poor, the Canada Assistance Plan and Provincial Responses to Income Supplementation," in J.S. Ismael, ed., *Canadian Social Welfare Policy*. Montreal and Kingston: McGill-Queen's University Press.

Hunter, Alfred A. 1988. "The Changing Distribution of Income," in J. Curtis *et al.*, eds., *Social Inequality in Canada: Patterns, Problems, Policies*. Scarborough: Prentice-Hall.

Iacobacci, Mario. 1987. "Overview," in S. Seward, ed., *The Future of Social Welfare Systems in Canada and the United Kingdom*. Ottawa: Institute for Research on Public Policy.

Irwin, Colin. 1988. "Lords of the Arctic: Wards of the State." Ottawa: Report for Review of Demography, Health and Welfare.

Jansen, Clifford, and Anthony H. Richmond. 1990. "Immigrant Settlement and Integration in Canada," paper presented at the Symposium on Immigrant Settlement and Integration, Toronto, May, 1990.

Jarvis, George. 1977. "Mormon Mortality Rates in Canada," *Social Biology*, 24: 294-302.

Jenness, Diamond. 1954. "Canada's Indians Yesterday; What of Today?" *Canadian Journal of Economics and Political Science*, 20, 1: 95-100.

Johnson, W.A. 1987. "Social Policy in Canada: The Past as it Conditions the Present," in S. Seward, ed., *The Future of Social Welfare Systems in Canada and the United Kingdom*. Ottawa: Institute for Research on Public Policy.

Jones, Charles, Lorna Marsden, and Lorne Tepperman. 1990. *Lives of their Own: The Individuation of Women's Lives*. Toronto: Oxford University Press.

Kalbach, Warren. 1987. "Ethnicity and the Labour Force: A Discussion Paper." Ottawa: Report for Review of Demography, Health and Welfare.

Kalbach, W.E., and W.W. McVey. 1979. *The Demographic Bases of Canadian Society*. Toronto: McGraw-Hill.

Kalbach, Warren E., and Madeleine A. Richard. 1988. "Ethnic-religious Identity, Acculturation and Social and Economic Achievement." Ottawa: Report for Review of Demography, Health and Welfare.

Kalbach, Warren E., and Madeleine A. Richard. 1989. "Ethnic Intermarriage and the Changing Canadian Family," in J. Légaré, T.R. Balakrishnan, and R. Beaujot, eds., *The Family in Crisis: A Population Crisis?* Ottawa: Royal Society of Canada.

Kalbach, Warren, and Madeleine Richard. 1990. "Ethnic Connectedness and the Gender Gap," paper presented at the meetings of the Canadian Population Society, Victoria, June, 1990.

Kallen, Evelyn. 1988. "Multiculturalism as Ideology, Policy and Reality," in J. Curtis *et al.*, eds., *Social Inequality in Canada: Patterns, Problems, Policies*. Scarborough: Prentice-Hall.

Kantrowitz, Barbara, and Pat Wingert. 1990. "Step by Step," *Newsweek*, Special issue on the 21st Century Family, pp. 24-34.

Kempeneers, Marianne. 1989. "L'Enquête sur la fécondité au Canada: un outil privilégié pour l'étude de l'activité féminine," in J. Légaré, T.R. Balakrishnan, and R. Beaujot, eds., *The Family in Crisis: A Population Crisis?* Ottawa: Royal Society of Canada.

Kempeneers, Marianne, and Marie-Hélène Saint-Pierre. 1989. "Discontinuité professionnelle et charges familiales: regards sur les données canadiennes," *Cahiers Québécois de Démographie*, 18, 1: 63-86.

Kennedy, Bruce. 1989. "Real Reform in Income Security," *Policy Options*, 10, 9: 9-12.

Kettle, John. 1980. *The Big Generation*. Toronto: McClelland and Stewart.

Kettle, John. 1990. "Introduction," in *Comments on "Charting Canada's Future"*. London, Ont.: Federation of Canadian Demographers.

Keyfitz, Nathan. 1982. *Population Change and Social Policy*. Cambridge: Abt Books.

Keyfitz, Nathan. 1985. "The Demographics of Unfunded Pensions," *European Journal of Population*.

Keyfitz, Nathan. 1986a. "Canadian Kinship Patterns based on 1971 and 1981 Data," *Canadian Studies in Population*, 13, 2: 123-50.

Keyfitz, Nathan. 1986b. "The Family That Does Not Reproduce Itself," *Population and Development Review*, 12, suppl.: 139-54.

Keyfitz, Nathan. 1987. "Canada's Population in Comparative Perspective," in *Contributions to Demography*. Edmonton: Population Research Laboratory.

Keyfitz, Nathan. 1988. "Some Demographic Properties of Transfer Schemes: How to Achieve Equity between Generations," in R. Lee, ed., *Economics of Changing Age Distributions in Developed Countries*. Oxford: Clarendon Press.

Keyfitz, Nathan. 1989a. "Aging is not the Whole Pension Problem," *Popnet*, 16: 5-8.

Keyfitz, Nathan. 1989b. "Reconciling Economic and Ecological Thinking on Population." IIASA Working Paper 89-27.

Keyfitz, Nathan. 1989c. "On Future Mortality." IIASA Working Paper 89-59.

Keyfitz, Nathan. 1990. "Effect of Mortality Uncertainty on Population Projections," paper presented at the meetings of the Population Association of America, Toronto, May, 1990.

Kosinski, L.A. 1981. "Federal Programs Directly Affecting Migration in Canada," in J.W. Webb *et al.*, eds., *Policies of Population Redistribution*. Ouli: Geographical Society of Northern Finland.

Krahn, Harvey, and Graham S. Lowe. 1990. "Young Workers in the Service Economy." Ottawa: Economic Council of Canada Working Paper No. 14.

Krishnan, Vijaya. 1987. "The Relationship between Income and Fertility: The Role of Immigrant Culture," in *Contributions to Demography*. Edmonton: Population Research Laboratory.

Krishnan, Vijaya, and K.J. Krotki. 1989. "Immigrant Fertility: An Examination of Social Characteristics and Assimilation," paper presented at the meetings of the International Union for the Scientific Study of Population, New Delhi, 1989.

Kritz, Mary M. 1987. "International Migration Policies: Conceptual Problems," *International Migration Review*, 21, suppl.: 947-68

Krotki, Karol J. 1990a. "International Migration and Canada's Ethnic/Linguistic Composition: Language Policy, Multiculturalism," in R. Beaujot, ed., *Facing the Demographic Future*. Ottawa: Royal Society of Canada.

Krotki, Karol J. 1990b. "Academic Research and Public Policy," in R. Beaujot, ed., *Facing the Demographic Future*. Ottawa: Royal Society of Canada.

Krotki, Karol J., and Dave Odynak. 1990. "The Emergence of Multiethnicities in 1981 and 1986: Their Sociological Significance." Edmonton: Population Research Laboratory Discussion Paper No. 63.

Kyriazis, Natalie. 1982. "A Parity-specific Analysis of Completed Fertility in Canada," *Canadian Review of Sociology and Anthropology*, 19, 1: 29-43.

Labourers' International Union of North America. 1990. "Immigration Levels for 1991-1995," paper submitted at the Immigration Opinion Forum, Toronto, 15 February 1990.

Lachapelle, Réjean. 1987. "L'avenir démographique du Canada et des groupes linguistiques." Ottawa: Report for Review of Demography, Health and Welfare.

Lachapelle, Réjean. 1988a. "L'immigration et le caractère ethnolinguistique du Canada et du Québec." Statistics Canada: Direction des études analytiques, Documents de Recherche No. 15.

Lachapelle, Réjean. 1988b. "Ethnic Diversity and the Evolution of Language Groups," paper presented at the Canadian Population Society, Windsor, June, 1988.

Lachapelle, Réjean. 1988c. "Quelques tendances démolinguistiques au Canada et au Québec," *L'Action Nationale*, 78: 329-43.

Lachapelle, Réjean. 1989a. "Evolution of Language Groups and the Official Languages Situation of Canada," in *Demolinguistic Trends and the Evolution of Canadian Institutions*. Ottawa: Secretary of State.

Lachapelle, Réjean. 1989b. "Evolution démographique des francophones et diffusion du français au Canada," paper presented at Université Laval, April, 1989.

Lachapelle, Réjean. 1990. "Effet de la mortalité, de la fécondité et de la migration internationale sur la structure par âge: une application du concept de population stable ouverte," paper presented at the Conference of European Statisticians, Ottawa, September, 1990.

Lachapelle, Réjean, and Jacques Henripin. 1980. *La situation démolinguistique au Canada: évolution passée et prospective*. Montréal: Institute for Research on Public Policy.

Lalonde, Marc. 1974. *A New Perspective on the Health of Canadians*. Ottawa: Health and Welfare.

Lanphier, C. Michael. 1979. "A Study of Third-World Immigrants." Discussion Paper No. 144. Ottawa: Economic Council of Canada.

Lanphier, C. Michael. 1988. "Irreversible Shift: Refugee Intake and Canadian Society," paper presented at the meetings of the Canadian Population Society, Windsor, June, 1988

Lapierre-Adamcyk, Evelyne. 1986. "Plaidoyer pour une recherche sur l'impact économique de la stagnation, voire de la décroissance démographique." Ottawa: Report for Review of Demography, Health and Welfare.

Lapierre-Adamcyk, Evelyne. 1987. "Mariage et politique de la famille," paper presented at the meetings of the Association des Démographes du Québec, Ottawa, May, 1987.

Lapierre-Adamcyk, Evelyne. 1989. "Le mariage et la famille: mentalités actuelles et comportements récents des femmes canadiennes," in J. Légaré, T.R. Balakrishnan, and R. Beaujot, eds., *The Family in Crisis: A Population Crisis?* Ottawa: Royal Society of Canada.

Lapierre-Adamcyk, Evelyne. 1990. "Faire face au changement démographique: la nécessaire participation des femmes," in R. Beaujot, ed., *Faire Face au Changement Démographique*. Ottawa: Royal Society of Canada.

Lapierre-Adamcyk, Evelyne, Pierre Lasserre, and Pierre Ouellette. 1988. "Démographie et productivité." Ottawa: Report for Review of Demography, Health and Welfare.

Laponce, Jean A. 1988. "Conseil au Prince qui voudrait assurer la survie du français en Amérique du Nord," *Cahiers Québécois de Démographie*, 17, 1: 35-48.

Latouche, Daniel. 1988. "Sur les limites des politiques démographiques et autres," *Cahiers Québécois de Démographie*, 17, 1: 3-6.

Lautard, E. Hugh, and Donald J. Loree. 1984. "Ethnic Stratification in Canada, 1931-1971," *Canadian Journal of Sociology*, 9, 3: 333-44.

Lavoie, Yollande. 1972. *L'emigration des Canadiens aux Etats-Unis avant 1930*. Montréal: Presses du l'Université de Montréal.

Le Bourdais, Céline. 1987. "On est pauvre: on naît pauvre ou on le devient?" *Cahiers Québécois de Démographie*, 16, 2: 269-88.

Le Bourdais, Céline, and Hélène Desrosiers. 1988. "Trajectoires démographiques et professionnelles: une analyse longitudinale des processus et des déterminants." Ottawa: Report for Review of Demography, Health and Welfare.

Le Bras, Hervé. 1988. "The Demographic Impact of Post-War Migration in Selected OECD Countries." OECD Working Party on Migration.

Leclerc, Wilbrod. 1989. "Bring Back the City State," *Policy Options*, 10, 8: 14-17.

Lefebvre, L.A., Z. Zsigmond, and M.S. Devereau. 1979. *A Prognosis for Hospitals*. Ottawa: Statistics Canada Cat. No. 83-520.

Légaré, Jacques. 1990a. "Aging and Health," in R. Beaujot ed., *Facing the Demographic Future*. Ottawa: Royal Society of Canada.

Légaré, Jacques. 1990b. "Une meilleure santé plutôt qu'une vie prolongée: plaidoyer pour une réorientation d'une politique de santé pour les personnes âgées," manuscript.

Légaré, Jacques, T.R. Balakrishnan, and Roderic Beaujot. 1989. *The Family in Crisis: A Population Crisis?* Ottawa: Royal Society of Canada.

Legoff, Jacques. 1989. "Les conséquences économiques et sociales des évolutions démographiques en Europe," *Population et Avenir*, 593/594: 6-9.

Lesthaeghe, Ronald. 1987. "Preface," *European Journal of Population*, 3, 3/4: 277-79.

Lesthaeghe, Ronald. 1989. "Demographic Recruitment in Europe: An Exploration of Alternative Scenarios and Policies." Vrije Universiteit Brussel: Interuniversity Programme in Demography Working Paper 1989-5.

Lesthaeghe, R., H. Page, and J. Surkyn. 1988. "Are Immigrants Substitutes for

Births?" Vrije Universiteit Brussel: Interuniversity Programme in Demography Working Paper 1988-3.

Lévesque, Suzanne. 1988. "Facteurs économiques dans la détermination du taux de natalité," manuscript.

Levy, Michel Louis. 1988. "Europe et démographie," *Population et Sociétés*, No. 230.

Li, Peter S. 1988. *Ethnic Inequality in a Class Society*. Toronto: Wall and Thompson.

Liaw, Kao-Lee. 1986. "Review of Research on Interregional Migration in Canada." Ottawa: Report for Review of Demography, Health and Welfare.

Liaw, Kao-Lee. 1988. "Mobility and Migration Schedules of the Canadian Population by Selected Personal Factors." Hamilton, Ont.: McMaster University, QSEP Research Report No. 237.

Lithwick, N. Harvey. 1986. "Regional Policy: The Embodiment of Contradictions," in D.J. Savoie, ed., *The Canadian Economy: A Regional Perspective*. Toronto: Methuen.

Loaiza, Edilberto. 1989. "Socio-demographic Characteristics and Economic Attainment of Latin American Immigrants in Canada," Ph.D. thesis, University of Western Ontario.

Loh, Shirley. 1990. "Population Projections of Registered Indians, 1986-2011." Ottawa: Statistics Canada.

Lowe, Graham. 1986. "Job Line for Youth," *Policy Options*, 7, 5: 3-6.

Lupri, Eugen, and James Frideres. 1981. "The Quality of Marriage and the Passage of Time: Marital Satisfaction over the Family Life Cycle," *Canadian Journal of Sociology*, 6, 3: 283-306.

Lupri, Eugen, and Donald L. Mills. 1987. "The Household Division of Labour in Young Dual-earner Couples: The Case of Canada," *International Review of Sociology*, Series No. 2, 1987: 33-54.

Lynch, James J. 1977. *The Broken Heart: The Medical Consequences of Loneliness*. New York: Basic Books.

MacKenzie, Colin. 1989. "National Health Plan Becoming U.S. Option," *Globe and Mail*, 23 May 1989: A2.

MacKenzie, Thomas. 1984. "The Long-term Budgetary Problem," in *Report of the Policy Forum on Medicare in an Age of Restraint*. Kingston: John Deutsch.

MacLean, Brian D., A.B. Anderson, and Peter S. Li. 1988. "Rural Depopulation and the Saskatchewan Economy." Ottawa: Report for Review of Demography, Health and Welfare.

Manpower and Immigration. 1966. *Canadian Immigration Policy*, White Paper on Immigration. Ottawa: Queen's Printer.

Manpower and Immigration Canada. 1974. *Immigration Policy Perspectives*. Ottawa: Information Canada.

Mansbridge, Stanley H. 1987. "Social Policy in Canada: Past, Present and Future," in S. Seward, ed., *The Future of Social Welfare Systems in Canada and the United Kingdom*. Ottawa: Institute for Research on Public Policy.

Manton, Kenneth G. 1987. "The Population Implications of Breakthroughs in Biomedical Technologies for Controlling Mortality and Fertility," in T.J. Espenshade and G.T. Stolnitz, eds., *Technological Prospects and Population Trends*. Boulder, Colorado: Westview Press.

Marcil-Gratton, Nicole. 1988. "Les modes de vie nouveaux des adultes et leur impact sur les enfants au Canada." Ottawa: Report for Review of Demography, Health and Welfare.

Marcil-Gratton, Nicole, and Jacques Légaré. 1987. "Being Old Today and Tomorrow: A Different Proposition," *Canadian Studies in Population*, 14, 2: 237-41.

Marr, William. 1986. "Are the Canadian Foreign-Born Under-Represented in Canada's Occupational Structure," *International Migration*, 14: 769-75.

Marr, William L. 1987. "Canadian Population Policy: Some Constraints and Parameters," in *Contributions to Demography*. Edmonton: Population Research Laboratory.

Marr, William L., and M.B. Percy. 1985. "Immigration Policy and Canadian Economic Growth," in J. Whalley, ed., *Domestic Policies and the International Economic Environment*. Toronto: University of Toronto Press.

Marr, W.L., and D.G. Peterson. 1980. *Canada: An Economic History*. Toronto: Gage.

Marsden, Lorna R. 1972. *Population Probe*. Toronto: Copp Clark.

Marshell, Katherine. 1987. "Women in Male-dominated Professions," *Canadian Social Trends*, 7: 7-11.

Maslove, Allan, and David Hawkes. 1989. "The Northern Population," *Canadian Social Trends*, 15: 2-7.

Mason, Greg, and Wayne Simpson. 1988. "An Exploration of the Micro-foundations of Internal Migration in Manitoba." Ottawa: Report for Review of Demography, Health and Welfare.

Massey, Douglas. 1988. "Economic Development and International Migration in Comparative Perspective," *Population and Development Review*, 14, 3: 383-414.

Mathews, Georges. 1984. *Le choc démographique*. Montréal: Boréal Expresse.

Mathews, Georges. 1988. "Le vieillissement démographique et son impact sur la situation des personnes âgées et les services qui leur sont offerts." Montréal: INRS-Urbanisation.

Mathews, Georges. 1989. *Politiques natalistes européennes et politique familiale canadienne*. Montréal: INRS Études et Documents No. 59.

Matras, Judah. 1989. "Demographic Trends, Life Course and the Family Cycle: The Canadian Example, Part I," *Canadian Studies in Population*, 16, 1: 1-24.

Matras, Judah. 1990. "Demographic Trends, Life Course and Family Cycle, The Canadian Experience, Part II," *Canadian Studies in Population*, 16, 2: 145-62.

Matthews, Ralph. 1988. "Issues in Regional Development," in J. Curtis *et al.*, eds., *Social Inequality in Canada: Patterns, Problems, Policies*. Scarborough: Prentice-Hall.

Maxwell, Judith. 1987. "Introduction" and "Closing Remarks," in *Aging with Limited Health Resources*. Ottawa: Economic Council of Canada.

Maxwell, Judith. 1990. "The Economic Role of Women," *Au Courant*, 10, 4: 12-13.

McCormack, Thelma. 1988. "Public Policies and Reproductive Technology: A Feminist Critique," *Canadian Public Policy*, 14, 4: 361-75.

McCullum, John S. 1985. "What is Wrong with UISP," *Policy Options*, 6, 10: 15-17.

McDaniel, Susan. 1985. "Implementation of Abortion Policy in Canada as a Women's Issue," *Atlantis*, 10, 2: 74-91.

McDaniel, Susan. 1986. *Canada's Aging Population*. Toronto: Butterworths.

McDaniel, Susan. 1987a. "Demographic Aging as a Guiding Paradigm in Canada's Welfare State," *Canadian Public Policy*, 13, 3: 330-36.

McDaniel, Susan. 1987b. "Fertility, Family and Feminism: Towards a Reconceptualization of Canadian Childbearing," in *Contributions to Demography*. Edmonton: Population Research Laboratory.

McDaniel, Susan. 1987c. "Women's Roles and Reproduction: The Changing Picture of Canada in the 1980's." Waterloo, Ont.: Department of Sociology.

McDaniel, Susan. 1988. "The Changing Canadian Family: Women's Roles and the Impact of Feminism," in S. Burt *et al.*, eds., *Women in Canada*. Toronto: McClelland and Stewart.

McDaniel, Susan. 1989. "Reconceptualizing the Nuptiality/Fertility Relationship in Canada in a New Age," *Canadian Studies in Population*, 16, 2: 163-85.

McDougall, Barbara. 1990. "Speech." Opinion Forum on Immigration, Toronto, 15 February 1990.

McInnis, R. Marvin. 1980. "A Functional View of Canadian Immigration," paper presented at the annual meetings of the Population Association of America, Denver, 1980.

McKeown, T., *et al.* 1972. "An Interpretation of the Modern Rise of Population in Europe," *Population Studies*, 26: 345-82.

McKie, Craig. 1987. "Lifestyle Risks: Smoking and Drinking in Canada," *Canadian Social Trends*, 4: 20-26.

McLaren, Angus, and Arlene Tigar McLaren. 1986. *The Bedroom and the State: The Changing Practices and Politics of Contraception and Abortion in Canada, 1880-1980*. Toronto: McClelland and Stewart.

McNeill, William H. 1986. *Polyethnicity and National Unity in World History*. Toronto: University of Toronto Press.

McNicoll, Geoffrey. 1986. "Economic Growth with Below-Replacement Fertility," *Population and Development Review*, 12, suppl.: 217-37.

McNiven, James D. 1987. "The Efficiency-Equity Tradeoff: The Macdonald Report and Regional Development," in W.J. Coffey and M. Polèse, eds., *Still Living Together*. Ottawa: Institute for Research on Public Policy.

McQuillan, Kevin. 1989. "Discussion," in J. Légaré, T.R. Balakrishnan, and R. Beaujot, eds., *The Family in Crisis: A Population Crisis?* Ottawa: Royal Society of Canada.

McQuillan Kevin. 1990. "Family Change and Family Income in Ontario," in L.C. Johnson and D. Barnhorst, eds., *Children, Families and Public Policy in the 90s*. Toronto: Thompson Educational Publishing.

McRoberts, Kenneth. 1989. "Making Canada Bilingual: Illusions and Delusions of Federal Language Policy," in D.P. Shugarman and R. Whitaker, eds., *Federalism and Political Community*. Peterborough, Ont.: Broadview Press.

McSkimmings, Judie. 1990. "The Farm Community," *Canadian Social Trends*, 16: 20-23.

Melvin, James R. 1987. "Regional Inequalities in Canada: Underlying Causes and Policy Implications," *Canadian Public Policy*, 13, 3: 304-17.

Mendelson, Michael. 1987. "Can We Reform Canada's Income Security System?" in S. Seward, ed., *The Future of Social Welfare Systems in Canada and the United Kingdom*. Ottawa: Institute for Research on Public Policy.

Merrick, Thomas W. 1986. "World Population in Transition," *Population Bulletin*, 41, 2.

Méthot, Suzanne. 1987. "Low Income in Canada," *Canadian Social Trends*, 4: 2-7.

Mickleburgh, Rod. 1991. "Doctors Hoping for Better Deal," *Globe and Mail*, 16 January 1991.

Millar, Wayne J. 1988. *Smoking Behaviour of Canadians 1986*. Ottawa: Health and Welfare.

Millar, Wayne J., and John M. Last. 1988. "Motor Vehicle Traffic Accident Mortality in Canada, 1921-1984," *American Journal of Preventative Medicine*, 4, 4: 220-30.

Mirabelli, Alan. 1989. "Family Issues and Family Policy," *Transition*, June, 1989: 9-10.

Mitchell, Rick. 1989. *Canada's Population from Ocean to Ocean*. Ottawa: Statistics Canada Cat. No. 98-120.

Mix, P., and M. Gagnon. 1990. "Preliminary Hospital Statistics," *Health Reports*, 2, 2: 177-80.

Moen, Phillis. 1989. *Working Parents: Transformation in Gender Roles and Public Policies in Sweden*. Madison: University of Wisconsin Press.

Montigny, Gilles. 1990. "Reading Skills," *Canadian Social Trends*, 19: 22-24.

Moore, Eric G. 1989. "Editorial Introduction," *Population Research and Policy Review*, 8, 1: 1-4.

Moore, Maureen. 1987. "Women Parenting Alone," *Canadian Social Trends*, 7: 31-36.

Moore, Maureen. 1988. "Female Lone Parenthood: The Duration of Episodes," *Canadian Social Trends*, 10: 40-42.

Moore, Maureen. 1989a. "Dual-earner Families: The New Norm," *Canadian Social Trends*, 12: 24-26.

Moore, Maureen. 1989b. "Female Lone Parenting over the Life Course," *Canadian Journal of Sociology*, 14, 3: 335-52.

Moore, Thomas Gale. 1986. "Comment," *Population and Development Review*, 12, suppl.: 243-44.

Mori, G.A., and B. Burke. 1989. *Educational Attainment of Canadians*. Ottawa: Statistics Canada Cat. No. 98-134.

Morin, Richard. 1986. "Les conditions de logement des vieux." Ottawa: Report for Review of Demography, Health and Welfare.

Morin, Richard, Damaris Rose, and Jael Mongeau. 1988. "La formation des ménages chez les jeunes." Ottawa: Report for Review of Demography, Health and Welfare.

Muhsam, Helmut V. 1979. "The Demographic Transition: From Wastage to Conservation of Human Life," in *Population Science in the Service of Mankind*. Ordina: IUSSP.

Murphy, Kevin, Mark Plant, and Fins Welch. 1988. "Cohort Size and Earnings in the U.S.A." in R. Lee, ed., *Economics of Changing Age Distributions in Developed Countries*. Oxford: Clarendon Press.

Myers, Robert J. 1990. "Should Social Security's Age for First Benefits or for Full Benefits be Changed," paper presented at the conference of National Academy of Social Insurance, Washington, January, 1990.

Myles, John. 1981a. "The Aged and the Welfare State," paper presented at meetings of the International Sociological Association, Paris, July, 1981.

Myles, John. 1981b. "Social Implications of Canada's Changing Age Structure," manuscript.

Myles, John. 1984. *Old Age in the Welfare State: The Political Economy of Public Pensions*. Boston: Little, Brown.

Myles, John. 1986. "Social Security and Support of the Elderly: The Western Experience." Ottawa: Carleton University, Sociology and Anthropology Working Paper No. 86-3.

Myles, John. 1988a. "Social Policy in Canada," in E. Rathborne-McCuan and B. Havens, eds., *North American Elders*. New York: Greenwood.

Myles, John. 1988b. "The Expanding Middle: Some Canadian Evidence on the Deskilling Debate," *Canadian Review of Sociology and Anthropology*, 25, 3: 335-64.

Myles, John. 1989. *Old Age in the Welfare State: The Political Economy of Public Pensions*. Lawrence: University Press of Kansas.

Myles, J., G. Picot, and T. Wannell. 1988. "The Changing Wage Distribution of Jobs, 1981-86," *Canadian Economic Observer*, November, 1988: 4.1-33.

Nagnur, Dhruva. 1986. *Longevity and Historical Life Tables*. Ottawa: Statistics Canada Cat. No. 89-506.

Nagnur, Dhruva, and Michael Nagrodski. 1988. "Cardiovascular Disease, Cancer and Life Expectancy," *Canadian Social Trends*, 11: 25-27.

Nash, Alan. 1988. "Our Enterprising Immigrants," *Policy Options*, 9, 10: 18-23.

Nash, Alan. 1989a. "Can we Meet the Refugee Challenge," *Policy Options*, 10, 7: 21-26.

Nash, Alan. 1989b. "International Refugee Pressures and Canadian Public Policy Response." Ottawa: Institute for Research on Public Policy, Discussion Paper 89.B.1.

Nathanson, Constance A., and Alan D. Lopez. 1987. "The Future of Sex Mortality Differentials in Industrialized Countries: A Structural Hypothesis," *Population Research and Policy Review*, 6, 2: 123-36.

National Council on Welfare. 1988. "Sixty-five and Older: Profiles and Policies," in J. Curtis *et al.*, eds., *Social Inequality in Canada: Patterns, Problems, Policies*. Scarborough: Prentice-Hall.

Needleman, Lionel. 1986. "Canadian Fertility Trends in Perspective," *Journal of Biosocial Science*, 18, 1: 43-56.

Nessner, Katherine. 1990. "Profile of Canadians with Disabilities," *Canadian Social Trends*, 18: 2-5.

Neuwirth, Gertrud, *et al.* 1985. "Southeast Asian Refugee Study," manuscript report on the Three Year Study of the Social and Economic Adaptation of Southeast Asian Refugees to Life in Canada, 1981-83.

Ng, Roxana, and Alma Estable. 1986. "Immigrant Women in the Labour Force: Issues of Social, Economic and Demographic Concern." Ottawa: Report for Review of Demography, Health and Welfare.

Norman, Ross M.G. 1986. "The Nature and Correlates of Health Behaviour." Health Promotion Studies, Series No. 2. Ottawa: Health and Welfare.

Normandeau, Louise, and Victor Piché. 1984. *Les populations amérindiennes et inuit du Canada: Aperçu démographique*. Montréal: Presses de l'Université de Montréal.

Norris, Mary Jane. 1990. "The Demography of Aboriginal People in Canada," in S. Halli *et al.*, eds., *Ethnic Demography*. Ottawa: Carleton University Press.

Northcott, Herbert C. 1988. *Changing Residence: The Geographic Mobility of Elderly Canadians*. Toronto: Butterworths.

Northcott, Herbert. 1990. "Public Opinion Regarding the Economic Support of Seniors." Edmonton: Population Research Laboratory, Edmonton Area Series Report No. 67.

Novak, Mark. 1988. *Aging and Society*. Toronto: Nelson.

O'Higgins, Michael. 1988. "The Allocation of Public Resources to Children and the Elderly in OECD Countries," in J.L. Palmer and I.V. Sawhill, eds., *The Vulnerable*. Washington: The Urban Institute.

OECD. 1985. *Social Expenditure 1960-1990*. Paris: OECD.

OECD. 1988a. *Ageing Populations, The Social Policy Implications*. Paris: OECD.

OECD. 1988b. *Reforming Public Pensions*. Paris: OECD.

OECD. 1988c. *The Future of Social Protection*. Paris: OECD.

Okraku, Ishmael. 1987. "Age Residential Segregation in Canadian Cities," *Canadian Review of Sociology and Anthropology*, 24, 3: 431-52.

Olshansky, S. Jay. 1990. "Discussion on Forecasting Mortality and Health," paper presented at meetings of the Population Association of America, Toronto, May, 1990.

Oppenheimer, Valerie K. 1987. "A Theory of Marriage Timing: Assortive Mating under Varying Degrees of Uncertainty," manuscript.

Osberg, Lars. 1988. "Is it Retirement or Unemployment? The Constrained Labour Supply of Older Canadians." Ottawa: Report for Review of Demography, Health and Welfare.

Osberg, Lars. 1990. "A Distinct Canada," *Policy Options*, 11, 4: 13-14.

Owen, Brian E. 1986. "Effects of Demographic Shifts on Economic Activities." Ottawa: Report for Review of Demography, Health and Welfare.

Paillé, Michel. 1985. *Contribution à la démolinguistique québécoise*. Québec: Conseil de la langue française.

Paillé, Michel. 1989a. *Nouvelles tendances démolinguistiques dans l'Ile de Montréal 1981-1996*. Québec: Conseil de la langue française, Notes et documents No. 71.

Paillé, Michel. 1989b. "Aménagement linguistique et population au Québec," *Journal of Canadian Studies*, 23, 4: 54-69.

Pampel, Fred C., and J.B. Williamson. 1985. "Age Structure, Politics and Cross-national Patterns of Public Pension Expenditures," *American Sociological Review*, 50: 782-98.

Pamuk, Elsie R. 1985. "Social Class Inequality in Mortality in England and Wales," *Population Studies*, 39, 1: 17-31.

Parekh, Navin M. 1988. "Institutional Responses to Multicultural, Multiracial Work Force." Ottawa: Report for Review of Demography, Health and Welfare.

Parliament, Jo-Anne. 1987. "Increased Life Expectancies, 1921 to 1981," *Canadian Social Trends*, 5: 15-19.

Parliament, Jo-Anne. 1989a. "Women Employed Outside the Home," *Canadian Social Trends*, 13: 3-6.

Parliament, Jo-Anne. 1989b. "The Decline in Cardiovascular Disease Mortality," *Canadian Social Trends*, 14: 28-29.

Parliament, Jo-Anne B. 1990. "Labour Force Trends: Two Decades in Review," *Canadian Social Trends*, 18: 16-19.

Parliament of Canada. 1978. "Immigration Act 1976," *Canada Gazette*, Part III, Vol. 2, No. 8, 25-26 Elizabeth II, Chapter 52.

Passaris, Constantine. 1989. "The Immigration Cure," *Policy Options*, 10, 5: 28-30.

Patel, Dhiru. 1980. *Dealing with Interracial Conflict: Policy Alternatives*. Montreal: Institute for Research on Public Policy.

Patterson, E. Palmer, II. 1978. "Native Peoples and Social Policy," in S. Yelaja, ed., *Canadian Social Policy*. Waterloo, Ont.: Wilfrid Laurier University Press.

Pepall, W.M., and W.A. Sims. 1986. "The Impact of Selected Government Policies on Fertility Trends." Ottawa: Report for Review of Demography, Health and Welfare.

Péron, Yves, and Jacques Légaré. 1988. "L'histoire matrimoniale et parentale des générations atteignant le seuil de la vieillesse d'ici l'an 2000." Ottawa: Report for Review of Demography, Health and Welfare.

Péron, Yves, E. Lapierre-Adamcyk, and Denis Morissette. 1987. "Les répercussions des nouveaux comportements démographiques sur la vie familiale: la situation canadienne," *International Review of Community Development*, 18, 58: 57-66.

Péron, Yves, and Denis Morissette. 1986. "Incidence des nouveaux comportements familiaux sur l'aide aux familles." Ottawa: Report for Review of Demography, Health and Welfare.

Péron, Yves, and Claude Strohmenger. 1985. *Demographic and Health Indicators*. Ottawa: Statistics Canada Cat. No. 82-543.

Picard, André. 1989. "Quebec to Boost Paternal Leave for 3 or More Children," *Globe and Mail*, 14 September 1989.

Picard, André. 1991. "Quebec Birth Rate Multiplies," *Globe and Mail*, 5 January 1991: A2.

Picot, G. 1980. "The Changing Educational Profile of Canadians, 1961 to 2000." Ottawa: Statistics Canada.

Pike, Robert M. 1988. "Education and the Schools," in J. Curtis and L. Tepperman, eds., *Understanding Canadian Society*. Toronto: McGraw-Hill.

Platiel, Rudy. 1987. "An Uncertain Journey," *Globe and Mail*, 21 March 1987: D1, D8.

Polèse, Mario. 1987. "Patterns of Regional Economic Development in Canada: Long-term Trends and Issues," in W.J. Coffey and M. Polèse, eds., *Still Living Together*. Ottawa: Institute for Research on Public Policy.

Polèse, Mario. 1990. "Misplaced Priorities: A Review of Demolinguistic Trends and the Evolution of Canadian Institutions," *Canadian Public Policy*, 16, 4: 445-50.

Pollard, John H. 1979. "Factors Affecting Mortality and the Length of Life," in *Population Science in the Service of Mankind*. Ordina: IUSSP.

Ponting, J. Rick. 1988. "Native Peoples," in J. Curtis and L. Tepperman, eds., *Understanding Canadian Society*. Toronto: McGraw-Hill.

Population Reference Bureau. 1990. "1990 World Population Data Sheet." Washington: Population Reference Bureau.

Portes, Alejandro. 1990. "The Economics of Immigration," *Contemporary Sociology*, 19, 6: 853-55.

Potts, Margaret. 1989. "University Enrolment in the 1980s," *Canadian Social Trends*, 15: 28-30.

Presser, Harriet B. 1986. "Comment," *Population and Development Review*, 12, suppl.: 196-202.

Presthus, Robert. 1973. *Elite Accommodation in Canadian Politics*. Toronto: Macmillan.

Preston, Samuel H. 1984. "Children and the Elderly: Divergent Paths for America's Dependents," *Demography*, 21: 435-58.

Preston, Samuel H. 1986. "Changing Values and Falling Birth Rates," *Population and Development Review*, 12, suppl.: 176-95.

Preston, Samuel H. 1987. "The Social Sciences and the Population Problem," *Sociological Forum*, 2: 619-44.

Preston, Samuel H., Christine Himes, and Mitchell Eggers. 1989. "Demographic Conditions Responsible for Population Aging," *Demography*, 26, 4: 691-709.

Priest, Gordon. 1990. "The Demographic Future," *Canadian Social Trends*, 17: 5-8.

Prince, Michael J. 1985. "Startling Facts, Sobering Truths and Sacred Trust: Pension Policy and the Tories," in M. Marlove, ed., *How Ottawa Spends, 1985*. Toronto: Methuen.

Prince, Michael J. 1986. "The Elderly, Tax Policy and Income Security in Canada." Ottawa: Report for Review of Demography, Health and Welfare.

Prince, Michael J., and Jim J. Rice. 1989. "The Canadian Jobs Strategy: Supply Side Social Policy," in K.A. Graham, ed. *How Ottawa Spends*. Ottawa: Carleton University Press.

Pross, A. Paul. 1975. *Pressure Group Behaviour in Canadian Politics*. Toronto: McGraw-Hill.

Pryor, E.T. 1984. "1981 Census of Population: Demographic Highlights." Ottawa: Statistics Canada Cat. No. 92-X-535.

Raby, Ronald. 1990. "Redistribution de la population, migration interne et développement régional," in R. Beaujot, ed., *Facing the Demographic Future*. Ottawa: Royal Society of Canada.

Rachlis, Michael, and Carol Kushner. 1989. *Second Opinion: What's Wrong with Canada's Health-care System and How to Fix it*. Toronto: Harper and Collins.

Rajulton, Fernando, and T.R. Balakrishnan. 1988. "Developments in Nuptiality and Fertility in Canada." London, Ont.: Population Studies Centre.

Rajulton, Fernando, and T.R. Balakrishnan. 1990. "Interdependence of Transitions among Marital and Parity States in Canada," *Canadian Studies in Population*, 17, 1: 107-32.

Rajulton, Fernando, T.R. Balakrishnan, and Zenaida R. Ravanera. 1990. "Measuring Infertility in Contracepting Populations," paper presented at the meetings of the Canadian Population Society, Victoria, June, 1990.

Ram, Bali. 1990. *New Trends in the Family*. Ottawa: Statistics Canada Cat. No. 91-535.

Ram, Bali, and M.V. George. 1990. "Immigrant Fertility Patterns in Canada, 1961-1986," *International Migration*, 28, 4: 413-26.

Ram, Bali, Mary Jane Norris, and Karl Skof. 1989. *The Inner City in Transition.* Ottawa: Statistics Canada Cat. No. 98-123.

Rao, G. Lakshmana, Anthony H. Richmond, and Jerzy Zubrzycki. 1984. *Immigrants in Canada and Australia.* Volume One. *Demographic Aspects and Education.* Downsview, Ontario: Institute for Behavioural Research, York University.

Rao, K.V., and T.R. Balakrishnan. 1986. "Childlessness as a Factor of Fertility Decline in Canada." Ottawa: Report for Review of Demography, Health and Welfare.

Rao, K.V., and T.R. Balakrishnan. 1988. "Age at First Birth in Canada: A Hazards Model Analysis," *Genus,* 44, 1-2: 53-72.

Rappak, J. Peter, and Mary S. Rappak. 1990. "Analysis of the Demographic Implications of Varying Immigration Levels and the Age Structure of Immigrants," paper presented at the meetings of the Canadian Population Society, Victoria, June, 1990.

Rashid, A. 1989. *Family Income.* Ottawa: Statistics Canada Cat. No. 98-128.

Ray, Brian, and Eric Moore. 1989. "Access to Homeownership," paper presented at the meetings of the Canadian Population Society, Quebec, June, 1989.

Raynauld, André. 1989. "The Advancement of the French Language in Canada," in *Demolinguistic Trends and the Evolution of Canadian Institutions.* Ottawa: Secretary of State.

Regier, Henry A., J. Bruce Falls, and Chris E. Taylor. 1973. "The Population Factor in the Environmental Equation," in Conservation Council of Ontario and Family Planning Federation of Canada, *A Population Policy for Canada?* Toronto: CCO and FPFC.

Reitz, Jeffrey G. 1980. "Immigration and Interethnic Relationships in Canada," in R. Breton *et al.,* eds., *Cultural Boundaries and the Cohesion of Canada.* Montreal: Institute for Research on Public Policy.

Reitz, Jeffrey. 1988. "Less Racial Discrimination in Canada, or Simply less Racial Conflict? Implications of Comparisons with Britain," *Canadian Public Policy,* 14, 4: 424-41.

Review of Demography. 1989. *Charting Canada's Future.* Ottawa: Health and Welfare.

Rhyme, Darla. 1982. "Generational Differences Between the Canadian Born and Immigrants in Metropolitan Toronto." Downsview, Ontario: Institute for Behavioural Research, York University.

Ribaud, Michelle. 1988. "Labour-market Response to Changes in Cohort Size: The Case of France," *European Journal of Population,* 3, 3-4: 359-82.

Richmond, Anthony H. 1987. "Demographic Research and Public Policy: The Case of Immigration," in *Contributions to Demography.* Edmonton: Population Research Laboratory.

Richmond, Anthony H.. 1988. *Immigration and Ethnic Conflict.* New York: St. Martin's Press.

Richmond, Anthony. 1989a. *Caribbean Immigrants: A Demo-economic Analysis.* Ottawa: Statistics Canada Cat. No. 91-536.

Richmond, Anthony. 1989b. "Immigrants in Multicultural Canada," manuscript.

Richmond, Anthony, and Warren Kalbach. 1980. *Factors in the Adjustment of Immigrants and their Descendants*. Ottawa: Statistics Canada.

Richmond, Anthony H., and Ravi P. Verma. 1978. "The Economic Adaptation of Immigrants: A New Theoretical Perspective," *International Migration Review*, 12: 3-38.

Richmond, Anthony H., and Jerzy Zubrzycki. 1984. *Immigrants in Canada and Australia*. Volume Two. *Economic Adaptation*. Downsview, Ontario: Institute for Behavioural Research, York University.

Riley, Ron. 1990. "Hospital Morbidity, 1985-86," *Health Reports*, 1, 2: 249-52.

Roadburg, Alan. 1985. *Aging: Retirement, Leisure and Work in Canada*. Toronto: Methuen.

Roberts, Barbara. 1988. *Whence They Came: Deportation from Canada 1900-1935*. Ottawa: University of Ottawa Press.

Robertson, Matthew. 1986. "A Longitudinal Perspective on the Unemployment Experience of Principal Applicant Immigrants to Canada: 1977-1981," *Canadian Studies in Population*, 13: 37-56.

Robinson, Patricia. 1986. *Women's Work Interruptions*. Ottawa: Statistics Canada Cat. No. 99-962.

Robinson, Patricia A. 1989a. "French Mother Tongue Transmission in Mixed Mother Tongue Families," *Canadian Journal of Sociology*, 14, 3: 317-34.

Robinson, Patricia. 1989b. "Women's Work Interruptions and the Family: An Exploration of the Family History Survey," in J. Légaré, T.R. Balakrishnan, and R. Beaujot, eds., *The Family in Crisis: A Population Crisis?* Ottawa: Royal Society of Canada.

Robitaille, Norbert, and Robert Choinière. 1987. "L'accroissement démographique des groupes autochtones au Canada au XXe siècle," *Cahiers Québécois de Démographie*, 16, 1: 3-35.

Rochon, Madeleine. 1989. "La vie reproductive des femmes d'aujourd'hui," *Cahiers Québécois de Démographie*, 18, 1: 15-61.

Rochon, Madeleine. 1990. "Changes in Households, Housing and Families," in R. Beaujot, ed., *Facing the Demographic Future*. Ottawa: Royal Society of Canada.

Roemer, Milton I. 1985. "Social Policies and Health Care Systems: Their Effects on Mortality and Morbidity in Developed Countries," in J. Vallin and A.D. Lopez, eds., *Health Policy, Social Policy and Mortality Prospects*. Ordina: IUSSP.

Romaniuc, Anatole. 1984. *Fertility in Canada: From Baby-boom to Baby-bust*. Ottawa: Statistics Canada.

Romaniuc, Anatole. 1987. "Transition from Traditional High to Modern Low Fertility: Canadian Aboriginals," *Canadian Studies in Population*, 14, 1: 69-88.

Roos, Leslie L., and Noralou P. Roos. 1986. "Physician Discretion: Its Measurement and Importance." Ottawa: Report for Review of Demography, Health and Welfare.

Roos, Noralou P., Patrick Montgomery, and Leslie L. Roos. 1987a. "Health Care Utilization in Years Prior to Death," *Milbank Quarterly*, 65, 2: 231-54.

Roos, Noralou P., Evelyn Shapiro, and Betty Havens. 1987b. "Comments," in *Aging with Limited Health Resources*. Ottawa: Economic Council of Canada.

Roos, Noralou, et al. 1984. "Aging and the Demand for Health Services: Which Aged and Whose Demand?" *The Gerontologist*, 24, 1: 31-36.

Roos, Noralou, *et al.* 1986. "Variations in Physicians' Hospitalization Practices," *American Journal of Public Health*, 76, 1: 45-51.

Roseman, Ellen. 1990. "Poor Children in Canada," *Globe and Mail*, 13 October 1990: D1-D2.

Rosenbaum, Harry. 1988. "Return Inter-provincial Migration, Canada, 1966-1971," *Canadian Studies in Population*, 15, 1: 51-65.

Rosenberg, M.W., and E.G. Moore. 1988. "Population Redistribution of the Elderly and its Impact on Services and Government Financing." Ottawa: Report for Review of Demography, Health and Welfare.

Ross, Kathleen Gallagher. 1986. "Parent's Choice," *Policy Options*, 7, 7: 31-33.

Ross, Lia. 1989. *Canada's Youth*. Ottawa: Statistics Canada Cat. No. 98-124.

Roussel, Louis. 1979. "Générations nouvelles et mariage traditionnel," *Population*, 34, 1: 141-62.

Roussel, Louis. 1989. "Les changements démographiques des vingt dernières années: quelques hypothèses sociologiques," in J. Légaré, T.R. Balakrishnan, and R. Beaujot, eds., *The Family in Crisis: A Population Crisis?* Ottawa: Royal Society of Canada.

Rowe, Geoff. 1989. "Union Dissolution in a Changing Social Context," in J. Légaré, T.R. Balakrishnan, and R. Beaujot, eds., *The Family in Crisis: A Population Crisis?* Ottawa: Royal Society of Canada.

Royal Commission on the Economic Union and Development Prospects for Canada. 1985. *Report*, 3 vols. Ottawa: Supply and Services.

Ryder, Norman B. 1985. "A Population Policy for Canada," manuscript. Toronto: University of Toronto.

Ryder, Norman B. 1990. "Comparative Trends in Canadian and American Fertility," paper presented at the meetings of the Population Association of America, Toronto, May, 1990.

Samuel, T. John. 1984. "Economic Adaptation of Refugees in Canada: Experience of a Quarter Century," *International Migration*, 22: 45-55.

Samuel, T. John. 1987. "Visible Minorities in Canada," in *Contributions to Demography*. Edmonton: Population Research Laboratory.

Samuel, T. John. 1988a. "Family Class Immigrants to Canada, 1981-1984: Labour Force Activity Aspects." Population Working Paper No. 5. Ottawa: Employment and Immigration Canada.

Samuel, T. John. 1988b. "Immigration, Visible Minorities and the Labour Force in Canada: Vision 2000," paper presented at the meetings of the Canadian Population Society, Windsor, June, 1988.

Samuel, T. John. 1988c. "Immigration and Visible Minorities: A Projection," *Canadian Ethnic Studies*, 20, 2: 92-100.

Samuel, T. John. 1989. "Factors Affecting the Acceptance of Immigrants," manuscript.

Samuel, T. John. 1990. "Third World Immigration and Multiculturalism," in S. Halli *et al.*, eds., *Ethnic Demography*. Ottawa: Carleton University Press.

Samuel, T.J., and T. Conyers. 1987. "The Employment Effects of Immigration: A Balance Sheet Approach," *International Migration*, 25: 283-90.

Samuel, T. John, and Ronald Faustino-Santos. 1991. "Canadian Immigrants and Criminality," *International Migration*, 29, 1: 51-76.

Samuel, T. John, and Mikael Jansson. 1987. "Canada's Immigration Levels and the Economic and Demographic Environment, 1967 to 1987," paper presented at the conference of the Canadian Ethnic Studies Association, Halifax, October, 1987.

Samuel, T.J., and B. Woloski. 1985. "The Labour Market Experience of Canadian Immigrants," *International Migration*, 23: 225-50.

Schmahl, Winfried. 1987. "Social Policies for Reducing Demographically Induced Costs in Social Security," *European Journal of Population*, 3, 3-4: 439-57.

Schultz, T. Paul. 1986. "The Value and Allocation of Time in High-income Countries: Implications for Fertility," *Population and Development Review*, 12, suppl.: 87-107.

Science Council of Canada. 1976. *Population, Technology and Resources*. Ottawa: Science Council of Canada Report No. 25.

Science Council of Canada. 1988. "Environmental Peacekeepers: Science, Technology and Sustainable Development in Canada." Science Council of Canada, Ottawa.

Seward, Shirley. 1987a. "Demographic Change and the Canadian Economy: An Overview," *Canadian Studies in Population*, 14, 2: 279-99.

Seward, Shirley. 1987b. "The Relationship Between Immigration and the Canadian Economy." Ottawa: Institute for Research on Public Policy, Discussion Paper 87.A.10.

Seward, Shirley, ed. 1987c. *The Future of Social Welfare Systems in Canada and the United Kingdom*. Ottawa: Institute for Research on Public Policy.

Seward, Shirley. 1990. "Immigrant Women in the Clothing Industry," in S. Halli *et al.*, eds., *Ethnic Demography*. Ottawa: Carleton University Press.

Seward, Shirley, and Mario Iacobacci. 1987. *Approaches to Income Security Reform*. Ottawa: Institute for Research on Public Policy.

Seward, Shirley, and Kathryn McDade. 1988. "Immigrant Women in Canada: A Policy Perspective." Ottawa: Canadian Advisory Council on the Status of Women, Discussion Paper.

Seward, Shirley, and Marc Tremblay. 1989. "Immigrants in the Canadian Labour Force: Their Role in Structural Change." Ottawa: Institute for Research on Public Policy, Discussion Paper 89.B.2

Seward, Shirley, and Marc Tremblay. 1990. "Immigration and the Changing Labour Market," paper presented at the meetings of the Canadian Population Society, Victoria, May, 1990.

Shapiro, D.M., and M. Stelcner. 1987. "The Persistence of the Male-Female Earnings Gap in Canada, 1970-1980," *Canadian Public Policy*, 13, 4: 462-76.

Sharir, Shmuel. 1990. "On Population and Well-being: An Economist's View," in *Comments on "Charting Canada's Future"*. London, Ont.: Federation of Canadian Demographers.

Shaw, R. Paul. 1985. *Intermetropolitan Migration in Canada: Changing Determinants over Three Decades*. Toronto: NC Press.

Shaw, R. Paul. 1986. "Fiscal Versus Traditional Market Variables in Canadian Migration," *Journal of Political Economy*, 94, 3: 648-66.

Shea, Catherine. 1990. "Changes in Women's Occupations," *Canadian Social Trends*, 18: 21-23.

Shifrin, Leonard. 1985. "Income Security: The Rise and Stall of the Federal

Role," in J.S. Ismael, ed., *Canadian Social Welfare Policy*. Montreal and Kingston: McGill-Queen's University Press.

Shihadeh, Edward. 1990. "Immigrants and Migrants: Economic Consequences for Wives and Mothers," paper presented at the meetings of the Canadian Population Society, Victoria, June, 1990.

Shorter, Edward. 1975. *The Making of the Modern Family*. New York: Basic Books.

Shulman, Norman, and Robert Drass. 1979. "Motives and Modes of Internal Migration: Relocation in a Canadian City," *Canadian Review of Sociology and Anthropology*, 16, 3: 333-42.

Siegfried, A. 1937. *Le Canada, puissance internationale*. Paris: Librairie Armand Colin.

Siggner, Andrew J. 1986. "The Socio-demographic Conditions of Registered Indians," *Canadian Social Trends*, 3: 2-9.

Siggner, Andrew. 1989. "The Inuit," *Canadian Social Trends*, 15: 8-10.

Simeon, Richard. 1976. "Studying Public Policy," *Canadian Journal of Political Science*, 9, 4: 548-80.

Simmons, Alan B. 1988. "The 'New Wave' of Immigrants to Canada: Trends in Country of Origin and Implications for the Future." Ottawa: Report for Review of Demography, Health and Welfare.

Simmons, Alan B. 1989. "World System-linkages and International Migration: New Directions in Theory and Method with Application to Canada," *International Population Conference, New Delhi*. Liège: International Union for the Scientific Study of Population, Vol. 2: 159-72.

Simmons, Alan B. 1990. "The Social and Economic Impact of Immigration in Ontario," paper presented to the Immigration Opinion Forum, Toronto, 15 February 1990.

Simmons, J.W., and L.S. Bourne. 1989. "Urban Growth Trends in Canada, 1981-86." Centre for Urban and Community Studies, University of Toronto.

Simmons-Tropea, Daryl, and Richard Osborn. 1987. "Disease, Survival and Death: The Health Status of Canada's Elderly," in V.W. Marshall, ed., *Aging in Canada*. Toronto: Fitzhenry & Whiteside.

Simon, Julian L. 1981. *The Ultimate Resource*. Princeton, N.J.: Princeton University Press.

Simon, Julian L. 1986. "What About Immigration?" *Freeman*, 36: 8-16.

Simon, Julian L. 1990. *Population Matters*. New Brunswick, N.J.: Transition Publishers.

Simpson, Wayne. 1986. "Implications of Demographic Change for the Labour Market: Labour Supply, Unemployment and Earnings." Ottawa: Report for Review of Demography, Health and Welfare.

Smil, Vaclav. 1990. "Planetary Warming: Realities and Responses," *Population and Development Review*, 16, 1: 1-30.

Southam. 1990. *Broken Words*. Toronto: Southam News.

Spurgeon, David. 1988. *Understanding AIDS: A Canadian Strategy*. Ottawa: Royal Society of Canada.

Stafford, James. 1986. "Retirement Pensions: Reinforced Exploitation," in J. Dickson and B. Russell, eds., *Family, Economy and State*. Toronto: Garamond.

Stafford, James. 1987. "The Political Economic Context of Post-war Fertility

Patterns in Canada," in *Contributions to Demography*. Edmonton: Population Research Laboratory.

Stafford, James. 1990. "Regions and Migration," in *Comments on "Charting Canada's Future"*. London, Ont.: Federation of Canadian Demographers.

Stafford, James, and Brian McMillan. 1987. "Immigration and the Two Schools of Canadian Political Economy," paper presented at the meetings of the Canadian Population Society, Hamilton, June, 1987.

Standing Committee on Multiculturalism. 1987. *Multiculturalism: Building the Canadian Mosaic*. Ottawa: Queen's Printer.

Stasiulis, Daiva K. 1988. "The Symbolic Mosaic Reaffirmed: Multiculturalism Policy," in K.A. Graham, ed., *How Ottawa Spends*. Ottawa: Carleton University Press.

Statistics Canada. 1978. *Out of School – Into the Labour Force*. Ottawa: Statistics Canada Cat. No. 81-570.

Statistics Canada. 1984a. *Charting Canadian Incomes, 1951-1981*. Ottawa: Statistics Canada Cat. No. 13-581.

Statistics Canada. 1984b. *Canada's Young Family Home-Owners*. Ottawa: Statistics Canada Cat. No. 99-939.

Statistics Canada. 1984c. *Canada's Native Peoples*. Ottawa: Statistics Canada Cat. No. 99-937.

Statistics Canada. 1986a. *Report of the Canada Health and Disability Survey, 1983-1984*. Ottawa: Statistics Canada Cat. No. 82-555.

Statistics Canada. 1986b. *The Labour Force, May 1986*. Ottawa: Statistics Canada Cat. No. 71-001.

Statistics Canada. 1987. *Health and Social Support 1985*. Ottawa: Statistics Canada Cat. No. 11-612.

Statistics Canada. 1989a. *Health and Activity Limitation Survey*. Ottawa: Statistics Canada Cat. No. 82-608.

Statistics Canada. 1989b. *Life Tables, Canada and the Provinces, 1985-87*. Ottawa: Statistics Canada Cat. No. 84-532.

Statistics Canada. 1989c. *Births and Deaths*. Ottawa: Statistics Canada Cat. No. 84-204.

Statistics Canada. 1989d. "Special Tabulations for Population Projections based on 1986 Census and Fertility Rate of 1.7." Ottawa: Demography Division.

Statistics Canada. 1989e. *Youth in Canada*. Ottawa: Statistics Canada Cat. No. 89-511.

Statistics Canada. 1990a. *Population Projections for Canada and the Provinces and Territories, 1989-2011*. Ottawa: Statistics Canada Cat. No. 91-520.

Statistics Canada. 1990b. *Postcensal Annual Estimates of Population by Marital Status, Age, Sex and Components of Growth for Canada, Provinces and Territories, June 1, 1990*. Ottawa: Statistics Canada Cat. No. 91-210.

Statistics Canada. 1990c. *Income Distributions by Size, 1989*. Ottawa: Statistics Canada Cat. No. 13-207.

Statistics Canada. 1990d. *Canadian Economic Observer, December 1990*. Ottawa: Statistics Canada Cat. No. 11-010.

Statistics Canada. 1990e. *Income After Tax, Distributions by Size in Canada*. Ottawa: Statistics Canada Cat. No. 13-210.

Steinmann, Gunter. 1989. "Immigration: A Remedy to the Birth Dearth of the Western World?" University of Paderborn, Federal Republic of Germany.

Stelcner, Morton, and Natalie Kyriazis. 1990. "An Analysis of the Labour Force Behaviour of the Elderly in Canada, 1980," *Canadian Studies in Population*, 17, 1: 71-105.

Stoddart, Greg, and David Feeny. 1986. "Policy Options for Health Care Technology," in D. Feeny *et al.*, eds., *Health Care Technology*. Ottawa: Institute for Research on Public Policy.

Stolnitz, George J. 1987. "Conclusions," in T.J. Espenshade and G.T. Stolnitz, eds., *Technological Prospects and Population Trends*. Boulder, Colorado: Westview Press.

Stone, Leroy. 1983. "Course Notes for Soc 150: Canadian Population and Social Policy." London, Ont.: University of Western Ontario.

Stone, Leroy O. 1986a. "Implications of Recent Sharp Declines in Mortality Rates and Rapid Population Growth at Ages 80 and Above: A State of the Art Review." Ottawa: Report for Review of Demography, Health and Welfare.

Stone, Leroy. 1986b. "On the Demography of Dementia," manuscript.

Stone, Leroy O. 1988. *Family and Friendship Ties among Canada's Seniors*. Ottawa: Statistics Canada Cat. No. 89-508.

Stone, Leroy O. 1990. "Causes of Population Aging," paper presented at the Conference of European Statisticians, Ottawa, September, 1990.

Stone, Leroy O., and Susan Fletcher. 1980. *A Profile of Canada's Older Population*. Montreal: Institute for Research on Public Policy.

Stone, Leroy O., and Susan Fletcher. 1986. *The Seniors Boom*. Ottawa: Statistics Canada Cat. No. 89-515

Stone, Leroy O., and Susan Fletcher. 1990. "Population Aging and the Financing of Social Programs: A Review of the Conventional Wisdom," manuscript.

Stone, Leroy, and Hubert Frenken. 1988. *Canada's Seniors*. Ottawa: Statistics Canada Cat. No. 98-121.

Stone, Leroy, and Claude Marceau. 1977. *Canadian Population Trends and Public Policy through the 1980s*. Montreal: Institute for Research on Public Policy.

Storey, Keith J., and Mark Shrimpton. 1986. "A Review of the Nature and Significance of the Use of Long Distance Commuting by Canadian Resource Industries." Ottawa: Report for Review of Demography, Health and Welfare.

Strain, Laurel A. 1990. "Receiving and Providing Care: The Experiences of Never-married Elderly Canadians," paper presented at XII World Congress of Sociology, Madrid, July, 1990.

Streib, Gordon. 1990. "Young and Old: Who Owes Whom," presentation to Interdisciplinary Group on Aging, University of Western Ontario, April, 1990.

Strohmenger, Claude. 1986. "Démographie et santé des populations," *Cahiers Québécois de Démographie*, 15, 1: 3-10.

Surault, P. 1979. *L'inégalité devant la mort*. Paris: Economica.

Suzuki, David. 1989. "Birth Rate Threatens Earth's Survival," *Globe and Mail*, 11 November 1989: D11.

Swan, Neil. 1990. "Minutes of Standing Committee on Labour, Employment and Immigration," Issue No. 37.

Swartzman, Leora, Clive Seligman, and William McClelland. 1991. "Detecting

Gender Discrimination in University Salaries: A Case Study," *Canadian Journal of Higher Education*, forthcoming.

Swimmer, Gene, and Darlene Gollesch. 1986. "Affirmative Action for Women in the Federal Public Service," in M.J. Prince, ed., *How Ottawa Spends*. Toronto: Methuen.

Tabah, Léon. 1988. "The Demographic and Social Consequences of Population Aging," in *Economic and Social Implications of Population Aging*. New York: United Nations.

Taylor, Christopher. 1987. "Demography and Immigration in Canada: Challenge and Opportunity." Ottawa: Employment and Immigration Canada.

Teitelbaum, Michael S., and Jay M. Winter. 1985. *The Fear of Population Decline*. Orlando: Academic Press.

Teitelbaum, Michael S., and Jay M. Winter. 1988. "Population and Resources in Western Intellectual Traditions," *Population and Development Review*, 14, suppl.

Tepper, Elliot, 1987. "Demographic Change and Pluralism," *Canadian Studies in Population*, 14, 2: 223-35.

Tepper, Elliot. 1988. "Self-employment in Canada among Immigrants of Different Ethno-cultural Backgrounds." Ottawa: Report prepared for Employment and Immigration.

Tepper, Elliot. 1989. "Polyethnicity and the Canadian State," manuscript.

Termote, Marc G. 1987. "The Growth and Redistribution of the Canadian Population," in W.J. Coffey and M. Polèse, eds., *Still Living Together*. Ottawa: Institute for Research on Public Policy.

Termote, Marc. 1988. "Ce que pourrait être une politique de migration," *L'Action nationale*, 78, 5: 308-22.

Termote, Marc, and Danielle Gauvreau. 1985. "Le comportement démographique des groupes linguistiques du Québec pendant la période 1976-1981: Une analyse multirégionale," *Cahiers Québécois de Démographie*, 14, 1: 31-58.

Termote, Marc, and Danielle Gauvreau. 1988. *La situation démolinguistique du Québec*. Québec: Conseil de la langue française.

Ternowetsky, Gordon. 1986. "The Impact of Immigration on Unemployment, Poverty, Inequality and State Dependency: Counting the Costs." Ottawa: Report for Review of Demography, Health and Welfare.

The Economist. 1988. "People Shortage," *The Economist*, 8 October 1988: 59-61.

Thériault, J.-Yvon. 1989. "Lourdeur ou légèreté du devenir de la francophonie hors Québec," in *Demolinguistic Trends and the Evolution of Canadian Institutions*. Ottawa: Secretary of State.

Thornton, Arland, and William Axia. 1989. "Changing Patterns of Marital Dissolution in the United States: Demographic Implications," *International Population Conference, New Delhi*. Liège: International Union for the Scientific Study of Population, Vol. 3: 149-61.

Timlin, M.F. 1951. *Does Canada Need More People?* Toronto: Oxford University Press.

Tindale, Joseph A. 1988. "Income, Pensions, and Inequality in Later Life," in J. Curtis *et al.*, eds., *Social Inequality in Canada: Patterns, Problems, Policies*. Scarborough: Prentice-Hall.

Todd, Daniel. 1986. "Prairie Small-town Futures: The Development Dilemma." Ottawa: Report for Review of Demography, Health and Welfare.

Townson, Monica. 1987. "Women's Labour Force Participation, Fertility Rates and the Implications for Economic Development and Government Policy." Ottawa: Institute for Research on Public Policy, Studies in Social Policy.

Treas, Judith. 1987. "The Effect of Women's Labour Force Participation on the Distribution of Income in the United States," *Annual Review of Sociology*, 13: 259-88.

Tremblay, Marc, and Robert Bourbeau. 1985. "La mortalité et la fécondité selon le groupe linguistique au Québec, 1976 et 1981," *Cahiers Québécois de Démographie*, 14, 1: 7-30.

Trovato, Frank. 1986. "Mortality Trends and Differentials Among Immigrants in Canada." Ottawa: Report for Review of Demography, Health and Welfare.

United Nations. 1989a. *World Population at Turn of the Century*. New York: United Nations Population Studies No. 111.

United Nations. 1989b. *World Population Prospects 1988*. United Nations: Population Studies No. 106.

United States Commission on Population Growth and the American Future. 1972. *Population and the American Future*. Washington: U.S. Government Printing Office.

Ursel, Jane. 1986. "The State and the Maintenance of Patriarchy: A Case Study of Family, Labour and Welfare Legislation in Canada," in J. Dickinson and B. Russell, eds., *Family, Economy and State*. Toronto: Garamond.

Vaillancourt, François. 1985. "Income Distribution and Economic Security in Canada: An Overview," in F. Vaillancourt, ed., *Income Distribution and Economic Security in Canada*. Toronto: University of Toronto Press.

Vaillancourt, François. 1988. "The View of Immigration from Quebec," in C.M. Beach and A.G. Green, eds., *Policy Forum on the Role of Immigration in Canada's Future*. Kingston: John Deutsch.

Vaillancourt, François. 1989. "Demolinguistic Trends and Canadian Institutions: An Economic Perspective," in *Demolinguistic Trends and the Evolution of Canadian Institutions*. Ottawa: Secretary of State.

Vaillancourt, Yves. 1990. "Personal communication," letter dated 21 November 1990 from the Office of the Minister of State for Employment and Immigration.

Van de Kaa, Dirk. 1987. "Europe's Second Demographic Transition," *Population Bulletin*, 42, 1: 1-58.

Vanderkamp, John. 1988. "Canadian Post-secondary Enrolment: Causes, Consequences and Policy Issues." Ottawa: Report for Review of Demography, Health and Welfare.

van de Walle, Etienne, and John Knodel. 1980. "Europe's Fertility Transition: New Evidence and Lessons for Today's Developing World," *Population Bulletin*, 34, 6: 1-58.

Veevers, Jean E. 1980. *Childless by Choice*. Toronto: Butterworths.

Veevers, Jean E. 1986. "Sex Ratio Factors in the Lives of the Middle-Aged and Elderly Segments of the Population." Ottawa: Report for Review of Demography, Health and Welfare.

Veltman, Calvin. 1986. "L'impact de la ségrégation résidentielle sur l'équilibre linguistique au Québec." Ottawa: Report for Review of Demography, Health and Welfare.

Veltman, Calvin. 1988. "L'impact de l'immigration internationale sur l'équilibre linguistique à Montréal." Ottawa: Report for Review of Demography, Health and Welfare.

Verma, Ravi B.P., and Dave Broad. 1989. "Motivational Factors in Interprovincial Migration," paper presented at the meetings of the Canadian Population Society, Quebec, June, 1989.

Vlassoff, Carol. 1987. "Fertility and the Labour Force in Canada: Critical Issues." Ottawa: Institute for Research on Public Policy, Studies in Social Policy.

Wadhera, Surinder. 1990. "Therapeutic Abortions, Canada," *Health Reports*, 1, 2: 229-45.

Wannell, Ted. 1989. "Losing Ground: Wages of Young People, 1981-1986," *Canadian Social Trends*, 13: 21-23.

Watson, William G. 1986. "An Estimate of the Welfare Gains from Fiscal Equalization," *Canadian Journal of Economics*, 19, 2: 298-308.

Watson, William G. 1987. "Demographic Change, Provincial Fiscal Behaviour and Regional Economic Growth," *Canadian Studies in Population*, 14, 2: 209-22.

Watson, William G. 1988. "Demographic Change, Fiscally-induced Migration, and Regional Economic Growth." Ottawa: Report for Review of Demography, Health and Welfare.

Wattelar, C., and R. Roumans. 1988. "Objectifs démographiques et migrations: quelques simulations," paper presented to Réunion d'experts nationaux sur les aspects démographiques des migrations, 17-18 November 1988.

Wattenberg, Ben J. 1987. *The Birth Dearth*. New York: Pharas Books.

Weaver, Carolyn L. 1986. "Social Security in Aging Societies," *Population and Development Review*, 12, suppl.: 273-95.

Weaver, Sally M. 1981. *Making Canadian Indian Policy: The Hidden Agenda 1968-1970*. Toronto: University of Toronto Press.

Wein, Fred. 1988. "Canada's Regions," in J. Curtis and L. Tepperman, eds., *Understanding Canadian Society*. Toronto: McGraw-Hill.

Weiner, Myron. 1985. "International Migration and International Relations," *Population and Development Review*, 11: 441-57.

Weinfeld, Morton. 1986. "A Study of Ethnic Polities in Canada." Ottawa: Report for Review of Demography, Health and Welfare.

Weinfeld, Morton. 1988a. "Ethnic and Race Relations," in J. Curtis and L. Tepperman, eds., *Understanding Canadian Society*. Toronto: McGraw-Hill.

Weinfeld, Morton. 1988b. "Immigration and Canada's Population Future: A Nation Building Vision." Montreal: McGill University, Department of Sociology, Discussion Paper.

Weinfeld, Morton. 1990. "The Politics of the Birth Rate," *Policy Options*, 11, 3: 24-26.

Weller, Geoffrey R., and Pranlal Manga. 1983. "The Development in Health Policy in Canada," in M.M. Atkinson and M.A. Chandler, eds., *The Politics of Canadian Public Policy*. Toronto: University of Toronto Press.

Western Opinion Research. 1986. "Effects of Demographic Shifts on Public Policy Issues." Ottawa: Report for Review of Demography, Health and Welfare.

Westoff, Charles F. 1986. "Perspective on Nuptiality and Fertility," *Population and Development Review*, 12, suppl.: 155-70.

White, Pamela. 1990. *Ethnic Diversity in Canada*. Ottawa: Statistics Canada Cat. No. 98-132.

Wigdor, Blossom T., and David K. Foot. 1988. *The Over-Forty Society*. Toronto: Lorimer.

Wigle, D.J., and Y. Mao. 1988. "Income and Life Expectancy," in J. Curtis *et al.*, eds., *Social Inequality in Canada: Patterns, Problems, Policies*. Scarborough: Prentice-Hall.

Wilkins, Russell. 1979. *L'espérance de vie par quartier à Montréal, 1976*. Montreal: Institute for Research on Public Policy.

Wilkins, Russell. 1980. *Health Status in Canada*. Montreal: Institute for Research on Public Policy.

Wilkins, Russell, and Owen Adams. 1983. *Healthfulness of Life*. Montreal: Institute for Research on Public Policy.

Wilkins, Russell, and Owen Adams. 1989. "Health Expectancy Trends in Canada, 1951-1986," manuscript.

Wilkins, Russell, and Owen Adams. 1990. "Changes in Mortality by Income in Urban Canada from 1971 to 1986," *Health Reports*, 1, 2: 137-74.

Wilkinson, Bruce W. 1986. "Elementary and Secondary Education Policy in Canada: A Survey," *Canadian Public Policy*, 12, 4: 535-72.

Wilson, S.J. 1988. "Gender Inequality," in J. Curtis and L. Tepperman, eds., *Understanding Canadian Society*, Toronto: McGraw-Hill.

Winer, Stanley L., and Denis Gauthier. 1982. *Internal Migration and Fiscal Structure*. Ottawa: Economic Council of Canada 22-109.

Winn, C. 1985. "Affirmative Action and Visible Minorities: Eight Premises in Quest of Evidence," *Canadian Public Policy*, 11: 684-701.

Winn, Conrad. 1988. "The Socio-economic Attainment of Visible Minorities: Facts and Policy Implications," in J. Curtis *et al.*, eds., *Social Inequality in Canada: Patterns, Problems, Policies*. Scarborough: Prentice-Hall.

Wolf, Douglas A. 1988. "Kinship and Family Support in Aging Societies," in *Economic and Social Implications of Population Aging*. New York: United Nations.

Wolfson, Michael. 1986a. "Statis Amid Change: Income Inequality in Canada, 1965-1983," *Canadian Statistical Review*, February, 1986: vi-xxvii.

Wolfson, Michael. 1986b. "A Guaranteed Income," *Policy Options*, 7, 1: 35-45.

Wolfson, Michael. 1989. "Divorce, Homemaker Pensions and Lifecycle Analysis," *Population Research and Policy Review*, 8, 1: 25-54.

Wolfson, Michael. 1990. "Perceptions, Facts and Expectations on the Standard of Living," in R. Beaujot, ed., *Facing the Demographic Future*. Ottawa: Royal Society of Canada.

Wolfson, Michael C., and Brian B. Murphy. 1990. "When the Baby Boom Grows Old: Impacts on Canada's Public Sector," paper presented at the Conference of European Statisticians, Ottawa, September, 1990.

Woodley, Olive Lumby. 1989. "The Case for a Guaranteed Income," *Policy Options*, 10, 2: 6-10.

World Bank. 1984. *World Development Report 1984*. Washington: The World Bank.

World Bank. 1990. *World Development Report 1990*. Washington: The World Bank.

World Commission on Environment and Development. 1987. *Our Common Future*. New York: Oxford.

Wright, Robert E. 1988. "The Impact of Income Redistribution on Fertility in Canada," *Genus*, 44,1-2: 139-56.

Wrigley, E. Anthony. 1977. "Reflections on the History of the Family," *Daedalus*, Spring, 1977: 71-85.

Yelaja, Shankar A., ed. 1978. *Canadian Social Policy*. Waterloo, Ont.: Wilfrid Laurier University Press.

Ziegler, E. 1988. "Refugee Movements and Policy in Canada." Ottawa: Report for Review of Demography, Health and Welfare.

Ziegler, E. 1989. "Population Trends and Pronatalist Measures in Selected European Countries." Ottawa: Report for Review of Demography, Health and Welfare.

Zsigmond, Z., *et al*. 1978. *Out of School – Into the Labour Force*. Ottawa: Statistics Canada Cat. No. 81-570.

AUTHOR INDEX

367

SUBJECT INDEX

Education, 320; costs, 229, 258-59, 262; and gender, 262-63; literacy, 261; policy issues, 261-63; post-secondary, 259-61; primary and secondary, 258-59; trends, 258-61
Emigration, 104, 106, 113-14, 116
Environment, 17-18, 22, 26, 33-34, 90, 179, 189-90, 308
Ethnic origins, 297-305, 322-23; dis-crimination, 301-03, 322-23; policy issues, 302-05; socio-economic profiles, 300-02; *see also* First Nations peoples; Immigration; Visible minorities
Expected fertility, *see* Fertility

Families, 318-20; change in, 16, 77; and children, 244-45, 249-51, 318; common-law, 79, 81, 244, 246-47; dual-earner, 244-46; and elderly, 216, 251-52, 255; husband-wife, 244-46; income, 83, 243, 245, 248, 250-52, 275-76; and older children, 243; and policy, 239, 252-56; and population change, 16, 235-39; single-parent, 81, 244, 247-48, 319-20; types, 242-52, 318-19; young families, 243-44
Farm population, 158, 168
Fertility: cultural factors, 76, 83-85, 94-95; economic factors, 76, 82-83, 92-94; expected, 81-82; explana-tions, 76-77; French, 77, 83, 144, 191, 289; and gender roles, 83-87; historical, 73-78; and immigration, 118-19, 200-01; and income, 83, 319; and labour force participation, 85-87, 266; and language, 86; policy issues, 87-101, 311, 312-13; pro-jected, 180, 182; proximate factors, 78-82, 91-92; and religion, 83, 86; structural factors, 85-87, 95-99; timing, 80; trends, 16, 73-74, 311-12; *see also* First Nations peoples; Foreign-born; Quebec
First Nations peoples, 282-88, 321-22; demographics, 157, 282-86; fertility, 77, 285; mortality, 61-62, 70, 285;

policy issues, 286-88; socio-economic conditions, 282-86
Foreign-born, 135-36, 120-22, 161; fertility, 118-19, 300
France, 19-21, 90, 93-97, 191, 223, 238
Free trade, 160, 189

Gender differences, 267-74, 320-21; and discrimination, 272; educa-tion, 270; for foreign-born, 132; income, 246, 250-51, 270-74; labour force, 17, 186, 263-64, 269-70; and occupations, 270-71; policy issues, 268, 272-74; *see also* Fertility; Labour force; Low income; Mortality
Germany, 90, 225
Government and population, 7, 18, 25
Green Paper on Immigration, 22, 110
Guaranteed Income Supplement, 219-20, 223, 278

Health policy: development of, 62-63; policy issues, 63-71
Health: costs, 63-68, 230-31, 311; costs and aging, 65-66, 226-29; curative and preventive, 63, 66-68, 311; definition of, 68-69; and pro-longing life, 57, 69-70, 227; and retirement, 214, 232-34; survey, 69; *see also* Disability; Hospital stays; Medical Care Act; Mortality; Physi-cian consultations
Heart disease, 54
Home language, *see* Language
Hospital stays, 64-65, 69, 311
Households, 236, 318-20; single per-son, 247; types, 242-52
Human ecology, 34

Immigration, 313-15, 322; age struc-ture, 120, 204; business class, 123; classes of immigrants, 110-11, 123, 125-28, 314; and education, 122, 124, 128, 131, 139; and emigration, 106, 113-14, 116; and future growth, 115-20; future levels, 111, 148-51, 180-82; geographic distribu-